Austria in Literature

Studies in Austrian Literature, Culture, and Thought

Austria in Literature

Edited and with a Preface by
Donald G. Daviau

ARIADNE PRESS
Riverside, California

Ariadne Press would like to express its appreciation to the Austrian Cultural Institute, New York and the Bundeskanzleramt–Sektion Kunst, Vienna for their assistance in publishing this book.

.KUNST

Library of Congress Cataloging-in-Publication Data

Austria in literature / Edited and with a preface by Donald G. Daviau
      p.   cm. – (Studies in Austrian literature, culture, and thought)
"...Symposium at the University of California, Riverside, in 1997... The contributions in German were published as a special issue of Modern Austrian Literature (31, 3/4, 1998...), while those presented in English are contained in this volume."–Pref.
    Includes bibliographical references and index.
    ISBN 1-57241-065-5
    1. Austrian literature–20th century–History and criticism. 2. American literature–20th century–History and criticism. 3. Austria–In literature. I. Daviau, Donald G. II. Series.

PT3822. A748   2000
810.9'32436–dc21
                                                99-086608
                                                       CIP

Cover:
Art Director: George McGinnis

Copyright ©2000
by Ariadne Press
270 Goins Court
Riverside, CA 92507

All rights reserved.
No part of this publication may be reproduced or transmitted in any form or by any means without formal permission.
Printed in the United States of America.
ISBN 1-57241-065-5 (paperback original)

TABLE OF CONTENTS

Donald G. Daviau (University of California, Riverside)
Preface i

John Pizer (Lousiana State University)
Vienna as the Heart of Darkness: Wilhelm Raabe's "Lesser-
Germany Politics 1

Ester Riehl (Ohio State University)
Marie von Ebner-Eschenbach's *Božena*: A Czech Maid and
the Future of Austria..19

Jane Sokolosky (Washington University)
Fashion and Class in Rosa Mayreder's Fiction................................31

Matti Bunzl (University of Illinois at Urbana-Champaign)
Modes of Nostalgia and Figurations of "Austria" in the
Exil(auto)biographien of Richard Beer-Hofmann and
Stefan Zweig...48

Barbara Zeisl Schoenberg (Pomona College)
How "Belle" Was the "Belle-Époque" Really? Some Not
So "Belle" Reflections of Vienna in the "Belle-Époque"
Mirrors of Kraus, Altenberg, and Petzold.......................................60

Alexander Honold (Humboldt-Universität Berlin)
Endings and Beginnings: Musil's Invention of
Austrian History...75

Raymond L. Burt (University of North Carolina)
Subliminal Austria: Sigmund Freud in
World Literature...86

Ena Pedersen (Wadham College, Oxford)
On Galician Jews in the Habsburg Monarchy as Depicted
in H.W. Katz's Novel *Die Fischmanns*.. 103

Contents

Ian Reifowitz (University of Salford)
Nationalism, Modernity, and Multinational Austria in the
Works of Joseph Roth 120

Dagmar C.G. Lorenz (University of Illinois at Chicago)
Separate Reality, Separate Nations? Austria in the
Works of Jewish and Non-Jewish Authors 132

Michael P. Olson (Harvard University)
Robert Menasse's Concept of Anti-*Heimat* Literature 153

Karl E. Webb (Northern Arizona University)
Gerhard Roth's *Der See* and Josef Haslinger's *Opernball*:
A Comparative Treatment of Contemporary Austria 166

Gerald A. Fetz (University of Montana)
Post-Bernhardian Austria in Lilian Faschinger's
Magdalena Sünderin 179

Lynne Cook (University of New South Wales)
'Black Holes' in the Novels of Christoph Ransmayr:
An Astronomical Interpretation of Images of
Alternative Worlds in his Work 193

Pamela S. Saur (Lamar University)
Underground Austria 212

Horst Jarka (University of Montana)
American Writers and Austria in the 1930s 225

Rita Terras (Connecticut College)
Austria in the American Short Story 243

Geoffrey C. Howes (Bowling Green State University)
The Idea of Austria in Djuna Barnes' *Nightwood* 256

Jörg Thunecke (Nottingham Trent University)
Schlagobers and Blood: Vienna in John Irving's Novel
The Hotel New Hampshire 276

Gerd K. Schneider (Syracuse University)
"I Wept While I Was Dreaming" How to Survive the
Holocaust after the Holocaust in Jon Marans' Play
Old Wicked Songs 295

Susan C. Anderson (University of Oregon)
The Image of Austria in Literary Readings From
American Textbooks 309

Name Index 321

Preface

National image is important to every country and to the people living in it. After all, image to a country is the same as character to a person, so what the individual thinks of his homeland and how others regard it are important considerations, determining the standing of a nation in the world. In recognition of this fact, nations invest considerable sums of money abroad trying to create a favorable image, especially those countries which, like Austria, depend heavily on tourism for a part of their national budget and which welcome foreign investment. Indeed, image for Austria becomes even doubly important, for throughout its history the country has always stood in the shadow of Germany in the view of the outside world, where even the greatest Austrian accomplishments in all of the arts has generally been subsumed under the rubric of German literature, art, and music.

These reflections led to the Symposium at the University of California, Riverside, in 1997 on the topic "Austria in Literature." Colleagues from fifteen nations offered discussions of literary portrayals of Austria ranging in time from the nineteenth century to the present. The contributions in German were published as a Special Issue of *Modern Austrian Literature* (31, 3/4, 1998, 274 pages), while those presented in English are contained in this volume. All together the essays provide an important understanding of how Austria is perceived and described in its own literature as well as in the literatures of fifteen western and eastern countries from America to Russia.

The majority of articles here focus on the characterization of Austria and Austrians in Austrian and American literature. Most of the Austrian works discussed are by contemporary Austrian writers, while the American texts, except for a few from the post-World-War-II era, were written in the 1920s and 30s, a time when upper-class people still considered travel to Europe a necessary adjunct to their formal education.

There exist many travel accounts from the nineteenth century, partly resulting from the influx of important people into Vienna in 1815 to take part in the Congress of Vienna. There in a party atmosphere of wine, women, and song the reactionary decision was made under the urging of Emperor Franz I (II) and his devoted servant Chancellor Clemens von Metternich, who dominated and shaped the proceedings, to restore Europe to the general geographical contours and the aristocratic, feudalistic outlook that had prevailed before the

French revolution and the disruption caused by the territorial ambitions of the upstart Napoleon. Foreign writers of memoirs during the period up to the revolution of 1848 – usually referred to as the *Vormärz* or pre-March era – were generally dazzled by life in Vienna and either willingly or innocently overlooked the repressive side of the political system: the police state, the censorship, the lack of freedom of speech, and the industrial exploitation of the poor. Vienna in what has now come to be known as the Biedermeier period was presented in such accounts as a comfortable, happy, friendly place, and it was – if you were wealthy and could overlook the suffering of the poor and could afford to ignore the lack of individual freedom that forced citizens to live artificial lives and caused such deep feelings of dissatisfaction and discontent among academics, artists, and intellectuals. The Austrian writers of the time were prohibited by government edict from telling the truth about the social and political circumstances, and so the literature of the time in no way reflects contemporary life and conditions. Only seminal accounts, like *Austria as It Is* (1832) by Charles Sealsfield, who left his homeland and published his book in English in England, and "Austria and Its Future" (*Österreich und dessen Zukunft*, 1843), written by Viktor von Andrian but published anonymously for self-protection, dared to give a true picture of what it meant to live under the tyranny of the absolutist state. It is one of the most amazing cases of historical revisionism that the term Biedermeier, which was coined originally in Germany as a deprecating term to caricature Austrians in this era lacking in personal freedom, was changed into its polar opposite at the turn of the century and is now idealized as a warm, cozy, idyllic epoch in complete disregard of the historical facts. As a further distortion, the definition has been expanded to include the entire society, when in fact the term can refer only to a small group of wealthy and titled families that could afford the good materialistic life. True, this small minority of advantaged people did enjoy a splendid life even under the repressive system. Indeed, exactly the same situation recurred at the turn of the century. But, except for the fact that the country was at peace, life in general was bad, especially for writers, artists, journalists, and intellectuals and, of course, for the poor and disadvantaged. The social and political situation continued to worsen until the situation became intolerable and exploded in revolution in 1848, resulting in the end of Ferdinand's reign and Metternich's control.

With the new beginning under young Emperor Franz Joseph I,

much was promised but little actually changed. In effect the second half of the nineteenth century is a mirror image of the first half, with the one difference that writers enjoyed a little more freedom to express their discontent. In general, however, Franz Joseph followed the same misguided Habsburg policy of looking backward and trying to maintain the status quo, with the result that the progressive elements in the country turned to Germany, which was burgeoning with growth and new developments in all areas of life. Otto von Bismarck, the German "Iron Chancellor," refused to admit Austria into the new united Germany, even though it took a war and the defeat of Austria at Königgrätz in 1866 to convince the southern neighbor and former partner in the Holy Roman Empire that no further union was desired.

According to John Pizer, the German image of Austria in the second half of the nineteenth century, as publicized in the writings of the German author Wilhelm Raabe, completely supports Bismarck's position of excluding Austria from any role or voice in the new German empire. Vienna is described as corrupt, decadent, and indolent, so enervated and enervating, that even the energy of outsiders who visit there is sapped. Austrians, according to Raabe, suffer from indecision, are amoral, asocial, afflicted by a sense of malaise and uneasiness, and always seeking amusements to distract them from their discomfort. Austrian writers from Franz Grillparzer to Robert Musil depict Austrian "resolute irresolution." This negative image, along with the traditional German attitude of superiority toward the Austrians, has prevailed in Germany to the present day.

In the nineteenth century and continuing up to World War I, two basic concepts dating back to medieval times prevailed in Austrian society: the social hierarchy and the patriarchal society. As Ester Riehl shows, Marie von Ebner-Eschenbach, although an aristocrat herself, opposed these concepts. Her strong sense of humanity and social justice enabled her to regard the peasants and the disadvantaged as human beings. Through the figure of the servant woman Bozena, who though of lowly status and lacking in formal education displays noble bearing and conduct throughout her life, Ebner-Eschenbach exposes the fallacy of the principles of hierarchy and patriarchy.

Rosa Mayreder, one of the most intelligent and ardent feminists at the turn of the century, used the symbolism of women's fashion and dress in her works to unmask the patriarchy and motivate women to become more independent, as Jane Sokolowsky demonstrates. Bourgeois women wore clothes and shoes that made them suffer in order to find a husband to support them, a necessary pursuit in an age when women were not educated. Like Ebner-Eschenbach, Mayreder advocated education for women, not only for their own self-esteem and independence, but also, as she tried to convince men, because they would make better wives. But emancipation came slowly, and bourgeois wives continued to dress in uncomfortable clothes in order to play their role in representing their husband's importance and financial status to the world. Full equality for women remains an unfulfilled goal in Austria as in the rest of the world, and the patriarchal system continues to prevail; education, however, is now open to all women.

The turn of the century will forever represent that most glamorous era in Austrian history, when wealth or talent made possible a rich, refined life in which culture and aestheticism played a large role. The flourishing of talent in all of the arts in Vienna, indeed, in Austria in general, has no equal in Austrian cultural history. The Austrian fin de siècle was the Biedermeier era writ large, a dazzling, cultivated period, a sensuous and even somewhat decadent time, when beauty and fashion reigned in every aspect of life from home furnishings to dress, to lifestyle. The emphasis was on show, on the facade. Vienna – for the well to do – became a theater in which the wealthy and the talented played their self-appointed roles. Reality and politics meant nothing; the arts, the beautiful life everything.

This heady atmosphere, the result of a unique set of circumstances, proved to be a heyday for the artists and architects, because Vienna was building as never before. New mansions could be constructed in the inner city now that the wall had been removed, and they in turn required large paintings, stylish furniture, musical instruments, and sculptures. Anyone with talent aspired to contribute in one artistic field or the other. At the pinnacle stood the Burgtheater, famous European wide, and every would be writer aspired to create a play that would be performed there.

No figure better represents this aesthetic era than Stefan Zweig, who embodied the fin-de-siècle lifestyle in every aspect to a greater degree than any of his contemporaries. Independently wealthy and incredibly talented, he could live exactly the beautiful life of self-indulgence, self-fulfillment, and self-satisfaction that he wished. He did not squander his time, however, but was endowed with a strong work ethic which he followed all of his life. Writing was so central to his life that he placed it over every other concern and consideration, even over people. No one embraced and represented the fin de siècle better than Zweig, and so it is fitting that he made his greatest literary contribution by writing the biography of this age which he loved so much that he refused to abandon it. When, living in exile in Petropolis, Brazil in 1941, he came to the realization that his was a *World of Yesterday* that would never return, he preferred to end his life rather than to change and accept the new reality of the mundane world that he witnessed developing. Matti Bunzl compares the autobiographies of Zweig and Richard Beer-Hofmann, the first general, the second highly personal and nostalgic, to show the strong influence that life at the turn of the century exerted on those who could afford to participate in the good life it made possible.

Similarly, Joseph Roth, a close friend of Zweig's, who likewise was so enamoured of the turn of the century that he stubbornly remained a monarchist until his death in exile in Paris in 1938. Like Zweig, as Ian Reifowitz shows, Roth wanted to cling to the past and, in disregard of the historical facts, blamed modernity for the collapse of the monarchy. In his novels, as in his life, Roth took refuge in a nostalgic Habsburg myth, in a world gone by, because, again like Zweig, he could not face the thought of having to adapt to a new reality in the future.

This fin-de-siècle world of glitter and cultural refinement that perpetually fascinates all who know it also has its underside which is its antipode in every respect. The contrast between the wealthy and the poor was as great in Vienna then as it remains in most major cities today. Barbara Schoenberg examines some of the literature of the time that focuses on the life of the poor and disadvantaged, who lived ever so close to the opulent world around them and yet were as far removed from it as if they were on another planet.

Pamela Saur goes even further in showing the underside of Austria by showing the underground literally. She describes the sewers and relics of the past buried under Vienna and notes where the bones of history are kept. Underground Austria, in her view, not only represents death and the grave, but also serves as a metaphor for a past that has never been overcome and that therefore will not die. On another level, she brings the sewers and canals into association with Sigmund Freud's theories of the subconscious.

The figure of Freud as the subject of several novels is examined by Raymond Burt, who raises the question of how reliable fiction can be a transmitter of historical reality. Freud himself is portrayed favorably as a man on a hero's quest. In terms of Vienna, Freud is shown to have a love/hate relationship with both the city and the people. In these novels the image of Vienna is unflattering largely because of its strong current of anti-Semitism. Freud, as Burt reports, utters many negative views and even outright condemnation, as when, looking at a crowd, he remarks to his companion that they were the enemy who would cut our throats. Yet, when forced to leave Vienna in 1938 to go into exile in England, he was deeply saddened because he "loved the prison."

It is, in fact, one of the remarkable features of exiled Jews that most remained completely loyal Austrians who devoted their efforts to creating a favorable image of Austria and Austrians – whom they differentiated from Germans – in their host countries and lived only for the day when they could return home. The fact that they were not invited back after the war, were resented if they did return, and experienced great difficulty in regaining their possessions that had been confiscated, proved an even more bitter disappointment than having been driven into exile originally. Then they believed they were victims of the Nazis; after the war they found themselves victimized by those they had through all the years of exile believed to be the good Austrians.

Anti-Semitism was one of the features noted and condemned in the works of American writers who discuss Austria in the 1930s, as Horst Jarka shows. The portrayals range from the humorous to the serious. Robert Sherwood's comedy *Reunion in Vienna*, while satirizing the decrepit nobility, the Habsburgs, and psychoanalysis, also creates a myth of gay Vienna at a time when the adjective signified a mood and not a sexual preference. Similarly, Mark Twain, who liked to visit Vienna, noted the light-heartedness of the city. He described the deadly confrontation at the Palace of Justice in 1927 that resulted in the loss of more than ninety lives and commented that you would not know anything serious was occurring, judging by the joyful mood of life in Vienna. Others like Sinclair Lewis made similar remarks about the brief but violent February revolution in February 1934. The authors Kay Boyle, Frederic Prokosch, and Catherine Hutter, deal with the rise of Nazism and the postwar era. Of the three, according to Jarka, Hutter comes closest to the truth of the time. Prokosch's nostalgic and melancholy portrayal of village life shows Austria as a helpless country, lending credence to the myth of "Austria as the first victim of Hitler."

In the novels of other American authors, Vienna at the end of the Habsburg empire is depicted as a baroque museum, a facade with a splendid surface but with nothing of substance underneath. Geoffrey Howes shows this image of Austria in Djuna Barnes's *Nightwood*, Jörg Thunecke in John Irving's *Hotel New Hampshire*, and Rita Terras in short stories by Ray Bradbury, John Irving, Kay Boyle, Mark Twain, and Leo Rosten. Terras feels that American writers consider Austria a romantic backwater and describe it in fairytale terms. Most present the standard clichés about Austria, for example, the doddering old Emperor and the mad psychiatrist; only Irving and Rosten try to present a more accurate account. According to Rosten, World War II destroyed the romantic image of Austria for American writers. He himself was struck by what he perceived as a moribund city trying to appear frivolous but showing its sadness. According to Terras, he found Vienna congenial enough, all empty show and excessive politeness, but with cynicism evident behind the courtesy and contempt behind the charm. Is Vienna or any city that suffers from overexposure to floods of tourists any different today? How can any place maintain any semblance of authenticity under such conditions? Contemporary Austrian writers have also sharply criticized this situation, as will be seen.

The image of Austria presented in the United States in the various literary works of American writers is supplemented by Susan Anderson's discussion of the image of Austrian and Austrians gained by American students studying German. Her findings indicate that culturally Austria is often simply subsumed under Germany. When Austria is identified, the information is superficial. Only a good teacher who knows Austria would make the difference in what image and level of understanding students would gain about Austria in lower division German language classes.

The burgeoning growth of Vienna began in the 1860s with Franz Joseph's decision to tear down the wall around the city and replace it with the imposing Ringstrasse lined with impressive buildings in different architectural styles, a triumph of historicism which prevailed then as dogma in official Austrian art circles. This development attracted people from the eastern lands and territories of the monarchy to Vienna seeking jobs and opportunity. Some were journalists and writers, and newspapers and literary works proliferated. Ena Pedersen examines the Eastern Jewish perception of Austria through her analysis of H. W. Katz's novel *The Fischmans*, a view of the world as experienced by those at the bottom of society. Not only the hope of jobs brought the eastern Jews to Vienna, but also their perception of an idealized German culture based on their reading of Lessing and Schiller. Life in Vienna proved quite different and much harder than they had envisioned, as they had to fight for survival in a strongly anti-Semitic environment, trying to maintain their identity in the hostile world around them. Even the assimilated and acculturated Jews disliked them, because the eastern Jews retained their native manner of dress and culture, thus further arousing feelings of anti-Semitism.

Anti-Semitism looms large also in Dagmar Lorenz's overview of the life of Jews in Austria from the nineteenth century to the present. She, too, notes that for eastern European Jews Vienna was a mecca representing civilization, opportunity, and refinement. After 1945, however, Jewish exiles were not invited to return to Austria. Those who did return met with continued anti-Semitism and found Austrians generally unapologetic and without remorse for the Holocaust. Claims for restitution were often refused. Clearly the problem of anti-Semitism remains ongoing and deeply rooted in Austria, with no resolution in sight. Prejudice cannot be legislated.

Gerd Schneider illustrates another approach to this problem in his analysis of Jon Marans' play *Old Wicked Ways*, which again highlights anti-Semitism in Austria and addresses the question of how Jews can live in Vienna after the Holocaust. In the course of the discussions between the protagonist and antagonist, Americans are informed about the differences between Austrians and Americans in terms of mentality, politics, culture, and even in eating habits – Austrians savor their food, while Americans devour it. (This last claim seems dubious, at least it does not correspond with my experience.) Ultimately, the play's open-ending leaves the audience to ponder the question of whether Austria exists presently in a condition of sunrise or sunset. It is noteworthy that this same question was being asked at the turn of the century.

Criticism of Austria and Austrians has a long tradition among Austrian writers – such names as Johann Nestroy, Hermann Bahr, Karl Kraus, and Robert Musil come readily to mind – but never has the criticism been more vociferous and vicious than in the writings of such contemporary authors as Thomas Bernhard, Peter Handke, Joseph Haslinger, Elfriede Jelinek, Robert Menasse, Gerhard Roth, and Peter Turrini, who have refined political and social attacks into an art form. One might add, an art form that pays well, for the more vehemently these authors have denounced the government, the more prizes and awards they have been awarded. Handke complained that Austria was "the fat on which he choked" and showed his contempt for Austria by making his residence in France. Thomas Bernhard made a career of criticizing Austria, and his outstanding play *Heldenplatz* is as complete a catalogue of failings and problems and as severe an indictment of contemporary Austria as can be imagined. All of these authors, who serve as a conscience of Austria, are long on criticism but short on solutions. Unlike earlier times, contemporary writers feel that they have fulfilled their social duty by simply pointing out the problems. They feel no responsibility to offer any suggestions for improvement.

With Bernhard dead and Handke, who has emerged from his ivory tower, concentrating these days on the Serbien problem, the reigning critic today is Robert Menasse, whose views of Austria Michael Olsen seeks to define. In Menasse's opinion, Austria's major problem is the destruction of its authenticity; it remains a nation but is no longer a homeland (*Heimat*) because of being constantly overrun by vast numbers of tourists. Turrini noted the same problem in lamenting the "Hawaiianization of Austria."

Certainly Austrians make many concessions to tourism, and equally certainly this situation has a bearing on lifestyle and authenticity. But how does one avoid the problem when the income from tourism provides a vital contribution to the national economy? The issue of authenticity has a long history in Austria. Under Emperor Franz I (II) and Metternich, writers and intellectuals complained that people could not lead natural authentic lives because of the censorship, and the same held true for the remainder of the century. Hermann Bahr in his insightful analysis of Austrian life in *Wien* (1906) maintained that the Habsburgs only ever wanted artificial citizens in the form of obedient citizens, loyal not to the nation – patriots can cause revolutions – but to them personally. Up to World War I artificiality, aestheticism, and role playing were the dominant tendencies. To overcome this "Flight from Reality" (1960), to use the title of Hans Weigel's book on the major artists of the nineteenth century, motivates the writings of the contemporary authors critical of Austria.

The analysis of contemporary Austrian conditions in the writings of Menasse and Gerhard Roth is further discussed in the contribution of Karl Webb. These writers show that the image of Austria is divided into two parts: the superficial Sound-of-Music tourist image and the violent, subsurface destroying the fabric of the country. They describe the overall seediness and decay of the city environment and the society, dwelling on the homeless and drug addicts, problems with refugees, greedy doctors, and insensitive, brutal police. Both writers, according to Webb, explore the coarsening of Austrian life as a result of the fascist, nationalistic tendencies at all levels of society, which, lacking moral purpose or direction, is deteriorating and losing its cohesiveness.

This dire criticism has, of course, to be taken with a strong dose of salt. Karl Kraus in *The Last Days of Mankind* (1918) and others ever since have been predicting the imminent demise of Austria, but the country has always tenaciously muddled through every crisis and appears stronger today than it has been at any time in its recent history. As seen in Gerald Fetz's article, Antonio Fian takes a contrary view to that of all these authors and accuses them of playing apocalyptic games. One must bear in mind that a strong feature of the contemporary criticism is exaggeration, Bernhard's stock in trade which the others engage in as well. Such criticism is good business, for it attracts media attention, gains free publicity, and not only sells books, but also results in paying interviews, reading tours, and, of course, grants and awards. Austrian politicians are so used to being criticized that they pay no attention to these attacks but stay focused on what is truly important for them – staying in power. For its part, the public enjoys seeing their complaints eloquently voiced, just as Nestroy's and Kraus's readers did in their day, but it does not realistically expect that anything will be done.

Fetz's examination of Lilian Faschinger's works reveals many of the same problems that others have already rehearsed: family life with its repression of individual members, especially children, lack of intellectual life, creating a stifling environment for anyone who does not wish to follow the established norm, and the sorry state of contemporary political life. Faschinger, who follows in the footsteps of Bernhard, has the saving grace that she presents her critique with humor. She is also more consistent than most of the others, for, consistent with her negative view of Austria, she, like Handke, prefers to live in Paris.

The idea that Austria tries to stifle creativity goes back at least to the time of Joseph II, and the concept of the "Austrian fate" of authors has become an accepted commonplace in literary history.

However, to keep a balanced perspective, it must be mentioned that the Austrian government today supports the arts more generously than any other country and places no barriers on what is produced, including works critical of the very establishment that provided the money to produce and publish the works of art in all forms.

Repressive family life is another theme with a long history. No mention is made here of recent works such as Felix Mitterer's *Siberia*, which depicts how old people are shunted aside today and put into homes by their children in order to inherit the property and money. Nor is there any discussion of the anti-provincial (*Antiheimat*) writings of Franz Innerhofer, Gerd Jonke, Joseph Winkler, and Anna Mitgutsch, who describe the cruelty of life on the farm and dispel for all time the long held myth of the wholesomeness of provincial life as opposed to the decadence of Vienna. Finally, there is no contribution on Elfriede Jelinek, neither of her feminist works such as *The Lovers* (*Die Lieberhaberinnen*), *The Piano Player* (*Die Klavierspielerin*), and *Lust* (Lust), nor of her confrontations with the political past.

The most recent trend found among the new generation of writers is away from an almost obsessive preoccupation with Austria, with carping about Austrian faults, which was carried on mostly by the leftist or die-hard Marxist authors. As a corollary of this shift, the tendency is also away from the topic of overcoming the past, which has never been a major theme in any event, since the Austrians as official policy still endorse the myth of Austria as the first victim of Hitler. The authors who have recently emerged are introducing a variety of new themes, be it classical antiquity (Michael Köhlmeier, Inge Merkel, Elfriede Czurda), South America (Erich Hackl, Gloria Kaiser), detective stories (Gerhard Roth, Doron Rabinovici), multiculturalism (Barbara Frischmuth), and questing, be it in the classical past or in the frozen wastes of St. Joseph's land (Christoph Ransmayer).

Austrian literature is clearly in a transitional phase at the present time with no clear direction evident at the moment (See "Austrian Literature in Transition. New Authors – New Themes – New Trends," *Modern Austrian Literature*, Vol. 31, Nos. 3/4, 1998). One thing is apparent: Austrian writers are more widely traveled and worldly today than ever before. The government is generous in sponsoring reading and lecture tours. This broadening of perspective is resulting in works with wider horizons. Also the collapse of Marxism is eliminating the stock leftist viewpoint and creating more thoughtful, objective works. With a new generation of talented authors with broader vision and without the burden of so much baggage from the past, the future of Austrian literature, which is clearly the leading German-language literature today, should continue to be bright. How that situation will change the image of Austria both at home and abroad remains to be seen.

Donald G. Daviau

Vienna as the Heart of Darkness: Wilhelm Raabe's "Lesser-Germany" Politics

John Pizer

Before Otto von Bismarck and the Prussian army definitively settled the matter in 1866 and 1871, advocates of German unity in the nineteenth-century were divided into two primary camps. Some wanted a unification which included Austria, while others favored a "kleindeutsch" (lesser-Germany) approach which excluded the Habsburg lands. Among the latter group was one of Germany's greatest nineteenth-century prose stylists, Wilhelm Raabe. Raabe toured Austria in 1859, and his highly negative impressions not only solidified his lesser-Germany politics, but also found resonance in his own fictional oeuvre. In his tale *Keltische Knochen* (Celtic Bones, 1864-1865),[1] for example, Raabe portrayed the populace of Austria's capital city as corrupt and decadent, pursuing their frivolous pleasures even as they learn of their nation's defeat in battle in Italy. The novel *Gutmanns Reisen* (Gutmann's Travels, 1892) is set in Coburg, on the occasion of the first convention of the German National Association in 1860. In this historically authentic setting, Southern and Northern Germany are symbolically united through the whirlwind courtship and engagement of the young Northern German Wilhelm Gutmann and the Bavarian maiden Klotilde Blume, which takes place as the convention debates the greater vs. lesser Germany issue. While the convention wisely decides to endorse a lesser Germany, Wilhelm triumphs over his rival for Klotilde's affections. This rival, an Austrian named Alois Pärnreuther who had been Wilhelm's childhood hero for his activities in the 1848 revolution and in the battle over Schleswig-Holstein, reveals himself in Coburg to be hesitant, effeminate, and weak-willed both in his pursuit of Klotilde and of his greater Germany ideals. Wilhelm's triumph clearly signifies the victory of Prussian politics in Coburg, and, as the novel's conclusion makes clear, at Königgrätz as well.

Nevertheless, Raabe's most negative view of Austria is manifested in the novel *Der Schüdderump* (The Rumbledump, 1869-1870). In this tale, the lovely vivacious Antonie Häußler is rescued from the Krodebeck poorhouse by a group of agreeable, well-meaning but eccentric and rather powerless characters. Antonie's grandfather, Dietrich, a former resident of Krodebeck and now a wealthy resident of Vienna, comes back to Krodebeck to bring Antonie with him to Austria, and her benefactors are powerless to stop this move. Vienna is portrayed in the novel as enervated and enervating, imbued with a deep, mysterious corruption which subtly drains life away from even energetic outsiders like Antonie in a manner not unlike Joseph Conrad's Belgian Congo in *Heart of Darkness* (1902). Drawing on a variety of Raabe's works, particularly *Der Schüdderump*, this paper will elucidate Raabe's negative portrayal of Austria and its capital city and will show how this portrayal was connected to Raabe's political predilections.

Raabe's journey through Austria in 1859 was decisive for his decision to cast his lot with the lesser Germany faction of those who were striving for national unification. He sensed the Habsburg lands were both too fractious and too regressive to be included in a modern, cohesive, undivided German state. As Julia Bertschik has noted in connection with Raabe's trip: "Through a personal confrontation with a Viennese Regime perceived to be antiquated, within a multiethnic Austrian state which appeared to be unpatriotic, Raabe decided to oppose a 'Germanic-greater-Germany' politics of imperial unity under the leadership of Austria-Hungary."[2] These negative travel impressions found powerful expression in *Keltische Knochen*, the tale of a German journeying through Austria who experiences two archaeologists quarreling over the provenance of ancient bones found in Hallstatt, near Salzburg. The university "prosector" Zuckriegel believes the bones to be of Celtic origin, while his Berlin "Doppelgänger," Professor Steinbüchse, argues they were the skeletal remains of Germanic individuals.[3] The unearthing of Bronze and Iron Age relics at the Hallstatt site did indeed give rise to the debate around which the story is centered. Jeffrey Sammons has commented that the dispute had "nationalistic" overtones, but that Raabe found the matter "ridiculous."[4] This circumstance underscores the fact that Raabe's cautious embrace of a "lesser" but, ethnically speaking, relatively uniform Germany under Prussian leadership was not mixed by the racist, xenophobic blood-and-soil ideology characteristic of many German nationalists in the second half of the nineteenth-century. Raabe's sense of a pervasive corruption in the Habsburg multiethnic state had little to do with the empire's diverse population. Indeed, in works such as *Holunderblüte* (Lilac Blossom, 1863), also inspired by Raabe's trip through Austrian territory in 1859, non-Germanic groups – in the case of *Holunderblüte*, the Czechs and Jews of Prague – are portrayed in a rather sympathetic light.[5] However, as we will see, nineteenth-century Austria's multiethnic and multilingual character did contribute to Raabe's lesser-Germany orientation.

Raabe's touching picture of Prague in *Holunderblüte* strongly contrasts with his description of Vienna in *Keltische Knochen*. As a letter to his mother Auguste, dated 9 June 1859, makes evident, Raabe himself was not particularly bothered by the outcome of the battle of Magenta, a defeat for Austria at the hands of French and Piedmontese forces on 4 June 1859,[6] though the war caused him some inconvenience during his journey. Nevertheless, as the letter goes on to make evident, Raabe found the Austrian capital odd, indeed bizarre: "I remained in Vienna for three weeks and increased my wisdom and powers of perception in more than one respect. I saw what was of interest to me – often the drollest things: the 'Burgtheater,' the 'Esterhazykeller,' the 'Kahlenberg,' the 'Sperl,' the people of Vienna in places where – women don't go" (*Ergänzungsband* 2: 39). An example of the droll events experienced by Raabe in Vienna is reflected in the narrator's description in *Keltische Knochen* of a magician's ability at the Prater – visited by Raabe several times during his stay – to tear a living rabbit in half and present to an enthused public two thrashing, thumping bunnies, one in each hand. Indeed, this description serves as an illustrative prelude to the introduction of Zuckriegel in a violent confrontation with his Double, Professor Steinbüchse (9/1: 212).

More important for our purposes are Raabe's veiled epistolary references to the increase in wisdom and knowledge he gained "in more than one respect" as a result of his stay in Vienna. Given the decisiveness of this Austrian journey for the firm anchoring of Raabe's lesser-Germany politics, one can assume that Raabe's self-described elevated sagacity included insights into political issues such as what regions should be included in a unified fatherland. The following representation of Vienna by *Keltische Knochen*'s narrator makes it quite obvious that Raabe believed Austria and its domains should not be among these territories; if undisturbed by Austria's defeat at the battle of Magenta, Raabe was obviously amused but discomfited by Vienna's response to this loss:

> This dissolute Vienna – even in all its misery one could
> be amused at the way in which it sought to comfort
> itself under the burden of ever-increasing calamities.
> While the young, energetic child Italy burst loose from
> its diapers and threw its baby bottle at its old peevish
> Austrian nurse, Vienna, widely known to be less than the
> most virtuous city in the world, studied France's statis-
> tical-moral indexes. It found reassurance in the loosen-
> ing of all moral ties in the Gallic nation and awaited its
> salvation from the decrease of France's population,
> which must inevitably be the result of such ghastly
> decadence. (9/1: 210)

The decadent Viennese placed their hopes, as Raabe saw it, in the putative greater decadence of their strongest enemy in the Italian campaigns, the French.

Raabe's use here of extravagant metaphors and colorful imagery in portraying Austria as a haggard, passive nurse unable to control the tempestuous infant Italy is typical of the highly subjective character of his humor. As Wolfgang Preisendanz has noted, this "subjective re-fraction" not only strongly manifests the narrator's presence, but also imbues him with an authoritative voice vis-à-vis both the object of his description and his reader. Such a sovereign narrative mediation and its concomitant subject-object polarity are reminiscent of Romantic writers such as Jean Paul.[7] Though such stances are frequent in Raabe's oeuvre, he tends to resort to highly exaggerated, humorous troping when he is bent on conveying a strongly felt belief, whether this belief is of a political, sociological, aesthetic, or other ideological character. Thus, the hyperbole of the passage points to the vividness of Raabe's impression of Austria as hopelessly passive and listless in the face of what he, at least, regarded as a military calamity for that nation.

Of course, Raabe was not alone in his time in this general percep-tion of Austria's national character. His elder contemporary, the playwright Franz Grillparzer, who was himself a rather patriotic Aus-trian, portrayed in his drama *Ein Bruderzwist in Habsburg* (*Fraternal Strife in Habsburg*, 1848, revised 1849) the tragic hesitancy and passivity both of Emperor Rudolph II and his fraternal rival, Mathias. Enemies with regard to the status and power of Protestants in Austria immediately prior to the Thirty Years' War, the vacillation of both men when they are in power is shown to lead to this horrendous conflagration. Bruce Thompson has cogently summarized the agreement of critics that *Ein Bruderzwist in Habsburg* not only looks back at Austria's past, but also stands as a veiled commentary on its present political situation and even offers a hellish glimpse of its twentieth-century future.[8] Indeed, with the stability of his land evaporating before his eyes, the newly minted Emperor Mathias assumes an attitude much like that of the Viennese crowds observed by Raabe in 1859 and caricatured in *Keltische Knochen*; sensing his powerlessness to act, he yearns for the diversions he had enjoyed up to that point after being installed in power by Archbishop Melchior Klesel. Addressing his deceased brother Rudolph, he laments: "Those dreams of future deeds have disappeared/ As powerless as you, I stagger towards the grave/ I yearn for the open air, to distract myself."[9]

As the example of Grillparzer makes evident, Raabe's caustic portrayal of nineteenth-century Habsburg Austria's impotence, indecision, and search for distractions in the face of calamity – an ambience he would later personify in the figure of Alois Pärnreuther – clearly does not represent a unique outsider's perspective. Indeed, drawing on the work of scholars such as Claudio Magris and on Austrian literature from Grillparzer and Adalbert Stifter to Robert Musil, Kurt Bartsch has shown that Habsburg Austria – particularly in the nineteenth-century – was thoroughly permeated with such resolute irresolution, with paralysis in the face of the many crises in the multiethnic state, and that its authors consistently reflected this circumstance in their works.[10] Though Raabe experienced Vienna's attendant decadence only briefly, this exposure was enough to permanently determine his political perspective and influence his image of Austria in subsequent literary works.

Like Grillparzer, Raabe used historical events in the late sixteenth-century as a medium for reflecting on the politics of the nineteenth. The brief novella *Sankt Thomas* (St. Thomas, 1866) takes place on the African island named in the title. At the time of the narrative, this island was occupied by Spanish forces. In this unrelentingly cheerless tale, virtually devoid of the humor Raabe employed even in other works which dwell on bleak moments in human history, the small band of Spanish and Portuguese colonists are beset and eventually overcome by Dutch ships of war. However, the Dutch themselves soon succumb to plague, and the only victors are the island's native African inhabitants, who had hidden in the hills while rebelling against the Spanish. The Africans had aided the Dutch invaders, but are naturally overjoyed when all the Europeans on the island are killed or retreat from the outpost in the face of war and pestilence. As Hans Otto Horch has indicated in an article on this short work, Raabe saw in the Dutch-Spanish conflict a reflection of the Prussian-Austrian and German-Danish confrontations. In Horch's reading, Raabe's portrayal of the blacks as oppressed but ultimately victorious through the battle between two foreign powers foregrounds Raabe's desire, at the time of *Sankt Thomas*' composition, to see the inhabitants of Schleswig-Holstein allowed to determine their own destiny, unconstrained by the ambitions of Denmark, Austria, and Prussia. Ultimately, as Horch goes on to argue, the story is indicative of Raabe's lesser-Germany politics and his concomitant political antipathy toward Austria:

> Raabe belonged in 1866 to the active proponents of a 'lesser' solution to the German question and thus grew isolated in Stuttgart. Given the background of the historical narratives dealing with the events of the year 1599, these circumstances point to a fresh advocacy of the Netherlandic (and Black) battles of liberation against, respectively, the Spanish and Austrian Habsburgs.[11]

If Horch's surmise is correct – and documents concerning Raabe's activities at the time he was writing *Sankt Thomas* certainly support his theory[12] – then it is worth noting that the Spaniards of *Sankt Thomas* display the same fatalistic resignation Raabe found evident in Austria in 1859. To be sure, they put up a brave fight against the Dutch troops, but early in the siege the Spanish governor, Don Franzisko Meneses, realizes the hopelessness of their situation. He expresses his certainty at the inevitable demise of the colony in a chapter entitled "Die Galatea des Herrn Miguel Cervantes" (The 'Galatea' of Mr. Miguel Cervantes). The image of the governor with his torn and dusty uniform, his blackened hands and face, and his long dagger in this specific onomastic context and in connection with his futile attempt to stave off the Dutch is inevitably reminiscent of Don Quixote tilting at windmills, although he lacks the latter's imagination and optimism, and although the chapter title refers to a different work of the great Spanish novelist (9/2: 30-35). Meneses and his colonists do believe in the dreams and glory of the rigidly class-structured Spanish civilization, much as nineteenth-century Austrians held to their faith in the higher, universal order they saw concretized in the equally hierarchical and imperially ambitious Austrian state.[13] Like the Austrians, the fictional Spaniards cling to this utopian image despite clear signs of impending imperial demise.

As Horch indicated in the above-cited passage, Raabe resided in Stuttgart during the composition of *Sankt Thomas* and felt isolated in his lesser-Germany politics. The majority of Stuttgarters of the time were adherents of the German Confederation, and thus in favor of a powerful, influential Austria. Raabe was subject to considerable opprobrium as a result of his views. In a letter to his mother and siblings, dated 11 September 1866, Raabe indicates a fear of denunciation and forced exile at the hands of the Swabians and their police, who were particularly antagonistic toward those who held pro-Prussian, anti-greater Germany sentiments following the conclusion of the Prussian-Austrian war (*Ergänzungsband* 2: 116-117). Throughout his residency in Stuttgart from 1862 to 1870, Raabe felt threatened as a result of his unpopular anti-Austrian perspective. Under such circumstances, it is easy to appreciate why Raabe would resort to employing an obscure sixteenth-century Spanish colony as a cipher for nineteenth-century Austria.

The veiled character of Raabe's negative image of Austria is also evident in *Der Schüdderump*. To be sure, key passages in the novel take place in contemporary Vienna and not in a metaphorically hidden distant place and time. Nevertheless, the role of the city as an *agent* of fatal corruption and decadence is far from obvious. Some critics see the portrayal of Vienna in the novel as simply symptomatic of Raabe's antipathy toward all big-city life, full of a cold impersonality, an empty social superficiality and egotism which stands in contrast to the communal harmony exemplified by the rural, agrarian Lauenhof from which Antonie Häußler is so abruptly, wrenchingly torn. In this respect, these critics believe, Raabe saw no real distinction between the Viennese and Berlin cityscapes. Rolf-Dieter Koll, for example, believes the Vienna of *Der Schüdderump* is "the emblem of societal superficiality, of a cold life lived in isolation and egotism, just as it was sketched in the house of the banker Götz in *Der Hungerpastor*, a connection which a self-quotation of the author [from this book-JP] clearly establishes."[14] The house to which Koll refers is located in the Berlin of *Der Hungerpastor*, and in describing one of the chambers in

Dietrich Häußler's Vienna home, the narrator of *Der Schüdderump* refers to a painting which had also hung in the room of Götz's wife (8: 273). Drawing on Raabe's allusion in the novel to the biblical sites "Ahala" and "Ahaliba" in connection with Berlin and Vienna, the respective localities of Dietrich Häußler's apprenticeship and sphere of influence as a wealthy speculator and nobleman, Dieter Kafitz finds both these capital cities allegorically transformed into generalized and timeless sites of corruption and sin.[15]

Certainly, Raabe's novels and stories consistently juxtapose a vanishing cohesive village life with the ruthlessness and divisiveness he saw in Germany's rapid urbanization in the late nineteenth-century. In one of the most celebrated episodes in all of Raabe's vast oeuvre, the idealist Velten Andres, one of the principals in the late novel *Die Akten des Vogelsangs* (The Documents of the Birdsong, 1896), gradually burns virtually every item of his childhood Vogelsang home during the course of a winter, and then allows what remains of the dwelling to be stripped apart at a bizarre street auction. Velten's motivations are complex and varied, but a central one is his refusal to allow the cherished site to remain in an area being rapidly transformed from a small, bucolic village into a large, soulless, materialistically oriented cityscape. In the very last paragraph in which Velten is involved in the narrative as a protagonist, he alludes to this change, to his knowledge that his old homestead has simply become "the 'new construction site,' one of the best in the new Birdsong" (19: 384). In the context of the novel and of Raabe's social perspective as well, the term "new Birdsong" conveys a subtle but clear repugnance at Germany's metamorphosis from a primarily rural to a primarily urban land. Nevertheless, during his student days in Germany's largest city, Berlin, Velten is able to find tranquility, moral support, and salubrious perspectives on life in the company of his landlady and the cultivated, aptly named des Beaux family. The Viennese atmosphere of *Der Schüdderump*, on the other hand, is irredeemably and unremittingly corrupt and corrupting.

Much more than Velten, Antonie Häußler is victimized largely as the result of the changes to which she is subjected as an adult because of her necessary move from her childhood domain. Her initial appearance in the novel is in the poorhouse of the town Krodebeck. She is brought there with her mother. The mother is near death, and the very sight of the cart bringing the impoverished former resident of Krodebeck and her child is enough to horrify the poorhouse's elderly female occupant. The vehicle thus becomes imbued with the resonance of death implied by the slang term which gave the novel its title, used to signify a wagon employed during the plague which delivered the pestilence's deceased victims to their mass graves. At an early stage, then, the eponymous conveyance, the rumbledump, becomes a central motif in the tale. However, after the death of Marie Häußler, her daughter Antonie is able to enjoy a rather happy, well-adjusted childhood. She is first raised by Hanne Allmann, the old woman of the poorhouse, and her herb-gathering friend Jane Warwolf, one of Raabe's numerous women-of-nature characters whose earth-bound wisdom casts into antithetical relief those big-city occupants spiritually impoverished through urbanization. After Hanne's death, the girl is cared for at the estate of her playmate Hennig von Lauen's mother Adelheid. Her primary guardians there are also gentle old folk, the dignified, deeply humane Karl von Glaubigern and the frail Adelaide von Saint-Trouin, who spends her time nostalgically immersing herself in the glory days of her noble French ancestors. Despite occasional inferences regarding life's mortal and evil aspects, little clouds the horizons of Antonie's youth until the arrival of her maternal grandfather. A sly, cunning, totally unscrupulous ne'er-do-well, he is able to first truly thrive, after years of poverty, in the Austrian empire. The circumstance that Austria provides the ideal environment for this corrupt individual is indicative of Raabe's continued animus toward this land. Because of the power, wealth, and insights Dietrich Häußler has gained there, the well-meaning but relatively feeble denizens of Krodebeck and the Lauen estate are helpless to prevent him from carrying out his wish to bring Antonie with him to Vienna. Thus, the arrival of his carriage in Krodebeck is associated with the return there, after a long, trouble-free period, of the rumbledump (8: 230).

Dietrich Häußler personifies most of the characteristics perceived by Raabe in Austria during his travels through the country in 1859. One of Raabe's biographers, Horst Denkler, notes that Raabe found Austria "amoral and asocial, corrupt and unpatriotic."[16] Häußler seems to incorporate even this latter quality, for he is described by Hennig as a "heimatloser Taugenichts" ("a good-for-nothing without a homeland"); even in contemporary times, the use of the similar term "vaterlandslose Gesellen" ("fellows lacking a fatherland") to characterize certain Germans clearly indicates a belief that their very lack of rootedness is unpatriotic. The reader's perception of this negative trait in Häußler is in no way mitigated by Jane Warwolf's response to Hennig that the new Austrian is "no longer a vagabond" (8: 192). Dietrich's lack of ethics is evident from the circumstance that he goads and manipulates Antonie and her Krodebeck circle into allowing him to take her back to Vienna (where he will ultimately try to induce her to marry a fellow swindler in order to further his business interests), even though it is obvious to him that his granddaughter accompanies him very unwillingly. His corruption becomes evident in the delineation of his Austrian business practices and lifestyle. His unsocial nature is revealed in glimpses back into his past as the Krodebeck village barber, where he brutally mistreated his wife in bouts of violent rage. Vienna is portrayed as an ideal milieu in which to hide this innate maliciousness, for its citizens wear the same false mask of charm and bonhomie which allows Häußler to thrive there. In Krodebeck, the superficial charm he displays upon his triumphant return succeeds only in hoodwinking the village pastor and his son, but they are themselves inherently corrupt and thus happy to accept the Austrian nobleman at face value.

As is evident from his characterization of Dietrich as a good-for-nothing without a homeland, Hennig is one of the Krodebeckers most strongly imbued with antipathy toward the village's ex-barber. In his helpless rage at the events leading toward Antonie's departure, he curses and screams about this powerful foe (8: 192-193). After Antonie's departure, Hennig becomes restless, and decides to undertake his own journey, which includes a visit to the Austrian capital. As much as the circumstance that its corrupt, stifling atmosphere literally draws life's breath from Antonie over time, Vienna's ability to seduce the young Junker Hennig into forgetting his early outrage and into deluding himself that Antonie's life at the home of her grandfather is not as miserable as it appears at first glance marks the city as a heart of darkness. To be sure, what most impacts Hennig is Vienna's famous gay frivolity rather than the more blatantly manifest malevolence and putrefaction characteristic of the Belgian Congo in Conrad's famous novella. As Johannes Klein has indicated in an article on *Der Schüdderump*, Vienna serves as a site where Antonie's world-theater style of fate, which would have been portrayed as a tragedy in the Middle Ages, is inevitably turned into a comedy, as she herself is fully aware.[17] It must also be recognized that Hennig, in spite of his indignant bluster at Dietrich's impending intrusion into Antonie's life, is both weak-willed and naive. He is accustomed to living his own life fully in accordance with the dictates of his mother Adelheid; his decision to undertake a European journey is his first genuine act of rebellion against her. His own feelings toward Antonie are informed neither by passion nor by love, and Antonie's recognition of this circumstance during the course of Hennig's stay in Vienna is as significant for her ultimate demise as the evil and corruption to which she is constantly subjected.

Nevertheless, Raabe uses the occasion of Hennig's sojourn in the Austrian capital to underscore what he saw as its baleful influence. Vienna's effect on Hennig is represented as the exploitation and perversion of a weak personality. To be sure, Vienna turns Hennig neither into a criminal nor a wastrel. Instead, he becomes infected with what Raabe saw as relatively subtle but deep-seated Viennese traits, traits he observed in his 1859 sojourn and briefly portrayed in *Keltische Knochen*, namely, passivity in the face of crisis, lassitude when action is required, a search for diversion in order to escape a looming exigency. Raabe represents this paralysis as gripping Hennig the moment he arrives in Vienna:

> The junker lit, on Viennese soil, the first of the cigars he had successfully smuggled in, a cigar of indecision and uneasiness. The light little clouds which curled up into the sky from the meadows and fields of Krodebeck all the livelong day were entirely different from those which vanished here in the stifling, dust-filled air. So there he was, the junker of Lauen, and he wasn't even in a hurry to find an inn. (8: 261)

Indecision, malaise, a sense of uneasiness – these for Raabe native elements in the Viennese atmosphere will infect Hennig during his entire stay in the Austrian capital, except at those moments when the town's amusements distract him from his discomfort. The murky, dank, oppressive, disabling milieu evoked by Raabe at the outset of Hennig's Austrian adventure is not unlike the landscape painted by Conrad at the end of his novella; this portrait underscores the incapacitating and decadent effects the Belgian Congo was shown to exert on Europeans susceptible to such power during the course of the narrative:

> Marlow ceased, and sat apart, indistinct and silent, in the pose of a meditating Buddha. Nobody moved for a time. "We have lost the first of the ebb," said the Director, suddenly. I raised my head. The offing was barred by a black bank of clouds, and the tranquil waterway leading to the uttermost ends of the earth flowed sombre under an overcast sky – seemed to lead into the heart of an immense darkness.[18]

The respective atmospheres of Vienna and the Belgian Congo produce the same enervation, the same collapse into corruption and indolence, in those who fall under their spell.

Hennig visits Antonie while Dietrich Häußler is away on business in Italy, and is, at first, genuinely shocked at her appearance (8: 274). Nevertheless, the longer he remains in Vienna, the more he adjusts to and enjoys the city. Thus, the succor he affords to his childhood friend consists in the simple attempt to amuse and divert her with caricatures of the city and its people, thereby demonstrating that what for Raabe was the Habsburg capital's chief occupation has become Hennig's own modus operandi with respect to Antonie. He hesitates to leave Vienna, and becomes increasingly baffled by its externalities. Raabe describes this confusing city and its inhabitants as happy to make no clear distinctions between delusion and reality, as cheerfully and lightly accepting what moralists and judges would find highly dubious, indeed criminal (8: 290). Hennig comes to enjoy the company of the city's nobility, and cannot recognize that the men are swindlers and the ladies frivolous and shallow in their perspectives concerning Antonie. Hennig makes a half-hearted proposal of marriage, which Antonie recognizes as an act of distorted compassion rather than love and therefore refuses. Finally, Karl von Glaubigern resolves to travel to Austria and rescue Antonie from Dietrich Häußler and his scheme to marry his granddaughter to a wealthy Viennese speculator in the hope of furthering his business interests. However, Glaubigern is too late; she dies shortly after his arrival from the combined effects of a broken heart and the stifling corrosive atmosphere of her environs.

In a book on Raabe published in 1930, Friedrich Röttger notes Raabe's relationship to Austria was a particularly interesting component of *Der Schüdderump*. He remarks that Hennig's visit to Austria takes place just prior to 1866 and the Prussian-Austrian war, and that

Raabe manages to strike a pacifistic tone in the novel even while making his sympathy for the eventual victors evident in exposing Austria's unsuitability for membership in a unified Germany. However, Röttger focuses primarily on the novel's allusions to the multiethnic, polyglot nature of the Austrian empire in analyzing its portrayal of the Habsburg lands.[19] *Der Schüdderump* does indeed refer to this aspect of Austria, and is illustrative of Raabe's fears about including Austria's different ethnic groups within a united Germany's borders. For example, a letter from Hennig to Krodebeck mentions the Austrian infantry's inability to comprehend German, which makes it inconceivable that Krodebeck and the Lauenhof could be ruled from Vienna (8: 280). Nevertheless, the novel clearly lends greater weight to what Raabe regarded as Austria's turpitude rather than to its national and linguistic diversity. In *Der Schüdderump*, Raabe sustained his lesser-Germany politics by showing what can happen to Germans – and, by extension, to Germany itself – when they are caught up in what he felt was the enervating moral morass of Austria and its capital.

Although Raabe was unwaveringly opposed to the inclusion of Austria in a greater Germany and had deep misgivings about the ethical tendencies of its inhabitants, Raabe himself did not consistently bear personal hostility toward the country, particularly after the battle of Königgrätz allayed all his fears regarding a possible "Großdeutschland." In a letter to the publisher Eduard Hallberger dated 10 April 1867 (six months before he began work on *Der Schüdderump*), Raabe offered the following political advice: "I would allow the concepts 'Prussian' and 'Austrian,' wherever possible, to recede into the background. On the other hand, through comparisons and contrasts, I would move national feeling against foreign lands as sharply as possible to the fore" (*Ergänzungsband* 2, 120). No doubt Raabe believed he followed this dictum even in *Der Schüdderump*, where overt political overtones are rarely present. In a novel written a number of years later, *Horacker* (1876), Raabe even poked fun at the German bourgeoisie's celebration of the victory over Austria. One of the principals in this tale of an escaped criminal – Cord Horacker – who had only stolen some lard and then ran away from his workhouse because of false rumors concerning his beloved – is the pompous teacher Neubauer. He spends much of his spare time composing an epic poem, a "Sixty-sixiad." As its title implies, this work is a paean to Prussia's recent victory over Austria. Neubauer is for Raabe the sort of humorless modern pedagogue whose advent in an increasingly militant

Wilhelmine Germany Raabe viewed with dismay; as Jeffrey Sammons puts it, he represents "the New Prussian Man as schoolmaster."[20] The reader experiences little about the contents of his ode, but the wife of the aging former teacher, Eckerbusch, a man whom Raabe represents as among the last of a dying breed of compassionate, good-humored educators, turns Bismarck's comment that the German schoolmaster won the battle of Königgrätz on its head in characterizing Neubauer, his poem, and indeed his entire fellow generation of teachers as fanatic, single-minded, stuffy, and misguided (12: 398). Julia Bertschik has trenchantly observed that Frau Eckerbusch exposes here the modern, rigidly disciplined, militaristic pedagogy Raabe regretfully felt was replacing the goal of a humanistic education ("Bildung") inherent in a vanishing National-liberal idealism.[21] By 1876 Raabe was clearly disappointed at the result of Prussia's ascendancy after the wars of 1866 and 1870-1871, and he uses an absurd, fictive poetization of the Austrian-Prussian conflict to ridicule not the former putatively corrupt enemy, but the bourgeoisie of the state Raabe had hoped would lead a united lesser Germany in a humane, enlightened fashion.[22]

This is clearly not the case with *Gutmanns Reisen*. If *Horacker* inverted Bismarck's famous maxim on the Prussian pedagogue's victory over Austria to equate this triumph with the defeat of tolerant, humane education in Germany, *Gutmanns Reisen* is Raabe's own paean to the Iron Chancellor. Indeed, in an often-quoted letter to the writer Wilhelm Jensen and his wife, dated 22 December 1891, Raabe calls this novel his "Bismarckias" (*Ergänzungsband* 3: 461). Unlike *Horacker*, it paints a retrospective picture of Germany, prior to the Second Empire and its stiff, intolerant militarism. Thus, Raabe ignored the dictum of the letter he wrote a quarter of a century earlier to Eduard Hallberger about the usefulness of allowing the concepts "Prussian" and "Austrian" to recede as far as possible into the background; they emerge as absolutely antithetical in both the novel's political discussions and in its characterizations. Of course, by the 1890s Raabe no longer had to be cautious about his feelings toward Austria and about his joy at the Prussian victory at Königgrätz which virtually ended the impetus for a "greater-Germany" solution to German unity. Raabe's circumspection in the Hallberger letter was certainly at least partly motivated by the circumstance that he composed it in 1867 in pro-Austrian Stuttgart and sent it to a Stuttgart address. Writing in Braunschweig to his friend Edmund Sträter in a letter dated 13 September 1897, Raabe could unabashedly proclaim: "The year eighteen hundred and sixty-six is and remains for me the most blessed in the entire history of our people" (*Ergänzungsband* 2: 396). What followed this putatively glorious year was disappointment for Raabe in Germany's sociocultural development. As Friedhelm Henrich has noted in an article on *Gutmanns Reisen*, this disappointment played a key role in inspiring Raabe to compose the novel.²³

Raabe joined the German National Association in May of 1860 and attended its first general assembly in Coburg, the historical event which provides the backdrop for *Gutmanns Reisen*, in September of that year. He was quite enthusiastic about the program put forward there by the Lesser Germany Liberals,²⁴ and this perspective is clearly evident in the novel. The opposing "Großdeutschland" principal finds its main advocate in the Austrian Alois Pärnreuther, and in several passages Raabe subtly alludes to a belief that Pärnreuther and his countrymen are not true Germans. When Gutmann senior chimes into a ditty about German women, German forthrightness, German wine, and German song, the hero of Viennese barricades and Hungarian meadows realizes his place is in bed rather than at the festive Coburg "Verbrüderungstisch" ("table of fraternization") where such tunes are being sung (18: 302-303). Alluding to his childhood hero's business affairs, Gutmann junior calls Pärnreuther a "half Hungarian," in contrast to the "authentic, pure Germans" among whom he numbers himself (18: 312); one could legitimately interpret this passage as indicative of Raabe's belief that Austria was too ethnically fragmented for inclusion in a unified fatherland. Willi Gutmann draws explicit parallels between his competition with Pärnreuther for Klotilde Blume's hand and the rivalry between Austria and Prussia (18: 338-339). When the Austrian magnanimously travels to the Northern German town where the Gutmanns reside in order to win the support of Frau Gutmann for her son's marriage, he implicitly equates the rebuff he received in the affair with the victory of Prussian earnestness over Viennese frivolity (18: 403, 407). Willi Gutmann's marriage to Klotilde Blume thus reflects allegorically the political implications of the Coburg convention.²⁵ As the novel's conclusion makes clear, the military victories attained by Bismarck in 1866 and 1871 make these implications a concrete reality; Austria is excluded from a united sovereign Germany, where Prussia attains dominant influence (18: 414-415).

Though he must swallow defeat in love and politics, Pärnreuther is never treated badly by his German rivals. In bidding the Austrian farewell after the convention, Pastor Nodt, an ardent "Kleindeutschland" advocate, strikes a conciliatory tone: "My dear Herr von Pärnreuther, if I am seeing things correctly, everything depends on you. So don't get angry, don't run off feeling hatred, remain with us, remain here as the dearest, best, most cherished and truest friend and companion of the family" (18: 398). After his visit to Austria in 1859, Raabe remained firm in his conviction that this land was too decadent, too corrupt, too inherently fractious and divided to be included in a united Germany. His literary representations of Austria were consistently negative, as was his personification of the nation in the figure of Alois Pärnreuther. Nevertheless, Raabe wrote *Gutmanns Reisen* in the 1890s, long after the possibility of a "greater Germany" had passed in the nineteenth century and long before it became a brief reality in 1938. If the novel is an allegory of the union of North and South Germany through the exclusion of Austria, then Nodt's speech can be seen to signal Raabe's desire that the Habsburg Empire should become a close friend of the now inextricably intertwined couple.

Louisiana State University

Notes

1. With one exception, all translations of the titles of Raabe's works are borrowed from Jeffrey L. Sammons' book *Wilhelm Raabe: The Fiction of the Alternative Community* (Princeton: Princeton UP, 1987) and are printed in Roman font. The one exception represents the title of a published English translation, and is given in italics. All translations of German citations are my own.

2. Julia Bertschik, *Maulwurfsarchäologie: Zum Verhältnis von Geschichte und Anthropologie in Wilhelm Raabes historischen Erzähltexten* (Tübingen: Max Niemeyer, 1995), 53.

3. Wilhelm Raabe, *Sämtliche Werke*, ed. Karl Hoppe et al. (Göttingen: Vandenhoeck & Ruprecht, 1960-), 9/1: 212-213. Hereafter cited in the text by volume and page number.

4. Sammons, 142.

5. To be sure, Raabe is regarded by some scholars as an anti-Semite because of his highly unflattering portrait of a Jew, Moses Freudenstein, in the most popular and widely discussed novel in his

oeuvre, *Der Hungerpastor* (*The Hunger Pastor*, 1863-1864). For a range of opinion on this issue, see Horst Denkler, "Das 'wirckliche Juda' und der 'Renegat': Moses Freudenstein als Kronzeuge für Wilhelm Raabes Verhältnis zu Juden und Judentum," *German Quarterly* 60 (1987), 5-18; Robert C. Holub, "Raabe's Impartiality: A Reply to Horst Denkler," *German Quarterly* 60 (1987), 617-622; Sammons, 73-87; Holub, *Reflections of Realism: Paradox, Norm, and Ideology in Nineteenth-Century German Prose* (Detroit: Wayne State UP, 1991), 185-190.

6. For a brief account of this battle and the events leading up to it, see C. A. Macartney, *The Hapsburg Empire 1790-1918* (London: Weidenfeld and Nicolson, 1968), 489-490.

7. Wolfgang Preisendanz, *Humor als dichterische Einbildungskraft: Studien zur Erzählkunst des poetischen Realismus*, 2nd ed. (Munich: Wilhelm Fink, 1976), 251-253.

8. Bruce Thompson, *Franz Grillparzer* (Boston: Twayne, 1981), 108-109.

9. Franz Grillparzer, *Sämtliche Werke: Historisch-kritische Gesamtausgabe*, ed. August Sauer (Vienna: Anton Schroll, 1927), I/6, 337.

10. Kurt Bartsch, "Literatur aus Österreich='österreichische' Literatur? Zum Problem ihrer eigenständigen Identität," *Studies in Modern Austrian Literature*, ed. B. O. Murdoch and M. G. Ward (Glasgow: Scottish Papers in Germanic Studies, 1981), 1-20.

11. Hans Otto Horch, "Historische Standortbestimmung vor Guinea. Zu Wilhelm Raabes Erzählung 'Sankt Thomas' (1865)," *Jahrbuch der Raabe-Gesellschaft*, 1986, 118-119.

12. As Bertschik (57) has noted, Raabe attended the second meeting of the general assembly of the German National Association at the very time (the summer of 1861) he was first occupied with composing *Sankt Thomas*, and two significant issues discussed at this meeting were Prussian-Austrian relations and the Schleswig-Holstein situation.

13. See Bartsch, 7-8.

14. Rolf-Dieter Koll, *Raumgestaltung bei Wilhelm Raabe* (Bonn: Bouvier, 1977), 126.

15. Dieter Kafitz, *Figurenkonstellation als Mittel der Wirklichkeitserfassung: Dargestellt an Romanen der zweiten Hälfte des 19. Jahrhunderts (Freytag, Spielhagen, Fontane, Raabe)* (Kronberg/Ts.: Athenäum, 1978), 186.

16. Denkler, *Wilhelm Raabe: Legende – Leben – Literatur* (Tübingen: Max Niemeyer, 1989), 89.

17. Johannes Klein, "Raabes 'Schüdderump,'" *Jahrbuch der Raabe-Gesellschaft* 1968, 12.

18. Joseph Conrad, *Complete Works* (Garden City: Doubleday, Page & Company, 1925), 16: 162.

19. Friedrich Röttger, *Volk und Vaterland bei Wilhelm Raabe* (Graz: Heinrich Stiasny's Söhne, 1930), 184-188. Of course, Röttger's focus is not surprising in light of Central European racial politics in the 1920s and 1930s.

20. Sammons, 138. In his otherwise excellent book Sammons errs on this page in describing Neubauer's work as "an epic poem on the recent Prussian victory over the Danes in 1866."

21. Bertschik, 118-119.

22. Though, as A. Weber has noted, Eckerbusch is, like Raabe himself, a self-proclaimed complete adherent of the North German League and in agreement with Bismarck's policy of unifying Germany by military force. See Weber's essay "Lehrerfiguren in Raabes Horacker," *Formen realistischer Erzählkunst: Festschrift for Charlotte Jolles*, ed. Jörg Thunecke (Nottingham: Sherwood Press Agencies, 1979), 216-232, esp. 219.

23. Friedhelm Henrich, "'Wunsiedel und die Gründung des Deutschen Nationalvereins.' Polarität und Komplexität in Wilhem Raabes 'Gutmanns Reisen,'" *Jahrbuch der Raabe-Gesellschaft*, 1991, 8.

24. On Raabe's association with the National Association and his involvement in the Coburg meeting, see Heinrich Leonard, "Wilhelm Raabe und der Deutsche Nationalverein," *Wilhelm Raabe und sein Lebenskreis: Festschrift zum 100. Geburtstag des Dichters namens der Gesellschaft der Freunde Wilhelm Raabes und der Verlagsanstalt Hermann Klemm A. G.*, ed. Heinrich Spiero (Berlin-Grunewald: Hermann Klemm, 1931), 43-49.

25. For a more detailed explication of this allegory, see Kafitz, 209, and Henrich, 23.

Marie von Ebner-Eschenbach's *Božena*: A Czech Maid and the Future of Austria

Ester Riehl

The novel *Božena* (1876) has usually been read as a tale of sin and atonement. Early in the novel the title character spends one night with a lover. Her absence from the house where she is responsible for Rosa, her employer's daughter, allows Rosa to run away and elope, causing her to be disowned by her father. Božena spends the remainder of the novel caring for Rosa and her daughter Röschen, and she also manages to reinstate Röschen's inheritance. The most common reading of *Božena* argues that the entire plot is motivated by Božena's guilt: because her "sin" allowed Rosa to run away, she must spend her life atoning for it. At the beginning of the twentieth century Gabriele Reuter explained this interpretation:

> Božena, the robust plebeian maid, has but one fault. That fault lies in her actions of one night, when she put her own happiness above her responsibilities to the child of her master. That sin is atoned only through her lifelong self sacrifice.[1]

Critics have continued to accept this interpretation of Božena's motivation. "[Božena] knows that regret does not suffice in atoning for a crime. The author repeatedly expresses this idea."[2] This argument suggests that since Božena's alleged sin is responsible for Rosa and Röschen's disinheritance, she must atone for that sin by getting it back.

That interpretation is unsatisfactory primarily because Božena's alleged sin does not cause Rosa to run away. Heide Beutin disagrees with the above interpretation, explaining, "These interpretations assume (as does the author) that guilt can indeed be identified in Božena's life."[3] Beutin concludes that Božena probably would not have tried to stop Rosa from leaving, had she been there. Rosa runs away and is disowned because of her father's inflexibility, while Röschen is denied her inheritance because of the greed of her grandfather's second wife and daughter. The origins of these unfair proceedings do not lie within Božena's responsibilities.

The actions of the rest of the characters, however, make it easy to assign guilt. After the deaths of his son and his first wife, Leopold Heißenstein remarries in hopes of having another son to carry on the family name and the family business. He already has a daughter, Rosa, from his first marriage. Rosa's rebellious elopement with the army officer Fehse enrages her father, who cuts her out of his will and decrees that he has but one daughter, Regula, from his second marriage. Božena follows Rosa and her husband, and she stays with them until their untimely deaths. She then returns to the Heißenstein household with Rosa's young daughter Röschen, begs forgiveness for running away, and hopes for a place in the family for Heißenstein's granddaughter. By now, Heißenstein is old and dying, and he rues his anger at his older daughter. He tells his wife and daughter that they must right the wrongs committed against his granddaughter, but dies before he can officially alter his last will and testament. They do not follow his wishes, though they do provide for Röschen's physical welfare and education.

The rest of the novel focuses on Božena's quest to reinstate Röschen's inheritance. Her quest is not motivated by a sense of guilt, but out of love for Rosa and Röschen, and a desire for justice. She finally succeeds when Regula buys the estate of the financially bankrupt Earl von Rondsperg. After Röschen and the Earl's son fall in love, Božena convinces Regula to give the estate to Röschen as a wedding present.

If it is not guilt that motivates Božena to help Rosa and Röschen, another motivation must be found. That motivation comes from her maternal concern for their welfare. Božena's role as mother contrasts both with Heißenstein's role as father and Nannette's role as mother. Heißenstein and Nannette both use their positions as heads of family to exercise power over others and use people for their own ends. As a mother figure to Rosa and Röschen, Božena is also the head of a family, but she uses that position very differently. A servant, she does not have the kind of economic and social power the Heißensteins do. Her power comes from love and morality.

One definition of family, that of the traditional "ganzes Haus,"* describes it as a group of people living and working together, and includes servants or individuals who are not blood relatives.[4] Using this definition, Božena belongs to the Heißenstein family and plays a specific economic role, though not necessarily an emotional one. Modern connotations of the word "family," however, imply emotional attachment and love. These modern connotations began to achieve prominence in the late eighteenth century, when people began expecting "an atmosphere of warmth and intimacy" from families.[5] The Heißenstein family presents an intersection of these two forms of family. While Heißenstein sees the family as a means to promote his economic activity (he wants a son who can take over the business), Božena's relationships with Rosa and Röschen are based on an emotional attachment and maternal responsibility.

Božena's role as matriarch, however, is not without problems. She is a mother who is allowed no life of her own. Not only must she deny her sexuality, but she must devote her life totally to her child. As a servant in the Heißenstein household, she already has little privacy or personal freedom. Servants, though members of the extended family in the *ganzes Haus*, had little independence. Moreover, Božena's dual role as servant and mother reinforces the notion that women are to dedicate their entire lives to their children and have no other self. Her "power," as well, is limited to the household, and in this way reinforces the notion of "separate spheres." In the ideology of separate spheres women are assigned a role only in the home and family and can only hope to influence the outer world through private interaction with their husbands or fathers. Božena does have the power to influence her employers, and her child's future depends on it. Her power is limited by the long process of winning her employers' trust and respect. Without their cooperation Božena can do little to help Röschen.

These private matters may seem to have little to do with the state of affairs in the Austrian Empire, but philosophers have long made a connection between the family and the state. Aristotle traced the origins of the state to familial organizations, explaining that "the most natural form of the village appears to be that of a colony from the

---

* I use the German term "ganzes Haus" (literally, whole house) because it more specifically describes the familial situation than the English term, "household."

family."[6] "Following Aristotle, most writers said that the household was the precursor of the state; it was a form of political organization that existed before the state and out of which the state evolved."[7] In a similar fashion, proponents of nationalism have often invoked the family as a precursor or model of the nation. Using familial terms to articulate political love for the nation, argues Benedict Anderson, implies natural ties to the nation.[8] Ernest Renan has called the nation a "spiritual family."[9] Anne McClintock points to a connection between family and nation within nineteenth-century modes of understanding:

> [T]he family offered an indispensable figure for sanctioning social *hierarchy* within a putative *organic unity* of interests. Since the subordination of woman to man, and child to adult, was deemed a natural fact, other forms of social hierarchy could be depicted in familial terms to guarantee social difference as a category of nature.[10]

Nineteenth-century bourgeois ideology posited the family as a natural unit, whose form was designated by "natural" principles. Linking the allegedly organic origins of the nation to the apparently organic origins of the family provided a familiar basis for the new ideology of the nation. Moreover, basing the idea of nation and state on the notion of a "natural" hierarchical, patriarchal family, allows for the same kind of hierarchy to exist in state and nation.

It is therefore quite striking that the most important family in *Božena* is a matriarchal family, in which relationships are based on love and caring rather than domination. A state or nation based on this kind of family would look very different from the Austrian Empire as it existed in Ebner-Eschenbach's lifetime. Carl Steiner comments that the Revolution of 1848 provides "historical background" for the novel.[11] I would argue that the revolution plays more than a background role, since the relationships between Czechs and German Austrians are central to the novel. Indeed, the issues of the Revolution and the Czech independence movement have numerous parallels in the novel.

This connection appears in *Božena* as the private issues of family and mothering are linked to political issues of state and nation. Such personal issues do play a large role in Ebner-Eschenbach's novel, but critics have largely ignored the political issues it addresses. The plot centers on private issues of family and mothering and only briefly mentions the changes going on in the Austrian Empire. The brevity of the direct statements on the Revolution and the changes it wrought do not, however, mean that political issues provide only a background to the novel. Written almost thirty years after the Revolution, the novel's plot centers on issues related to national identity and the role of Czechs in the Austrian Empire.

The novel clearly demarcates bad and good characters along national lines. Without making blatant political statements, the title character, who embodies goodness, fairness and honesty, is Czech, and her adversaries are German. The Czech nationalist leader František Palacký (1798-1876) claimed that the struggle between Germans and Slavs formed the central issue in Czech history. "The ideological form of this conflict had been expressed in the struggle of Slavic principles of democracy, equality and liberty with the principle of German feudalism, based on the distinction between the lord and his subject."[12] Palacký elevated those "Slavic principles" over German feudalism and sought the legitimization of the Slavic nation, but not the subjugation of Germans. Palacký was invited to represent Bohemia at the new German National Assembly in Frankfurt in 1848, since "The assumption was that, as of old, Bohemia was part of Germany."[13] Palacký declined that invitation, explaining in a letter:

> The rights of nations are in truth the rights of Nature. No nation on earth has the right to demand that its neighbors should sacrifice themselves for its benefit, no nation is under an obligation to deny or sacrifice itself for the good of its neighbor. Nature knows neither dominant nor underyoked nations.[14]

Palacký maintained that Slavic interests could best be served by continued association with a reformed Austrian Empire. He believed the world was moving toward increased centralization, requiring that smaller nations seek protection in mutually beneficial federations. International relations, he argued, "should be based on the idea of the natural right of nations to exist."[15]

Later in 1848 the First Slavonic Congress issued its manifesto to the nations of Europe. This manifesto, drafted by Palacký, again demanded national independence. It contrasted the militarism of Germanic states against the independence and peace desired by Slavic nations. It criticized "Latin and Germanic nations" which had "ensured independence for their own States by the might of the sword," and based their statecraft "mainly . . . on the right of superior force."

> On the other hand, the Slavs, among whom liberty was ever cherished the more fervently as they showed little aspiration for conquest and dominion, and among whom the desire for independence always prevented the formation of a higher central power of any kind, fell in the course of the ages, people after people, under alien dominion.[16]

Not only do Slavs desire liberty and independence for nations, continues the manifesto, but for individuals as well.

> The Slav . . . remains true to his natural character and the principles of his forefathers. He demands neither conquest nor dominion, but he asks for liberty for himself and for all others: he demands that liberty shall be unconditionally recognised as the most sacred right that man possesses. Therefore we Slavs reject and hold in abhorrence all dominion based on main force and evasion of the law; we reject all privileges and prerogatives as well as all political differentiation of classes; we demand unconditional equality before the law, an equal measure of rights and duties for all.[17]

Despite its inflated political rhetoric, this manifesto expresses the ideal views of some prominent Czech leaders, and it represents a challenge to the traditional organization of Austrian society at national, social and individual levels.

The division drawn along national lines in *Božena* is also drawn along gender lines. A central theme in the novel is the conflict between patriarchy and matriarchy. Such a theme is not surprising, since many other studies of matriarchy appeared in Ebner-Eschenbach's lifetime. Grillparzer's *Libussa*, though not published until 1872, had been performed in part in 1840. Given her personal contact with Grillparzer, it seems reasonable to assume that Ebner-Eschenbach knew about his work on the drama before it was published. Bachofen's *Mutterrecht* (1861) was widely read and debated, and

Bachofen himself corresponded with Lewis Henry Morgan, author of *Ancient Society* (1877). Friedrich Engels, in turn, based his understanding of ancient matriarchal societies on Morgan's work and outlined it in *Origin of the Family, Private Property and the State* (1884). While these texts explore the idea of matriarchy through mythical, sociological and historical perspectives, Ebner-Eschenbach imagines the establishment of matriarchal society in the world she knows. Contemporary issues such as class and national struggles play central roles in the founding of her vision of matriarchy.

Her form of matriarchy provides a contrast to a hierarchical and unyielding patriarchy. Leopold Heißenstein rules his family with little regard for the wishes of his wife and children. The first two paragraphs of the novel reveal most of the pertinent information on him. The reader is immediately told Heißenstein's full name, his occupation (wine merchant), and that the Heißenstein family has successfully run the wine business for many years. He is an astute businessman. He has a son. The reader receives no information on the father's feelings for his son, only that the son will fulfill the role his father has prepared for him. The son's name is not important; it is important only that he will carry on the family name. The Heißensteins have lived in Moravia for generations, but he is still considered an outsider. And it is clear that he has not gone out of his way to make contact with people. He is respected for his business skills, but not particularly well-liked.

The emphasis on Heißenstein's name accompanies his emphasis on possessions, notably, his wine business. His grief at the death of his son centers on his disappointment that his hard-earned wealth will no longer carry his name. He tries to circumvent this problem by passing the family name through his daughter. He tries to convince his future son-in-law to change his name after marrying:

> Heaven had taken away his son, but his honorable firm must continue to thrive. It was therefore his unwavering decision that he would give his daughter's hand in marriage only to the man who would agree to adopt the name Heißenstein and to take over the leadership of the business.[18]

Insisting that his daughter keep her maiden name and pass it on to her children presents a challenge to the patriarchal order. When a woman marries, she leaves her father's control and becomes the property of her husband. Keeping her own name can signify some independence from her husband. Heißenstein, however, is not concerned with his daughter's individual identity, but with ownership. He wants to ensure that his property will continue in his name.

Eventually his name is carried on, though not in the way he had intended. Rosa names her daughter Leopoldina Rosa Fehse, joining the names of her grandfather Leopold, her mother Rosa, and father Fehse. While naming a son after his father is quite common, naming a daughter after her mother is not. Carrying her mother's name, Röschen (or "Little Rosa") is part of a new lineage. Röschen embodies a new tradition and becomes part of a new kind of family that is not based on power and domination.

Ebner-Eschenbach's novel also challenges the hierarchy of Austrian society. Božena seems to transcend her role as servant, and her character exudes a sense of nobility. The narrator assigns attributes to Božena that raise her above her station of plebeian maid. Early in the novel, when *Božena* and Nannette engage in a heated argument, the narrator compares the scene to one in the *Nibelungenlied*: the fight between Brunhild and Kriemhild at the cathedral of Worms. This comparison of Božena and Nannette to the mythical characters of Brunhild and Kriemhild elevates Božena's character in two ways. First, it puts Nannette and Božena, employer and maid, on even terms with each other: they fight like equals. Second, it compares them both to royalty. Likening a lowly maid to royalty ignores class boundaries. Comparing the Czech Božena with a royal character out of Germanic myth crosses national boundaries as well.

Božena is repeatedly described in regal terms. One Sunday afternoon when she goes out dressed in her best clothes, she emanates nobility again: "She was lovely and majestic in this splendor; a strong and mighty figure" (31). Even the old Count von Rondsperg sees her qualities. "He declared her to be one of the most sensible people he had ever come across" (195), and he refers to her as a "Countess Libussa" (196), again emphasizing the mythic majesty of her character. And this from the man who is offended when the farmers who used to be his serfs fail to stand up and remove their hats when he walks by. While arguing with Regula, convincing her to give the Rondsperg estate back to Ronald, Božena's strength is clear: "The maid stood there, surrounded by a wonderful, quiet and proud majesty. Her statuesque figure seemed to grow, her entire being breathed power, and her voice rang of iron" (261). As much as Božena has regal characteristics, however, she is still plebeian. This contradiction challenges traditional class distinctions that disregard individual character while recognizing only economic lineage.

Božena's role is not, however, without problems. Being mother and servant at the same time reinforces the notion that women exist only to serve and support their families. In many ways, Božena plays the role assigned to women in the ideology of separate spheres since she has only a supportive role in the household. She can hope to influence the decisions of other people but does not have the power to act on her own. Her life is defined by the boundaries of the household.

Her kind of mothering, however, provides a stark contrast to the kind of mothering Nannette provides for Regula. While Božena seeks only to regain what rightfully belongs to Röschen, Nannette attempts to better her daughter's position without regard to Röschen's rights. Her attitude toward her maternal duties is clearly expressed on the night Rosa elopes. Nannette sees Rosa on the night she elopes. The description of what Nannette sees and thinks makes it clear that she knows that she should stop Rosa, but she chooses to let her go.

> ... Now, now she sees it all; the glowing lantern sends a shaft of light to the ground. A figure dressed in a white riding cloak steps into the light – that figure seems to support, to lead a second figure ... For an instant they are both clearly illuminated in the light, then they disappear into the darkness. Nannette recognized them ... And her conscience called out to her: Avert disaster – save the household from shame and humiliation. Go on! Wake your husband – one word – a cry from him would lead the confused child back home. There is still time – do your duty!
>
> What duty? Preparing the way for her own daughter – that is her duty! ... (67)

Nannette returns to bed and tells no one what she saw. The next day, she feigns surprise when others notice that Rosa is missing.

Nannette continues actively to hinder a reconciliation, hiding behind the mask of maternal responsibility. She delays in placing advertisements seeking information on Rosa's whereabouts, and fails to summon the lawyer when Heißenstein requests his presence (presumably to alter his will). Then she refuses to accept any responsibility toward her husband's granddaughter. "'Above all, I have to heed my responsibilities toward my daughter,' declared Nannette. 'Parental responsibility is the highest responsibility'" (112). Božena believes the same thing but does not let her parental responsibilities hurt anyone else. Nannette believes her responsibility toward her biological offspring justifies any action she might take to help her daughter.

Though neither Regula nor Röschen was involved in the actual events that led to Rosa's disinheritance, the final confrontation comes between them. Regula, though she benefits from the disinheritance, did not cause it. She is not personally responsible for something her parents did when she was only a young child. Still, since she finds herself in an unjust situation, it is Regula who has the responsibility in the end to rectify that situation. This problem of responsibility is also relevant to the question of national rights. Those people holding power within the Austro-Hungarian Empire in Ebner-Eschenbach's lifetime were not personally responsible for the actions that led to the subordination of other nationalities to the German and Magyar powers. Those in power, however, continued to benefit from an unfair system and therefore had some responsibility to change it. Not because they were responsible for its origin, but because they were responsible for its perpetuation.

The way the two mothers in the novel, Nannette and Božena, care for their children can be compared to two forms of nationalism. Nannette sees her responsibility only to her biological offspring, and seeks to better her daughter's position, no matter what the cost to others. This attitude is similar to the kind of chauvinistic nationalism that seeks to dominate other nations. Božena, on the other hand, tries only to regain what has been taken from her adopted daughter and restore her rights within the family.

Božena is Czech and plebeian, and she embodies the values and the character of the ideal Slav. If she can be viewed as Röschen's mother, then Röschen's marriage into a noble family forms a union between Czech plebes and the German nobility. Perhaps this should be viewed as a new class in society in which Röschen and Ronald represent a new order. Ronald retains his title, but that title is meaningless without hard work to improve the estate. And he is not able to maintain the estate without Röschen's help. In a similar way, the novel suggests that Austrians of all nationalities must work together for the economic and social improvement of the empire. Röschen "inherits" the Rondsperg estate, not because of the power of her father, but through the strength of her mother. The power invested in the Czech maid/mother Božena challenges both traditional patriarchal family structure and the notion of the superiority of German nationals in the Austrian Empire.

Ohio State University

Notes

1. Gabriele Reuter, *Ebner-Eschenbach* (Berlin: Schuster & Loeffler, 1904), 70; my translation.
2. Edgar Groß, Nachwort, *Božena*. (Frankfurt/Main: Ullstein, 1984), 278; my translation.
3. Heidi Beutin, "Marie von Ebner-Eschenbach: *Božena* (1876). Die wiedergekehrte *Fürstin Libussa*," *Romane und Erzählungen des bürgerlichen Realismus. Neue Interpretationen*, ed. Horst Denkler (Stuttgart: Reclam, 1980), 250; my translation.
4. Ingeborg Weber-Kellermann, *Die deutsche Familie* (Frankfurt/Main: Suhrkamp, 1980), 16.
5. Beatrice Gottlieb, *The Family in the Western World from the Black Death to the Industrial Age* (New York: Oxford University Press, 1993), 261.
6. Aristotle, *Politics*, trans. Benjamin Jowett, *Infoshare*, CD-ROM (Full Circle, 1994), 2.
7. Gottlieb, 232.
8. Benedict Anderson, *Imagined Communities. Reflections on the Origin and Spread of Nationalism* (London: Verso, 1983), 131.
9. Ernest Renan, "What is a nation?" 1882, *Nation and Narration*, ed. Homi Bhaba, (New York: Routledge, 1990), 19.
10. Anne McClintock, "Family Feuds: Gender, Nationalism and the Family." *Feminist Review* 44 (Summer 1993): 64.
11. Carl Steiner, *Of Reason and Love: The Life and Works of Marie von Ebner-Eschenbach (1830-1916)* (Riverside, CA: Ariadne Press, 1994), 151.
12. František Kutnar, "František Palacký and the Development of Modern Czech Nationalism," *East European Quarterly* 15 (1981), 10.
13. Golo Mann, *The History of Germany Since 1789*, 1958, trans.

Marian Jackson (New York: Praeger, 1968), 98.

14. František Palacký, "Letter Sent by František Palacký to Frankfurt." 1848. *The Slavonic and East European Review* 26 (1948), 306.

15. Kutnar, 11.

16. František Palacký, "Manifesto of the First Slavonic Congress to the Nations of Europe." 1848. *The Slavonic and East European Review* 26 (1948), 309.

17. Palacký, "Manifesto," 310.

18. Marie von Ebner-Eschenbach, *Božena*. 1876. (Frankfurt/Main: Ullstein, 1984), 56. All quotations from the novel are my translations from this edition.

Vienna in Literature: Fashion and Class in Rosa Mayreder's Fiction

Jane Sokolosky

Career, lifestyle, and morals contribute to one's prestige and status in society and consequently signify one's social class. Rosa Mayreder (1858-1938)[1] utilizes career, home, and daily life to present her fictional characters as representative of *fin-de-siècle* Vienna. The image of Austria that she creates accurately reflects the middle classes of turn-of-the-century Vienna. To better understand Mayreder's texts, we must, however, ask how her characters respond to these social classes? How do they support or subvert the reigning social structures?

The sociologist René König maintained in his 1967 study *Kleider und Leute (A la mode. On the Psychology of Fashion,* 1973): "One's self-presentation in society, one's self-affirmation inwardly and outwardly, and also one's appropriate rank and sought-after distinction from the next person are determined to such an amazing extent by the secret power that we refer to with the simple word: fashion."[2] In this sociohistorical discussion of class in Mayreder's fiction, I concentrate on fashion as a marker of class. I explore how Mayreder's attention to fashion presents an accurate image of fashion trends and social codes in turn-of-the-century Vienna. We will see how Mayreder's fiction clearly substantiates the importance of fashion for society and how her characters' attitudes towards dress codes reflect their attitudes towards bourgeois lifestyle.

I.

Scholarship on Mayreder that tries to encapsulate her mentality in succinct sound-bites inevitably mentions the fact that Mayreder refused to wear a corset at the age of eighteen. In her autobiography *Mein Pantheon (My Pantheon)* she writes: "My resentment towards the corset as a means of overall confinement grew so great in the course of time that I simply stopped wearing it at the age of eighteen – to the great annoyance of those around me who considered my decision a definite lack of good manners."[3] For the late twentieth-century woman this might seem like the only logical thing to do when faced with the thought of wearing an undergarment made out of whale bone or steel wires that would restrict one's waist to an average of eighteen inches when tightly-laced. But for the late nineteenth-century woman of all classes this was an essential part of her wardrobe. Going without a corset was scorned as being immoral and completely against the norm. At eighteen women entered society.[4] They went to their first balls with the intent of finding a husband and were encouraged to pay meticulous attention to their attire so as to attract men. Wearing corsets was an important part of this new phase in their lives. Yet Mayreder refused to follow this trend (and still she found a husband and married at the age of 23). This act of defiance shows not so much a lack of interest on Mayreder's part in fashion, but rather a conscious decision to speak out against the conventional attitudes towards women's clothing and its role in society.

In *The Theory of the Leisure Class* (1899) Thorsten Veblen explains that in the aristocracy it was male dress that emphasized conspicuous consumption and conspicuous leisure.[5] But this did not suit the hard-working, self-made bourgeois man. Since the bourgeois man was concerned with hard work, order, and diligence, it was left to the woman to take over the role of conspicuous consumption. While the men worked, amassed wealth, and reinvested it, women took over the fashion world and practiced ostentatious consumption.[6] In Vienna, women's fashions were mainly influenced by Paris and men's by London.[7] Working with ideas of divergent male and female virtues, König proposes divergent foreign influences on men's and women's fashion. He suggests that men's fashion came from London because London was the birthplace of Puritanism. The Puritan work ethic was consistent with the ideals of bourgeois diligence and consequently Viennese men adopted their strict, dark, somber clothes. Men's clothing was also practical. There were rules about the proper shirt or gloves for specific occasions, but the white shirt was always appropriate, and accessories served mainly as a statement about one's social standing. König goes on to posit that since Paris was not affected by rampant Puritanism, creative, colorful women's fashions were created there.[8] In *Seeing through Clothes* (1978) Anne Hollander maintains that men wore black to separate themselves from women and ally themselves with clerical, professional, and commercial aspects of life.

Fashion histories state, however, that women too wore black, especially in winter and during the day, even though the etiquette books suggested that women wear light colors to suit their tender fine complexions.[9] The fact that many etiquette books were written by men reminds us that men's fantasies are not necessarily consistent with actual styles worn by women.

The creative, colorful women's fashion to which König refers is the extensive array of fashions that upper-middle-class women needed for various social engagements.[10] There was a prescribed set of rules and guidelines for proper attire for morning, afternoon, and evening events. There were visiting, ball, dinner, reception, walking, evening, street, traveling, spring, and outdoor toilettes, as well as house gowns and calling costumes. In *Die Ordnung der bürgerlichen Welt. Verhaltensideale und soziale Praktiken im 19. Jahrhundert (The Ordering of the Bourgeois World. Ideals of Behavior and Social Practices in the Nineteenth Century*, 1994) Ulrike Döcker quotes from one source that explains the functions of some of the outfits: "The negligée and déshabillé are reserved for the early morning hours, the house and street dress for shopping, at home, and bad weather, the afternoon and visiting dress only for those hours of the day, the evening, ball, and party dress for especially festive occasions."[11] One etiquette book from 1891 recommends that a woman change at least three times a day and devotes three chapters each to home, calling and social attire.[12] There were usually specific fashion rules that bourgeois women were expected to follow for public appearance and in the home. Attendance at different theaters at different times of the day required different necklines, colors, fabric, jewelry, gloves, and hats.[13] These minute details of fashion could only be followed by wealthy women who had ample time and money to spend on fashion. The procedure for dressing according to the latest fashion in corsets, crinoline, and bustles involved much time (especially when a woman was expected to change three times a day!).

The impracticality of women's clothes was obvious. The long trains hindered easy movement and collected dust. The over-sized hats, dangerous hat pins, precarious high heels, and veils that inhibited one's sight were often cited as dangerous to women's health. Mayreder's contemporary, Irma von Troll-Borostyáni, believed that women's clothing clearly showed lack of reason and suggested that women should have been called mentally inferior because of their clothes not their brains.[14] That at the end of the nineteenth century sexologists often addressed foot fetishes in their theoretical analyses does not come as a surprise, since bourgeois fashion believed in an aesthetic of the female foot. Shoes should make women's feet small, since wide feet were plebeian.[15] Troll-Borostyáni even called shoes instruments of martyrdom (*Marterinstrumente*).[16] But of course the ultimate instrument of torture was the corset. Mayreder was not alone in her condemnation of the corset. Many men of her time spoke out against it. Veblen was most likely referring to the old mode of construction which fashioned corsets out of whale bone, feathers, ropes, ties, and steel when he insisted that it was a means to "crucify the flesh."[17] *Die Frauenkleidung* (*Women's Clothing*, 1900) by Dr. C. H. Stratz and *Die Kultur des weiblichen Körpers als Grundlage der Frauenkleidung* (*The Culture of the Female Body as a Basis for Women's Clothing*, 1903) by Paul Schultze-Naumburg were well known works addressing the corset controversy. An article in the journal *Die Gartenlaube* (*The Arbor*) explained why women should protect themselves from such clothing: "Only foolish women who are unworthy of their calling can approve of fashion that not only ruins their bodies, but also causes the stunted growth of their offsprings."[18] Reducing women to the role of childbearer leads some current researchers to emphasize the misogynist nature of such criticisms. In *Fashion and Eroticism. Ideals of Feminine Beauty from the Victorian Age to the Jazz Age* (1985) Valerie Steele maintains that Schultze-Naumann's argument was anti-feminist and racist because he is against the corset on the grounds that it impairs childbearing – woman's "natural" role. According to Steele, corsets most likely did not sever the liver or displace organs as the *Gartenlaube* (*The Arbor*) suggested, and at most they may have caused problems in breathing or constipation.[19] She believes that Schultze-Naumann only condemns the corset in order to put women back into their role in the "traditional hierarchy of sexes, classes, and races." Turn-of-the-century women like Troll-Borostyáni or Mayreder tended, however, to emphasize the restrictive nature of such garments and the damage they do to women's health without specifying any damage to potential offspring.

II.

Mayreder's fictional characters show a range of attitudes towards fashion. Many of her stories make no mention of the characters' clothing or their attitudes towards the reigning styles. Others exercise caustic criticism of fashion guidelines. The young girl Emmy in *Mit Dreizehn Jahren* (*At Thirteen*, 1896) complains about the problems her sisters and mother have getting dressed for Sunday church services.[20]

The dresses do not hang right; their hair does not look right; and the veils, gloves, and handkerchiefs always seem to be lost. The sheer number of glitches leads Emmy to conclude that "it was clear that our dear God highly disapproved of all the fussing over clothes for church" (*At Thirteen* 35). Furthermore, when Emmy's sisters check over her appearance they find her feet too big: "My God, what big feet the child has" (36). Once in church, Emmy cannot concentrate on the services because of her feet. The cobbler always makes her boots too small even though it is obvious that her feet are growing: "her feet had a peculiar tendency to grow longer, but they couldn't be stopped, no matter how hard anyone tried" (38). Mayreder directly addresses the absurdity of trying to control the size of women's feet in order that they conform to the bourgeois ideal of physical beauty.

The topos of the impracticality of women's clothing also appears in Mayreder's fiction. In *Sein Ideal* (*His Ideal*, 1894) the thirty-year-old school teacher August marries the nineteen-year-old Emilie whom he envisions as the ideal bourgeois housewife and mother. August continually voices his wish that his wife conform to his ideals of feminine beauty, but on their honeymoon it is precisely this idealized beauty that hampers the couple's enjoyment of an afternoon walk. August admires the birds and the flowers in the fairy-tale like forest, while Emilie concentrates on her "pretty little honeymoon boots" (emphasis on little) to make sure they stay clean. When she realizes that her elegant honeymoon dress has torn, she complains to August in tears: "It's easy enough for you to climb mountains in your male attire, but not for me with my long dress and skimpy shoes!" (*His Ideal* 205). Emilie expresses quite accurately the problems with women's clothing. The exchange between August and Emilie alludes to the role of fashion in the idealized and contradictory image that men have of women. August loves her for her beautiful appearance in her bourgeois clothes, yet at the same time he wants her to enjoy the rigorous hike. He answers her complaint by matter-of-factly stating that she should have taken more appropriate clothes for a trip to the mountains. But there were few alternatives for an upper-middle-class woman. In Mayreder's 1903 novel *Pipin. Ein Sommererlebnis* (*Pipin. An Adventure One Summer*) Elmenreich – an aging bachelor – similarly points out the impracticality of women's attire. When he sees the young unmarried Eugenie out in the woods for a walk, he warns her that she is wearing the wrong clothes for hiking (*Pipin* 142). Eugenie does not reply to his comment, because she is acutely aware of women's fashions. She does not intend to do any hiking, she is dressed for a rendezvous in the woods. Her conventional attitude about women's fashion mirrors her attitude toward the contemporary upbringing of young women: Her and her parents' one goal for the summer is to find her a husband who can support her financially. Eugenie dresses and lives according to the bourgeois social codes of turn-of-the-century Vienna.

Mayreder also portrays alternatives to the typical Viennese woman's attire. In *Das Stammbuch* (*Relatives*, 1895) Mayreder offers a portrait of a woman whose character is defined by her attire, an attire that does not conform to the turn-of-the-century fashion code. The man who meets her on vacation feels an attachment to her that he has never felt before to a woman, i.e., he feels friendship for her. He is so quickly attracted to her, "because she is wearing a short skirt, roughly made boots, not sewn but stapled, because she hides her figure in a baggy blouse, and without a second thought lets her hands and face be touched by the sun" (*Relatives* 69). This woman wears no corset, no shoes with heels, and she does not protect herself from the sun to achieve the white complexion typically sought by upper-class women. The man praises her because she defies the turn-of-the-century dress code. In *A Critique of Femininity*, a collection of theoretical essays, Mayreder champions relationships between men and women based on friendship, and it is safe to assume that she approves of this woman's attire as well.

The previous examples show the inappropriateness of long dresses for hiking and the contradiction inherent in the importance of clothes for church, but they also allude to the utter importance of clothes for the women attending church and the young bride. In fact, fashion functions in Mayreder's fiction primarily to create the characters' identities. Whereas at one time the official dress regulations and sumptuary laws forced people to dress according to their social estate, in the late nineteenth century no such laws existed; indeed after 1776 the fashion regulations (*Kleiderverordnung*) were no longer observed, but the growing bourgeoisie continued to use fashion as a means of separating themselves from other classes.

In 1905 Georg Simmel writes in *Die Philosophie der Mode* (*On the Philosophy of Fashion*) that fashion is "a device that divides classes accordingly and works like a number of other entities, above all honor, whose double duty it is to hold together a class while at the same time distinguishing it from others."[21] One's wealth and prestige determined one's relationship to the bourgeoisie. The man's wealth must therefore be visible on his wife, so that society can judge his success.[22] As Veblen emphasized in 1899:

> The high heel, the skirt, the impracticable bonnet, the corset, and the general disregard of the wearer's comfort which is an obvious feature of all civilized women's apparel, are so many items of evidence to the effect that in the modern civilzed scheme of life the woman is still, in theory, the economic dependent of the man, that, perhaps in a highly idealized sense, she still is the man's chattel. The homely reason for all this conspicuous leisure and attire on the part of women lies in the fact that they are servants to whom, in the differentiation of economic functions, has been delegated the office of putting in evidence their master's ability to pay.[23]

Women displayed their new fashions, i.e., their husband's wealth, in private and in public. Walks in city parks afforded the opportunity to show off the latest fashions. Indeed, the large Viennese park known as the Prater was considered the "rendezvous of the fashionable world."[24] Women were expected to be current with the latest fashion trends, many of which were started by Empress Eugénie and her friend Pauline Countess Metternich. A man's wealth was most clearly noticed by his accessories. The type of scarf, gloves, watch, and walking stick were significant to determine a man's status. A tie clip, cufflinks, and a well-groomed beard were outward markers of the bourgeois man.[25]

Since appearances were so vital to the bourgeoisie, fashion assumes an important role for an individual's identity, for one's self-presentation. Mayreder offers small details of dress that help situate the individual in a certain social class. Her novel *Pipin* provides excellent examples of such. In fact, the narrator's description of the character's clothes always precedes the entrance of the character onto the scene or into the dialogue. In her autobiography *Mein Pantheon* (*My Pantheon*) Mayreder writes that this story is based on a group of acquaintances who were involved in the theosophy society surrounding Rudolf Steiner and Marie Lang. She admits that *Pipin* was meant to parody this group. For my argument the novel is especially significant when one considers Mayreder's statement about the story's personal nature because the story is meant to depict a real upper-middle-class circle of friends at the turn of the century. This identifiably autobiographical aspect suggests that Mayreder's literary works are based squarely on her experience; the ubiquitous attention to fashion must parallel real life.

Pipin is set in a resort spa town in the Austrian mountains. The fictional characters are a group of acquaintances who have met there on summer vacation. The story unfolds through the letters that the narrator writes to her husband who has remained in the city. She reports on young Eugenie's attempts to find a husband, the conflict between the successful Dr. Kranich, the flamboyant Count Hermosa, and the eternal pessimist Dr. Elmenreich, as well as on the group's fascination with a wandering prophet, and on the young wealthy bachelor Pipin who tries to orchestrate the comings and goings of the group. Eugenie, the twenty-five-year-old woman who must find a husband before the summer vacation is over and who is therefore very clothes conscious, finds in Dr. Arthur Kranich someone who shares her interests in fashion. The narrator comments with surprise about the discussion of fashion trends that takes place between a man and a woman, since this seems to defy the common *fin-de-siècle* perception that fashion belongs to the women's sphere. But Kranich, who also has strong opinions about food and the reform movement, crosses this border and enters women's realm. He discusses with Eugenie

> clothing and hairstyles with phrases and expressions, as if he himself were a lady or a tailor. He critiqued her outfit from head to foot, praised and scolded as only a professional could. With a swift slight of hand he even lifted up the hem of her skirt to scrutinize her undergarments. (*Pipin* 39)

Fashion is also paramount to Count Hermosa's character; his outward appearance contributes greatly to his self-representation. Although, unlike Kranich, the Count engages in no conversations about fashion, the reader learns much about his dress. One can recognize him by his white flannel suit with the bright blue cummerbund and by his numerous rings with wonderful jewels. Another one of his trademarks is his "wonderfully groomed hands and his slender, delicate fingers" (78). However, this appearance only serves to hide his poor financial state. He defies Veblen's assumption that "our apparel is always in evidence and affords an indication of our pecuniary standing to all observers at the first glance."[26] The Count had arrived at the stage of Schnitzler's Casanova in *Casanovas Heimfahrt* (*Casanova's Homecoming*) who still travels but whose accommodations are no longer so luxurious, who prefers to be invited to stay with friends and acquaintances, and whose clothes are worn but were once of the highest quality. Mayreder exposes the Count even further when Pipin assumes the task of packing for the Count:

> With perspiration on his brow Pipin packed for half a day. He packed his suits of white flannel, of yellow raw silk, of silver gray worsted wool. He packed his cummerbunds and ties, the white shirts, the colorful shirts, the embroidered shorts, the checkered stockings, silver brushes and ivory combs, perfume vials, manicure sets, a limitless number of boxes and cases. (242)

Mayreder describes the Count's wardrobe with such detail as if the Count were being undressed. By showing the reader everything, she exposes the Count, who throughout the story assumes a rather secretive attitude towards the others. The power afforded by one's clothes may outlast one's actual worth, but not when the author chooses to lay bare the banality and superficiality of fashion itself.

The significance of clothes to a person's identity is best exemplified by comparing literary figures who have different opinions on fashion. The novel *Idole. Geschichte einer Liebe* (*Idols. A Love Story*, 1899) tells the story of Gisa, a young bourgeois daughter, whose love for a successful young medical doctor goes unreciprocated. Gisa's girlhood friend Nelly, who believes that marriage serves to improve one's social standing and has little if anything to do with love or friendship, represents Gisa's complete opposite. Nelly's and Gisa's divergent attitudes towards clothes clearly expose the basic dissimilarity between the two women. For Nelly clothes constitute a significant part of her personality. Her conversations with Gisa often deal with clothes and fashion. One of her pre-marital dilemmas is the right dress to wear to a tryst with a young military officer. She wants to be attractive, but she realizes that clothes can draw too much attention, so she chooses the more discrete dress so as not to stand out. Later the reader learns of her extensive toilettes and the fancy furnishings for her new home. Gisa, on the other hand, shows no interest in fashion. She dislikes attending parties and balls and even when she dreams about her first love, she does not contemplate what to wear to impress him. In discussions about church and women's education, Mayreder shows the reader that Gisa's interest lies in a relationship based on love and companionship, not in one based on material possessions. Nonconformity to fashion codes parallels nonconformity to social codes.

Sonderlinge (*The Odd Ones*), which appeared in Mayreder's 1896 collection *Aus meiner Jugend. Drei Novellen* (*In My Youth. Three Novellas*), offers two other main characters whose views on fashion vary greatly. The successful twenty-five-year-old civil servant lawyer Traugott has attitudes towards fashion that resemble Nelly's, whereas Friedrich, who was a classmate of Traugott's and was raised in a bourgeois household but left it to live independently and become a basket weaver, has opinions more similar to Gisa's. The story centers on Traugott's attempts to marry his boss's daughter Merene, who would much rather marry the anti-bourgeois Friedrich.

Traugott's greatest concern is being part of the upper-class society, and clothes are essential to mark his adherence to this group. The first paragraph of the story introduces Traugott by describing him as he promenades for two hours in the late afternoon: "very carefully dressed, hat, coat, and shoes painstakingly brushed, only the finest gloves, a walking stick with a silver handle" (*The Odd Ones* 171). Traugott displays those accessories necessary to his class and for his public image. When his boss invites him for dinner he deliberates over which suit to wear in order to make the right impression. He decides against his best suit in favor of "the average one that was still quite formal compared to the president's suits" (175). Traugott also pays attention to hygiene and cleanliness. One morning in his office when he has completed all his work for the day, Traugott cleans the nails of his fine white hands. This attention to cleanliness is characteristic of the upper middle class which is freed from manual labor. Mayreder mentions clean hands and fingernails for many of her characters, male and female. As minute a detail as it may appear, Döcker explains: "cleanliness signals the very rational nature of the middle class; it is proof of higher education and a greater aptitude for social relationships, and so it is a means to distinguish oneself in society."[27]

Cleanliness was equated with good health and sound reason, both of which defined the bourgeois man. Traugott's heightened sense of being an upstanding citizen forces him to adhere to the social guidelines for clothing and hygiene. Friedrich, who has no desire to follow the social norms, also has no interest in contemporary fashion. When Traugott first sees him from a distance, he can only make out a "young man dressed in an outfit that seems both country-like and 'fantastic'" (*The Odd Ones* 196). As soon as they are engaged in conversation, Traugott asks in an accusing tone "Where have you come from wearing that strange outfit? You look comical enough in these high boots, short trousers, and this little jacket! Why are you dressed so peculiarly, Alfons?" (198). Friedrich ignores Traugott's comments on his attire and instead corrects Traugott for calling him by his "old" name Alfons instead of his chosen name Friedrich. Clearly a name carries a certain amount of importance for Friedrich and his identity, but clothes do not. In the 1878 edition of Knigge's etiquette book *Über den Umgang mit Menschen* (*Practical Philosophy of Social Life, or, The Art of Conversing with Men*) one is warned not to dress in a "fanatastic" manner.[28] By using this exact word "fantastic," Traugott emphasizes Friedrich's lack of interest in subscribing to social norms.

That Friedrich defies the rules of fashion and society's insistence on following such rules is especially evident one day when he appears at Traugott's office asking for help. He storms into the office unannounced and angrily complains about Traugott's office workers: "This despicable mob! . . . . They stand there and stare just because I have taken the liberty of dressing my own body according to my own style. They don't even allow their fellow creature this one paltry freedom" (208). Unlike Gisa whose character ignores any discussion of fashion, Friedrich speaks openly against the narrow-minded office workers and eschews fashion ideals.

The wandering prophet in *Pipin* evokes similar attitudes towards clothes, but he does not practice outright criticism. Besides the clothes on his back – a shirt, a yellow cotton cloth worn on that "place where other Europeans wear a tie," a broach which serves as a tie clip, and a camel's hair coat (84) – he owns one other shirt and two handkerchiefs (242). This unusual attire indeed draws attention to him, but the upper-middle-class vacationers in *Pipin* merely show curious interest in the man, as opposed to the open disdain of the office workers in *The Odd Ones*. Deviance from the norm as practiced by Friedrich and the prophet emphasizes how adherence to dress codes situates a person in a certain social class and contributes directly to one's prestige. In *Illustrierte Sittengeschichte. Das bürgerliche Zeitalter* (*Illustrated History of Manners and Customs. The Bourgeois Age*) from 1912 Eduard Fuchs explains: "Fashion is a public act. It is the poster on display with which one shows how one officially intends to approach this business of public morals."[29] Clearly Friedrich and the prophet intend to defy norms of fashion.

As we have just discussed, fashion can reveal a person's attitudes towards public morals. It also influences people's opinions of each other, it determines how we judge others. Mayreder concentrates mainly on men's perception of women as shaped by the women's attire. First Lieutenant von Zedlitz in *Idols. A Love Story* provides an excellent example of adoration for women based solely on outward appearances. The female narrator exclaims in exasperation:

> Around his conversations there hovered a cloud of incense which honored all things feminine, sweet little feet in little patent leather boots, delicately raised skirts from which peek out embroidered slips, pliable waists that one could encircle with one's hands, majestic bosoms whose silk coverings burst the seams at every movement. (86)

In his praise of women, von Zedlitz concentrates solely on women's appearance. He emphasizes those aspects – the cute little feet, the waists small enough to get one's hands around – that were most problematic and received the most criticism from Mayreder and her male and female contemporaries. August in *His Ideal* also pays close attention to women's clothes. What he remembers of his wife from the ball when he first fell in love with her is how she looked ". . . in her little white dress with the barely visible youthful bosom" (201). Only later when he wants to divorce her does he recall that she actually was not so intelligent (*geistreich*). Indeed, the image of Emilie's clothes and body dominates August's understanding of her to the extent that it conceals her true nature from him. Once he sees through this, he lives the life of a disappointed man in a relationship he cannot dissolve.

The long-term effect of fashion on others, as with August and Emilie, is not so drastic in Mayreder's short story *Onkel Bautz* (*Uncle Bautz*), but the immediate influence of fashion on others is central to the story. When Uncle Bautz surprises Jenny early one morning he finds her trying on a new negligée that she has purchased for her husband's return from a business trip. Jenny wants to change into something more appropriate, but Uncle Bautz insists that she looks fine and that she should just sit down and enjoy his visit. Thinking that Uncle Bautz has confused the negligée with society attire (*Gesellschaftstoilette*), Jenny joins him without changing. She is moved to ask Uncle Bautz why he never married and suggests to him that he dress a little more stylishly. This turns into a conversation about the sad events of Uncle Bautz's past which included his marriage to an actress who left him as well as his attempted suicide. The conversation ends with a kiss. The next day Jenny's friend Adele visits her in the morning and finds Jenny dressed more for going out than for a morning at home. She was not wearing her typical batiste dress, but a dark wool dress with a high collar, with which she tries to conceal her body. Jenny has convinced herself that the negligée was the cause of her intimate encounter with Uncle Bautz. Her response is to don something that hides her figure and suggests nothing. When Uncle Bautz returns, he too has changed his appearance. He has taken Jenny's advice and changed his hairstyle and purchased a new hat. Both characters have been confronted with the power of fashion to influence others. Jenny's awareness makes her more self-conscious; Uncle Bautz's gives him more confidence.

The inappropriateness of women's fashion for women's lifestyles and the importance afforded fashion in creating one's identity are issues Mayreder addresses in her criticism of turn-of-the-century society. We have seen how she judiciously uses fashion as a marker of class and class attitudes. She demonstrates fashion's role in defining one's personality and finds fault with it for obscuring one's true personality. Some of her characters subscribe to fashion codes of her time. Some serve to criticize the role fashion plays. Through closer analysis it becomes evident that Mayreder uses fashion as an outward display of her characters' inward convictions concerning bourgeois norms. Her characters adhere to fashion trends that match their bourgeois attitudes. The more clothes-conscious they are, like Traugott in *The Odd Ones* or Nelly in *Idols*, the more idealistically bourgeois the character. Those characters who defy the fashion code stand out conspicuously in Mayreder's depictions of the Viennese upper-class milieu that mercilessly judged people by their clothes. Like Tonio Kröger, whom the hotel porters tried to place according to his appearance – "[they] looked him up and down, deliberately scrutinizing him from the part in his hair down to his boots, obviously trying hard to categorize him according to a certain bourgeois hierarchy in order to give him the respect he deserves"[30] – so, too, are Mayreder's anti-bourgeois characters Friedrich in *The Odd Ones* and the tanned woman vacationer in *Relatives* objects of scrutiny. They represent two of Mayreder's more creative figures because they differ from the social norms; they break with convention. They exercise criticism of the society that Mayreder herself struggles to improve.

Brown University

Notes

1. Rosa Obermayer Mayreder was a prominent writer and activist in turn-of-the-century Vienna. She was a founding member of the General Austrian Women's Association and editor of its journal. She co-founded the Associated Art School for Women and Girls and founded the first Austrian chapter of the International Women's League for Peace and Freedom. Mayreder published two collections of theoretical works – *Zur Kritik der Weiblichkeit* (*A Critique of Femininity*, 1905) and *Geschlecht und Kultur* (*Sex and Culture*, 1923). Her fictional works include two collections of short stories: *Aus meiner Jugend* (*In My Youth*, 1896) and *Übergänge* (*Transitions*, 1897), two novels – *Idole. Geschichte einer Liebe* (*Idols. A Love Story*, 1899) and *Pipin. Ein Sommererlebnis* (*Pipin. An Adventure One Summer*, 1903) – as well as plays, fables, sonnets, and aphorisms.

2. René König, *Kleider und Leute*, 1967. Translated into English as *A la mode. On the Psychology of Fashion*. Trans. F. Bradley (New York: The Seabury Press, 1973). Quoted in Gerda Buxbaum, *Mode aus Wien. 1815-1938* (*Viennese Fashion. 1815-1938*). (Vienna: Residenz Verlag, 1986). This and all subsequent translations in the text and in the footnotes are my own.

3. Mayreder, *Mein Pantheon* (*My Pantheon*), 59-60: "mein Groll gegen das Mieder als Werkzeug der Beschränkung stieg im Laufe der Zeit so weit, daß ich es mit achtzehn Jahren einfach ablegte – zum beständigen Ärgernis meiner Umgebung, die darin einen Mangel an Sittsamkeit erblickte...."

4. Ulrike Döcker, *Die Ordnung der bürgerlichen Welt. Verhaltensideale und soziale Praktiken im 19. Jahrhundert* (*The Ordering of the Bourgeois World. Ideals of Behavior and Social Practices in the Nineteenth Century*) (Frankfurt/Main: Campus, 1994), 260. Döcker divides the nineteenth-century woman's social development into five phases. Childhood lasted until the age of thirteen. From thirteen through seventeen one was con-

sidered a "Mädchen" (girl). In the third phase from seventeen until twenty-five at the latest, the woman was to prepare for marriage and find a suitable husband, in rare instances a woman could receive job training. Until thirty-five or forty a woman was called a young wife and thereafter she was an "alte Ehefrau" (an old married woman).

5. Thorstein Veblen, *The Theory of the Leisure Class* (1899; NY: Penguin, 1994), 170-171.

6. König, 160.

7. Traude Hansen, *Wiener Werkstätte Mode. Stoffe. Schmuck. Accessoires* (*Viennese Workshop. Fashion. Material. Jewelry. Accessories*) (Vienna: Brandstätter, 1984), 183. See also Buxbaum.

8. König, 157.

9. Döcker, *Die Ordnung*, 144. For illustrations of fashions from the late nineteenth century see Stella Blum, ed., *Victorian Fashions and Costumes from Harper's Bazaar: 1867-1898* (NY: Dover, 1974). Although this was published in the United States the styles were international and the journal reached audiences in Europe as well as in the United States. It was mainly for wealthy women since "not only were most of the fashions shown impractical for any sort of housework, but many of the gowns were so constructed that it would have been impossible for a woman to dress herself without assistance" (vii).

10. See Buxbaum; Ludmila Kybalová, ed. *Das große Bilderlexikon der Mode. Vom Altertum zur Gegenwart* (*The Large Picture Lexicon of Fashion. From Ancient Times to the Present*) (Gütersloh: Bertelsman, 1966), especially pp. 293-320.

11. Döcker, *Die Ordnung*, 150.

12. Paul von Schönthan, *Die elegante Welt. Handbuch der vornehmen Lebensart im gesellschaftlichen und schriftlichen Verkehr. Mit zahlreichen Briefmustern, Lexikon des guten Tones, Denksprüchen, Toastentwürfen und Fremdwörterbuch* (*The Elegant World. A Handbook of Proper Etiquette for the Social and Written Context. With Numerous Sample Letters, A Lexicon of Good Taste, Thoughtful Phrases, Toasts and a Foreign Dictionary*) (Berlin, 1891). Quoted in Döcker, *Die Ordnung*, 152.

13. Buxbaum, 303.

14. Christa Gürtler, ed. *Irma von Troll-Borostyáni. Ungehalten. Vermächtnis einer Freidenkerin* (*Irma von Troll-Borostyáni. Indignant. The Legacy of a Freethinker*) (Salzburg: Otto Müller, 1994), 211-214.

15. Valerie Steele, *Fashion and Eroticism. Ideals of Feminine Beauty from the Victorian Era to the Jazz Age* (NY/Oxford: Oxford UP, 1985) 114-116.
16. Gürtler, 218.
17. Veblen, 184. See also Buxbaum; Steele, 161-191.
18. Quoted in *Fascimile Querschnitt durch die Gartenlaube* (*Facsimile. A Trip through the Arbor*) (Bern; Scherz, 1963), 214.
19. Steele, 170. See also David Kunzle, *Fashion and Fetishism* (Totowa, New Jersey: Rowman and Littlefeld, 1981). Davies sees a direct correlation between declining fertility rates and tight-lacing. Mel Davies, "Corsets and Conception: Fashion and Demographic Trends in the Nineteenth Century," *Comparative Studies in Society and History* 24 (1982), 611-641.
20. See Hugh McLeod, "Weibliche Frömmigkeit--männlicher Unglaube? Religion und Kirchen im bürgerlichen 19. Jahrhundert," *Bürgerinnen und Bürger. Geschlechterverhältnisse im 19. Jahrhundert* (*Women and Men. Relationships between the Sexes in the Nineteenth Century*), ed. Ute Frevert (Göttingen: Vandenhoeck & Ruprecht, 1988), 134-156.
21. Georg Simmel, *Die Philosophie der Mode* (*On the Philosophy of Fashion*, 1905), *Gesamtausgabe Band 10* (*Complete Works. Volume 10*), eds. Michael Behr, Volkhard Krech, and Gert Schmidt (Frankfurt/Main: Suhrkamp, 1995), 12. Also in Silvia Bovenschen, *Die Listen der Mode* (*The Ruse of Fashion*) (Frankfurt/ Main: Suhrkamp, 1986), 182: "ein Produkt klassenmäßiger Scheidung und verhält sich so wie eine Anzahl anderer Gebilde, vor allem wie die Ehre, deren Doppelfunktion es ist, einen Kreis in sich zusammen und ihn zugleich von anderen abzuschließen."
22. Heidi Rosenbaum. *Formen der Familie. Untersuchungen zum Zusammenhang von Familienverhältnissen, Sozialstruktur und sozialem Wandel in der deutschen Gesellschaft des 19. Jahrhunderts* (*Family Structures. Research on the Connection between Familial Relationships, Social Structures and Social Change in Nineteenth Century Germany*) (Frankfurt/Main: Suhrkamp, 1982), 342.
23. Veblen 181-182.
24. *The Newest Plan and Guide to Vienna and Environs* (Vienna: R. Lechner, 1909), 126. See also Otto Friedländer, *Letzter Glanz der Märchenstadt. Das war Wien um 1900* (*The Final Sparkle of the Fairy Tale City. Vienna around 1900*) (Vienna: Gardena Verlag, 1969). This was originally published in 1948 under the title *Letzter Glanz der*

Märchenstadt. Bilder aus dem Wiener Leben um die Jahrhundertwende. 1890-1914 (*The Final Sparkle of the Fairy Tale City. Pictures from Viennese Life at the Turn of the Century. 1890-1914*).

25. Lucie Hampel, "200 Jahre Mode in Wien," *200 Jahre Mode in Wien. Aus den Modesammlungen des Historischen Museums der Stadt Wien* (*200 Years of Viennese Fashion: From the Clothes Collection of the Historical Museum of the City of Vienna*) (Vienna: Freunde der Hermesvilla, 1976), 19-30. Buxbaum, Döcker, and Steele deal with accessories as well.

26. Velben, 167.

27. Döcker, *Die Ordnung*, 104.

28. Adolph Freiherr Knigge, *Über den Umgang mit Menschen. 16. Originalausgabe. Eingeleitet und aufs neue verbessert von Karl Goedeke* (*Practical Philosophy of Social Life, or, The Art of Conversing with Men*) (Hannover: Hahn'sche Buchhandlung, 1878), 49.

29. Eduard Fuchs, *Illustrierte Sittengeschichte. Vom Mittelalter bis zur Gegenwart. Das 3. Band. Das bürgerliche Zeitalter* (*Illustrated History of Manners and Customs. The Bourgeois Age*) (Munich: Langen, 1912), 189.

30. Thomas Mann, *Tonio Kröger* (1903) in *Die Erzählungen* (Frankfurt/Main: Fischer, 1986), 340.

Modes of Nostalgia and Figurations of "Austria" in the *Exil(auto)biographien* of Richard Beer-Hofmann and Stefan Zweig

Matti Bunzl

Richard Beer-Hofmann – the famous poet, close friend of Schnitzler and Hofmannsthal, and "member" of *Jung Wien* – had to flee his native Vienna in August 1939. With him was his beloved wife Paula (née Lissy), who was suffering from an acute heart ailment. Bound for the United States, Paula Beer-Hofmann's condition worsened during a layover in Zürich, where she passed away in October of the same year. Richard Beer-Hofmann was forced to continue his journey to the New World on his own, living out the rest of his days in relative contentment in New York, where he died in September 1945.

In the wake of his emigration and the loss of his wife, Beer-Hofmann's literary output markedly changed upon his arrival in the United States. In the decades before his escape, he had been hard at work on *Die Historie von König David* (The History of King David), a monumental dramatic trilogy, which sought to reclaim the cultural and political relevance of Old Testament narratives for an uncertain age. Beer-Hofmann had published the dramatic prologue *Jaákobs Traum* (Jacob's Dream) in 1918 (it was premiered in the Vienna Burgtheater in 1919) to great acclaim. Much like the cycle's next installment, *Der junge David* (The Young David, 1933), it had presented a hopeful poetic vision of Jewish national and cultural affirmation in the context of a burgeoning Zionist movement.

Beer-Hofmann had continued work on *Die Historie von König David* up to the moment of his emigration (delivering bits and pieces to an eager audience on the way), but when he settled in New York in late 1939, he abruptly abandoned all work on the biblical cycle, turning instead to a free-flowing memoir (whose loose prose style stands in marked contrast to the strict poetic framework of the *Historie*) devoted to a celebration of his forty-year marriage to his wife Paula. The resulting text was *Paula. Ein Fragment* (Paula. A Fragment), published posthumously in 1949 (edited by Otto Kallir, following Beer-Hofmann's precise specifications).

In this article I argue that *Paula* enacts a "fragmented geography of nostalgia" – an intensely personal and purposefully disjointed mode of commemoration that takes idiosyncratic temporal, spatial, and symbolic reference points as the foundations for generative acts of the writer/reader's remembrance. In thus demarcating a complex and contradictory hermeneutic field of nostalgia, *Paula. Ein Fragment* marks a radical formal contrast with other, more canonized, texts of German/Austrian émigrés – Stefan Zweig's *Die Welt von Gestern (The World of Yesterday)* most prominent among them. In this light I present my reading of Beer-Hofmann's biography/ autobiography in the context of a discussion of Zweig's memoir and the specific modes of nostalgia deployed therein.

Over the last few years the "literary genre" (if it can be called that) of exile autobiography has become a prominent topic within German literary studies. In this context several scholars have begun to develop typologies of this form of exile literature. In this sense Richard Critchfield observes that the preponderance of exile autobiographies tend to narratively construct themselves as representatives of an entire generation, while Michael Winkler has noted that exile autobiographies often double as the depiction of an entire epoch.[1] Erich Kleinschmidt, on the other hand, has focused on the tendency toward formal conservatism in the genre of exile autobiography.[2]

As Mark Gelber has noted, all these characteristics fully apply to Stefan Zweig's famous memoirs of a European, published two years after the author's suicide in Brazil in 1942 under the title *Die Welt von Gestern (The World of Yesterday)*.[3] Indeed, Zweig himself had noted in the preface that *Die Welt von Gestern* was not so much the narrative of his own life as that of "an entire generation."[4] As early as June 1939 Zweig had specified this conception of the text in a letter to Felix Braun, noting that the memoir he was planning was "not an autobiography, but a farewell (*Abgesang*) to the Austrian-Jewish-bourgeois culture that had culminated in Mahler, Hofmannsthal, Schnitzler, Freud."[5] Zweig, born in Vienna in 1881, clearly saw himself as an integral member of that uniquely creative generation, whose irretrievable *Lebenswelt* he sought to evoke and celebrate when writing *Die Welt von Gestern*. It is in that sense that the text often realizes the narrative *ich* as part of a collective *wir*, signifying Zweig's notion of his role in "our generation."

Much of the narrative structure and the mode of nostalgia enacted in *Die Welt von Gestern* is predicated on this premise. In the final analysis Zweig attempted a comprehensive account, not so much of his life (Zweig's "self," in fact, is often curiously absent), but of the cultural fields which sustained it. In this manner Zweig was eager to utilize many of the specificities of his own life as inroads toward the formulation of social and historical generalities – a practice that is particularly evident in the treatment of his family. As he noted, "Their way of life seems to me to be so typical of the so-called 'good Jewish bourgeoisie,' ... that in telling of their quiet and comfortable existence I am actually being quite impersonal."[6] In conjunction with Zweig's deep attachment to the world he chose to describe in that manner, the resulting "sociological" treatment constructed a kind of "absolute" historical context against which individual lives (Zweig's and that of his interlocutors) could be set.

In turn, this narrative style – with its constitutive recourse to the authority of historical "fact" (this, ironically, in the face of the absence of crucial historical data at the time of the completion of *Die Welt von Gestern*) – enacted a mournful mode of nostalgia, which set the present age against a past whose irretrievable loss was exacerbated by its narrative constitution as a singular moment in humankind's cultural development. Consider, for example, the book's famous opening passage in light of *fin-de-siècle* Vienna's construction as an idealized spatio-temporal reference point:

> When I attempt to find a simple formula for the period in which I grew up, prior to the First World War, I hope that I convey its fullness by calling it the Golden Age of Security. Everything in our almost thousand-year-old Austrian monarchy seemed based on permanency, and the State itself was the chief guarantor of this stability. The rights which it granted to its citizens were duly confirmed by parliament, the freely elected representative of the people, and every duty was exactly prescribed .... Everyone knew how much he possessed or what he was entitled to, what was permitted and what forbidden. Everything had its norm, its definite measure and weight .... In this vast empire, everything stood firmly and

immovably in its appointed place, and nothing would change in the well-regulated order. No one thought of wars, or revolutions or revolts. All that was radical, all violence, seemed impossible in an age of reason.[7]

As the cultural historian of *fin-de-siècle* Vienna Steven Beller has argued, this introductory statement, in its historicizing and objectifying voice, sets the tone for Zweig's persistent, unreflected nostalgia – a nostalgia, which can only be sustained through the constitutive repression of the great social, political, national, and cultural chasms that not only divided turn-of-the-century Vienna, but also ultimately caused the demise of the Habsburg Monarchy at large.[8] If, as Beller puts it, Zweig thus "claimed for Vienna and the Viennese a musicality, theatricality, love of the arts, and a *Gemütlichkeit* which seem at times written for the Austrian Tourist Office,"[9] his representation of *fin-de-siècle* Vienna, ultimately (re)wrote – through "objective," narrative fixing – the historical period under question at the very moment of its nostalgic constitution. In the final analysis the text of Zweig's *Die Welt von Gestern* functioned as a forum of "absolute" memory of turn-of-the-century Vienna, transporting along with the biographical and social material presented an essentially closed interpretive framework anchored in the mournful nostalgia of total historical loss.

In contrast to Zweig's biography of his age, Richard Beer-Hofmann's *Paula, Ein Fragment*, actively resists the narrative construction of such "totalized" nostalgia. Where Zweig sought to capture the flavor of *fin-de-siècle* Vienna's socio-cultural fields, Beer-Hofmann opted for an intensely personal account, focused on his wife of forty years, Paula, and their relationship. And even within this limited realm, Beer-Hofmann eschewed any notion of totality. Rather, he deliberately conceived his memoir as a fragment, explicating on the rationale in the book's preface written in January 1944:

> "Paula, ein Fragment" is the title that should one day connect the content of these pages. – "Fragment" – because: how many or how few, how large or how small the pieces that I may leave, what is attempted here *must* remain in its innermost form a "fragment," *can* not be anything else, *may* not be anything else . . . . Thus, much might seem in a state of imbalance, emphasized too strongly, only touched fleetingly, indistinct and de-

> scending into darkness, others outlined too sharply, in glaring light – some, already said, will be repeated once more tiredly, gaps will be wide, much will remain capricious, restless, confusing, but – however it may be – it will be no more capricious, no more restless, no more confusing, no darker, no *more* incomplete work (*Stückwerk*) than life itself.[10]

Indeed, on first view, *Paula. Ein Fragment* may seem like an inchoate collection, merging into a five-part structure family genealogies, a few sustained narratives (such as the story of the servant Vinzek, a major figure of Beer-Hofmann's youth, and the account of Alcidor, Paula's grandparents' dog), descriptions of numerous, seemingly unconnected micro-events and, what appear to be, random observations. Furthermore, the book is characterized by a radical anti-chronology, which avoids factual and historical continuity and/or specificity in favor of a commemorative intertextuality in which particular strands of memory generate others in mutually constitutive fashion. The book's third "chapter," entitled "Herbstmorgen in Österreich," for example, is anchored in Beer-Hofmann's discovery of a seven-page manuscript completed while vacationing in Alt-Aussee in 1935. The text, which Beer-Hofmann shares with the reader, spurs a host of other memories – summers in Aussee, the trip to Italy with the family in 1903, and the trip to Denmark with Paula in 1896 – which are then related in loose fashion to complete the chapter. Given this overall narrative structure, *Paula. Ein Fragment* hardly emerges as a sustained effort in "conventional" autobiography (in ironic reversal to Zweig's situation, Beer-Hofmann actually had the personal and historical material at his disposal to construct a "seamless" autobiography/ biography of himself and Paula).

Nevertheless, it would be wrong to proclaim the absence of structuring principles in *Paula. Ein Fragment*. Rather than residing in such totalizing endeavors as the nostalgic reconstruction of an entire social framework, however, they emerge in what I would call two "interpretive nodes," signifying, in turn, specific spatio-temporal and symbolic reference points in the author's life: the fateful meeting of Beer-Hofmann and Paula Lissy on 5 December 1895 (which stands in metonymic relation to Beer-Hofmann's figuration of their relation at large) and the author's complex identification with the archangel Michael (which gestures to Beer-Hofmann's self-understanding as *exculpator dei*). As I will show in the following analysis, these two nodes of reference (which also signal the two components Richard Sheirich has identified as the constitutive aspects of Beer-Hofmann's life and work)[11] not only structure *Paula*, but effectively enact what I will call Beer-Hofmann's "fragmented geography of nostalgia."

Within the internal economy of *Paula. Ein Fragment*, the centrality of Beer-Hofmann's initial meeting of his future wife is clearly evident in the heading of the book's first (and longest) part – titled, with rather unusual precision, after the date of the fateful event ("Donnerstag, Der fünfte Dezember, 1895"). More importantly, however, a close reading of the entire text reveals the moment thus put into discursive play as the book's main axis, organizing all other depictions along its vectors. In this manner the initial meeting functions as a looking-glass, structuring all events in Paula's and Beer-Hofmann's lives in temporal (and symbolic) relation to this moment of recognition. In this sense Beer-Hofmann regarded all aspects of his (and his ancestors') lives as part of a meaningful trajectory that had its preordained telos in his meeting with Paula, while viewing all events following their encounter in light of the relationship's realization: "My soul wants to take its place – already it fills me – everything that was, it was a path to this moment – everything that was before must leave me."[12] "How can I leave from here – leave the place where *this* was met upon me? Must stay – what connects me to this glance must not tear. Something has taken my hand, and holds me."[13]

Along with Beer-Hofmann's conception of the individual as part of a larger generational structure (a notion initially articulated in the famous "Schlaflied für Mirjam" (Lullaby for Mirjam, 1897) and developed further in the novel *Der Tod Georgs* (The Death of George, 1900), as well as the dramatic works *Der Graf von Charolais* (The Count of Charolais, 1904) and *Die Historie of König David*),[14] this understanding of the nature of his encounter with Paula ultimately explains the careful depiction of Beer-Hofmann's ancestry (as well as the evocation of Paula's familial background – the two aspects taking up nearly half of the entire book). As Beer-Hofmann noted in relation to the long account of his family history and youth in Moravia which opens the book:

> Page after page has been filled, and Paula's name has still not been mentioned. I tell of my fathers and ancestors, of people, times, and places alien to her and seemingly

> unconnected. And still: as Paula and I see each other for the first time, she is sixteen, I am twenty-nine – tender memories of early childhood, happy years of youth, impetuousness and carefree joy of my adolescence . . . all that has to come *with* me on the long journey to her.[15]

But if Beer-Hofmann's and Paula's fateful encounter thus anchors *Paula. Ein Fragment* as the overarching relational moment of temporal structuration, a second, seemingly less prominent, interpretive node emerges in conjunction with the figure of the archangel Michael, who serves both as symbolic and spatial signifier of Beer-Hofmann's role as *exculpator dei* – the self-image the author had developed in the course of conceiving *Die Historie von König David*.[16] Just as the Jewish *Volk* was chosen to bear witness to God's greatness by proclaiming his name throughout the epochs, Beer-Hofmann came to understand his poetry as the result of divine calling and to see his role, in analogy to the Jews' ancient and noble function as *exculpator dei*, as that of a prophet, chosen to reveal God's word.

In *Paula. Ein Fragment* the image of the archangel Michael appears prominently toward the end of the book. Introduced in covert reference to Beer-Hofmann's identification with the mythical figure, he is characterized (following the book of Daniel) as the "angel," who is "entrusted with the protection of Israel."[17] It is in one of the book's most moving fragments (depicting a fleeting moment just prior to Beer-Hofmanns' escape from Vienna in 1939 and placed right after the discussion of the archangel Michael) that the symbolic and spatial significance of the figure is anchored retrospectively in a complex web of references:

> We drive back in the late morning. . . . At the Michaelerkirche traffic slows down, we have to wait. . . . She looks up to St. Michael: "They did not take the Hebrew letters off the sign". . . . I look at the clock, and it is noon, and at once it pulses through me: how we first met here at noon, and St. Michael in Salzburg, and in Eppan, and at the engraver on the Rotenturmstraße, and the embroidered picture of St. Michael that she gave me on a birthday, and, shaken, I'm thinking how quickly our life passed by . . . she . . . slips the glove off her right hand . . . and then she holds my hand . . . and I feel that, what-

ever may come upon us, even if we have to go to foreign lands – as long as my hand can rest in hers, I am safe – nothing can happen to me. I bend over her hand, my lips are quietly touching her finger and move the bright, honey-colored bishop's ring that has become a bit too large for her. She feels it, and she glances at the ring: "When you bought it on the Markusplatz in Venice it was too big as well.... And you asked me, if I would wear the ring once in a while – and I said: Always. And you said: Don't promise that, don't say always – what do you know about what may come – you are so young! Now, I'm no longer young – and I always wore it, and everything that did come was good – that you know – my Richard – don't you?" – "Yes."[18]

This passage, which unites the celebration of Beer-Hofmann's and Paula's relationship with the author's self-understanding as *exculpator dei* (symbolized by the privileged figure of the archangel Michael, as well as his trans-religious representations) in one interpretive node, enacts a spatio-temporal and symbolic order, effectively structuring the memorial topography evoked in *Paula. Ein Fragment*. In this manner the passage anchors the spatio-textual relevance of the Michaelerkirche and the Michaelerplatz (presented as privileged spatial reference points in the depiction of Beer-Hofmann's first encounter with Paula),[19] much as it inscribes the description of the family's trip to Italy in 1903 (along with the protracted retelling of Beer-Hofmann's purchase of the bishop's ring in Venice)[20] in an overarching, relational teleology. Similarly, the introduction of Tycho Brahe, introduced as Beer-Hofmann's initial guide toward an understanding of the relationship between God and humanity (and presented within the textual economy of *Paula. Ein Fragment* in conjunction with Beer-Hofmann's narrative of his and Paula's trip to Denmark in 1896),[21] as well as the description of his collection of medals from the Order of St. Michael and his experience with the Jewish engraver[22] all function as constitutive elements of this larger interpretive node, yielding a structural, yet fragmentary coherence to *Paula* and the life paths it seeks to represent.[23]

In the final analysis the book's interpretive nodes (the event of 5 December 1895 and the image of the archangel Michael) thus enact a textual grid whose temporal (relational vis-à-vis Beer-Hofmann's and

Paula's fateful encounter), symbolic (signified by such signs as the archangel Michael, as well as such iconic representations as Paula's bishop's ring), and spatial (in reference to meaningful sites, in turn, often gesturing to the symbolic imagery associated with the archangel Michael) axes not only constitute each other in mutual ways, but also reveal Beer-Hofmann's remembrance work as an individualized project of complex, generative association.

Olga Schnitzler's description of Beer-Hofmann's mode of remembrance during his exile gestures to this associative memorial topography: "What could be taken from the one who left here? His life had flourished here, his work had matured here. He carried thousands of memories, countless images with him ... relationships – with streets, houses, people – that had formed him ... because every foot was laden with experience."[24]

What emerges from this vivid account of Beer-Hofmann's mode of memory in conjunction with my reading of the interpretive nodes of *Paula. Ein Fragment* is the affirmative nature of the remembrance work generated at the fragmentary sites of Beer-Hofmann's memorial field. In the final analysis the author regarded the work of memory as a generative process, capable of providing retrospective, if fragmentary, coherence to lives that were always the conglomeration of seemingly disjointed historical "events." It was in that sense that the very process of generative memory was capable of enjoining the satisfaction that, as Beer-Hofmann put it in the preface of *Paula. Ein Fragment*, came with the "devout remembering that inspires happiness."[25]

This process of generative and affirmative remembrance (and the memoir it generated) gestures in turn to a specific mode of nostalgia. Other than the nostalgia enacted in Zweig's *Die Welt von Gestern*, however, Beer-Hofmann avoids the totalizing circumscription of an idealized (and unattainable) past. Rather, his mode of nostalgia – what I figure as a "fragmented geography of nostalgia" – is forward-looking, in the sense that it takes seemingly disjointed sites of memory as the starting points for the affirmative remembrance work which can lend retrospective coherence and meaningfulness to human lives. My notion of a "geography of nostalgia" (as enacted in Beer-Hofmann's mode of remembrance) thus ultimately takes its cue from Pierre Nora's concept of *lieux de mémoire*[26] with which it shares a concern for the evocative (and affirmative) nature of temporally, spatially, and symbolically actualized sites of memory. Analogous to Nora's account of the cultural complexity underlying (and generated by) the co-articulation of various *lieux de mémoire*, it is ultimately the inherently fragmented nature of the sites of memory underwriting Beer-Hofmann's "geography of nostalgia" that engenders the complex webs of memorial intertextuality which (re)constitutes and sustains human experience at the moment of its retrospective realization.

When during his American exile, Beer-Hofmann participated in a conversation on the predicament of uprootedness, he remarked with serene calm: "Why do I need roots – I have wings."[27] This statement goes far in illuminating Beer-Hofmann's mode of generative and affirmative (because always already fragmented) nostalgia. In marked contrast to Stefan Zweig's (and other authors') hermetic construction of a narratively fixed, stable, "objective," and absolute past whose irretrievable loss invariably signals despair with the present age, Beer-Hofmann's "fragmented geography of nostalgia" enacts a radically subjective process of remembrance work – a memorial hermeneutic that employs temporal, spatial, and symbolic representations of the past as the basis for the associative constitution of viable contemporary *Lebenswelten*. It was in that sense that Beer-Hofmann valued the "wings" that allowed the successful transplantation to his American exile (shortly before his death he willingly received American citizenship, calling it "a proof of human sympathy, of understanding and recognition")[28] over the sentimental longing for the "roots" whose irretrievable loss ultimately caused Zweig's suicide in 1942. While the present analysis thus points to the two authors' contrary modes of nostalgia as textual evidence for their divergent psychological states during exile, it also suggests why Zweig's *Die Welt von Gestern* (marked by the totalizing structure and absolutist interpretive framework characteristic of much of *Exilautobiographie*) fails to convince from a literary point of view (while remaining one of the most compelling "historical" accounts of *fin-de-siècle* Vienna). In contrast, it is Beer-Hofmann's "fragmented geography of nostalgia" (while "disappointing" in its disregard of biographical and historical specificity and continuity) that renders *Paula. Ein Fragment* a continuously fascinating piece of exile literature – a piece whose larger significance we are just beginning to appreciate.

University of Illinois at Urbana-Champaign

Notes

1. Richard Critchfield, "Einige Überlegungen zur Problematik der Exilautobiographie," *Exilforschung* 2 (1984), 51. Michael Winkler, "Exilliteratur als Teil der deutschen Literaturgeschichte betrachtet," *Exilforschung* 1 (1983), 363. See also Mark Gelber, "*Die Welt von Gestern* als Exilliteratur," in Mark Gelber and Klaus Zelewitz eds. *Stefan Zweig: Exil und Suche nach dem Weltfrieden* (Riverside: Ariadne Press, 1995).

2. Erich Kleinschmidt, "Schreiben und Leben: Zur Ästhetik des Autobiographischen in der deutschen Exilliteratur," *Exilforschung* 2 (1984), 32. See also Gelber, "*Die Welt von Gestern* als Exilliteratur."

3. Gelber, "*Die Welt von Gestern* als Exilliteratur," 148.

4. Stefan Zweig, *Die Welt von Gestern: Erinnerungen eines Europäers*. The English renditions are taken from *The World of Yesterday: An Autobiography by Stefan Zweig*. Harry Zohn, Introduction (Lincoln: University of Nebraska Press, 1964), xvii.

5. Quoted in Gelber, "*Die Welt von Gestern* als Exilliteratur," 148.

6. Zweig, *Die Welt von Gestern*, 19.

7. Ibid., 14-15.

8. Steven Beller, "The World of Yesterday Revisited: Nostalgia, Memory, and the Jews of Fin-de-siècle Vienna" in: *Jewish Social Studies* 2, 2 (Winter 1996), 37-53.

9. Ibid., 38.

10. Richard Beer-Hofmann, *Paula. Ein Fragment* (Paderborn: Igel Verlag, 1994), 7-8. All translations of Beer-Hofmann are my own.

11. Richard M. Sheirich. "*Frevel* and *der erhöhte Augenblick* in Richard Beer-Hofmann: Reflections on a Biographical Problem," *Modern Austrian Literature*, 13, No. 2 (1980), 1-16.

12. Beer-Hofmann, *Paula. Ein Fragment*, 115.

13. Ibid., 116.

14. See also Matti Bunzl, "The Poetics of Politics and the Politics of Poetics: Richard Beer-Hofmann and Theodor Herzl Reconsidered," *The German Quarterly* 69(3) (1996), 277-304.

15. Beer-Hofmann, *Paula. Ein Fragment*, 30.

16. See also Sheirich, "*Frevel* and *der erhöhte Augenblick* in Richard Beer-Hofmann: Reflections on a Biographical Problem."

17. Beer-Hofmann, *Paula. Ein Fragment*, 225.

18. Ibid., 227-228.

19. Ibid., 113, 114, 122.
20. Ibid., 139-142.
21. Ibid., 173-174.
22. Ibid., 225-227.
23. See also Esther N. Elstun, "Richard Beer-Hofmann as (Auto) Biographer: *Paula*," 129, *Richard Beer-Hofmann: His Life and Work* (University Park: The Pennsylvania State University Press, 1983).
24. Olga Schnitzler, *Spiegelbild der Freundschaft* (Salzburg: Residenz Verlag, 1962), 129. My translation.
25. Beer-Hofmann, *Paula. Ein Fragment*, 7. Translation in Esther N. Elstun, *Richard Beer-Hofmann: His Life and Work*, 82.
26. Pierre Nora, "Between Memory and History: *Les Lieux de Mémoire*," *Representations* 26 (Spring 1989), 7-25.
27. Olga Schnitzler, *Spiegelbild der Freundschaft*, 129.
28. Cited in Esther N. Elstun, *Richard Beer-Hofmann: His Life and Work*, 29-30.

How "Belle" Was the "Belle-Époque" Really? Some Not So "Belle" Reflections of Vienna in the "Belle Époque" Mirrors of Kraus, Altenberg and Petzold

Barbara Zeisl Schoenberg

In past years the Viennese "belle-epoque" has held a fascination for cultural historians and literary critics who have at once focused on the birth of modernism and recorded the dying gasps of the Austrian monarchy in the last decade of the nineteenth and the pre-World-War years of the twentieth century. As the titles of some of the well-known works written on the period seem to suggest – *Vienna's Golden Autumn, The Austrian Mind, The Hapsburg Mythos, A Nervous Splendor* – scholars interested in the *fin-de-siècle* have been skeptical of the fragile façades and fleeting glimmer of golden gaiety, and have probed under the surface in attempts to uncover the malaise, the deeply-rooted psychological and artistic problems of late Viennese bourgeois society which were suspected of lurking beneath.

Until recently, however, both cultural historians and literary critics exploring the Viennese "belle-époque" have focused primarily on the intellectual and artistic impulses which originated almost exclusively out of high bourgeois culture and have failed to address works which reflect issues of concern to a broader spectrum of society, in most cases avoiding those which deal with severe social problems altogether. Thus the secondary literature on the Austrian "belle-époque" defines it as a period of refinement, critical introspection and morbidity, as "a center of impressionist thought around 1900,"[1] an era whose creative artists espoused aesthetic principles far removed from the socially engaged Naturalism advocated by a Zola in France, or Hauptmann, Holz, Kretzer or Bleibtreu in Germany. Furthermore, "belle-époque" Vienna is usually pictured as a kind of hallowed sanctuary, a bourgeois porcelain tower, where, as one critic asserts, "there never ever was such a thing as Naturalism,"[2] and into which the misery of the lower classes could not easily penetrate.

This feature of embellishment or systematic "covering up" of the more sordid reality which lay beneath the surface of Viennese everyday life can perhaps best be illustrated in a fictional account by Heimito von Doderer, written after World War II, entitled "Eine Person von Porzellan" (A Person Made of Porcelain). This short piece tells the shocking story of a delicate, charming little would-be seamstress, by all appearances "so bright and clean and delicate and white, that when you looked at her, you seemed, by contrast, to be completely covered by filth."[3] At the conclusion of the narrative, however, this pure and dainty, immaculately and stylishly clad little innocent turns out to be an insane and brutal murderess, one who rips apart the putrid flesh of her dead victims "nodding and moving up and down, resting and going at it again, like a vulture with its fallen prey."[4]

The tension between "Schein" (appearance) and "Sein" (reality), outward decorum and inner truth, the disparity between the prim and proper, polished externals of clothing and demeanor vis-à-vis the more sordid, less perfect picture which lies beneath, so graphically contrasted in Doderer's story, is not a new theme and has been a favorite topic with writers over the ages and with Austrian writers of the *fin-de-siècle* in particular. In fact, such was the particular focus in Vienna during the last decade of the nineteenth and the pre-World-War years of the twentieth century. But in contrast to the shockingly brutal and repulsive turn of events of Doderer's postwar "Eine Person von Porzellan," a perusal of the literature produced by some of the more prominent "belle-époque" writers like Bahr, Hofmannsthal, Beer-Hofmann, Schnitzler, Andrian demonstrates an utter lack of such graphically raw or ugly scenes. We are thrust into an artificial, porcelain world of house balls and coach rides, illicit love affairs and duels, elegance and decorum, a spectrum of muted colors and momentary, fleeting impressions, of neurasthenia, soul searching, and musings – lifestyles which reflect luxury, comfort and a great deal of leisure time. Only with rare exceptions – which will be the focus of this essay – do we find a portrayal of the underclass, the proletariat, depictions of the harsh realities of daily life, the mistreatment and exploitation by the bourgeoisie of those who made their elegant lifestyle possible. We also do not find the kinds of problems which beset our contemporary world exactly one hundred years later, such as spousal and child abuse, violent crime and abject poverty.

Is it because these problems did not exist in the Viennese "belle-époque"? Was it that "belle-époque" writers were so sheltered and they themselves so dependent upon, and part and parcel of their bourgeois milieu, as to be insensitive to or even unaware of these social issues? Or was it an intentional suppression, an aesthetic program whereby the reader was meant to be protected from hearing about anything ugly, vulgar or distasteful, as Hubert Ehalt in "Geschichte von Unten" (History From Underneath) maintains:

> There flourished... an intellectual history, at the core of which was a cultural concept which was oriented to the consciousness of the upper and educated classes, and which by focusing on aesthetic works and highly stylized institutions [art, science, religion, law] left the life and the culture of the "common people" completely out of sight)?[5]

Ehalt's thesis certainly seems to be corroborated in the following excerpt from a 3 March 1895 edition of the *Arbeiterzeitung* in which an elegant, programmatic snobism is caricatured, and child abuse and poverty are glossed over and dismissed as trivial and unsuited for the domain of art:

> "Don't you find the painting absolutely disgusting, my lady?" the lieutenant asked the Senator of Commerce's wife with a yawn.
> "But why, dear Lieutenant? You see, I find the painting very interesting. You see, I find it quite modern. You know – social question, Naturalism, Impressionism ... The child is dirty, probably doesn't even know how to read or write, gets beaten a lot and very little to eat."
> "... But that contradicts all traditional ideas about art ... dirt, beatings. Art has to deal with the ideal ... art is supposed to edify and entertain ..."
> "I find poverty extremely interesting, but I don't want to see it in a painting. The main thing anyway is one's digestion. And dirty children spoil one's appetite."[6]

Reflecting a similar mind-set, most examples of "belle-époque" literature demonstrate that indignities, social injustices, and abuse were made to appear innocuous by being swept under Persian carpets, tucked behind elegant wall hangings, and obfuscated by lavish descriptions of soirées, summer holidays and clandestine rendezvous. However, an examination of some of the lesser-known primary sources which document the "belle-époque" reveals not only that grave social problems existed, but also that some of the more socially-engaged writers of the period actually addressed these very issues in their work, though they were sometimes severely attacked because of it, as was often the case with the critical and scrupulous word-purist Karl Kraus. Also, writers who voiced such criticism were frequently not taken seriously, like the scurrilous, "inclined to perversity"[7] and "decadent coffee-house scrivener,"[8] Peter Altenberg, or they were not even recognized, either in the realm of "belle lettres," or in the secondary literature, as has been the fate of Alfons Petzold, whose autobiographical novel, *Das rauhe Leben* (The Rough Life), has received little if any critical attention to date.

Because of this lacuna in scholarship it is my intention to "crack" the porcelain exterior of "belle-époque" literature, and expose the underside, the inelegant and unseemly image of Vienna as an oppositional force to the cliché of the "charming, graceful Vienna"[9] traditionally represented in "belle-époque" collections and critical appraisals. I shall examine lesser-known texts by Kraus, Altenberg, and Petzold which reveal the great frequency of sexual assaults, abuse, and violent crimes during the Viennese "belle-époque," similar to those enumerated, for example, by Hilde Spiel who in her essay "Die Dämonie der Gemütlichkeit" (The Demonical in the Guise of Coziness) points up "the symptomatic familial crimes of Vienna around the turn of the century, incest, patricide, fratricide and juvenile delinquency."[10]

In *Wien - Spektrum einer Stadt* (Vienna - Spectrum of a City), Hilde Spiel reports the sadistic tendencies of the Viennese when she relates that "in the oldest chronicles of Vienna animal torture, public quarreling, deeds of blood and guerrilla activities abound."[11] Spiel searches for the source of this "unfeeling brutality of the Viennese"[12] and wonders from a modern perspective why callous brutality seems repeatedly to regenerate itself, always hiding under a mantle of feigned innocence: "Beneath the mantle of graceful demeanor the deadly dagger lies hidden." After tracing the long-standing tradition of baiting and violent crimes, contrary to what one might expect, Spiel concludes from statistical evidence that in modern times violent crimes have somewhat abated when compared to the great frequency of sexual assaults and violent crimes which existed during the years of the belle époque!

In *Wolken drohen über Wien* (Clouds over Vienna), memoirs written in 1948 about growing up in Vienna during the early years of the twentieth century, Otto Friedländer seems to verify Spiel's assertions when he recalls the heinous crimes which were reported daily in the press, warnings of a world full of despair and hopelessness for children, musings which demonstrate that there indeed was something very rotten in the state of "belle-époque" Vienna. "An evil spirit is going through the world," Friedländer writes, "You can't read the newspaper without reading about 'a corpse in a suitcase'... The journalists have set phrases for the appropriate occasion:... 'a horrifying scene in plain view,'... 'advanced putrifaction'... 'Where has the left thigh gone to?'... 'The motive of the crime is unclear.' 'Sensationalism of the press,' the people say. Well, yeah... but those are real facts – the press didn't make them up!"[13]

Friedländer continues his probe into the past with a list of atrocities, criminal activities recollected as commonplace events:

> Every day mothers abuse their children to death... Children run up to policemen in the streets seeking protection from abuse which they can no longer endure. Children run away, supposedly on account of a yearning for adventure – in truth because they are afraid of being beaten... Daily you read about pupils killing themselves... the parents are making their homes a hell. Children aren't afraid of school, they're just so afraid of their parents, they'd rather kill themselves.

While Spiel denounces the propensity for violence inherent in the Viennese by presenting factual and verifiable details from chronicles and histories, Friedländer's accounts are more personal, and may therefore seem to be unreliable since they are based on private experiences. However, Friedländer's memories are supported by a review of the newspapers of the time, as suggested by the excerpt in the *Arbeiterzeitung* cited above, and can be confirmed in almost any of Kraus's numerous tirades against the sensationalism of the press and the perversion of the judicial system in such essays as "Sittlichkeit und Kriminalität" (1902, Morality and Criminal Behavior) or in many of the publications of *Die Fackel* (The Torch).

A prime example which combines both child abuse and the unscrupulous sensationalism of the press is the piece entitled "Interview mit einem sterbenden Kind" (Interview with a Dying Child), in which Kraus reproduces the newsclipping about a mother who threw herself and her little son out of a fourth-story window and whose other little son jumped out after her and survived his brother and mother by twelve hours. An irate Kraus comments:

> He lay in a pool of blood and had to give information to the police reporters and to the representative from the exclusive edition of the Vienna Illustrated News ... The report is authentic. They have it first-hand, they're proud of that. This is worse than unbelievable. A child is telling the interviewer how he jumped out of the window ... The press is wrestling with death, struggling to get to the deathbed sooner, so that they can be sure to get all the valuable information. In view of such theatricality, all hatred and contempt for the press is silenced. Nothing remains but sorrow.[14]

Because Kraus was more a caustic satirist than a lyric poet, a most outspoken critic both of the escapism of "belle-époque" writing and the depravity of the press, I would like to focus our attention instead on the prose poet and author of lyrical sketches whom Kraus consistently admired and championed, and even suggested as recipient for a high literary prize: Peter Altenberg.[15] Except for the mounting critical attention given Altenberg's *Ashantee*[16] in recent years, the socially-engaged side of Altenberg – the numerous sketches in which he expresses indignation at the blatant social injustices he perceived in the world about him – have received markedly little critical attention.

An examination of some of the better known of Altenberg's sketches presents the reader with a closely detailed map of the inner and outer machinations of a bourgeois world, vested with most of the selfsame superficial qualities usually listed as trademarks of the "belle-époque": elaborate fashions and lavish decor, elegance, grace, and a great amount of leisure time. The world of the bourgeoisie – "the world order of the Philistines,"[17] the era of refinement and culture, of "good manners" (LA 140), and "well-brought-up people" (S 111), lifestyles of affluence and ease – are punctiliously depicted in Altenberg's work. Through glimpses into parks, villas and vacation spots, we encounter the basic structure of bourgeois society, the family unit, with all its prototypes and appendages, as Altenberg notes in his poetic sketch of the bourgeois maiden and her entourage: "She was spoiled from day one by governesses, maids, cooks, parents, brothers, uncles, visitors – yes, even by the seamstress when she tried on her clothes."[18]

Shimmering colors and elegant fashions which rival those painted by Klimt abound in Altenberg's sketches and are unmistakable representations of a refined, perfectionist bourgeois world intent on outward decor and façade, as mirrored in his stylized description of a mondaine "with reddish-brown hair and a silk dress which changed back and forth from lilac to green,"[19] or the following word-portraits of the finest in dress design: "She wore a wide, light-blue dress with tiny white dots" (WS 31), or "At his right sat his little golden-blonde sister dressed in velvet the color of puréed chestnuts with a blouse made out of the same material" (WS 86-87). And the styles continue, on and on, captivating the reader with their beauty and sensual appeal. Always written between the lines of such idyllic tableaux, however, is the understated suggestion of a dire lack of communication between the parties, conflicts between the rich, leisure class and their servants, and even exploitation: men who take advantage of women, parents who misunderstand children, forcing them into social ties and bourgeois strictures which threaten their well-being and stifle their claims to happiness and self-fulfillment.

Although Altenberg's first published work, *Wie Ich Es Sehe* (1896), may contain only rare and muted allusions to a more sordid world of struggle, poverty, and abuse, subsequent works, such as *Ashantee*, written scarcely a year later, in 1897, or later works which appeared during the years 1902 to 1910, reveal a world replete with inequities, social injustice, oppression and racist attitudes.

Both the piercing realist Kraus and the lyrical Altenberg underscore and confirm such attitudes as an accurate reflection of the status quo. In "Der Neger" (The Negro), for example, Kraus writes that he once knew a black man,

> who was subjected to the boorishness of an entire city. He didn't only give the impression of being a gentleman, but he also acted like one when they let loose and attacked him with their innate meanness: "Hey, little black guy, why don't you wash yourself?

> Git on home, black man, you're dirtying up the whole city! Hey, when I catch hold of you, just wait and see what you'll look like after I get through with you, black Chinaman. Wow, Bejeezus, a crazy Indian! You Ashantee, you damned, untrustworthy..."[20]

The racist attitudes exposed by Kraus in these satirical snippets – where the black man is mistaken for other potentially exotic misfits in a racially pure and uniform society – a black Chinese and a mad Indian – need no further comment.

In *Ashantee*, Altenberg expresses both his malaise and his concern for a group of touring African nationals, over 100 members of an Ashanti village on exhibit for more than a year – from the summer of 1896 through October, 1897 – in the Prater zoo! Defending their human rights and objecting to the Africans having to squat when eating in confined, primitive areas, where the only civilized "comforts" were an occasional "piss-pot" in the corner, Altenberg documents the unfeeling reactions of Viennese passers-by to the abject poverty and ignominy of the exploited natives. Described by Altenberg are the elegantly-dressed Viennese drawn there to observe these abused Ashanti, as Andrew Barker maintains, "less out of anthropological curiosity than by the prurient desire to observe and mingle with 'naked savages.'"[21] In the sketch "Akolé," for example, we note interior monologues and language snippets which reveal a bigoted social outlook expressed by park visitors who muse about a frightened Ashanti maiden:

> She's really proud, really not very appealing. What is she even thinking of, that little Moor? She doesn't even want to look at us... Hey, you've got to be friendly, little darling, nobody's going to hurt you... No, no, no, no, come on, now, don't get your back up... What an arrogant brat. Farewell. You can't get her to do anything. Goodbye, little Moor, don't put on airs... So long.[22]

The less than pretty picture of "belle-époque" Vienna highlighted in *Ashantee* is tarnished even further in later Altenberg sketches which suggest that alongside the more blatant abuses suffered as a result of racism and xenophobia, human rights were violated on a daily basis;

for on the underside of the seductive but corrupt, morally bankrupt, leisurely way of life of the bourgeoisie was, of course, the suppression and exploitation of the lower classes, who worked almost ceaselessly to make this exalted world possible (ML 207; 234). Altenberg notes, "Behind the lit-up windows you feel the people exhausted from work. Especially the girls, who are using up the precious years of their youth ... Behind the lit-up windows an exhausted humanity labors, in order not to starve in the ensuing days, in the next weeks,"[23] and he understandingly defends "the despair of hysterical, overburdened young mothers, harrassed by work, who are despondent over their fate and who curse the world" (ML 95).

In numerous sketches Altenberg decries the common practice of bourgeois women to take advantage of and mistreat their servants, commiserating, for example, with "The governess who sat silently by ... oppressed by the miserable treatment which she received from those around her" (BL 92). Repeatedly our attention is drawn to exploited servants who are subjected to indignities and who are seen to be constantly at the beck and call of their masters or mistresses, scapegoats of bourgeois appetites, discontentment and whims, as suggested in the following statements: "The lady of the house came home from the opera and nevertheless quarreled with the chambermaid" (P 184), "I used to be very strict with my servants, but since I've met Karl, I'm amazingly nice to them" (P 176); "You don't defend flower vendors or girls who sell champagne. You seduce that kind and exploit them, and then you throw them away like lobster shells or lemon rind" (P 199).

In addition to criticisms concerning exploitations and the pitiable mistreatment of the servant class are numerous sketches intended to arouse outrage because they demonstrate the extremes of abuse, brutality and violence present in Altenberg's society. He felt these conditions were a direct result of the oppression of the working class by the bourgeoisie. Repeatedly we read of battered and abused children who, Altenberg suggests, owe their sufferings directly to the exploitation and ruthless ambitions of the leisure class. Furthermore, Altenberg frequently links such abuse directly to the bourgeois lifestyle together in one and the same utterance: "Here (in reference to the world of nature) no little children will be abused, no one wants to be a privy-councillor out here"[24] (WT 313). Of course, paradoxically, these sensitive insights into a less than perfect world in which servants are mistreated and the working class exploited are rarely perceived by members of the underclass themselves but are always told in the third person – always from a bourgeois vantage point.

Altenberg's depictions of lower-class violence include seduction, rape (WT 318, ML 178), and child abuse. We are told of a girl who, while giving birth on a cold stone floor of a stall, accidentally crushed the skull of her newborn. The woman was tried and convicted for the "crime," while her innocent seducer sat detachedly in the courtroom, "handsome and coarse" (P 161). We read about pimping and extortion (ML 161) and are repulsed by the story of a mother, sentenced to four years in prison, who had tortured her four-year-old daughter to death (ML 95).

There is also a sketch about a woman who abused and beat her child to death because her own father had beaten her, as had her husband, and this was the only lifestyle she knew (ML 178). We take note of still another sketch dated 3 May 1907, which depicts the brutal slaying of an illegitimate child by a mother who had covered its body with burning coals and who was subsequently set free because the child did not die directly, as in an axe slaying, from the murderous act, but indirectly, a few days later, from the effects of the burn (ML 187)! We are informed of a mother who had abused her three-year-old daughter by splitting her lip with an iron spoon. While reopening the wound and inflicting pain repeatedly in the same fashion, she had prevented the cries of the child from being heard by covering its face with a pillow. Altenberg notes that the mother had been subsequently set free (BL 10)!

We are told, furthermore, about the five-year-old daughter of a mother of nine children, who was discovered washing the vestibule at 6 A.M. in sub-zero temperature dressed only in a shirt. Altenberg relates that when the judge reprimanded the mother, who had taken the child back from its well-to-do foster parents in order for it to help her with her work, the mother had scornfully replied, "When eight starve, the ninth can starve with them; why should she have it better than me?!" (NA 53). With abhorrence we note also the tale, in the selection ironically entitled "Cristentum 2" (Christianity 2), of the little five-year-old child, who, out of fear of her father, had testified, "Papi lieb" (daddy good), and had exonerated both her parents accused of child-abuse charges. Altenberg clarifies that the child had so testified because her parents had threatened her, "if she told the truth, they would stick a red-glowing iron nail up her 'Popo,' which no doctor would ever be able to see or prove" (F 161).

Further examples of extreme brutality and violence are the cases of a nine-year-old gypsy girl beaten to death because she had cried too much over the absence of her mother, who had been incarcerated,[25] and that of a young girl who had been threatened with murder either by shooting, or by "throwing caustic acid over that heavenly visage of springtime" (V 121). We shudder at yet another child abuse case about a mother who "had undressed her little stepdaughter till she was completely naked, had beaten her all over her body with a pipe, and had prevented her from screaming by hitting her on the mouth" (LA 206). Because there was no precedent in the law which pertained to torture and abuse of stepchildren (LA 206), however, the mother was set free!

Another lonely voice worthy of mention who, like Kraus and Altenberg, offers a richly detailed account of how the lower echelon of Viennese society lived during the Viennese "belle-époque" can be found in *Das rauhe Leben* by Alfons Petzold, a semi-autobiographical account of a youth growing up in the tougher sections of Vienna, the "wild-west"[26] and rowdy districts of Ottakring, Simmering and Hernals. The novel, a most unusual mixture of a picaresque novel without a prankster, and a novel (*Bildungsroman*) of education starring a proletarian hero, is a grimly realistic account which spans the years of the "belle-époque" from the time of the Crown Prince Rudolf's suicide in 1889, when the main character is six years old (RL 36-37), through brief "real-time" interruptions in the narrative, to the time of a "hot August evening in 1908" (RL 285). The hero, one Alfons Petzold, who, Hitchcock-like, makes cameo appearances either by others calling his name or by periodic personal descriptions of himself,[27] pens his first disillusionment and initial observation of the discrepancy between reality and illusion, and then continues his narrative by presenting one disillusionment after the other: poverty, starvation and degradation at every turn. Because, as a result of his frailty, his deformity and living with his sickly mother, whom he must help support, Petzold is exposed to the most grueling suffering and abuse, which he describes in great detail, the reader gains insight into a very different world than the usual "belle-époque" fare: a world of small businesses and factories, flophouses and public lavatories, and the callous treatment of underprivileged laborers.

Not immune to strongly anti-Semitic sentiments, such as his aversion for the "fat Jewesses, hung with glittering jewels"[28] – a prejudice which he readily and repeatedly expresses – the main character proceeds through a series of reversals of fortune, spiraling lower and lower to the very depths of disease, poverty and exhaustion, to ultimately living with petty thieves and vagabonds in the "Free Hotel of 'The Golden Rats,'" (p. 227) their name for the vaulted tunnels of the freezing sewers of Vienna.

Repeatedly Petzold takes up the banner of the underprivileged in his work, and what makes this work so remarkable when contrasted with more well-known texts of "belle-époque" literature is the almost total exclusion of the bourgeois world of leisure, luxury, and seduction. Although the disparity between the two worlds is frequently a topic for socialist diatribe, the reader is granted only rare glimpses into that glittering world of privilege and excess, as in the following passage where the hero longs for the unobtainable:

> How I envied the well-fed and warmly-clothed people whom I saw go laughing and talking into the brightly-lit restaurants, which offered the best of food and drink and entertainment! I saw all this on my way home, hungry, to the garret where my mother sat, hungry and stiff with cold, and thought of the carriages filled with furs and warm wraps which I had seen standing in long rows in front of the brilliantly-lighted palaces, and the gaily-attired people seen through an occasional open door.[29]

But perhaps the most poignant example, highlighting the disparity and inequity which existed between the two very distinct worlds of the Viennese "belle-époque," is demonstrated in the following bitter lament by Petzold, who had his own dreams of an improved social order and better world for the underclass, of which he was both suffering representative and spokesman:

> From day to day I became more embittered, and my disgust at life, my hatred of the execrable social order which was to blame for my miserable state of health, and my contempt for its laws grew from day to day ... I divided mankind into two camps. One, much the smaller, was composed of the rich and powerful ... Had they any sympathy? Did they feel any charity for their disinherited brothers and sisters in the opposite camp, from which the bitterest misery rose like a huge cloud

obscuring sun and stars? ... Did they at least recognize the disgrace of their parasitic existences, did they make any effort ... to suppress their shrill laughter and their servants' cries of misery, to change the latter's angry growling into timid laughter and quiet singing? ... On the contrary, they carried their accursed behavior to the limit, their manners became more and more refined, their demand for luxuries knew no bounds, nor their inordinate desire for the very latest sensation. To satisfy these cravings it was no longer sufficient that hundreds of their fellow creatures should be ruined; thousands and tens of thousands of us who had no rights were now their victims. The most hidden signs of poverty found me painfully clear-sighted; everywhere I saw its mark. I was driven to look for it in the faces of children ... In my mind I inscribed an archive of proletarian misery containing picture after picture, each more sad, more shameful, more horrible than the other.[30]

In conclusion, the writers who have been the focus of my attention in this paper – Kraus, Altenberg and Petzold – present the reader with unusual, lesser-known views of "belle-époque" Vienna. Bitterly at odds in their work are the oblivious, pleasurable life-styles of the bourgeoisie and the disillusioned and resentful existences of the working class who toil tirelessly to make possible the former's dreams and extravagances. Exposed are two mutually exclusive worlds, one superficial and cosmetic, the other ugly and often violent, disparate social spheres whose severe problems were rarely confronted, if even acknowledged, in the Viennese, not-so-"belle," "belle-époque."

Pomona College

Notes

1. Wolfgang Nehring "Möglichkeiten impressionistischen Erzählens um 1900," *Zeitschrift für Deutsche Philologie* 100 (1981), 164.
2. Ibid.
3. Irmgard Feix and Ernestine Schlant, *Gespräche, Diskussionen, Aufsätze* (New York: Holt, Rinehart and Winston, 1969), 125.
4. Ibid., 128.

5. Hubert Ch. Ehalt, ed. *Geschichte von Unten* (Wien: Hermann Böhlau, 1984), 13.
6. "Das Modell," *Arbeiterzeitung*, Vol. I, Sunday, 3 March, 1895, 287.
7. Peter Altenberg, *Märchen des Lebens* (Berlin: S. Fischer, 1924), 51. Hereafter references to this work will be cited in the text as ML.
8. Jost Hermand, "Peter Spinell," *Modern Language Notes 79* (1964), 440-441.
9. Hilde Schmolzer, *Das böse Wien* (München: Nymphenburger, 1973), 7.
10. Hilde Spiel, "Die Dämonie der Gemütlichkeit" in: *Wien-Spektrum einer Stadt* (München: Biederstein, 1971), 191.
11. Ibid., 190.
12. Ibid., 195.
13. Otto Friedländer, *Wolken drohen über Wien* (Wien: Ring Verlag, 1949), 14-16.
14. Karl Kraus, "Interview mit einem sterbenden Kind," in: *Magie der Sprache*, Heinrich Fischer, ed. (Munich: Suhrkamp Taschenbuch, 1987), 167.
15. Karl Kraus, "Blutiger Ausgang einer Faschingsunterhaltung," in: *Magie der Sprache*, 47.
16. Andrew Barker, "Unforgettable People from Paradise!": Peter Altenberg and the Ashanti Visit to Vienna of 1896-1897." In *Research in African Literatures*, Vol. 22, No. 2, Summer 199; Marilyn Scott, "A Zoo Story: Peter Altenberg's Ashantee (1897)," *Modern Austrian Literature* Vol. 30, No. 2 (1997), 48-64.
17. Peter Altenberg, *Neues Altes* (Berlin: S. Fischer, 1911), 83; *Mein Lebensabend (Berlin: S. Fischer, 1919)*, 140; *Semmering* (Berlin: S. Fischer, 1913), 111. Hereafter references from these works will be cited in the text as NA, LA, S.
18. Peter Altenberg, *Fechsung* (Berlin: S.Fischer, 1916), 139. Hereafter references from these works will be cited in the text as as F.
19. Peter Altenberg, *Wie Ich es sehe* (Berlin: S. Fischer, 1922), 28. Hereafter citations from this work will appear in the text as WS.
20. Karl Kraus, "Geschlecht und Lüge," in: *Magie der Sprache*, 18.
21. Andrew Barker, 57.
22. Peter Altenberg, *Ashantee* (Berlin: S. Fischer, 1897), 38. Hereafter citations from this work will appear in the text as A. I will also be citing from the following editions: Peter Altenberg, *Was der Tag mir*

zuträgt. (Berlin: S. Fischer, 1902); *Pródromos* (Berlin: S. Fischer, 1906); *Bilderbogen des kleinen Lebens* (Berlin: Eric Reiss, 1909). Hereafter citations from these works will appear in the text as WT, P , BL.

23. Peter Altenberg, *Vita Ipsa* (Berlin: S. Fischer, 1919), 237. Hereafter citations from this work will appear in the text as V.

24. Other examples of such linkages are "No little children are abused here, no one wants to become a Senator out here" (F 109), or "No little children are abused here, out here nobody yearns for riches and prestigious positions" (ML 30).

25. Peter Altenberg, *Nachfechsung* (Berlin: S. Fischer, 1916), 101. Hereafter citations of this work will appear in the text as NF.

26. Alfons Petzold, *The Raw Life*. Translated by E. Bennett (London: George Allen & Unwin, Ltd., 1926). Hereafter citations from this work will appear in the text as RL. Petzold refers to Ottakring as the "wild west" quarter of Vienna on 117.

27. Petzold, 90; 137; 145; 184; 291; 111; 179; 180; 212; 213; 251; 267. The hero tells of his deformity, 238; red hair, 115; girlish face, 150; etc. With these personal characterisitics we encounter inconsistencies: Petzold refers to himself as an only child, 146, yet in the beginning he states he has a sister and she is referred to later as married, 215 and 218.

28. Ibid., 309. Other anti-Semitic references and overtones can be found on pp. 30, 71 88, 109, 136, 152, 186, 240, 277, 291. Interestingly, all these anti-Semitic remarks do not appear in the 1940 (!) edition published by Adolf Lufer Verlag, Wien/Leipzig.

29. Ibid., 121-122.

30. Ibid., 306-307.

Endings and Beginnings: Musil's Invention of Austrian History

Alexander Honold

In the beginning there is the ticking of a mechanical clock. What does it sound like? What does it say? The clock says "tick-tock," sure, but what is the problem with that? The problem is that there is no reason at all, considering the physical experience, to distinguish between two different sounds produced by the pinion of the watch. Nevertheless we do not perceive its sound as a monotonous "tock-tock-tock," which would correspond to the real acoustical phenomenon. Instead of hearing what is to be heard, we insist on having the impression of a tick-tock, tick-tock, a repetition of two alternate sounds. This phenomenon, if my reading of Frank Kermode's book on narrative endings is right, must be considered as a decisive element for the rise of what we are still used to calling "literature." "Of course," he says, "it is we who provide the fictional difference between the two sounds; *tick* is our word for a physical beginning, *tock* our word for an end.... The fact that we call the second of the two related sounds *tock* is evidence that we use fictions to enable the end to confer organization and form on the temporal structure."[1]

Rethinking Kermode's argument now, this example offers many observations that can help us to understand how narration works, and that is, how beginnings and endings are used and what they are needed for. Auditory sensations like the ticking of a clock appear almost meaningless on their own, without any semantic structure. So we humanize them with fictions; and this happens not only with such simple perceptions, but even to the most complicated events. What we do is organize them, restructure them temporally. Just as we possess a spatial coordinate system that tells us what is right or left, above and below, we need a temporal scanner system that tells us what is going on subsequently. I am still with Kermode with my first thesis:

To understand things that happen, we have to put a certain beginning and an ending to them.

Thus, beginnings and endings are not "the real thing," they are ours, they emerge when we face and interpret the world outside. This idea of temporal scanning probably somehow reminds you of Immanuel Kant, especially of his intention to find what he called "the transcendental conditions of perception," that is, preexisting structures that determine our daily experience. What I termed scanning, Kant called "Schematismus" (a pattern). It is not from experience, Kant argued, that we are given the notions of space and time. As these organize everything that man is able to perceive, they must precede our experience. The only thing that experience can do is to apply and confirm the patterns it was generated by. So far, all that does not sound exceedingly dramatic, and we learned to live as Kantian beings long ago; so let us simply take Kant's conceptualizations of time and space for granted, and the narrative patterns of beginning and ending along with them.

But things look different if we take a critical case, that of the principle of causality. From eighteenth-century Empiricism to the early twentieth century, causality was regarded as a linkage of two events as cause and effect: A causes B. This assertion can at least include two different propositions. The first one is the assertion of what we could call "weak" causality, and it says: B would not have happened if A had not happened before. For example: "The king died and then the queen married again." Weak causality just argues that things occur one after the other and that you cannot change the order of a given time sequence. Now, the alternative concept, as you might have guessed, is that of "strong" causality, in which B follows A necessarily. If we have any given A, we are able to predict its B. This concept of strong causality was valid first and foremost in empirical science, at least until Einstein and Heisenberg came along. The course of a billiard ball, for example, is strictly determined by the way it was struck. The impulse at the beginning already provides all the necessary information to predict the final results. In this case, the relation between cause and effect can be proved, and, what is even more, the whole arrangement can be repeated and controlled anywhere at any time. Operating with this notion of strong causality, we presume a closed artificial system, with totally known initial conditions, and its final results perfectly conforming with the expectations. Of course, things do not work this way, and whoever has played billiards, knows that not even that game does. What scientists try to omit, and in fact have to omit, is the influence of any disturbing element of uncertainty and singularity. In this sense, causality tries to eliminate blind chance, while history and our methods of producing historical knowledge are based on matters of contingency. History positively depends on the intervention of new, disturbing elements that can change the whole story; and so does narrative.

Nevertheless our approach to history has also to do with the desire for explanations and reasons, for causes and effects. To explain events of the past, means to search for initial conditions and final results. When we are trying to understand what is going on we have to find out: When did it start? And, to what end? So we are asking for a narrative that explains to us how our billiard ball of history finds its way through. Thus, my second observation is: Science and history offer singular models of actions and happenings that lead from a beginning to an end, and both of these models have been "disenchanted" as fictions or sheer arrangements – and, by the way, this is where "Postmodernism" gets into it. Causality, in the strict sense of necessity, came to its limits with Heisenberg's principle of indeterminacy, whereas our understanding of history was questioned by the discovery of its basic narrative or rhetorical ingredients. Although these fictions and narratives are still more or less useful, they cannot claim objectivity or absolute validity anymore.

It is important to keep in mind the trivial fact that whatever we can experience hardly fits into those patterns, be it a scientific one or a narrative one, because "reality" is an open signifier for something without beginning or end. We are just part of a chain of circumstances that is causeless and unpredictable. I dare say: as human beings we are not able to experience origins or last things at all, and that is exactly why we are so desperately trying to fix them or manipulate them. Transforming reality into a text is like following a modest thread entangled in an always-already existing web. But we are tempted anyway to identify the text's limits with those of history itself, as the Bible does: whatever happens in history, be it human or divine, happens between the beginning and end of the book of books, that is, within the limits of time defined by Genesis and Revelation. The A and O, Alpha and Omega, were regarded for a long time as symbolic demarcations, because all that can be written and read is confined by the limits of the alphabet.

I would like to sum up what we have seen so far. The patterns of beginning and ending provide a narrative framework that transforms the eternal flux of disparate events into something that deserves being called a plot. Thus, plotting works as a chaining together of events that can achieve different degrees of intensity, ranging from mere chronological order to the assertion of strong causality.

With these questions in mind, it is time to begin, or to begin again, or perhaps I should better say: to put an end to these tiring and exaggerated preliminary remarks, passing over to the realm of literature. Let us enter Musil's invention of Austrian history – in fact, we already stepped into it some time ago. It is precisely Musil's occupation with causality and contingency that I have tried to sketch so far; and when we talk about Musil's philosophy, we do not deal with a particular theoretical or ideological approach, but with problems located in the triangle of science, history, and literature.

The beginning and ending of a novel can be determined on at least two different levels: first, they are defined by the interval that covers writing time, and in this case, a great deal of a lifetime as well; second, there is another interval that covers the area of written text, framed by its first and last words. To examine the endings of *Der Mann ohne Eigenschaften (The Man without Qualities)* seems easy and difficult at the same time, for the simple and sad reason that when Musil's writing was interrupted by death, there was no final chapter authorized by the writer's hand. For a long time, scholarship and publishing efforts were mainly dedicated to the purpose of posthumously bringing this immense fragment to an end. Musil critics spent thousands of pages discussing whether the love story of Ulrich and Agathe would have come to an unhappy ending or not, and whether a showdown of violence and anarchism would have been privileged on the very last pages or, on the contrary, a sign of utopian hope. But even the posthumous papers published in the second volume of Frisé's edition could not put an end to such speculation. The only thing that can supply some indications for that nonexistent ending, is to study those parts of the narrative framework Musil himself had finished and published in his lifetime. All that we know about the novel's mysterious ending, we know by its beginning and we know it from the beginning.

When did Musil start writing *The Man without Qualities*? A few short fragments date from the very beginning of the century, outlining some of the characters we meet again in the final version, such as Moosbrugger, Clarisse and Walter, and the protagonist himself.

Nevertheless, Musil's project took shape only when he was confronted with the experience of the First World War and the collapse of the Austro-Hungarian Empire.

I think we cannot understand the novel's basic structure unless we take into account its deep addiction to the world of ancient Austria, or "Kakanien," to fin-de-siècle Vienna and its culture of decadence. Two of the protagonists, Ulrich and his friend Walter, are introduced as having joined the fin-de-siècle-generation and its glorification of youth. On the other hand, that youth of the century's first decade was surrounded by an atmosphere of historicism and eclecticism. In spite of intellectuals like Freud, Ernst Mach, Otto Wagner or Ludwig Boltzmann, Vienna was not exactly a place of modernity, but a fortress of traditionalism, the old-fashioned capital of an Empire that showed undeniable symptoms of decline. The outbreak of World War I in August 1914 only accelerated this decline, which culminated in the emperor's death in 1916 and at last in the military defeat in 1918. Finally, Vienna ceased to be the "Imperial Capital and Royal City," as it is called in the first chapter of *The Man without Qualities*.[2]

Therefore August 1914 is a crucial point for the creation of Musil's novel as well as in history itself. For Musil, the beginning of war is regarded first and foremost as an ending, as a symbol of social and cultural change. To understand what exactly enabled most people to affirm the declaration of war enthusiastically, historians as well as novelists have tried to analyze its preceding circumstances. When interviewed by Oskar Maurus Fontana in 1926 about his work in progress, Musil emphasized that the central issue he wanted to focus on in his novel was the outbreak of war, because that event provided a key to his understanding of the prewar period. As he declared in that interview, his purpose was a genealogical one, he intended to demonstrate the different and even contradictory tendencies that finally resulted in war.

And again we get stuck in the predicament of causality. "Die Frage nach der Ursache," that is, to be in search of a first cause that could be made responsible for the whole process; as Musil puts it, this is an absolutely useless undertaking. It is simply everybody and everything, he says, that has to be taken into account, so that you cannot isolate one single man or one single nation as being decisive. And that is why his novel of prewar Viennese society disperses, splitting into dozens of places and sequences, often interrupted by reflections and digressions which demonstrate the author's analytical – and satirical! – capacity.

There is a chapter (Chapter 83), one of the famous ones, which is entitled: "Seinesgleichen geschieht oder warum erfindet man nicht Geschichte?" In the recent translation by Sophie Wilkins and Burton Pike, it says the following: "Pseudoreality prevails, or: Why don't we make history up as we go along?"[3] (And I have to admit that it sounds even more precise than the original.) It seems to be one of Musil's special tics to show us his hero most extensively whenever he is on his way home. In this chapter we meet Ulrich after a visit to Clarisse's house, returning slowly to the inner sections of town. The chapter starts when he leaves the tram for a little walk, rethinking the argument he had with Clarisse. It has been her yearning for carrying out something really spectacular (actually she starts planning Moosbrugger's rescue), her being crazy about great historic events which brings Ulrich to an attitude of radical scepticism as regards history. And his scepticism is focused especially on the question of causality. Is it not an absurd fiction, Ulrich states, to think of history as a billiard ball that follows its predestined, linear course? As if we only had to know all the initial conditions well enough in order to be able to calculate the whole process and its results; or, given the final results, to figure out all the factors and circumstances they were caused by? I am going to quote just one of these passages or digressions:

> The course of history was therefore not that of a billiard ball which, once it is hit, takes a definite line – but resembles the movement of clouds, or the path of a man sauntering through the streets, turned aside by a shadow here, a crowd there, an unusual architectural outcrop, until at last he arrives at a place he never knew or meant to go to. Inherent in the course of history is a certain going off course.[4]

A nice aphoristic observation indeed. But what is the reason for Ulrich's occupation with this sophisticated and misleading subject? First, his reflection is not as misleading as it seems to be: Ulrich's *bonmot* that history should be invented or simulated is exactly the credo of the Austrian "Parallelaktion" which fills the novel's first volume; and it also describes the relation Musil's novel establishes to its own "raw materials." On a second level, Ulrich's reflection is not misleading because it is misleading, namely misleading Ulrich; when he stops thinking about history at the end of the chapter, he realizes that he has lost his way, too. Thereby he confirms exactly what he has said about the similarity of progression and digression, or, of making history up as he goes along, as *he* is going off course.

Finally we should recognize that Ulrich's reflection and even the metaphors he uses do not pertain exclusively to this fictional character, they are part of the author's thinking, and for Musil the problem of causality is not an academic one. As we saw, this question only arose in the postwar situation, so that the whole passage can be read as an anachronistic insert from after the war. There are two metaphors Ulrich suggests for replacing the mechanical pattern of the billiard-ball: the way of history is like the way of a flaneur walking through the streets – which happened to be Ulrich himself; or, and this is a strange comparison, like the movement of the clouds. Does the movement of the clouds have anything in common with the course of history? Let us suppose that weather-forecasting probably was not as reliable in the twenties as it is today; so what makes meteorological phenomena comparable to the contingency of historical events is that they are almost unpredictable. To respect contingency means to admit that history is not predictable, that it cannot be processed by sheer deduction. A beginning can thus give us initial conditions, but it cannot determine what follows, although everything that actually follows is determined. A beginning therefore could be described as a starting point, "from which, remarkably enough, nothing develops" ("woraus bemerkenswerter Weise nichts hervorgeht").[5] So, why not start this beginning with the unpredictable *per se*, the movement of the clouds? "A barometric low hung over the Atlantic. It moved eastward toward a high-pressure area over Russia without as yet showing any inclination to bypass this high in a northerly direction."[6]

It took a long time to arrive here at the very beginning, to reach the novel's famous first words and the initial conditions they provide. Is there really nothing that develops from this beginning? Nothing but more than 2,000 pages. But is there anything that supplies the answer to our question about the possible ending?

As every "tick" is followed by its "tock," Frank Kermode's book on narrative endings was echoed by Edward Said's study on beginnings. Said points out that one of literature's primordial merits is its capacity of deliberate beginnings, of constructing beginnings. We do not have to speculate about origins anymore, Said writes; there is no origin, but there are lots of beginnings and a variety of ways to begin. On the one hand, there are the solemn ones, beginnings which do not just fall in medias res but try to emphasize in advance the kernel of the whole story; those beginnings pretend to be not only beginnings but principles, so that what follows can be deduced from this logical basis. For example: "It is a truth universally acknowledged, that a single man in possession of a good fortune must be in want of a wife" (Jane Austen's *Pride and Prejudice*). As that novel is about prejudice, it performs prejudice, in spite of its ironic mode: a beginning that claims to predestine all the following action.

The other way to begin emerges when irony and the self-consciousness of the narrator not only accompany the run of narrative but disturb and almost destroy the plot that is being told. The paradigm for this category is *Tristram Shandy*. A beginning that is postponed "with a kind of encyclopedic, meaningful playfulness which ... delays one sort of action for the sake of undertaking another."[7] But even in cases like that, Said declares, "the beginning is always a first step from which ... *something follows*."[8] Unfortunately, *The Man without Qualities* is not discussed in Said's study, so that it is up to us now to give evidence to that judgment.

Musil's first chapter seems to be located right in the middle between the solemn beginnings and ironic playfulness; in fact, it is a battlefield occupied by both of them. While nearly the whole first paragraph neglects and frustrates our conventions of beginnings with astronomical and meteorological details, its last phrase is willing to reconcile us to tradition: "It was a fine day in August 1913." ("Es war ein schöner Augusttag des Jahres 1913.")[9] It is only from both aspects together that we receive some indirect information about the novel's subsequent course and its ending. The first chapter mainly designates what M. Bakhtin called a chronotopos, it indicates that the following action starts in Vienna, capital of Austria-Hungary, in August 1913. Reading this in 1930 or later, it was almost impossible not to be reminded of what happened one year later. Now the crucial point in Musil's beginning is that he manages to say two things that are absolutely contradictory at the same time. He says: Look at our pretty town dozing in its peaceful summertime, there is no reason at all to be suspicious or scared. Not even the clouds are showing any inclination to move eastward toward that Russian high-pressure area, so to speak. But only a few moments later an accident happens that disturbs this sunny opening. Just as the accident that ends this beginning results from an unpredictable urban traffic system, the end of the novel would have been marked by the collective accident of war.

We know that the final point of the story would have been reached exactly when Ulrich's sabbatical year was reaching its end. In his very last years of writing, Musil tried to postpone, I guess almost unconsciously, this troublesome ending by repeatedly rewriting chapters that took place in previous parts of the story; that is, to extend both his hero's "leave of absence from his life" ("Urlaub von seinem Leben")[10] and Musil's own symbiosis with the world he had created. When Lyotard started to propagate the end of the master narratives, *The Man without Qualities* was one of his chief witnesses. But Musil's main problem was not the ending of narrative but rather the narrative of an ending. Referring to Kermode's book once more, it reminds us that to narrate "the end" was a central theological problem. As the last things were supposed to be transcendental, how could they be inserted into such inferior matters like narrative? What takes place in modernity, then, is a secularization of this everlasting apocalyptic imminence. Kermode says literature converts imminence into immanence, into small endings, so to speak. It seems to me that we can find something quite similar in Musil's novel: Although he was obviously hindered from reaching the final point, the showdown in August 1914, the plot offers small endings, like the first chapter's accident, like the telegram informing Ulrich about his father's death, or, at the end of the last volume published in Musil's lifetime, a series of four chapters entitled: "A great event is in the making" ("Ein großes Ereignis ist im Entstehen.")[11] That was the point when the "Parallelaktion" tried to put a deliberate ending to its own history, in vain, as we know, because they were confounding endings with results.

In a diary note from September 1939 in Geneva, Musil recognized: "In my career as a writer, I never succeeded in going beyond beginnings" ("Ich habe nie etwas über die Anfänge hinausgeführt.")[12] When World War II started, not a single soul would care about those remote times that preceded the first one. Musil still did, for his own biography and his way of writing were too deeply and too persistently challenged by the experience of war. What was all the traditional lore of how to tell stories good for, when it was confronted with a new, technological warfare that did not operate in terms of individual fighting but of statistical destruction? The imminence of death did not appear as a personal fate anymore, but as a question of simple calculations.

Do you remember that conversation in the first chapter immediately after the accident, when individual suffering is countered by anonymous statistics? "People dispersed almost as if justified in feeling that they had just witnessed something entirely lawful and orderly. 'According to American statistics,' the gentleman said, 'one hundred ninety thousand people are killed there every year by cars and four hundred fifty thousand are injured.'"[13] Not even American statistics can be as enormous as Musil's imagination was. Lots of critics have not been able to find any convincing explanation for these totally mistaken and exaggerated numbers. I have to admit, I did not even try to find some American statistics which could reach an amount like that. But I received some statistics from Manfried Rauchensteiner, the director of the Museum of Military History in Vienna. In the first year of war, the Austro-Hungarian troops had had very high losses: exactly 490,000 wounded and 190,000 killed, counting from a beautiful day in August 1914 – a crucial point that does not appear at the ending of Musil's novel, but that lies buried under its beginning.

Nothing but beginnings? Musil's narrative achieves what Austria failed to do: preparing for an end that is still hard to tell.

Humboldt-Universität Berlin

Notes

1. Frank Kermode, *The Sense of an Ending. Studies in the Theory of Fiction* (New York, 1967), 44.

2. *Die Reichshaupt und Residenzstadt Wien: recte Robert Musil, Der Mann ohne Eigenschaften*, Adolf Frisé, ed. (Reinbek: Rowohlt, 1978), 9; *The Man without Qualities*. Translated by Sophie Wilkins and Burton Pike (New York: Alfred Knopf, 1995), 3.

3. Musil, *The Man without Qualities*, 388; "Seinesgleichen geschieht oder warum erfindet man nicht Geschichte?": *Der Mann ohne Eigenschaften*, 357.

4. Musil, *The Man without Qualities*, 392. "Der Weg der Geschichte ist also nicht der eines Billiardballs, der, einmal abgestoßen, eine be-

stimmte Bahn durchläuft, sondern er ähnelt dem Weg der Wolken, ähnelt dem Weg eines durch die Gassen Streichenden, der hier von einem Schatten, dort von einer Menschengruppe oder einer seltsamen Verschneidung von Häuserfronten abgelenkt wird und schließlich an eine Stelle gerät, die er weder gekannt hat, noch erreichen wollte. Es liegt im Verlauf der Weltgeschichte ein gewisses Sich-Verlaufen." *Der Mann ohne Eigenschaften*, 361.

5. Musil, *The Man without Qualities*, 3; *Der Mann ohne Eigenschaften*, 9.

6. Musil, *The Man without Qualities*, 3. "Über dem Atlantik befand sich ein barometrisches Minimum; es wanderte ostwärts, einem über Rußland lagernden Maximum zu, und verriet noch nicht die Neigung, diesem nördlich auszuweichen." *Der Mann ohne Eigenschaften*, 9.

7. Edward W. Said, *Beginnings. Intention and Method* (New York: Columbia University Press), 44.

8. Ibid., xvi.

9. Musil, *The Man without Qualities*, 3; *Der Mann ohne Eigenschaften*, 9.

10. Musil, *The Man without Qualities*, 44; *Der Mann ohne Eigenschaften*, 47.

11. Musil, *The Man without Qualities*, 1078; *Der Mann ohne Eigenschaften*, 994.

12. Musil, *Tagebücher*, Adolf Frisé, ed. (Reinbek: Rowohlt, 1983), volume I, 943.

13. Musil, *The Man without Qualities*, 5. "Man ging fast mit dem berechtigten Eindruck davon, daß sich ein gesetzliches und ordnungsgemäßes Ereignis vollzogen habe. 'Nach den amerikanischen Statistiken,' so bemerkte der Herr, 'werden dort jährlich durch Autos 190.000 Personen getötet und 450.000 verletzt.'" *Der Mann ohne Eigenschaften*, 11.

Subliminal Austria: Sigmund Freud in World Literature

Raymond L. Burt

In undertaking the task of examining the image of Austria in literature, one is faced with two distinct areas of investigation: one within Austrian literature itself, i.e. works primarily addressed to an Austrian audience, and one examining the image of Austria in world literature. The former as an intercultural dialogue between artist and audience may challenge the cultural identity of the reader, whereas the latter may be the sole or significant source of information about Austrian culture to which the reader has been exposed.

Regardless of one's choice, one will discover that the examination of an "Österreichbild" in a literary tradition is related to the general question of the viability of fiction as a transmitter of historical reality. Inquiries into the image of Austria in literature are, in effect, a focus on a particular period of history, a particular political entity, or a specific milieu in Austria's cultural and ethnic history. The question becomes: To what extent is the representation of Austria in fictional works related to the "real" Austria?

This article will focus on the image of Austria as represented in world literature. To enhance my chances of finding a "reality-based" representation of Austria, I will focus on one of its most famous sons, Sigmund Freud. The advantage of having a historical person as a point of reference is that I am generally assured of managable chronological and geographic parameters, specifically Freud's Vienna from the late nineteenth century to shortly after the Anschluss. The major disadvantage of focusing on a historical character in a literary work is that I step squarely into the postmodern no-man's-land between "fiction" and "reality."

In recent decades the "reality" question has been banned by the deconstructionalist theorists, who, together in symbiotic harmony with many postmodern novelists, have gone so far as to challenge the very notion of a comprehensible reality. Assertions of the impossibility of effectively portraying historical events in literature matched similar developments in the field of historiography, in which all historical narrative accounts were viewed as a product of the historian's creative selection and the combination of a necessarily incomplete set of data. If all historical narratives are viewed as primarily subjective, revealing more about the historian than about their chosen topics, and if all fiction is self-referential with no possibility of any connection to experiential reality, then the task of seeking in literature meaningful images of a geographical, political, cultural and historical entity is futile.

At this point I am reminded of the (undoubtedly historically inaccurate) anecdote of Galileo's last words which served as his final rebuttal to a forced recantation foisted on him by the Church's theological purists. Faced with the power of the dominant paradigm, he had to acknowledge the current theories of the earth-centered solar system, despite his own observations to the contrary. "And yet it moves," he muttered on his deathbed, referring to the earth. We, when faced with a well-argued and ensconced literary theory which asserts the impotence of literary narrative to depict historical reality, might point to the plethora of historical narratives, biographies and resurgence of interest in the historical novel and mutter: "And yet . . ."

Granted, it is simplistic to paint the literary critical environment in such dogmatic tones, just as it is not true that Galileo faced a Church totally committed against heliocentric theories. Currently in the discussion of the historical narrative, critics are seeking a middle path between the deconstructionalist view of the ultimate referential meaninglessness of literature and the now defunct position which saw the narrative form as an objective and accurate transmitter of historical reality. For example, Hayden White, in *The Content of Form*, seeks to reconcile the two extremes. According to White, any one set of historical events can find a variety of narrative forms. These forms, or story types (comical, tragic, farcical) are derived from a particular culture, and their use in a historical narrative produces meaning independent from the set of historical events. "It is the choice of the story type and its imposition upon the events that endow them with meaning."[1] White views the historical narrative as a method of testing a culture's system of meaning production against any set of 'real' events. This ability of a society to imbue historical facts with meaning posited in its genre forms places historical narrative into the realm of allegory. Narrative always says one thing (the historical content) and means another (the culturally determined literary code).

White's theoretical considerations approach the fiction/non-fiction boundary by examining the non-fictional forms. From the fictional side we have Linda Hutcheon's *A Poetics of the Postmodern* which identifies the growing interest in historical themes in postmodern literature. Her 'historiographic metafiction' finds a middle path, on the one hand, by validating the historical fiction's connection to actual historical events and, on the other, by subverting the use of history in narrative. This paradox is essential in recognizing a historical grounding of the narrative as well as the artificial construction which that narrative provides.

An author, by introducing a historical figure well known to the readers, is (to use White's terminology) applying some of the meaning codes that figure has acquired in the mind of the culture. The author's creative manipulation of the historical personage within the fictional framework (à la Hutcheon) may provide the reader with insights into our own time as well as that of the novel's subject. With a historical figure like Sigmund Freud, who, as one of the major shapers of the contemporary intellectual landscape, evokes a wide spectrum of perceptions in readers, an author taps into a wealth of associations, including that complicated relationship Freud had with his homeland.

With his use of cultural manifestations in his theoretical writings and the fact that his case studies have been praised for their artistic or literary quality, not to mention the fact that his psychoanalytic theories have been applied as a literary interpretive method themselves, Sigmund Freud is inevitably bound up with Western culture of the twentieth century. His life has been the subject of major biographies, notably by his protégé Ernest Jones, whose work has served as the source for many of the fictive accounts, and more recently by Peter Gay. Freud himself, was hostile to the prospect of being subjected to a biographer's attention, and in anticipation of such, occasionally committed his papers, letters, and other biographical fodder to the flame. In a letter to his fiancée in 1885 he states: "As for the biographers, let them worry, we have no desire to make it too easy for them. Each one of them will be right in his opinion of 'The Development of the Hero,' and I am already looking forward to seeing them go astray."[2]

When Arnold Zweig approached him in 1936 about composing a biography, Freud responded with an even more revealing comment: "Anyone who writes a biography is committed to lies, concealments, hypocrisy, flattery and even to hiding his own lack of understanding, for biographical truth does not exist, and if it did, we could not use it."[3]

As we have seen, this is very much in synch with modern literary theory. However it seems odd that Freud rejected the narrative form of biography as a viable undertaking, when his own work, especially the case histories, depended on narrative as an accurate revealer of truth. As suggested by Madelon Sprengnether, the founder of psychoanalysis may have feared that since his own self-analysis (his own interpretation, if you will) is intrinsically involved in the development and justification of his theories, any alternative interpretation of his life, might undermine the credibility of his life's work.[4] She shows that the two major biographers (Jones and Gay) both sustain the self-image created and propagated by Freud himself. This image is of a man who struggles against formidable odds, facing his own personal demons, in order to wrest the truth from them.

It is ironic that Freud vehemently rejected the objectivity of the traditionally "non-fictional" narrative form on the basis of its necessary fiction, for now there are ample narrative interpretations of his life which arise within the fictional genres of novels, screenplays, dramas, speculative fiction, literary fragments and even a detective story. That the story of Freud's life is conducive to literary interpretation was perhaps first pointed out by Thomas Mann on the occasion of Freud's eightieth birthday. In his address, entitled "Freud and the Future," Mann took his lead from an article in the journal *Imago* that identified a pattern in biographical writing in which legend formats were used to shape the narrative. According to the unnamed journal writer, this strategy facilitated the reader's comprehension of the new by its association with the familiar. Mann transformed this line of thought into the assertion that the artist is one that perceives the mythical in the individual. This perspective has been reintroduced by Elizabeth Wesseling who, in acknowledging the postmodern chaotic view of history, points to the "myth method." Wesseling demonstrates that, contrary to the assumed rift between historical novels and postmodern novels, the tendency in contemporary literature has been toward increased literary treatments of history: "It is furthermore remarkable that these subtle historical references are yoked to mythical motifs. This combination conjures up parallels between historically situated persons and events and transhistorical archetypal structures.[5]

Michael Palencia-Roth has gone so far as to make a case for the "mythical novel" as a twentieth-century genre form. In examining the nature of myth and its relationship to the novel, he identifies the function of myth as that of expressing the inexpressible through its ability to transmit antithetical concepts. Although his examples predate postmodern writers, he does draw support for his view of myth in literature by turning to Freud.[6] In "The Antithetical Sense of Primal Words," Freud acknowledges that dreams allow contradictions and antitheses to coexist without difficulty. This capacity for accepting antithetical images comes from the subconscious and is thus basic to the human mind. Whereas Palencia-Roth connects this trait to myth as a transmitter of the transcendent, we might see here one of the underpinnings of postmodernism's receptivity to paradox. Novels which take historical events or characters and present them in a manner which contradicts the traditional historical understanding, may still offer a transcendent "truth." One could connect this to a human ability described by John Keats as "negative capability" or the capacity to face the inexplicable without "any irritable reaching after fact and reason."[7] This ability seems appropriate to the postmodern historiographic metafiction.

There are roughly two approaches in the use of Sigmund Freud as a literary character: an author places him as either the main character, making some aspect of his life the focus of the work, or as the antagonist. The former includes works such as Irving Stone's *The Passion of the Mind*, Jean Paul Sartre's *The Freud Scenario*, Henry Denker's *A Far Country*, and Anthony Burgess' *The End of the World News*. Among the latter, I include the following: Joshua Sobol's *Weinigers Nacht*,[8] Irvin Yalom's *When Nietzsche Wept*, D. M. Thomas' *The White Hotel*, and Nicholas Meyer's *The Seven Percent Solution*.

As to the image of Austria which appears in this literature, we cannot expect a flattering one. Freud's existing letters and his conversations with colleagues and friends attest to his negative opinion of Austria, or more specifically, of Vienna, both as Imperial capital and the capital of the Republic. That Freud's Vienna should be portrayed in this literature as a hotbed of anti-Semitism is no surprise. As Peter Gay points out in his biography of Freud: "Vienna never wholly ceased to be for him the theater of hardship, repeated failure, prolonged and hateful solitude, unpleasant incidents of Jew-hatred."[9] But Gay also gives credence to the speculation by Freud's son Martin that his rejection of Vienna concealed a strong love of the city. Bruno Bettelheim in his essay "Two Views of Freud" posits the idea that Freud's hatred was the product of a frustrated deep love for the city which had become increasingly open in its anti-Semitism.[10] Whatever the reason, Freud himself admits the love-hate relationship upon his final departure from the city in 1938: "The feeling of triumph which freedom brings is strongly mixed with sadness, since one loved the prison. . . ."[11]

In another view, psychoanalysis is a product of the particularly Viennese environment. This view was adamantly rejected by Freud. Ernest Jones quotes Freud who has shunned a colleague because he "was stupid enough to say that the idea of a sexual etiology for the neuroses could only arise in the atmosphere of a town like Vienna."[12] Nevertheless, the connection between the birth of psychoanalysis and *fin-de-siècle* Vienna has allies even among Freud's supporters. This connection is most eloquently expressed in Bettelheim's essay, "Freud's Vienna." Here Bettelheim paints a picture of a city schizophrenically balanced between the old Imperial, baroque past and the new modern Ringstrasse façade, ever in denial about its political decline, with a ruling family shaken by the Oedipal struggle and the ultimate suicide of Crown Prince Rudolf, as well as the assassination of the estranged Empress Elisabeth. Franz Josef, thus succumbed to his work neurosis, while the artists and poets reflecting the cultural malaise delved ever deeper into the twin obsessions of *eros* and *thanatos*. If Freudian psychoanalysis is grounded ultimately in the validity of its founder's self-analysis and if Freud's psyche is intrinsically linked to his Viennese environment as such a love/hate relationship would indicate, then we could expect that the image of Vienna in this literature to be more than just a perfunctory backdrop.

In the works I have chosen, the spectrum of the intermixture of psychoanalysis, Freud's psyche and the role of Vienna ranges between these two extremes: On the one hand, the development of the new view of the mind is a product of an introspective and neurotic Freud, who is entangled in a love/hate relationship with Vienna, a city which symbolizes a culture in need of psychoanalytic healing; on the other, Freud appears as great thinker, who has tapped into the universal truth of the workings of the mind. He symbolizes authority. He just happened to live in Vienna.

In Joshua Sobol's play, *Weinigers Nacht*, we find Otto Weiniger on the night of his suicide on 3 October 1903. Sobol has various personages from Weiniger's past replay key points in his life. Weiniger had played a role in the split between Freud and his friend Wilhelm Fliess. In a single scene Sigmund Freud steps out of the audience and onto the stage performing a psychiatric interview of sorts.[13] Freud asks short questions, eliciting longer responses from Weiniger. In the confrontation Freud's role is much like that of the father in Kafka's *Das Urteil*, and indeed there is an analogy drawn between Freud and Weiniger's father. After a few questions he lies down on the couch asking Weiniger to make observations about Freud's work. Weiniger's critique focuses on flaws in Freud's theories, which he views as being related to Judaism. Freud's hesitancy to assert a dogmatic truth, as revealed in his relativism and his amoral stance of rejecting guilt, for example, is labeled by Weiniger as derivative of Jewish thought. Suddenly Freud, with renewed vigor, jumps up and assumes the dominant role. Freud condemns Weiniger by accusing him of stealing Fliess's ideas. He thus turns Weiniger's weapon against him by insisting on his guilt. This confrontation becomes at once that of Weiniger pitted against his father, his religious tradition, and the scientific authority represented by Freud. This scene is bracketed by conversations between Weiniger and his *Doppelgänger*, who introduces it as an all-or-nothing contest of Oedipal consequences.

In *Weinigers Nacht* the images of anti-Semitism are impersonal, elemental, and ominously swelling to a cataclysm. From the thousands and thousands of candles flickering in the windows of a dark Vienna, lit in celebration of the appointment of Karl Lueger as mayor, to the statement that the city is a liberal, democratic paradise sitting on a volcano of anti-Semitism. These images form the unavoidable background to the tragedy of Weiniger's fate. The title in English, "The Soul of a Jew," indicates the representational function of the main character. Otto Weiniger's major work, *Geschlecht und Charakter*, was a turn-of-the-century best seller, which served as a catalyst in the growing debate of the "Jewish question." Weiniger's suicide, as the culmination of the play, is symbolic of the tragic fate of European Jews who sought assimilation but were swept away by the tides of ethnic and racial extremism.

In Irvin Yalom's *When Nietzsche Wept*, Friedrich Nietzsche arrives in Vienna in 1882 for medical treatment. Lou Andreas-Salomé secretly enlists the aid of Dr. Josef Breuer to attempt to cure Nietzsche's troubled soul under the guise of treating his physical ailments. Breuer, Freud's mentor and discoverer of the basic psychoanalytic technique of the "talking cure," engages Nietzsche in philosophical and psychological dialogue during months of intense treatment. The author thus juxtaposes the philosophy of Nietzsche with the birth of the psychoanalytic theory. One wonders if Breuer is merely the stand-in for Freud in a hypothetical meeting of two of the greatest influences on the early twentieth century. Unfortunately the historic timeline did not accommodate such a possible encounter. The twenty-five year old Freud does appear as a supporting character, and in his first appearance the author endows him with the aura of future greatness. Breuer spots the young medical intern from his fiacre: "Breuer looked out at the pedestrians hurrying home from work, mostly men, each carrying a black umbrella and dressed much as he was – dark fur-lined greatcoat, white gloves, and black top hat. Someone familiar caught his eye. The short, hatless man with the trim beard, passing the others, winning the race!"[14]

In the first conversation between the two friends, Freud is introduced to Breuer's discovery of the "talking cure." Freud also attempts to interpret Breuer's recurring nightmare, convinced that dreams contain a hidden key to the psyche, a reference to his later groundbreaking work *The Interpretation of Dreams*. It is evident that there is an identification of the two men in the novel. Breuer refers to Freud as a younger version of himself. Freud confesses that he chose his fiancée using Breuer's wife as a model. The younger colleague has practically become a member of the Breuer household, as we see in his first visit. He takes a bath, changes into Breuer's clothes, goes to check on the children, and engages the wife in confidential discussions. Freud serves as confidante throughout the novel and offers the approaches Breuer should take in treating Nietzsche. Breuer shares his revelations with Freud, revelations which contain the seeds of many psychoanalytic theories. Breuer thus functions as intermediary. Similar to the representation of Freud by Denker and Sartre, Breuer is presented as entrapped by his own troubled neuroses: fear of death, difficulties with his father, and sexual obsession. Breuer's treatment of Nietzsche turns into a confrontation with his own torment. The result of this confrontation is the birth of psychoanalysis, but as Yalom points out in the author's note, it is Freud who pursues the new theories, not Breuer.

The Vienna of *When Nietzsche Wept* is strictly background to the internal duet of its main characters. The coffee house milieu, the Ringstraße, *Neue Freie Presse*, and Viennese culinary delicacies appear as historic stage settings and props. The most extensive description details the Jewish section of the *Zentralfriedhof*, the main cemetery in Vienna. Anti-Semitism also lurks in the wings but is present only in references to it as a growing political force.

D. M. Thomas takes special pains to acknowledge his use of Freud in his novel, *The White Hotel*. He begins the book with a note that outlines his view of Freud: "One could not travel far in the landscape of hysteria – the "terrain" of this novel – without meeting the majestic figure of Sigmund Freud."[15] He acknowledges that his Freud is fictional but that certain credence is given the historical Freud. One third of the book is written as if it were one of Freud's case histories. Thomas praises Freud's case histories as "masterly works of literature" and proves his point by creatively incorporating a fictional version of this Freudian genre into his postmodern novel. Freud here, is the psychotherapist, the invisible, observant analyst hidden from the view of the patient on the couch. His presence in the novel is mostly in the form of letters, and in the case study of the main character, Lisa Erdman, under the pseudonym Anna G, David Cowart shows how *The White Hotel* exposes the shortcomings of the Freudian method in its inability to encompass the entirety of the main character's mental and emotional disorders.[16] Traditional psychoanalysis falls short in its rejection of the paranormal. The main character's neuroses result not only from events in her past, but also from those yet to occur. Vienna, in this novel, is as invisible to the reader as is the figure of Freud. Lisa Erdman moves between Vienna, Milan, and Kiev, but the most decisive locations are the surreal White Hotel and the horrific massacre at Babi Yar.

On the more popular level, Nicholas Meyer presents us with a new adventure of Sherlock Holmes in his two-million-copy bestseller *The Seven-Per-Cent-Solution*. This novel had perhaps the widest exposure of any in the group, and its author was nominated for an Academy Award for Best Adaptation of a novel into a screenplay. Thus as a medium for the projection of an image of Austria, this work is perhaps the most significant. In this action-packed romp in Vienna, we have the collaboration between Sigmund Freud and Sherlock Holmes in solving a kidnapping case. Anti-Semitism is reduced to the form of a young ruffian with a sabre-scarred face, whom Freud challenges and defeats 6-3 in a set of indoor tennis. The two protagonists are presented as equals, even to the point of using the same methodology. Holmes aids Freud with a patient under hypnosis, and at a crucial point in the plot Freud applies his psychoanalytic theories to Holmsian deductive techniques to save the day. Both men are depicted as misunderstood "prophets by their homelands."

The Vienna through which Sherlock Holmes and Sigmund Freud pursue a kidnap victim is at first seen through the eyes of Dr. Watson who has never been to the city before, and little detail is mentioned. Later it does receive a brief descriptive summary outlining the typical *fin-de-siécle* image. However, as the identification of Freud and Holmes is cultivated, so too is that of Vienna and Victorian London. The coffee houses are likened to London's clubs, and the Danube to the Thames. Vienna is thus to Sigmund Freud, what London is to Sherlock Holmes.

Among the works which focus on Freud as the protagonist, the first book I wish to mention is the one least interesting for my purposes. Irving Stone spent five years of detailed research for his historical novel of Freud's career, *The Passions of the Mind*. In its recounting of Freud's life, it closely follows its well-documented sources, and the novel borders on the claim of biography. As such it dishes up meticulous detail and references to Vienna to the extreme. Even internal dialogue is not safe from them as Stone has Freud react to his fiancée: "Her delighted laughter rang in his head like the bells of St. Stephan's."[17] Stone is capable of long, descriptive passages of the city which are rivaled only by conscientious guidebooks. For example, a brief excerpt of Freud's walk to a meeting with Professor Brücke provides a visual feast of the city: "After he had passed the Zum Hl. Josef pharmacy, with ornate chemical jars in its windows, he turned left into the Taborstrasse, passing the fine shops, coffeehouses and restaurants that had been built for the Vienna World's Fair of 1873 and continued to prosper. At the corner of the Obere Augartenstrasse he could see through the trees to the French pavilion-like buildings in the park. At the corner of the Grosse Pfarrgasse was a four-story house, its top floor held up on either side by plaster torsos of two Amazons with heroic breasts and the classical headdress of the ancient Greek women."[18] Should the reader, after completing the 800 pages, desire more information about Vienna, Stone has included in the appendix a three-page collection of local color and custom under the title "This is Vienna." The novel strives not only for the veracity once accorded historical narrative, but also to place the reader in Freud's footsteps, lets the reader hear the historic conversations and taste the *Melange* and the *Schlagobers*.

Henry Denker's play, *A Far Country*, focuses on Freud as the pioneer, struggling to take science onto a path not yet explored. Like Stone, his image of Freud is painted by one who has no doubts about this pioneer's ultimate contribution. It is a look back to the difficult origins of a great movement, and the play reflects the self-image propagated by Freud.

A less successful screenplay than the one offered by Meyers, but by all standards a better literary interpretation of Freud is provided by Jean-Paul Sartre, published now under the title *The Freud Scenario*. This work was, oddly enough, commissioned in 1958 by John Huston, who wished to direct a film showing Sigmund Freud as the pioneer of the mind, an adventurer. For a Hollywood approach, which Huston said he wished to present as a detective story, he turned to the most unlikely screenwriter. Sartre's overlong script presented a neurotic, nose-picking, father-hating Freud. It was sent back for a rewrite and came back even longer and with scenes even more abhorrent to Hollywood tastes than the earlier version. Huston, with help from two other more conventional screenwriters, finally produced his film, which Sartre disowned.[19]

In the original screenplay Freud is the modern day Everyman, caught in the transformation of the defunct traditional values and the search for new ones. Sartre openly draws a connection between Freud and the Faust legend. Faust was falsely praised by the local peasants for his efforts in healing them from the plague, when in fact his conscience reminds him that he, indeed, did more harm than good. Freud, also seeking to heal the modern plague, is condemned by his contemporaries. The cure is perceived as the plague, and he is accused of seeking the dark path of superstition, hypnotism – the fraudulent method, a parlor game. In Sartre, the Faustian motif is woven into the narrative. Faust/ Freud becomes increasingly remote from colleagues, friends and family in his obsessive pursuit of truth. His new mentor, Wilhelm Fliess, whose ironic, cold Prussian airs contrast with the Viennese *joie de vivre*, gains influence by encouraging Freud to press on, when all others try to bring him back into the fold of acceptability. On his deathbed his estranged patron and early supporter, Theodor Meynert, confesses that he himself did not have the courage, but that Freud should not give up and should make a pact with the devil to achieve his goals. Fliess, with Mephistophelian charm, is characterized as having "demonic eyes." As in *Faust* the devil is presented in the guise of the traveling scholar. The analogy is intentional, and Sartre even has Fliess suggest a blood pact between the two. The scene occurs on a bridge over the Danube and Fliess offers Freud a ring engraved with snakes. Mephisto/Fliess asks him to join him in knowing Nature's secret: that sexuality drives the world. Freud hesitates, because in "this soft, debauched city, . . . will whisper daily: he's a dirty Jew, he's a pig like all Jews." Fliess counters: "We shall have omnipotence, Freud. We shall know their hidden instincts, the sources of what they call Good and Evil, and we shall dominate them through Reason."[20] Fliess's function is to push Freud to the extreme limits. But like Goethe's Faust, Sartre's Freud finds salvation through intercession by a female. His Gretchen, Cäcilie,[21] is the epitome of innocence seduced. She is a ten-year-old in the body of a young woman who is constantly replaying the dark seduction in her past. Together the two explore the nature of the subconscious, and together they exorcise their own personal demons – the psychoanalytic method is born.

An anti-Semitic Vienna is prominent in the *Freud Scenario*, but it is characterized as the product of the social subconscious. In an early scene, staged as a street scene on the Ringstraße, Freud and his fiancée, Martha observe two vendors, each with his own following. The first has two cardboard cutout wrestlers, who seem to be magically moving. Freud explains that there are hidden strings and that someone in the crowd is controlling one of the wrestlers. Martha doesn't wish to shatter the illusion and says: "Explanations! Explanations! You want to find the reason for everything." Freud in searching the faces of the crowd notes that "they all look as if they're hiding something."[22] The next vendor is hawking booklets called the story of the Jew and the Pig. He cries out: "Buy the Protocols of the Elders of Zion. How the Jews aim to control the universe. Lament the child eaten by a rabbi."[23] The stage directions indicate that the vendor "is totally unconcerned about what he is doing. He thinks only of selling them and does not even understand what he is saying." Again Freud surveys the crowd and finds that the faces are the same as the others. Perhaps he is again looking for the one who is pulling the strings. When Freud confronts one of the customers, the man cannot understand his anger. Upon seeing the pedestrians along the Ringstrasse, (officers, fine ladies, and fine gentlemen in frock coats), Freud tells

Martha: "Look. The enemy. When the time comes, they'll hunt us down mercilessly and cut our throats. If we allow them to do so."[24]

Freud is the crusader, the avenger of wrongs. Sartre takes from the biographies Freud's identification with Hannibal taking his revenge on the Romans for wrongs done to his father. After the presentation of his findings to the Medical Society, Freud is booed and ridiculed, yet Sartre has a proud, undefeated Freud turn the tables on the taunting crowd which has turned to anti-Semitic rhetoric. He revenges an old wound, by knocking the top hat of the ringleader into the gutter and saying: "Dirty anti-Semite, pick it up," a direct reenactment of his father's disgrace which he had witnessed as a boy.

Here Vienna is the Vienna of neurosis which rejects Freud in anti-Semitic vehemence when he reveals his theory of the sexual origins of neurosis. Sartre's Freud exclaims: "Vienna is rotten! Everywhere hypocrisy, perversion, neurosis! . . . We'll cleanse this city or we'll blow it to smithereens."[25]

In Anthony Burgess' *End of the World News*, the entire tale of Freud's career is presented in flashbacks from the point at which the prophet is wiping the dust of his hometown from his sandals; that is, we first meet Freud after the Anschluss and follow him on his journey to London. The narrative continually drifts back in dreamlike connections to various episodes in his life. Freud must face his own neurosis and overcome it, but instead of this process giving birth to the new psychoanalysis, it is presented as having cosmic ramifications, as Freud says: "And if I'm right . . . the world will come to an end and then start all over again – a new world. Men and women will know themselves for what they are, for the first time. It will be a terrible shock to the world. And to me."[26] From this point on, the imagery in the novel takes a strongly messianic flavor. When he is first contacted by Carl Jung, Freud remarks: "Well – the Gentiles have at last heard the word of the Lord" (B 150). Those who accept the new theories are said to be converted, like St. Paul. Freud attempts to calm his Viennese disciples, who are upset at the growing recognition of Jung and the Swiss contingent, by stating: "I have to spread the light" (B 188). Alfred Adler draws the analogy of Jung being Joshua to Freud's Moses, but, perhaps like Jesus' disciples, he misunderstands the scope of Freud's mission. Freud/Christ states that "We do not know the day or the hour" (B 232). As for Jung, Freud defends him, saying, "He believes." To which Adler replies, parroting the Nicene Creed: "He believes . . . in Jung, the Züricher almighty, creator of heaven and earth" (B 234). Ultimately as Adler and Wilhelm Stekel become heretics in Freud's eyes, they reject him as "supreme pontiff" and begin the "reformation" (B 244). As the new psychoanalytic Jungian school takes the front stage, Freud's message is relegated back to the Old Testament which is summed up by Jung as: "Thou shalt believe in the sexual aetiology of the neuroses, thou shalt believe that thou didst desire thy mother in infancy, thou shalt have no other God but thy avenging father who has come hither to shear off thy testicles" (B 261).

As Freud's cancer of the jaw worsens so that each spoken word is like a "station of the cross" (B 306), Freud is forced to silently endure seeing his kingdom 'not' come. In a dream as Moses, he hurls down the commandment tablets at Jung and Adler, only to have the tablets crumble to dust. The final blow occurs when his own daughter reveals to him that she is taking his theories into new territory, positing the origin of all neurosis in the birth trauma. Ultimately her equating the womb with the tomb seems to be borne out in the death of Freud, who, in a morphine-induced illusion at the moment of his death, is once again a young child, standing before his youthful, nude mother: "'Come, darling. Come to mamma,' she called. A small naked child crawled out of the light and into the comforting darkness" (B 368).

The End of the World News begins with a detailed description of the Nazis in Vienna and the Freud household subjected to extortion, threats and terror. As they finally leave Vienna, Burgess' Freud says: "No more Nazis. No more Vienna. Seventy-five years of it. An ungrateful hypocritical antisemitic obscurantist vicious frivolous stupid brutal detestable city. No more Vienna. But his eyes brimmed" (B 20). Vienna, which as the new Jerusalem had fathered and mothered the new movement, represents Freud's ultimate failure. By far this depiction of the city is the most condemning, yet its final word is that of his love for Vienna.

In the above discussion, I have grouped the works according to a simple distinction: Freud as an antagonist or as the protagonist. Returning to Hayden White's synthesis of the earlier 'objective' historical narrative and the innate 'subjectivity' of all narrative by his positing an 'objective' content in a 'subjective' form, the works considered here cover a variety of genres: drama, novels, and screenplay. Nevertheless, the genre forms are less important than the mythic pattern expressed in the use of Freud in the works. In those with Freud as the antagonist, we find an epic clash of titans. Freud/Breuer wrestle with

Nietzsche's soul, Weiniger and Freud for the Jewish soul, Freud/Holmes with the forces that ultimately lead to the World Wars, and Freud's psychoanalytic methods clash with the postmodern paradoxes and challenges to the self presented by Lisa Erdman. In these struggles, Austria and the Viennese *fin de siècle* serve more or less as background. References to anti-Semitism foreshadow the rise of National Socialism and the Holocaust, but generally these references are balanced by positive local color.

In those works with Freud as the protagonist, the mythic pattern is that of the hero's quest and the Faust legend. Freud wears many masks: Hannibal, Orpheus, Faust, Moses, and Christ. The shifting roles cast doubt on the nature of Freud's ultimate accomplishment. An image of Vienna also becomes more problematic as the city becomes the antagonist. Vienna is the patient who, rejecting Freud's diagnosis of its sexual neurotic maladies, projects its problems onto Freud and persecutes him. It is represented as an anti-Semitic, Christian Rome, requiring a new-Jewish Hannibal to storm its walls, but it is also Jerusalem, the birthplace of the new religion of psychoanalysis.

Thomas Mann concluded his essay on Freud by mythologizing Freud's life. He referred to him as the "pathfinder towards a humanism of the future," and compared him to Faust, the venerable Faust of the final segment of *Faust II*. In quoting Faust's utopian vision at the Zuider Zee, Mann prophesizes a similar future for a humanity grounded on the work of Freud. With this comparison, Mann has, perhaps unknowingly, anticipated the postmodern skepticism and ambiguity in regard to Freud's legacy. For behind Mann's optimistic appraisal, is the elderly blind Faust, who only thought that he was listening to the dike workers reclaiming lost land from the sea's depths, when in actuality the sounds he heard came from Mephistopheles' Lemures digging his grave. Fictional interpretations, by offering alternative mythical reformulation, call into question our image of Freud, his contributions to intellectual history, and his relationship to Austria.

University of North Carolina at Wilmington

Notes

1. Hayden White, *The Content of the Form: Narrative Discourse and Historical Representation* (Baltimore: Johns Hopkins University Press, 1987), 44.
2. Sigmund Freud, *Letters of Sigmund Freud, 1873-1936*, ed. Ernest L. Freud, trans. Tania and James Stern (New York: Basic Books, 1961), 152-153.
3. Sigmund Freud, *The Letters of Sigmund Freud and Arnold Zweig*, ed. Ernest L. Freud, trans. Elaine and William Robson-Scott (New York: Harcourt, Brace & World, 1970), 127.
4. Madelon Sprengnether, "Reading Freud's Life," *American Imago* 52.1 (Spring 1995), 10.
5. Elisabeth Wesseling, *Writing History as a Prophet: Postmodernist Innovations of the Historical Novel* (Utrecht: John Benjamins, 1991), 80.
6. Michael Palencia-Roth, *Myth and the Modern Novel: Garcia Marquez, Mann, and Joyce.* (New York: Garland, 1987), 15.
7. In a letter dated 22 December 1817.
8. This is the only work I am using in German. The English translation was not available to me.
9. Peter Gay, *Freud: A Life for Our Time* (New York: W. W. Norton, 1988), 10.
10. Bruno Bettelheim, *Freud's Vienna & Other Essays* (New York: Alfred A. Knopf, 1990), 46.
11. Letter dated 5/6/1938 to Max Eitingon. Quoted in Harald Leupold-Löwenthal, *Handbuch der Psychoanalyse* (Vienna: ORAC, 1986), 170. Translation mine.
12. Ernest Jones, *The Life and Work of Sigmund Freud* (New York: Basic Books, 1961), 542.
13. Joshua Sobol, *Weinigers Nacht* (Vienna: Paulus Manker, 1988), 38-43.
14. Irvin D. Yalom, *When Nietzsche Wept* (New York: Harper Perennial, 1992), 30.
15. D.M. Thomas, *The White Hotel* (New York: The Viking Press, 1981), vii.
16. David Cowart, *History and the Contemporary Novel* (Carbondale and Edwardsville: Southern Illinois University Press, 1989), 144.
17. Irving Stone, *The Passions of the Mind: A Biographical Novel of*

Sigmund Freud (New York: Doubleday, 1971), 19.

18. Ibid., 22.

19. The movie, released in 1962, is titled *Freud, The Secret Passion* and stars Montgomery Cliff in the main role.

20. Jean Paul Sartre, *The Freud Scenario* (Chicago: University of Chicago Press, 1985), 235.

21. Based on the real life Bertha Pappenheim, known in the case studies as Anna O.

22. Sartre, 29.

23. Ibid., 30.

24. Ibid., 32.

25. Ibid., 257

26. Anthony Burgess, *The End of the World News: An Entertainment.* (New York: McGraw-Hill, 1983), 94. Henceforth cited in the text as B with page number.

"Dear Kaiser Franz Joseph, you understand us and we understand you – and every man must help himself": On Galician Jews in the Habsburg Monarchy as Depicted in H. W. Katz's Novel *Die Fischmanns* (1937)

Ena Pedersen

Adapting themselves to the milieu of the people or country where they live is not only an external protective measure for Jews, but a deep internal desire. Their longing for a homeland, for rest, for security, for friendliness urges them to attach themselves passionately to the culture of the world around them. And never was such an attachment more effective – except in Spain in the fifteenth century – or happier and more fruitful than in Austria. Having resided for more than two hundred years in the Imperial city, the Jews encountered there an easy-going people, inclined to conciliation, under whose apparent laxity of form lay buried the identical deep instinct for cultural and aesthetic values which was so important to the Jews themselves.[1]

On the following pages of his autobiography, *The World of Yesterday* (*Die Welt von Gestern*), Stefan Zweig goes on to describe the great importance of Vienna for the Jews and the equally immense and well-known importance of the Jews for Austrian culture and social life. It is an idyllic description of peaceful ethnic coexistence as Zweig himself experienced it in Vienna in the years preceding the First World War; a picture of a society more concerned with the program of the Hofburg Theater and the Wiener Oper than the politics of the day or developments on the stock market. But is this really a picture of *"The World" of Yesterday*? Would it not be more correct to designate it a depiction of *Vienna of Yesterday*? How, for example, was Austria experienced by the Jews in the remote provinces of the vast Habsburg Monarchy, where there was no Hofburg Theater and no mutual interest in, or indeed knowledge of, literature and music to create the kind of symbiosis between Jews and non-Jews described by Zweig? In order to gain an insight into the life of these Jews and into their image of Austria, we must thus turn elsewhere, for example, to the works of the well-known writer Joseph Roth, to whom I shall return later, or to Henry William Katz – an Austrian-Jewish writer in exile only recently rediscovered after having been forgotten by scholars and critics for nearly fifty years. Katz's first novel, *Die Fischmanns (The Fishmans)*, for which he was awarded the inaugural Heinrich Heine Prize in 1937, and the Eastern European Jewish perception of Austria and the Austro-Hungarian Monarchy presented in his novel, will be the main focus of this examination.

Henry William Katz, or Herz Wolf Katz as he was originally called, was no stranger to the environment he was depicting. Born in 1906 in Rudki, a small shtetl in Galicia – one of the Habsburg Empire's most backward provinces – Katz grew up in an orthodox Jewish environment. In 1914 the outbreak of the First World War and the approaching Russian army put him and his family to flight. After a long journey they reached Germany, where they settled in the town of Gera, approximately sixty kilometers south of Leipzig. Here Katz spent his childhood and youth, experiencing the conflict between his growing personal love of Germany and German culture and his exposure to increasingly anti-Semitic influences during the Weimar Republic. While distancing himself rapidly from his orthodox background and beliefs, Katz became involved in the work of the local Social Democratic Youth Group (*Sozialistische Arbeiterjugend*). Soon he also began to write short stories, poems, and reports dealing with the worker's lot for local newspapers.

In 1932 this interest in journalism led to his employment as the youngest editor of the Berlin newspaper *Die Welt am Montag (The World on Monday)*, a position, however, which he had to abandon less than a year later when forced into exile in France by Hitler's accession to power on 30 January 1933. Highly disappointed with both the left-wing parties lack of resistance and the German population's acceptance of Hitler and his policies, Katz turned to writing literature in the few remaining hours after each day's battle to secure his livelihood. Mentally he returned to the world of his early childhood, the Galician shtetl, with its primitiveness and its conflicts between the Polish,

Ukrainian, and Jewish groups inhabiting the area. His first novel, *Die Fishmans*, is a tribute to the Eastern European Jews and their fight for survival in a largely anti-Semitic environment. Katz himself said of the origin of this novel: "The idea of writing a book about the Fishmans ... came to me as I sat a hundred feet away from my countryman Hitler and listened to his diatribe against the Jews. He especially railed against immigrated Jews."[2] Having himself twice become the victim of anti-Semitism in such different environments as the Galician shtetl and German society, Katz felt the urge to demonstrate the effects of persecution from the victims point of view. His novel *The Fishmans* thus forms the beginning of a Jewish family saga starting in the Eastern provinces of the Habsburg Empire at the turn of the century and closing with the life and fate of the Fishman family in Germany at the end of the Weimar Republic. In his second novel, *Schloßgasse 21 (No. 21 Castle Street)*, which was published in New York in 1941, Katz analyses the political climate of the Weimar era and the psychological make-up and social background of the average Nazi adherent. In particular, he succeeds in describing the situation of German as well as Eastern European Jews and the internal conflicts within the German Jewish community.

In April 1941 Katz, his wife Friedel, and their one-year-old daughter were brought to America by the American rescue scheme "Operation Emergency Rescue" led by the Quaker Varian Fry in Marseilles. Upon arrival in New York, Katz again found himself facing the task of acquainting himself with a foreign language and culture, having previously had to adjust first to the German, then to the French, and now to the American mentality. He soon realized the impossibility of earning a living by writing in English for the American market, as he was not only unfamiliar with the language, but was also dealing with topics of no interest whatsoever to the American population. With not only his own family, but also his parents-in-law to support, he therefore decided to take up work in factories, in the beginning working at a lathe and operating a chewing gum machine, later employed by a small food manufacturing company of which he eventually became vice-president. On 6 June 1992, Henry William Katz died in Florida.

In Katz's novels the narrative perspective is of particular importance. Both *The Fishmans* and *No. 21 Castle Street* have a "worm's-eye-view," presenting a view of the world as it is experienced at the bottom of society. Yet in no way are they merely expressions of self-pity or accusations against an unjust and cruel world. At the same time, it is made clear by the narrator that the characters are not merely characters in their own right but representatives of the social group to which they belong. The story of the Fishman family is told by the young Jacob Fishman who, from his present adult position, inserts occasional comments to explain or clarify events and the motivation for the characters' actions. A pronounced characteristic of the novel's narrative technique is thus the mixture of the innocent and ignorant young Jakob Fishman's point of view and the adult, now better informed and experienced, narrator's clarifying comments which, then, frequently lead to critical remarks about the treatment of the Galician population. For example, a description of the muddy and primitive roads leading to and from the shtetl contrasted with the nearby paved roads unknown to the shtetl inhabitants causes the adult narrator to realize that the latter were constructed by the government for war purposes and not for the local population's benefit.

The story, which contains many autobiographical features, proceeds chronologically from the year 1905 when Jacob's parents, Lea and Yossel Fishman, are married, until Lea's sudden death in Germany in 1914. The narrative style is characterized by an impressionistic use of images illustrating Jewish life and tradition in Strody, the fictitious shtetl in which the Fishmans live. Thus, the matchmaker who arranges Lea and Yossel's marriage, descriptions of the Jewish wedding, the Sabbath, the weekly market, interaction between Jews and non-Jews, and the importance of religion play a significant part in the novel. Parallel to this apparently inner-Jewish idyll, however, are generational conflicts and disputes between spouses caused by disagreements as to the position and future of the Jews in this part of the Habsburg Empire. But what exactly was the relationship of these Jews, living as they were on the margin of Austrian culture and society, to the Monarchy and to the Emperor Franz Joseph himself, and what characterized everyday life as his subjects?

One of the features of life in the shtetl, as Katz depicts it, is the severe tension between the Jewish, Polish, and Ruthenian groups inhabiting the area. As far as possible Jews and gentiles attempt to live separate lives in the shtetl – or, in other words, the Jews try to stay away from the gentiles because they are very much aware of the physical danger of interaction. Thus, the gentiles to a large extent determine the general pattern of life, and the Jews for their part attempt to maintain their own identity and to conform to the hostile reality surrounding them. Each group has its own traditional way of life and they are separated not only physically but even more by an impenetrable wall of mutual prejudice. Whether they like it or not, however, the isolation of the shtetl makes them interdependent and they are forced to interact on two regular occasions: the weekly market day and when the traveling Jewish merchant visits the peasants to sell his goods. The shtetl and the market place are initially described as idyllic and peaceful: "The husbands of these squatting peasant women stood by their little horses or leaned against their wagons and gazed dreamily and silently at the surrounding world. This world was called Strody. I can still picture these men: prominent cheek bones, thick moustaches, the obstinate hair hanging down, covering their foreheads and eyebrows."[3] This idyll, however, is destroyed as soon as a Jew enters the market place and the atmosphere turns cold and hostile:

> When the Jew came by, one who wanted neither to buy nor sell, one who only passed that way, there was an ominous hissing and cursing:
> "Hey, Jew, haven't you spit your life out yet?"
> "Not yet, Mister Peasant," the Jew would say. He would laugh, embarrassed. He would make a sort of obeisance. A deep one. (F 8)

During his visits to the peasants, Yossel, who after his marriage to Lea has become a pedlar, faces the same hostility. Before his encounter with the peasant he contemplates the best approach, knowing that although they are interdependent, he, the Jew, must break the ice and trade on the peasant's terms. He realizes that their differences in occupation and educational background are among the main causes of their clashes: "All day long they work with grasses and stones, with earth and wood, and then some Jew comes along and frightens them with his cleverness...." The Jews of Strody are too clever for the peasants who live hereabouts," Yossel brooded. "The contrast is too violent, that's why we can't get along with each other." (F 83).

The novel thus points to the existence of mutual prejudices between Jews and gentiles and by no means imputes the responsibility for their bad relationship entirely to the gentile peasants. Yossel's prejudices mostly concern the peasants' simple character and ignorance, a rather condescending attitude perhaps, but nonetheless understandable considering the generally high level of literacy and education among the Jews in stark contrast to the often illiterate peasants. The peasants' prejudices, on the other hand, were influenced by superstition and by the Jews' economic role, particularly the common Jewish occupation of tax collector and innkeeper. By depicting unjust and irrational outbursts of violence against the Jews – such as when the young peasant Janek permanently damages Yossel Fishman's eyesight in a fit of rage because the local prostitute, Marischka, has cheated him of the "goods" he paid for – the novel does, however, level a severe criticism at gentile society's tendency to place the Jews in the position of the eternal scapegoat. [4]

In his novel Katz attempts to explain the psychological mechanisms underlying anti-Semitism, but by no means pardons such behavior. Instead, showing the background to such antagonism, he analyses the psychological make-up of pogromists and the effect of constant persecution on the victim's personality. By depicting the obsequious way in which Yossel approaches the peasant, for example, Katz takes a direct stand against anti-Semitic clichés and stereotypes rather than denying their existence altogether. Yossel's behavior, which on the surface corresponds to the anti-Semitic stereotype of the Jewish pedlar, is subsequently explained as a means for the Jewish individual to survive in a hostile gentile community. In order to survive Yossel, then, in reality a humble and somewhat helpless man, must adopt this second rather fawning personality when carrying out his professional duties. Through scenes such as this Katz invites the reader to look beyond the surface of anti-Semitic stereotypes to discover their origin and see them in their proper historical and sociological context. When seen as a cultural phenomenon, then, anti-Semitism is a self-perpetuating process in which Jews inevitably become the stereotypes created of them by non-Jews in an attempt to repudiate gentile prejudice against them. Thus Yossel, for example, is forced to become more fawning in his attitude towards the peasant if the latter shows great hostility. This, on the other hand, only confirms and intensifies the peasant's anti-Semitic prejudice that Jews are fawning and dishonest people, and the process becomes a vicious circle of which there is no way out.

Considering the conditions under which the Jews live, it is no major surprise that they do not feel closely attached to their shtetl. The world outside the Jewish part of the shtetl is conceived of as "feindlich" (hostile) and the nature of the surroundings is described in very objective and realistic terms. Indeed, Katz's descriptions form a marked contrast to the romanticized picture given in much shtetl literature by Yiddish writers such as Scholem Aleichem and in early German-language ghetto literature by, for example, Leopold Kompert and Salomon Kohn who, having themselves left the shtetl, created a nostalgic picture of it as the pure and orthodox environment of the Jewish people. Instead, *The Fishmans* describes Strody and its surroundings in the following way:

> The summer was dry and withered, and I heard dull detonations. It thundered often, and the lightning struck often, for lightning-rods were as little known as electricity, gas or the movies. But there was a sharp penetrating odor of wheat and oats. And the wide-lying, deep-dunged fields competed with the stink of fish and onions and the beggarly poverty of the small villages. (F 5)

This primitiveness of life in the eastern part of the Monarchy and the constant threat of anti-Semitism soon leads to discussions about emigration in the Fishman family. They are not deeply regretful about leaving Strody but rather concerned as to whether or not they will find a better future elsewhere. The two main arguments in the discussion are represented by Malke and Leib Fishman, the narrator's grandparents. Malke insists on emigration to a supposedly enlightened western country, such as Germany, as the only solution to the Jewish question in eastern Europe, basing her belief in a better future on the idealistic views of tolerance and acceptance expressed by German writers such as Lessing and Schiller. The naiveté of Malke's idealization of Germany becomes clear in the slightly ironic scene in which, when confronted with the question of whether Lessing lives in Berlin, Malke must confess that unfortunately her idol is already dead – a statement implying that Lessing's high ideals and hopes for a Jewish-non-Jewish symbiosis in Germany died with him. Leib, on the other hand, represents the more fatalistic and deterministic view that their Jewish origin and not their place of residence is what determines the Jews' living conditions:

> "Oh, nonsense!" said Leib, mistrustfully. "Do you really believe that it's better somewhere else? You don't get

> peace for the asking even in the west. To be a Jew
> means just that: never to hear an insult, to play the deaf-
> mute, to master yourself everywhere. For a young man it
> isn't easy, I know it, I haven't forgotten it yet. But in
> time you get used to it . . ." (F 102)

Of significance to the discussion, however, is also the Jews' knowledge of worse conditions elsewhere, for example in Russia where
severe pogroms took place from 1881 onwards after the assassination
of Alexander II, often with the Russian government's blessing. The
Kishinev pogrom from 6 to 8 April 1903 is one such instance. Despite
the Habsburg Empire's neglect of the eastern provinces and the
Galician Jews' own resistance to modernization, which they rightly
feared would lead to assimilation, the Jews' conditions in Galicia were
not as catastrophic as in Russia, and it is therefore no coincidence that
the two pogroms described in the novel are not experienced by the
Fishmans themselves but are related by refugees from Russia. The
Jews impute this state of relative security to the rule of Emperor
Franz Joseph himself. In their awareness he assumes the role of their
personal protector, and his presence guarantees them relatively
humane conditions: "'And suppose, God forbid, Franz Joseph should
die tomorrow?" asked my father. "What then, when he finally dies?
It's no sort of life here, with the peasants! Only yesterday . . ." and he
began to lament and upbraid' (F 127-28). At the same time, these Jews
who are so distant from Franz Joseph and Vienna in every way consider themselves to have a particularly intimate relationship with their
emperor – a relationship based on the one aspect of life with which
they themselves know how to identify, the experience of suffering:

> On innumerable occasions I witnessed in my childhood
> how the Jewish soul, which identifies itself wholly and
> instantly with every sad heart everywhere in the wide
> world, which has so much empathy for every sufferer,
> pitied the venerable Kaiser. Alas, he was powerless even
> within his own family, so weak is earthly power. No one
> paid any attention to him, everyone in the Hofburg
> lived, married, loved, and died as he pleased. "Dear
> Kaiser Franz Joseph, you understand us and we under-
> stand you – and every man must help himself." (F 104)

As the end of the quotation suggests, the reality of the Jews' situation, despite immense sympathy for the emperor, is geographical and political distance from the center of power in Vienna, and at the end of the day the Jews must fight their own battles. Admittedly there is a representative of the Monarchy's central power in Strody to whom they can turn for help. The *Bezirkshauptmann* (official) in the center of the shtetl is to be consulted whenever problems arise. Unfortunately, he is a rather incompetent and uninterested elderly gentleman whose outward appearance strongly resembles that of Emperor Franz Joseph and whose internal state is just as sick and weak as that of the Monarchy itself on the eve of the First World War:

> The said district captain was a jovial, smiling aged official whose chin for ever dangled over his throat. He was a man on the tip of whose nose Dr. Spiegel could read off the index of his arterio-sclerosis. He looked like the tired official of a firm on the point of bankruptcy. His side-whiskers, the one striking feature in his appearance, were more than irreproachable – they looked exactly as if they had been clipped from one of those pictures of His Majesty, the good old people's Emperor, which had as their object to endear him to the mixture of races that he ruled. (F 40-41)

After the attack on Yossel which damages his eyesight, the assimilated Jewish doctor, Dr. Spiegel, who has studied in Vienna and therefore is more likely to find the *Bezirkshauptmann's* favor than the ordinary shtetl Jews, approaches the official in an attempt to appeal for justice and for measures to be taken against the increasing anti-Semitism. The *Bezirkshauptmann*, however, shows greater interest in the increasing number of water rats in the shtetl and takes his recent orders to "reign with a mild hand" and get along with all minority groups very literally. So literally indeed that he refuses to interfere in their affairs, suggesting that if he were to help the Jews, the Polish, Ruthenian, and German minorities would also approach him with "unreasonable" requests for help, as if these groups, too, were victims of persecution and not in fact the perpetrators themselves. Dr. Spiegel's efforts thus amount to nothing apart from the promise that the local policeman, Róman, will pay extra attention to the events in the shtetl. However, having been acquainted with Róman earlier – a thin and rather fragile young man whose self-confidence is twice as great as his efficiency – the reader already knows how much value this promise will be to the local Jews. The Austrian authorities and their policy towards the primitive Galician province, then, are generally described as slack, indifferent, and even corrupt as the young Jakob realizes when the hygienic conditions in the packed 'cheder' – the religious school for Jewish boys – are being controlled by governmental inspectors. The adult narrator sarcastically comments on the inspectors' lax morals: "These governmental descents enabled me to discover at the age of four, and with the help of the older boys, a certain peculiarity about the State power; to wit, that it was not inevitably and by its nature open-eyed, but that it could, at bidding, half or even completely close its eyes" (F 121-22). This selective "blindness," however, which enables the Jews to keep their "cheder," does not reflect mutual understanding and helpfulness but rather a form of exploitation allowing for continuous contempt and prejudice despite the personal gain.

In view of all this misery caused by anti-Semitism, ignorance, prejudice, and poverty, one would expect *The Fishmans* to be an extremely depressing novel taking the reader from one description of suffering and adversity to the next. Fortunately this is not the case or the reading of the novel would surely be unbearable. Instead, the novel is imbued with an atmosphere of great warmth and love within the Jewish environment which helps the Jews to compensate for the outward hostility. Deprived of a mother country in which they feel sheltered and protected, they thus create their own sense of belonging within the family and the Jewish community. This can be seen, for example, when Yossel leaves for America, where he goes to seek his fortune, having been persuaded by his mother that there is no future for young people in Galicia: "There the dear familiar faces are, there stands the Fishman family. Here is Yossel's homeland, and he must say farewell, must tear himself away from us" (F 149). In a broader sense, the Jewish community forms the framework of security, and here the religious context plays a major part, for example in the scene describing the Strody Jews' flight on a hay cart from the approaching Russian troops at the outbreak of the First World War. This day happens to be Yom Kippur, the highest Jewish holiday, and the Strody Jews decide to spend the day praying despite the thunder of cannons from the nearby front. Here, the synagogue is defined as the Jews' true mother country by the narrator when he says: Here, in the synagogue, was the true Fatherland, the homeland of the Jews' (F 224), whereby the Jewish community is defined as religious rather than one of common fate (*Schicksalsgemeinschaft*).

It is of major importance, however, that the failure of the Austro-Hungarian Monarchy to provide a mother country for the Jews is not ascribed entirely to the treatment they receive here but is in fact also explained as Jewish fate. Early on in the novel, the young narrator reflects on the nature of identity and belonging and arrives at the following conclusion:

> I have spent many an hour wondering whether my life would have taken another turn if Strody had not been my birthplace. Today I am of the belief that it is all one where I, the Jew, came into the world. The fact that I was born a Jew was the decisive factor in my life. For it is not only the Jews of Strody who are persecuted. (F 6)

In other words, being born a Jew is invariably connected with persecution and the experience of uprootedness, and yet a main feature of both of Katz's novels is the search for a place where one can belong, a place that not only tolerates you, but accepts you and welcomes you into the heart of its native population. In *The Fishmans*, Austria-Hungary fails to provide such a secure haven, but during one of his trips to the hostile peasants Yossel quite clearly defines the nature of the country the Jews are longing for:

> Dreamily, in a rapture of anticipation, . . . he must have thought about a far-off land to flee to, a land where even a Yossel Fishman could lead a peaceful life; where one is a human being first, and then a Jew; where the peasants, too, are cleverer than in this land, and where a Fishman is worth as much as a peasant. (F 99)

America, then, forms the major contrast to Strody and Galicia and appears to be the manifestation of Yossel's vision of tolerance and peaceful coexistence. Indeed, the change that slowly begins to take place in Yossel's personality after his arrival in New York is quite remarkable. He becomes a spiritually free and outgoing person who even after half a year in his new country of residence marvels at the fact that no one in New York calls him "Sheeny" (F 161). Katz's image of America suggests a society in which the individual is too busy surviving and creating a life of his or her own to have the time for, or even the interest in, anti-Semitic outbursts. At the same time, the confrontation with the hectic life in New York is an overwhelming and frightening experience for Yossel who, like many other Jewish emigrants in the city, tries to compensate for his confusion by retreating to a world governed by Jewish values and religion.

Most importantly, however, America is presented as a society whose existence is based on the voluntary coexistence of different ethnic groups, unlike the Austro-Hungarian Monarchy whose population structure is determined by the haphazard outcome of wars and political agreements. The presence of a large Jewish community in the eastern parts of the Empire, for example, resulted from the Polish partitions between 1772 and 1795, whereby the Habsburgs acquired not only land, but also a Jewish ethnic group which they had no desire whatsoever to welcome as their subjects. Compared with the Habsburg Monarchy, America thus forms the country of Yossel Fishman's dreams. Unfortunately, after saving his hard-earned money for two years to send for his family, the First World War breaks out and Yossel, worried about the fate of his family in war-torn Europe, decides to return to Strody to find them. Upon arrival he is immediately called up for military service in the Austro-Hungarian army. Meanwhile, his wife Lea and the two children have fled to Germany, where Lea dies when the narrator is only ten years old. This, then, is how the first novel ends – the narrator Jakob Fishman orphaned in a foreign country and with a father facing the unknown fate of a soldier. Of his youth in Germany Jakob says: "What followed was a youth filled with passionate dreams of a homeland, of taking root, of friends, of an irreplaceable mother ... They were the Jewish dreams of a Jewish boyhood ... How I longed and implored my way through to all this, how I struggled – and how I was betrayed!" (F 293).

At this point, however, the question arises to what extent Katz's representation of Galician Habsburg Jews' relationship to the Empire is typical or whether it perhaps offers a different perspective on the idea of Austria as a potential Jewish mother country? As was obvious from the opening quotation, Stefan Zweig, speaking from a Viennese standpoint, certainly believed in a symbiosis between Austrians and Jews. Another Austrian writer who immediately comes to mind is Joseph Roth who, because of the great resemblance between his and Katz's biographies, offers an even better basis for comparison. Like

Katz, Roth was born into a Jewish family in Galicia, spent his childhood and early youth in the eastern part of the Habsburg Monarchy, and arrived in Vienna at approximately the same time as Katz settled with his family in Germany. Both writers opted for exile in France from 1933 onwards – an experience which destroyed Roth but which Katz managed to survive. A comparison between Roth's and Katz's views of the Habsburg Empire is thus of great relevance because they both, unlike Zweig, actually experienced life in the Galician shtetl and because the image of Jews in and from Eastern Europe plays a significant role in both writers' works. Of even greater interest, however, are the surprising differences in their perceptions of Jewish identity in Austria despite the obvious biographical similarities.

Joseph Roth's life-long infatuation with the Habsburg Empire and with Emperor Franz Joseph in particular is well-known and also strongly manifested in his work. In novels such as *The Radetzky March* (*Radetzkymarsch*) and in his short story *The Bust of the Emperor* (*Die Büste des Kaisers*) Roth presents a nostalgic picture of an empire which despite its former greatness is about to dissolve, and the only thing the characters can do is to watch it happen. Thus, in *The Radetzky - March*, the clear-sighted and realistic Count Chojnicki predicts the end of the Monarchy:

> "Naturally!" replied Chojnicki. "In literal terms, it [the monarchy] still exists. We still have an army" – the count pointed at the lieutenant – "and officials" – the count pointed at the district captain – "but the monarchy is disintegrating while still alive, it is doomed! An old man, with one foot in the grave, endangered whenever his nose runs, keeps the old throne through the sheer miracle that he can still sit on it. How much longer, how much longer? This era no longer wants us! This era wants to create independent nation states!"[5]

In Strody, at the remote eastern border of the Monarchy, the general feeling of decay as seen in *The Radetzky March* has not yet pervaded the atmosphere. And yet even here, the westernized Dr. Spiegel does sense the approaching catastrophe:

> Doktor Spiegel shrugged his shoulders. It suddenly occurred to him that in a few years this country would

perhaps no longer be Austrian. Perhaps the war would bring realization to the century-old struggle and faith of the Polish nation. Warsaw would no longer be subject to the rule of the Tsars, nor Galicia to that of Franz Joseph (F 191).

Both Count Chojnicki and Dr. Spiegel are marginal characters to the action and are thus suitable as observers of events through whom prophetic sentiments can be uttered. In both cases this is done with hindsight. In *The Fishmans*, however, the collapse of the Monarchy is not considered particularly tragic because the Jews do not feel closely connected with it in any case. Their only feeling of loyalty concerns the figure of Emperor Franz Joseph – an image which is also famously depicted in Roth's *The Radetzky March* in the scene describing the Jews of Galicia presenting Franz Joseph with a Torah scroll to show him their devotion – but to the Fishmans, the Empire as such has not represented the secure haven they were looking for. Herein also lies the major difference between Katz's and Roth's perceptions of Austria. To Roth the Habsburg Monarchy represents the optimal and ideal form of government for the Jews because it is comprised of a large number of minorities and different ethnic groups. In this way, the Jews do not make up *the* minority in a predominantly gentile population and are thus more likely to avoid the exposure to anti-Semitism. This idea is expressed nostalgically in *The Bust of the Emperor*, for example, where not only the advantages of the Monarchy compared with the nation state, as Roth saw it, are shown, but also the strong feeling of homelessness and sentimental longing experienced by the narrator after the collapse of the Empire: "My old mother country was a big house with many doors and many windows for many kinds of people. The house was split up, divided, destroyed. I have no more to do there. I am used to living in a house, not in cabins."[6]

Katz, on the other hand, rejects the Austro-Hungarian Monarchy as the ideal state form for the Jews and indeed for all the other ethnic groups, too, precisely because of its multi-ethnicity and multi-nationality. The Jewish lack of *Vaterlandsgefühl* (patriotism) for the Monarchy is ascribed to the lack of a uniform culture through which all minorities can be united and to which everyone belongs on equal terms. In *The Fishmans*, the narrator explains it in the following way:

> One must know the history of ... this land in order to appreciate why neither the Jews, nor the local Poles and Ruthenians of the period prior to 1914, could have a definite concept of the word "Fatherland," such as is current, let us say, among the inhabitants of a unified national and cultural territory like Germany or France. (F 103)

And later he says: "Since they did not see before them a powerful, protective State, there was really no reason why they should see a Fatherland" (F 104). In other words, a true mother country is a place where one can feel protected and secure and where one is part of the dominant culture and mentality. It is therefore interesting that both Roth and Katz find such an atmosphere within the Eastern European Jewish environment at a time when both have been deprived of the countries they respectively regarded as their mother countries. They do not, however, necessarily understand the Eastern European Jewish family as a literal entity but rather as a metaphysical concept signifying the values lost to them as successors of these Eastern European Jews. The way back is blocked by their own assimilation and by the fact that the shtetl in its original form no longer exists – a situation, however, which at the same time facilitates a metaphysical idealization of the shtetl as the secure and protected haven for the individual exposed to an otherwise chaotic and hostile world.

Keeping this in mind, it is curious that Katz mentions Germany as an example of such a secure place, considering that at the time of writing, he himself had only recently been forced into exile by that very country. And yet it may not be that strange. After all, Katz had come to Germany at the age of seven and had been assimilated into German culture to the point where he felt more associated with Germany and the German Social Democratic Party than with his Jewish background. Although he never tried to disguise or deny his inheritance, his Jewishness was not the main focus of his life, and when the Nazis came to power in 1933, the pain at having to leave the country was intensified by the remembrance of the years of struggle to "conquer" German culture and win the German people's acceptance. Thus, although he originally came from the Habsburg Empire, Katz's perspective at the time of writing is that of an assimilated German Jew who only reluctantly left the country he considered not only to be his mother country, but also the foremost representative of western "Bildung" (education in its broadest sense) and enlightenment. The narrator's remark when going into exile at the end of Katz's second novel, *No. 21 Castle Street*, can therefore be seen as highly autobiographical: "Only the homeless can understand me.... With fierce effort I had made Germany mine, and she had made me hers. That today she was disgraced, besmirched, could not change my past.... I hated the Nazis, but I loved Germany.... And now I had to leave her...."[7] Katz thus presents successful integration as the optimal solution from a Jewish point of view and yet, on the basis of the events before and after 1933, he is forced to admit the futility of assimilationism however painful this is.

Henry William Katz never returned to settle in Germany. From 1941 onwards he was building up a life for himself and his family in America which he eventually came to regard as his home. By then, having changed cultures and languages three times, every time believing it to be the last, Katz had developed his own concept of *Vaterland* (native country) saying: "My native country is where I am allowed to stay alive." In America, he felt that he was given not only the right to live, but also a fair chance in life, and thus, highly disappointed with political developments in Europe and their catastrophic consequences for the Jews, Katz ironically enough opted for the kind of multinational and multi-ethnic society advocated by Joseph Roth a decade earlier. Having experienced the increasing anti-Semitism of the Weimar Republic himself, Katz was by no means blind to the failure of Jewish assimilation in Germany described very well in his second novel. But that, as noted by the narrator at the end of *The Fishmans*, is quite a different story.

Wadham College, Oxford

Notes

1. Stefan Zweig, *The World of Yesterday* (London, 1943), 27.
2. Henry William Katz, *Die Fischmanns* (Berlin: Quadriga, 1994), 249. (My translation since the postscript was not added until the German edition in 1994). Unless otherwise stated, further quotations from the novel will be taken from the English translation *The Fishmans*

(London; Constable & Co., 1938) and cited in the text by F for Fishmans and page number.

3. Henry William Katz, *Die Fischmanns*, 16 (my translation).

4. For a discussion of the concept of the ghetto in *Die Fischmanns* see Ena Pedersen, "Persecution, Exile, and the Mental Ghetto: On Henry William Katz's Novel *Die Fischmanns* (1937)," in Anne Fuchs, Florian Krobb, eds. *Ghetto Writing: Traditional and Eastern Jewry in German-Jewish Prose* (Columbia SC: Camden House, 1998).

5. Joseph Roth, *The Radetzky March (Penguin; London, 1995)*, 161.

6. Joseph Roth, *Die Büste des Kaisers (The Bust of the Emperor)*. In: Fritz Hackert, Klaus Westermann, eds. *Joseph Roth Werke* (Köln/Amsterdam, 1989-1991), Vol. 5, 675. My translation.

7. Henry William Katz, *No. 21 Castle Street* (London, 1942), 477.

Nationalism, Modernity, and Multinational Austria in the Works of Joseph Roth

by Ian Reifowitz

In the waning years of his life Joseph Roth grew more and more alienated from the world around him. This essay follows the process of his alienation through his depiction of multinational Austria-Hungary and his juxtaposition of the Monarchy to what he saw as Modernity. Roth first began to discuss the Dual Monarchy in his fictional works and essays in 1927, and continued to do so until his death in 1939. Throughout these years he praised the world of Austria-Hungary and preferred it to the one that had emerged after its destruction in 1918. Between 1927 and 1932, Roth presented an insightful and relatively balanced picture in which he noted both Austria's strengths and weaknesses. After 1933, the year that began with Hitler's seizure of power in Germany, Roth's nuanced portrait of Austria transformed into an idealized version of a multinational paradise that barely resembled the reality of the past. However, throughout the entire period from 1927 to 1939, Roth consistently opposed his Austria to Modernity. It was the modern world and the ideas brought in its wake – nationalism, democracy, equality – that destroyed his world. Thus Roth became the enemy of Modernity.

Joseph Roth was born 2 September 1894, in Brody, a city close to the Galician-Russian border. He was raised in a Jewish family, although he was baptized as an adult. Eastern Jews (*Ostjuden*) figured prominently as characters in many of his works, as did the setting of Galicia itself. Brody, in fact, was almost 75 per cent Jewish in 1900, as high a percentage as any city in Austria.[1] During the Great War Roth served in the Habsburg Army and applied for Austrian citizenship after it ended. He had to apply for it because citizenship in the Austrian Republic was based on *Heimatrecht* according to the Treaty of St. Germain. Roth's *Heimatrecht* lay in Brody, his birthplace, which made him a Polish rather than an Austrian citizen after the breakup of the

Monarchy. Roth actively expressed his Austrian identity by claiming citizenship in the new Republic as opposed to Poland or Germany, where he actually resided after the war.[2] He spent much of the interwar period outside Austria, first in Berlin before he fled to Paris in the 1930s, but always remained involved in Austrian politics and continued to write about Austria.

Roth's writings on Austria during the 1920s and 30s represented the archetype of the interwar body of literature described by Claudio Magris as *Der Habsburgische Mythos (The Habsburg Myth)*.[3] Roth, Stefan Zweig, Franz Csokor, Franz Werfel and others were assimilated, cosmopolitan Jews who grew up in Habsburg Austria. They were young men during WWI and were left after November 1918 with a profound nostalgia for the relative calm and security of their pre-war youth. Their writings portrayed Austria under Franz Joseph as a golden age of tolerance and freedom, especially when compared to the insecurity Central European Jews felt with the rise of Nazism and racial anti-Semitism in the 1930s.

As a very young man, Roth had been a socialist and a critic of the Monarchy. In the years after its destruction his attitude began to change. In a 1927 essay, "Juden auf der Wanderschaft" (Jews on their Wanderings), Roth discussed Austria-Hungary at length in print for the first time. He condemned the idea of the nation-state as an invention of Western European intellectuals imposed on Central and Eastern Europe. The fall of Austria-Hungary, unfortunately, had confirmed the victory of the nation-state. However, had the Monarchy been well-governed, nationalism would not have been able to defeat it, and its success could have presented an alternative to the nation-state. Roth's youthful hostility towards the Monarchy had begun to soften by 1928, as seen in "Seine k. und k. apostolische Majestät" (His Imperial and Royal Majesty). In these essays Roth praised the idea of a multinational state, but he also recognized Austria's failure to become a successful one before 1918.[4]

In *Der Stumme Prophet (The Silent Prophet)*, written in 1928, Roth condemned modernity in the form of feminism and the breakdown of traditional gender roles in the 1920s. He censured another aspect of modernity – nationalism – personified by the tribal attitudes of university students. The novel also presented a picture of Austria, not through the semiautobiographical character, Friedrich Kargan, but through an elderly aristocrat, Herr von Maerker, to whom Kargan accorded the measure of respect due a man advanced in years.

In discussing Habsburg Austria, von Maerker observed, "In my time, when the man was more important than his nationality, the possibility existed of making a homeland for all out of the old monarchy. It could have been the prototype in miniature of a real future world."[5] Roth used the conditional tense and talked of the possibility of what Austria could have been. In his later works he discussed the Monarchy as if it had actually become a true homeland for all its nations, destroyed only by the blind forces of modernity.

Von Maerker offered insight into Roth's own feelings regarding the end of the Monarchy. He endorsed the old man's assessment, but the idea of Austria's mission against nationalism did not yet obsess Roth. He expressed his detachment from this idea through von Maerker:

> Even his sadness was accompanied by serenity. His somber obituary on his fatherland did not prevent him from enjoying to the full and with mild deliberation his black coffee and thin cigarette, and it seemed he enjoyed life more and more because it still continued beyond his own time . . . The destruction of the monarchy had put an end only to the active period of his life . . . but he continued to live on as the passive observer of a new era which, though it did not please him at all, did not bother him in the slightest because it did not in any way concern him.[6]

Roth, although he lamented the Monarchy's fall and criticized the modern world that replaced it, discussed Austria here in a more balanced and emotionally disengaged fashion than he did in his later works. The process of Roth's alienation from reality had not yet begun.

The next five years saw the Great Depression and the rising tide of National Socialism in Germany. From early on Roth had spoken out against the Nazi party. Through his vigilant condemnations of Nazism, seen in a number of essays he wrote while living in Berlin, including "Vom Attentäter zum Schmock" (1930, From Assassin to Immoral Journalist), "Bekenntnis zu Deutschland" (1931, Allegiance to Germany), "Ursachen der Schlaflosigkeit im Goethejahr" (1932, Causes of Insomnia in the Year of Goethe), and "Die nationale Kurzwelle" (1932, The National Short-Wave), Roth came to gradually embrace the old Monarchy.[7]

In *Radetzkymarsch* (1932, *The Radetzky March*), his masterwork, Roth placed Austria-Hungary on center-stage, portraying both the majesty and the folly of the Habsburg Monarchy under Franz Joseph. Roth followed three generations of the Trotta family, loyal servants and Austrian patriots. The grandfather, Joseph Trotta, saved the Emperor's life at the Battle of Solferino in 1859 and was ennobled for his heroism. The grandfather's son, Franz, became a civil servant and eventually a District Commissioner, while his son, the grandson, Karl Joseph, served as a young army officer in the years leading up to 1914. Through their service to the Emperor, the Trottas, who had descended from Slovene peasant stock, became anational Austrians. The Trottas represented Roth's ideal Austrians and demonstrated the difference between his vision of a supranational Austrian identity and the national identity of today's virtually ethnically homogeneous Austrian nation-state.

Although Roth did not shower the old Austria with unconditional praise in *Radetzkymarsch*, he clearly juxtaposed it to modernity. On the one hand, he condemned the outdated system of dueling and honor in the army that led to the death of Karl Joseph's best friend. Roth also exposed the backwardness of the Emperor himself and used as a metaphor for the dynastic state the man who burned candles in the Hofburg rather than install electric lights.

However, Roth also praised the charming inconsistencies of old Austria. For example, although married ladies were not supposed to commit adultery, exceptions could be made for a particularly beautiful woman unfortunately married to an ill man. Roth favorably contrasted even the Habsburg bureaucracy, which he admitted was Byzantine, with the cold, heartless efficiency of modern government. Roth longed for a world where traditions mattered, and, if not every decision was rational, it was at least human.

Roth described the coming end of the Monarchy through Count Chojnicki, who predicted that Franz Joseph's death would lead to disintegration into its national components. Chojnicki fulminated against democrats, socialists and nationalists, the three major political elements in the post-1918 world in which the author lived. Chojnicki lamented that a dynastic state was doomed in the modern world of nationalism.

> This age has no use for us. This age wants to form independent national states. People no longer believe in

> God. Their new religion is nationalism. Nations don't go to church, they go to independence meetings instead. Monarchy, our Monarchy, is founded on piety, on the belief that God chose the Habsburgs to reign ... No other sovereign is that, so dependent on the grace of God and the piety of the people. The German Emperor could still reign even if God were to abandon him. Perhaps by the grace of his people. But the Austro-Hungarian Emperor must not be forsaken by God. And God has forsaken him! [8]

Through Chojnicki, the author acknowledged that Austria-Hungary was not paradise, that its army and government were grossly inadequate. In *Radetzkymarsch* Roth demonstrated that, as late as 1932, he still maintained a balanced view of the past, something he was unable to provide in his later works.

Radetzkymarsch presented Emperor Franz Joseph and also District Commissioner Trotta, the son of the hero of Solferino, as relics of a dying age. The Commissioner's son Karl Joseph, who perhaps also represented Franz Joseph's successor, Emperor Karl, "saw the ages roll toward each other like rocks and he ... the Lieutenant, was crushed between them."[9] The Great War destroyed both Karl Joseph and the state Emperor Karl inherited after Franz Joseph's death in 1916. Emperor Karl himself died in 1921 at the age of thirty-one.

Karl Joseph's death stood as a metaphor of Roth's vision of the paternalistic role played by the Habsburg Monarchy itself. During a battle at the war's outset, the young lieutenant was killed by a bullet to the head as he attempted to bring water back from a well to his platoon of thirsty Ukrainian peasants. The enemy was pounding the well with gunfire, but the scared and exhausted peasants had grown desperate and wanted to run towards the water. Karl Joseph tried to protect his benighted Ukrainians from the guns by getting the water himself, just as the dynasty tried to care for its 'backwards' peoples while shielding them from harm. His mission, like that of the Habsburgs, ended in failure and with the death of the missionary.

Radetzkymarsch showed Roth at the height of his powers. It offered a highly nuanced depiction of Austria and reflects a balance between nostalgia and reality. In an article he wrote in 1932, the year he wrote *Radetzkymarsch*, Roth expressed his regret over the passing of Austria-Hungary. He remarked that the Monarchy had allowed him a multi-layered identity. He was able to be a loyal member of the German nation and a supranational Austrian, or even a citizen of the world, all at the same time.[10] His portrayal of Austria in *Radetzkymarsch* demonstrated that Roth, despite his sadness over the fate of his fatherland, remained in touch with reality in 1932.

Shortly after *Radetzkymarsch*, Roth wrote *Stationschef Fallmerayer (Fallmerayer the Station Master)*, published in 1933. It followed the life of the station master for the Imperial Railway in an Alpine town two hours south of Vienna. The trains represented the possibilities for progress that modernity offered, but also its potential to disrupt the lives of those it touched. The story began with a train wreck that brought the beautiful Countess Walewska into Fallmerayer's station and his life. He took her into his family home to care for her injuries and fell in love with her. After her recovery she returned to Russia and left Fallmerayer devastated.

He would never have seen her again except for the outbreak of war, which took Fallmerayer away from his wife and children and sent him to Russia, where he eventually found himself at the Countess' house. The two disregarded their spouses (the Countess' husband was presumed dead in the war) and became lovers. However, the husband finally returned and reclaimed his marital position, shattering Fallmerayer's paradise. Roth's antihero in the story is modernity itself, represented by the trains. The railroads gave Fallmerayer a job and a means to provide for his family, but the wreck awakened him from his banal existence and showed him what seemed to be a more fulfilling life. In the end, that better life, for which he had exchanged his secure existence, proved little more than an illusion. When the illusion shattered, Fallmerayer was left homeless.

In the essay *Der Antichrist* (1934, *The Antichrist*), Roth proclaimed his absolute hatred for modernity. He railed against every kind of technological advance. For example, he criticized the impact of telephones by arguing that people could more easily lie to one another when not speaking face to face. Motion pictures were illusions compared to the reality of seeing a live performance in a theater. Modern buildings were built with glass, steel, and chromium instead of the more natural bricks and stone. Roth condemned both the crass capitalism of Hollywood and the unspiritual materialism of Soviet Communism. He denounced war, racism, poor working conditions, environmental pollution, and, above all, nationalism. Perhaps in a swipe at Nazi Germany, Roth castigated those who blindly supported their country even when it behaved immorally. In a crowning denunciation of modernity, Roth asserted "Modern men, indeed, are distinguished from men of the ancient world chiefly by the fact that they have already introduced Hades, the realm of shadows, into the living world."[11]

In 1935 Roth wrote *Die Büste des Kaisers (The Bust of the Emperor)*, in which he followed *Der Antichrist's* unceasing tirade against modernity with a tale of unconditional praise for the Habsburg Monarchy. The protagonist was Count Franz Xaver Morstin, a Galician aristocrat whose family had emigrated to Poland from Italy during the Renaissance. However, he considered himself neither a Pole nor an Italian, rather "Like so many of his peers in the former Crown Lands of the Austro-Hungarian Monarchy, he was one of the noblest and purest sorts of Austrian, plain and simple. That is, a man above nationality, and therefore of true nobility."[12] He was both the archetypal Austrian and nobleman because he aided all those who asked for help, no matter their nationality or religion. The Count symbolized Roth's idealized depiction of Austria and personified his vision of a supranational Austrian identity.

The Count despised modern politicians for trying to politicize the peasants of his native village, who were concerned not with national self-determination or democratic rights but rather with their material well-being. Furthermore, he maintained that the priorities of his peasants reflected those of most people, whether modern politicians accepted it or not.

The First World War destroyed the old Count because it destroyed his fatherland, Austria-Hungary. The Count remarked "Now I am homeless and have lost the true home of the eternal wanderer – the old Monarchy."[13] He was unable to adjust to needing a passport to travel across what had been provincial borders within the old Monarchy.[14] The Count also reviled the social conventions of modernity, particularly what he saw as the less discretionary fashion sense of women in the 1920s.

The Count then turned to the causes of his beloved Monarchy's destruction. He decried nationalism's role, citing Grillparzer's epigram "'From humanity, via nationalism, to bestiality.'"[15] Roth, as narrator, noted that, "It had been discovered ... that in order to possess individuality as a citizen every person must belong to a definite nationality or race."[16] The Count held the Austro-Germans largely responsible for the monarchy's demise, and praised the Slavs and Jews of the outlying Crownlands as bulwarks of the Imperial system. In his late works Roth consistently and unfavorably contrasted the modernity of Vienna and the cities with the simple backwardness of his native Galicia. He failed to offer any of the Empire's deficiencies as a state, such as its anachronistic army and government, as reasons for its demise. The balanced view of Austria presented as recently as *Radetzkymarsch*, written only three years earlier, was absent from *Die Büste des Kaisers*.

Roth linked nationalism with the *petit bourgeoisie* created by modern society. He claimed that nationalism was the recourse of 'losers': primary school teachers who wanted secondary school classrooms, apothecaries' assistants who wanted to practice medicine, tooth pullers who could not be dentists, low level bureaucrats and, in a nod to Hitler, budding artists rejected by the academy. Modernity robbed these Austrians of their pride by giving them expectations they could not fulfill. Their failure led them to look to racial nationalism for acceptance and affirmation.

The story climaxed in a conflict between the Count and the new democratic regime of Poland, to which Galicia was awarded after the war. Some years after 1918, the Count placed outside of his home a bust of Franz Joseph that he had received before the war. It was the gift of a grateful local artist who, thanks to the Count's assistance, had procured a position at the Academy of Arts in Vienna. The village peasants saw the bust as perfectly natural, in fact they assumed Franz Joseph himself had freed Poland. However, a visiting government official disapproved, and ordered the bust removed. The Count decided to give Franz Joseph an Imperial burial.

In this mythologized depiction, the preparations and funeral ceremony represented the supranational harmony the Empire inspired. A Ukrainian built the coffin, a Pole forged a double eagle and a Jew inscribed the blessing. At the funeral, three pastors, representing the three Galician faiths, offered prayers as the coffin, draped with the Imperial black and gold flag, was lowered into the ground. The villagers grieved for their loss. "The crowd began to sob as though the Emperor Franz Joseph and with him the old Monarchy and their old home had only then been buried."[17] Finally, the Count lamented in his memoirs, "I hate nationalism and nation-states. My old home, the Monarchy, alone was a great Mansion with many doors and many chambers, for every condition of men. This mansion has been divided, split up, splintered. I have nothing more to seek there, I am used to living in a home, not in cabins."[18]

The Count's comments reflected the author's complete and utter alienation from the world in which he lived. Furthermore, they were strikingly personal when compared to the detached criticism of that world by von Maerker, Roth's witness to Habsburg Austria in *Der Stumme Prophet*, written seven years earlier. In addition, von Maerker was a supporting character in *Der Stumme Prophet*, while the Count was at the center of *Die Büste des Kaisers*, and served as the character who spoke for Roth himself. Unlike von Maerker, who lived on happily in the post-Habsburg world, the Count had "nothing more to seek," and thus no reason to live. The years between these two works had witnessed the Great Depression and the accession of Adolf Hitler to power. The problems of the modern world did not personally concern the character of von Maerker in 1928. However, by 1935 they had come to obsess Joseph Roth.

Roth returned to Galicia for the setting of *Das falsche Gewicht (The False Scales)*, written in 1937 and set in the pre-1914 period. The novel detailed the attempt by an Austrian bureaucrat to impose a modern, standardized system of weights and measures on the markets of a Galician border district. The *Eichmeister (Calibrator)*, Herr Eibenschutz, arrived intent on bringing rational order to the town's backward marketplace. However, after spending some time in the province, Eibenschutz became 'corrupted' by the more traditional, more human ways of doing business. He found himself unable to arrest Mendel Singer, a poor trader with a wife, children, and, like all the other traders, illegal scales. However, Piotrak, Eibenschutz's newly arrived gendarme, insisted the law be enforced and Singer pay his fine or go to jail. Eibenschutz protested but eventually gave in to Piotrak, to the rule of law. Roth punished Eibenschutz for his inhuman enforcement of the law by ending the novel with his murder.

This criticism of Austria's attempt to enforce the letter of the law, to be a *Rechtsstaat (state of laws)*, made little sense in light of Roth's praise for the Monarchy as a home for all its nations. Austria's ability to provide that home depended on its consistent and systematic application of the laws, as well as the modern principle of equality before the law.

In *Die Kapuzinergruft (The Emperor's Tomb)*, written after the Anschluss of 1938, Roth brought back the Trottas of *Radetzkymarsch* through the descendants of the brother of the hero of Solferino. The protagonist was Karl Joseph Trotta's second cousin, Franz Ferdinand, whom the story followed from the prewar period through the Anschluss. Although of an inferior literary quality to *Radetzkymarsch*, *Die Kapuzinergruft* is more compelling because it showed the depths of Roth's personal anguish.

Roth once again depicted the Monarchy as a land of harmony among all its nations, this time through the close friendship between Franz Ferdinand's cousin Joseph Branco, a Slovenian farmer and traveling chestnut salesman, and the Galician Jewish cabbie Manes Reisiger. Trotta praised Reisiger as a primeval sort of man, as if he were a wondrous relic from a better age. Trotta contrasted the modern world with this man's primitive honesty and admitted he craved the Jew's realness. In his description of Reisiger, Roth displayed his preference for the traditional Galician-Jewish life he had abandoned in order to become an assimilated urbanite. By 1938, Roth had become alienated not only from the world around him, but from his own self, from the man he had chosen to be.

Roth, through his protagonist, declared his complete and total alienation from the rest of the world. "I saw myself, as I had for so long since my return from the war, as someone who was wrongly alive."[19] Furthermore, he declared "I am not a man of my time, in fact I find it hard not to declare myself its enemy."[20] Sadly, he referred to the old Monarchy, which by this time had been gone for two decades, as home. After the Anschluss Roth literally perceived himself to be homeless. He knew that the only home he longed for would never be rebuilt, thus he felt his homelessness was permanent.

Trotta was unable to escape the past, and named his son Franz Joseph Eugen, evoking his dead Emperor and his dynasty's greatest military hero. Roth used a female character, Trotta's wife Elizabeth, to personify the modern world, as he had done in *Der Stumme Prophet*. The baubles and trinkets Elizabeth constructed represented the dishonesty of modernity. Their flashy design gave them a value that belied the fact that they consisted of worthless material. Roth contrasted the grounded, real value system of the old world, in which its substance determined an object's worth, with that of a modern world that valued form and style over substance. Elizabeth proved herself the ultimate modern woman by forsaking her husband and child for another woman and seeking fame in Hollywood, the evil heart of Modernity. Roth's mysogynistic depiction of women reflected his preference for a traditional hierachy in which people, including women, knew their place.

Finally, by 1938, the end had come for Trotta, and for Roth as well. In the final scene he wandered down to the Kapuzinergruft after hearing that Nazi Germany had absorbed the last remnants of Austria. When the Capuchin brother asked why he had come, Trotta replied "I want to visit the sarcophagus of my Emperor, Franz Joseph I." When he began to cry out "Long live the Emperor!" the brother scolded him to lower his voice for fear of the Nazis. His spirit broken, he asked "So where could I go now? I, a Trotta?"[21] His alienation from the world around him was complete.

By the late 1930s, Roth had escaped into the past because he was unable to face the present, let alone the future. In his depiction of Austria-Hungary, he described a world that had never really existed. His growing alienation from reality represented a tragic but consistent thread in his writing. Roth was doubly alienated from his chosen homeland, first as a Galician-born Jew in the Republic of Austria, and finally as a supranational Austrian in a land of rampant German nationalism. The triumph of the modern world of mass politics and intolerant nationalism over his traditional, cosmopolitan Habsburg Austria, made complete by the events of 1938, left Roth without hope, and without a place in the world in which he lived. Joseph Roth drank himself to death within twelve months of the Anschluss.

Georgetown University

Notes

1. For more biographical information on Roth, see David Bronsen, *Joseph Roth: eine Biographie* (Köln: Kiepenheuer & Witsch, 1974). In English see Sydney Rosenfeld, "Joseph Roth," in: *Major Figures of Modern Austrian Literature*, ed. Donald G. Daviau (Riverside, CA: Ariadne Press, 1988), 341-369.

2. See Edward Timms, "Citizenship and 'Heimatrecht' after the Treaty of Saint-Germain," in *The Habsburg Legacy*, Ritchie Robertson and Edward Timms, eds. (Edinburgh: Edinburgh University Press, 1994), 161-162.

3. Claudio Magris, *Der Habsburgische Mythos in der Österreichischen Literatur* (Salzburg: O. Müller, 1966).

4. For more on Roth's early reflections on Habsburg Austria, see C.E. Williams, *The Broken Eagle: The Politics of Austrian Literature from*

Empire to Anschluss (New York: Barnes & Noble, 1974).
  5. Joseph Roth, *Der Stumme Prophet*, in *Werke*, Vol. 4 (Köln: Kiepenheuer & Witsch, 1989), 922.
  6. Ibid., 923.
  7. Williams, 101.
  8. Joseph Roth, *Radetzkymarsch*, in *Werke*, Vol. 5 (Köln: Kiepenheuer & Witsch, 1989), 290.
  9. Ibid., 336.
  10. Joseph Roth, *Frankfurter Zeitung*, April 17, 1932. He also criticized history for its cruelty towards his fatherland in an article in *Österreichische Bücher*, July 6, 1932. (cited in Bronsen, 59.) As a Galician-born Jew, Roth's identification with the German nation pointed out the tremendous attraction of the German language and culture for Eastern Jews.
  11. Joseph Roth, *Der Antichrist*, in *Werke*, Vol. 3 (Köln: Kiepenheuer & Witsch, 1989), 573.
  12. Joseph Roth, *Die Büste des Kaisers*, in *Werke*, Vol. 5 (Köln: Kiepenheuer & Witsch, 1989), 655.
  13. Ibid., 663.
  14. The inability to adjust to new national borders appeared again with the chestnut roaster Joseph Branco in *Die Kapuzinergruft*, and clearly reflected Roth's own personal discomfort towards the post-1918 political situation.
  15. *Die Büste des Kaisers*, 660.
  16. Ibid.
  17. Ibid., 675.
  18. Ibid.
  19. Joseph Roth, *Die Kapuzinergruft*, in *Werke*, Vol. 5 (Köln: Kiepenheuer & Witsch, 1989), 342.
  20. Ibid., 227.
  21. Ibid., 346.

Separate Reality, Separate Nations?
Austria in the Works of Jewish and Non-Jewish Authors

Dagmar C. G. Lorenz

Austria, particularly Vienna, played an important role in the imagination of Jewish intellectuals of the Habsburg Empire and the Second Republic. During and after the era of Emancipation and Assimilation many Eastern European Jews championed the ideals of acculturation and assimilation and embraced the German language as their medium for realizing their aspirations of becoming citizens with equal rights and equal social status. Although the different phases of immigration since the Compromise Agreement of 1867 had often led to conflicts between Austrian Gentiles, assimilated Jews, and unassimilated newcomers, by the end of World War I the integration of the sons and daughters of most Jewish immigrants into Viennese society was close to being a *fait accompli*.[1] In the minds of many East European Jews, Vienna, renowned for its high culture and its social diversity, had become a synonym for civilization and good taste. Along with Paris and New York, Vienna signified opportunity and refinement.

In his autobiography Elias Canetti writes that in Bulgaria his parents frequently spoke German with one another, reminiscing about their studies in Vienna, their erstwhile dreams of becoming actors, and, most of all, their memories of the *Burgtheater*, the court theater.[2] This type of appreciation for things Viennese and the loyalty for the Austrian Emperor, who was considered the protector of the Jews as one of the many nations of his multi-nation realm, was characteristic of Habsburg Jewry. The positive attitude toward the House of Habsburg was based on the relatively favorable situation of Austrian Jews since Joseph II's Edict of Toleration and the ensuing gradual improvement of their position, which ultimately included Austrian citizenship. In the First Republic Jewish citizens enjoyed complete equality for the first time. However, only a decade later the process of integration was reversed by the so-called Anschluss, the annexation of Austria by Nazi Germany, in 1938. In the *Kristallnacht*, the pogram of November 9/10, 1938, the Jewish institutions and social networks were destroyed.

Less enthusiastic than other critics about the strides Jewish citizens had made, Marsha Rozenblit describes the situation prior to these traumatic events as follows: "Austria never did accept them [the Jews]. After the First World War, the Jewish community of Vienna grew to over 200,000. At the same time antisemitism flourished in the First Austrian Republic. Demands to remove the Jews became especially shrill after the rise of Hitler to power in Germany in 1933." Yet, Rozenblit also concedes that one of the "positive achievements of nineteenth-century Viennese Jews" was having forged a "Jewish and a European identity" (Rozenblit 196). In fact, one of their achievements was the formation of Viennese culture, in the creation of which, as Egon Schwarz points out, "Jews played an eminent, indeed, a crucial role."[3]

The rebuilding of Austrian society did not include plans to restore Vienna's Jewish culture and community; not even an invitation to return was extended to Jewish exiles. Those who did come back were expected to conform to the dominant culture. "In Austria the Jews were allowed to live again, conditionally, if they were inconspicuous and well-behaved, however, they were only welcome as Austrians, not as Jews, the Austrian Chancellor Julius Figl declared.[4] This notwithstanding, the postwar Jewish community, initially considered a transitional solution, established itself permanently, and Jewish intellectuals once again were an integral part of Viennese cultural life. Some of them articulated specifically Jewish points of view and experiences and made a profound impact on contemporary Austrian culture. The very complexity of the contemporary Jewish culture and literature in Austria reflects, as Sander Gilman notes, "a 'real' Jewish cultural presence. 'Real' in the sense that the debates, the schisms, reveal a living and breathing cultural entitity."[5]

It was not uncommon for Austrian Jews who had gone into exile during the Nazi era and returned thereafter to hold on to their earlier positive outlook on assimilation and integration. Hans Weigel and Hilde Spiel, for example, were strongly identified with Austria as their homecountry, with Vienna, their native city, and German, their native and literary language. Because of their intense fondness for Austria's landscapes and the cityscape and ambiance of Vienna – not necessarily of the people – some former exiles were willing to overlook even blatant instances of anti-Semitism.[6] In their often autobiographical works many of them conjured up the events and places of their youth, creating a nostalgic scenery made up of memories.[7] On the basis of these memories and yearnings they identified as citizens of Vienna, as Austrians, and within this framework, as Jews. Some even took a conciliatory position during the most scandalous political debate of the mid-1980s,[8] the "Waldheim Case," as Simon Wiesenthal termed it.[9]

During the 1980s and 1990s the discrepancy between the Jewish and the Gentile Austria-experience became the focal theme in the works of authors and filmmakers who had grown up after 1945 but who defined their work through the Shoah and the post-Shoah Jewish experience in Austria. In their portrayal of their Vienna experience they reveal the profound impact an environment experienced as xenophobic and hostile, which was at the same time aesthetically and culturally appealing, had on them. These authors, among them Nadja Seelich, Ruth Beckermann, Robert Menasse, and Robert Schindel, came from a wide variety of backgrounds. With all of them the analysis and discussion of their relationship with the Austrian public and the experience of otherness plays a significant role in their essays, literary works, and films. A recurrent theme is the seemingly insurmountable dividing line between the children of Holocaust survivors and exiles and those of the Austrian mainstream as it reconstituted itself after World War II, denying and glossing over the past.

Jews and Jewish-identified authors born in Austria after the Shoah have positioned themselves increasingly in opposition to and apart from the majority culture. In their unwillingness to define themselves exclusively in terms of Austria's Jewish past or against the legacy of the Nazi era, they established and cultivated an attitude of scepticism and resistance which became a part of their identity as writers and intellectuals. They expressed their sense of identity through non-canonical literature: turn-of-the century and interwar Jewish writing as well as contemporary literature and public debates and events involving Jewish concerns. By absorbing an alternative discourse they emphasized the distance between themselves and the children non-Jewish Austrians, the majority of whom they considered implicated in the crimes committed against the Austrian Jews of the previous generations. By assuming the position of the children of Holocaust survivors, they defined young Austrian non-Jews as the children of perpetrators and mass-murderers.

By contrast, the majority of the older generation of authors, many of whom had taken an active part in the intellectual life of the Second

Republic, even though they remained permanent residents or citizens of their countries of exile – Erich Fried, Jakov Lind, Georg Kreisler, and Frank Zwillinger – positioned themselves according to ideologies that reflected more traditional notions of individual and group identity. These included Marxist models, linking fascism, middle-class identity, as well as bourgeois notions of the individual. The latter concept was strongly supported by the Humanist ideal transmitted in the *Gymnasium*, the traditional college preparatory schools. None of these paradigms provided for a separate Jewish identity, let alone a Jewish nationalist one. As a consequence, the attitude toward Jewish concerns on the part of Jewish Social Democrats and Communists as well as political conservatives, inasmuch as Jewish identity is discussed in their works at all, is ambivalent at best. Compared to members of the younger generation, Ruth Beckermann and Doron Rabinovici, for example, representatives of the prewar generations ideologically as different as Simon Wiesenthal, Erich Fried, and Hans Weigel speak a similar language when discussing Jewish topics and concerns.

Only few authors, notably Friedrich Torberg and Jean Améry, embraced a distinctly Jewish outlook. While these authors were viewed by their contemporaries, non-Jews and supporters of assimilation alike, with criticism and some trepidation, the post-Shoah generation of Jewish authors was receptive to their works. Along with authors of the early to mid-twentieth century who had written extensively about the problem of being Jewish in German-speaking cultures, Schnitzler, Wassermann, Roth, and Sperber, the strong Jewish voices of the survivors of Austro-fascism, National Socialism and the Holocaust, provided models for Jewish writing in today's Austria.

The 1980s, marked by increasing anti-Semitic activities in Austria, e.g. the bomb attacks on the Schoeps department stores and Jewish cultural sites during the early eighties, and the events and polemics of the Waldheim election in the mid-eighties, were the era in which Austrian, mostly Viennese, Jews discovered, acknowledged, and defined themselves as Jews. They did so by setting themselves ideologically and discursively apart from mainstream positions, conservative and Leftist, and by articulating a Jewish-centered cultural and political discourse. The works of the early and mid-1980s deployed the already established dichotomy of Germans (or Austrians) versus Jews in a polemical and productive way. However, at the same time they subverted the hierachy of values that up until that time had determined the way in which things

Jewish were discussed in the German-speaking context; in anti-Semitic or philo-Semitic terms, neither one of which allowed for a Jewish agenda or Jewish agency.

In Nadja Seelich's film *Kieselsteine* (*Pebbles*), for example, Germans and Jews are configured as opposites.[10] While anti-Semitic and philo-Semitic films and literary works usually stereotyped Jews as an amorphous, homogeneous group without its own inner-group dynamics and differentiations, Seelich's work represents Jews from an insider's perspective. Hence her Jewish characters appear diverse, relating to numerous Jewish and non-Jewish groups and contexts. On the other hand, non-Jews, particularly Seelich's German protagonist, are portrayed as caricatures of Austrian- or Germanness. Ruth Beckermann, criticizing Seelich for excluding Austrians from the equation, posits "Juden und Österreicher," Jews and Austrians, as the pair of opposites that she is most interested in examining.[11]

Recently, in the 1990s, a discourse that transcends the oppositional models of the 1980s has evolved in the works of authors and intellectuals who are firmly grounded in the culture of the Second Republic. Treated as an axiom by most authors of the post-Shoah generation, the notion that between Jews and non-Jews in Austria insurmountable barriers exist, came under scrutiny by intellectuals firmly grounded in the culture of the Second Republic. In the lives of most of these younger authors such barriers seem less pronounced. In fact, in the personal lives of Jewish authors they did not exist to the same degree as their portrayal in in the literature and films of the previous decade suggests.

Of the 1940s generation, Robert Schindel, the author of the novel *Gebürtig* (1992, *Born – Where*[12]), stands out because his work challenges the binary opposition that structures the narratives and films in the works of his Jewish colleagues.[13] By sketching a complex network of relationships among Jews and Gentiles in contemporary Vienna and worldwide, and by exposing the anything but "pure" lineages of his protagonists, Schindel challenges the prevailing notion of a separate Jewish sphere.[14] Through the use of satire he exposes the incongruency between the ideological positions set forth in the works of his colleagues and associates and the reality Vienna Austrian Jews encounter on a daily basis. Matti Bunzl, who explored the everyday experience of young Jews in Austria, including his own perceptions, writes: "Without for a moment discounting or belittling the realities of anti-Semitism and right-wing politics, it is nevertheless true that Jews *can* live in contentment in contemporary Austria, because they have the ability to construct their lives within resistive spatio-temporal realms – or what I have called 'alternative geographies' and 'fantasmatic histories.'"[15] Schindel is aware of the literary strategies of forging identities of self-imposed otherness, identities through which the individual tries to transform or elude the Austrian here-and-now. *Gebürtig* thematizes a different path of coming to terms with Austrian and Jewish history by confronting the problem and the people to whom it is attributed, "the Austrians." He focuses on the blind spots that prevent many of his contemporaries from acknowledging the fact that rather than by the past or their ethnicity and philosophy, their actions may be motivated by desire and ambition.[16]

Schindel's novel signals a departure from earlier texts by Jewish authors who emphasized in almost mythological dimensions, the rift between Jews and Gentiles. Instead, Schindel traces the complex network of relationships between a group of intellectuals affected by the Holocaust, Jews and Gentiles, Austrians, Germans, and US citizens. Through their interaction, friendly or hostile, they have created a multiply interconnected sphere in the present. The medium through which they accomplish personal and societal change is language. Beyond their mutual attractions, aversions, and sexual contacts, their conversations and encounters undermine or establish boundaries between different individuals. Schindel's Jewish protagonist Danny Demant, for example, tells his Gentile lover Christiane Kalteisen about his Communist father who was killed in Mauthausen, and she reciprocates with an account of her Christian-Socialist father (35). Exchanges such as these solidify their relationship and allow for a love relationship that transcends the past. Conversely, the repressed childhood memories of Konrad Sachs, the son of the governor general of Poland, which emerge in the course of the novel, threaten to destroy this character's perfectly good marriage. Left untold, they foster a superficial allegiance to the Jewish author Emanuel Katz. To a certain extent Schindel adopts a psychotherapeutic model in his novel: articulation, getting things out in the open, enables individual characters to leave their neurosis-ridden world of old discourses and enter the present.

Gebürtig moves beyond rigid notions of group identity which were foregrounded by Jewish authors in the 1980s. Indeed, as is the case in the international settings of Robert Menasse's novels, the multicultural aspects of contemporary Central Europe and the global implications of the Shoah come into focus and cause the binary patterns to break down as a matter of course. Schindel embraces a paradigm of individual self-determination. Quoting Nietzsche, Danny Demant's twin brother Alexander proclaims the innocence of the post-Holocaust generations, the children of the victims and those of the perpetrators: "Which child would not have reason to cry about his parents." (339). By portraying a viable relationship between a Jewish man and a Gentile Austrian woman, Danny and Christiane, first in the isolation of an intensely erotic one-on-one relationship, then in an expanding social context, Schindel challenges former positions concerning post-Shoah Jewish and Gentile identity, notably those of his colleagues and collaborators Nadja Seelich and Ruth Beckermann. Throughout his narrative Schindel alludes to and parodies scenes from Seelich's film *Kieselsteine*, introducing, as in a roman à clef (to an extent *Gebürtig* is precisely that), figures representing real persons. Esther Lichtblau, for example, is a reflection of Ruth Beckermann. In the epilogue "Verzweifelte" (A Desperate People, 341-353), Schindel gives his own rendering of an episode in Beckermann's film *Die papierene Brücke* (The Paper Bridge). He reveals that he was one of the Jewish extras in the Theresienstadt episodes in Herman Wouk's World War II documentary *War and Remembrance* (1988).[17]

In her film sequence about the shoooting of Wouk's television series, Beckermann foregrounded Schindel as one of the participants in Wouk's venture. Schindel is shown as one who questions the genre of the documentary film, in particular Wouk's attempt to historicize the Holocaust in an artificial Theresienstadt setting built in Yugoslavia for the purpose of the film, because Czechoslovakian authorities did not allow any filming at Theresienstadt. Both Schindel and Beckermann question why Jewish characters are standardly represented by Jews, even by Holocaust survivors, while the ethnicity of non-Jewish characters is irrelevant. As a character in *Die papierene Brücke* (The Paper Bridge) as well as in his own novel *Gebürtig*, Schindel pokes fun at the American film director who has taken a fancy to his "nose that looked as if it had been modeled after the caricatures in *Der Stürmer*" (350). Moreover, he satirizes his own Jewishness and the Jewish speech patterns, which he generally avoids although he knows them well: "'Sch'ma Jisruel, my feet are cold, Sch'ma so cold are my feet, oh, my feet are so cold, oh so cold are my feet, Israel. Sch'ma Jisruel, my feet are so cold, so cold are my feet, Adonaj.' Well I think if my feet finally get warm and my head stays so wonderfully cold it could happen that rather than the Messiah there will come a beautiful feeling" (353). The competing paradigms of identity formation and avoidance discussed in *Gebürtig*, which include different language registers, Yiddish, Austrian dialect, Jewish-German, and High German, are reminiscent of the multiple roles open to Austrian Jews before the Nazi terror.

Sketching different positions and relationships among Jews and their professional and sexual interaction with Gentiles, Schindel reveals some of the choices available to the post-Holocaust generations: acceptance or rejection of the past, mourning, repression, or moving beyond the past. Taking the latter path, the novel suggests, could lead to the kind of close-knit Jewish and Gentile culture Austria had known before the Nazi era. Authors of the interwar period, including Hugo Bettauer, were aware of Vienna's unique culture in particular, a multicultural blend with a strong Jewish component. In his novel *Die Stadt ohne Juden* (1925, *The City Without Jews*) Bettauer shows a utopian Vienna without Jews as a provincial place without life and luster.[18] To illustrate the affinity Jews have for the rural Austria of the *Sommerfrischen*, the summer vacation spots, Friedrich Torberg tells the following anecdote about an encounter in the Salzburg mountains:

> Heinrich Eisenbach was a regular visitor at Ischl. Unshakably loyal, he belonged to the same geographic and artistic region as Amin Berg (Karl Kraus praised him as one of the great character actors of contemporary theater. For weeks he had been the only guest taking his coffee at the country inn ... Then, one day he noticed up there a person, obviously tourist who had been recommended at home to visit "Sophia's Double Panorama." Eisen bach took him by the hand and led him silently to the barrier on the opposite side. He pointed into the impenetrably gray rain curtain and said in the tone of a tour guide: "It is from this place, Sir, that the ancient Jews saw the Dachstein mountain."[19]

Of course, Schindel knows that the often debated, often idealized Austrian-Jewish symbiosis, if it ever existed, ended in 1938, and his work takes into account the Holocaust trauma. Beyond that, however, he explores both aspects of the past and their impact with a focus on Jewish identity in today's Austria. Without diminishing the suffering of individuals such as Katz who were traumatized by their traumatized parents, Schindel does not portray the tragic legacy of the Shoah as inescapable. He also shows that both aspects of the past, the Shoah legacy and that of National Socialism, can be and are exploited by the later generations for emotional and material gain.[20]

Schindel's assessment of Jewish life in Vienna differs from the views reflected in Seelich's *Kieselsteine* (1982) and Beckermann's autobiographical essay *Unzugehörig* (1989, Not Belonging) and film *Die papierene Brücke*.[21] Rather than relying on the fronts established in most Austrian (and German) texts about Jewish identity during and after the Shoah in German-speaking countries, Schindel thematizes the diversification of the Jewish discourse to reflect the range of choices open to Jews in Austria. Recent experience has shown that these may include positions as extreme as Peter Sichrovsky's endorsement of Jörg Haider and the FPÖ, the Liberal Party of Austria, an indication of the wide spectrum of viewpoints taken by Jewish intellectuals.[22] The diversity of possible positions in Schindel's novel reveals that the Jewish community in Austria is neither homogeneous nor static.

In his autobiography, *Von der Kunst, Österreicher zu sein* (About the Art of Being an Austrian), the diplomat and former exile Hans J. Thalberg stated that a deep moat separated postwar Jews and Austrians, similar to the "Tiefe Graben," the deep moat, between the Jewish Quarter and the Inner City.[23] Convinced that National Socialism was a popular mass movement, Thalberg did not trust the ideological reorientation in postwar Austria and Germany. He maintained instead that the emotional and intellectual gulf between Jews and non-Jews could not be bridged. Daniel Goldhagen's recent study, *Hitler's Willing Executioners*, supports Thalberg's views. Focusing on the tradition of anti-Jewish and anti-Semitic cultural attitudes in Central Europe, Goldhagen argues that in German-speaking countries (and not only there) the anti-Semitic tradition had become the norm. Sander Gilman's earlier analysis of anti-Jewish discourses *Jewish Self-Hatred* shows the deep level on which anti-Semitism functions.[24] Goldhagen rightfully contends that to qualify as an anti-Semite in the late nineteenth and early twentieth century, an Austrian or German did not have to articulate his/her anti-Semitism (as, indeed, many Nazis did not while fully supporting the measures taken against Jewish citizens; some of them, such as Eichmann and Hoess even denied that they were anti-Semites) – anti-Semitism was par for the course.[25] There was relatively little resistance to Nazism, and hardly any protest against the deportations.[26] Whether they were practicing Jews or not, individuals and groups perceived as Jews were targets of anti-Semitism.

Anti-Semitism caused Jewish and Gentile Austrians to relate to the country in which they lived and with which they identified in vastly different ways. This was the case even before the Nazi takeover, as a comparison of texts by Schnitzler, Kraus, Altenberg, Veza Canetti, or Broch with works by Doderer, Erika Mitterer, Rosegger, or Waggerl would show. After 1945 the memory of the Holocaust produced distinct perceptions and images of Austria in the literature and films by Jewish and Jewish-identified authors who viewed Austrian society with trepidation, hostility, detachment, or alienation and suspected danger lurking behind the idyllic façades of Austrian villages. Ilse Aichinger's poem "Ortesanfang" ("City Limits") is but one example:

> I do not trust the peace,
> the neighbor, the rose hedges,
> the whispered word.
> I heard that they put skins to the nuce,
> that they overturn benches before wintertime,
> that their cheers flew through the air....[27]

Of course there were exceptions: Hans Weigel, a former exile, painted a predominantly optimistic image of Austria. On the other hand, Ingeborg Bachmann, a non-Jew, was profoundly affected by the Jewish experience. She established an intertextuality with Joseph Roth, Paul Celan, and Jean Améry and viewed Austria with profound criticism. Her solidarity lay with the victims of the Nazis. Her protagonists speak as women oppressed by patriarchy, as Slovenians dominated by German-Austrian society, as Jews persecuted by the Nazis. She was opposed to the everyday fascism of the postwar era, and she escaped by embracing the life of a cosmopolitan and member of the jet-set, uprooted, but eluding the confines of nationality, ethnicity, traditional gender roles, race, and class. Such exceptions notwithstanding, there are, generally speaking, noticeable differences between the portrayal of Austria in the works of Jewish and non-Jewish authors.

As did earlier Jewish writers, authors after the Holocaust have thematized life in the city, particularly Vienna. Matti Bunzl asserts that "Vienna ... emerges as the one social space in Austria's cultural landscape which can sustain Jewish life (in terms of its size and the presence of a Jewish community), most Viennese Jews find genuine pleasure in their urban environment. As these urban sentiments are constituted in typical opposition to an imagined Austrian Other, this urban environment is in turn figured along very particular lines of difference, which at once reflect and reproduce specific Austrian-Jewish experience" (Bunzl: 66). Since the city is perceived as a space to socialize with like-minded people and other Jews, it assumes the quality of a place of centrality and safety. Indeed, the majority of Jews in Austria lived and live in Vienna. Counter to predictions, Vienna's Jewish community never ceased to exist and is currently expanding. Yet, Vienna, as portrayed by Ilse Aichinger, Elfriede Jelinek, Ruth Beckermann, Nadja Seelich, and Robert Schindel, is a problematic place, associated with past suffering, replete with memories of an anti-Semitic history and the Holocaust. At the same time, all of these authors show Vienna inseparably linked with Jewish history and their own lives. This is articulated, for example, by the voice-over in Beckermann's *Die papierene Brücke*. The narrator says that she knows every street, every pebble in Vienna and is unlikely to derive the same joy from any other place. This sentiment was shared by Hilde Spiel, who returned from England to Vienna: "I had an immortal love for Vienna."[28]

The older generation's love of Vienna derives from their euphoric recall of a golden age of Jewish and Gentile co-existence, either in the Austro-Hungarian Empire, captured by the image of a paternal Franz Joseph, e.g., Roth's *Die Büste des Kaisers* (*The Bust of the Emperor*) and *Radetzkymarsch* (*Radetzky March*) and Spiel's *Lisas Zimmer* (*The Darkened Room*). As Bunzl maintains, "the mediated memory of the Habsburg Monarchy plays a crucial role. Specifically, it is the ethnic pluralism embodied in the supra-national semblance of the crown that continues to serve as a reference point for contemporary Jews" (Bunzl: 68). Although more critical, authors of the postwar generations have resumed these topoi repeatedly, for example, Bachmann's *Drei Wege zum See* (*Three Paths to the Lake*) and Beckermann's *Die papierene Brücke*. None of them dismantled the lure of Habsburg entirely. Another reference point is interwar Central European Jewish culture, thematized in Friedrich Torberg's *Die Tante Jolesch* (Aunt Jolesch). Also for Torberg Vienna was the focal point. A decidedly Jewish voice, he inspired contemporary authors to explore their Jewish roots. Schindel, Menasse, Beckermann, and Seelich have indeed claimed interwar Vienna as their intellectual anchoring point, a time when Jewish life, secular and religious, prospered, despite rising anti-Semitism.

Authors who experienced the Nazi years envision Vienna and rural Austria as the now empty stage of past atrocities, for example, Aichinger's *Plätze und Straßen* (Squares and Streets), Lind's *Seele aus Holz* (*Soul of Wood*), and Klüger's *weiter leben* (continuing to live). However, most authors of this generation also remember positive experiences, namely, Aichinger in her later autobiographical texts and Torberg in *Auch das war Wien* (Also that was Vienna). Authors born after the Holocaust associate contemporary Austria primarily with the *Kristallnacht* pogrom and the Holocaust. They signal their contempt through the use of irony and satire and they emphasize their distance from "the Austrians."[29]

In the works of Austrian authors specific sites have traditionally played an important role. Gentile authors often refer to specific locations to evoke a sense of familiarity. The same alleys and squares, the same cozy Inner City coffee houses figure in Doderer's *Dämonen* (*The Demons*) and in Seelich's and Beckermann's films. Here they are sites where the unexpected – insults and attacks against individuals perceived as other – can and do occur. The only safety their protagonists can hope to attain is in their domestic spheres, in Schindel the apartment in the Halmgasse and in Beckermann the house in the Marc Aurel Straße with its long Jewish history. Also, the locations highlighted by Jewish authors are distinct. They include the Prater, Vienna's Second District, Café Museum, known from Canetti's autobiography, and other places associated with Jewish history. None of the semi-autobiographical protagonists associated with the Jewish past, be it Peter Henisch's protagonist Stein, Seelich's central character Hannah, or Schindel's twins, Danny and Sascha, is as self-assured as the characters in the works of non-Jews, for example Barbara Frischmuth's *Die Frau im Mond* (The Woman in the Moon): "Come, says Colombina, let us fly, and the panther spreads an invisible sail. While they fly along in the breath of the storm the city, strictly separated into quarters, lies beneath them. Only the branches of the trees soften the hard contours every once in a while."[30]

Jewish authors view the countryside with even greater trepidation than the city. They associate rural Austria with concentration camps – Mauthausen and Ebensee – and portray the rural population with a mixture of fear and contempt, for example, Robert Menasse's *Schubumkehr* (Reversal).[31] The very images that evoke a wholesome natural life in the works of Gentiles, suggest the opposite in Jewish texts. Elfriede

Jelinek's *Die Kinder der Toten* (The Children of the Dead) is a case in point. The novel immediately establishes a Jewish reference point through the Hebrew invocation preceding the text ("Let them come, Spirits of the Dead that were not seen for years, and bless their children").[32] The allusions to the past are indirect, but obvious. Images reminiscent of the Holocaust pervade the book, as do the allusions to guilt and destruction: "So much nature has been bestowed upon this country that, perhaps in order to repay its debt to nature, it has always treated its people rather carelessly" (14).

In *Die Kinder der Toten*, the *Bucklige Welt*, a hilly area southeast of Vienna, a popular vacation area, serves as the setting of a narrative about vampires and other undead. An inviting Austrian inn turns out to be a secret murder site, a scene of serial killings. There could be no greater contrast than between Jelinek's view of rural Austria and that of Barbara Frischmuth. Without idealizing it, Frischmuth configures the country as a refuge that offers respite from some of civilization's constraints, e.g., *Die Mystifikationen der Sophie Silber* (The Mystifications of Sophie Silber) and *Die Ferienfamilie* (The Vacation Family). She similarly depicts the open spaces of the Vienna Stadtpark in *Kai und die Liebe zu Modellen* (Kai or the Love of Models).[33] By contrast, Jelinek's *Die Ausgesperrten (Wonderful, Wonderful Times)* associates the Stadtpark with the lawlessness of the postwar era, black market and prostitution activities, and Seelich makes it the setting of an uneasy rendezvous between the daughter of Holocaust survivors and the son of a Nazi doctor in *Kieselsteine*.[34]

Schindel is intimately familiar with these works and addresses similar problems in *Gebürtig*, namely, how to relate to Austria and the Austrians. Most Jewish and Jewish-identified authors articulate their alienation from "the Austrians," but are also unwilling or unable to embrace a traditional Jewish life. Some began only recently to deal with their Jewish background, e.g., Mitgutsch and Henisch, and face the task of inventing their own Austrian-Jewish identity. Others grew up with an awareness of their Jewish identity and turned to Austrian Jewish literature for role models. This literary tradition, almost destroyed by the Nazis, continued to be repressed in the school curricula after the war. Beckermann describes the "secret book treasure," the literary canon which she and her friends acquired as forbidden reading during physics and chemistry classes:

First came Schnitzler and Zweig. Also they were secret allies against the daily infamy of the old and young, against the crucifix on the classroom wall and the rod in the bag. No matter how different our chosen writers were, they named the stale atmosphere we felt without being able to express it. Schnitzler discussed everything that mattered to us in his drama *Professor Bernhardi* and particularly in his novel *Der Weg ins Freie* ... then came Sartre. His essay about the Jewish questions was new – and he spoke to us. To us as Jews ... We did not understand the sentences of Sarte, Améry, and Camus, but we did understand that their texts had something to do with our feelings of being thrown into an existence without an emotional safety net. We understood Améry when he equated the loss of his home country with the loss of certainty.[35]

From their own experience and from this literature the Jewish postwar intelligentsia constructed their perception of Austria as a nation of anti--Semites. They took issue with the Gentile public who repressed and denied their Nazi past. They portrayed them as perpetrators who continued to adhere to Nazi principles, e.g., the Witkowskis in Jelinek's *Die Ausgesperrten*, as hedonists without a conscience, e.g., Seelich's *Kieselsteine*, or showed Austria as a treacherous country, always at the verge of extremism. None of these authors placed stock in the democratic structures of the Second Republic. Rather, they pointed out the Austrians' lack of remorse about their participation in the Holocaust. They exposed the Austrian's refusal to make proper restitutions, made public the attacks on Jewish life and property since the postwar era. They debated Kurt Waldheim's presidential campaign and his involvement in the deportations of Jews. They publicized the threat to Jews and other minorities by Jörg Haider's FPÖ and right-wing or neo-Nazi militias. They criticized Austrian industry for providing Arab countries with weapons and poison gas and decried their government's persistent refusal to surrender property confiscated from Jewish owners during the Nazi era. They took issue with the gentrification and commercialization of Aryanized real estate in former Jewish quarters and decried the appropriation of Vienna's Jewish history for the tourist industry and as a lucrative intellectual and academic export article. In other words: they acted as Austria's conscience. The majority of Jewish intellectuals in

Austria live with the awareness of Austrian guilt. They view their lives in Austria as tenuous and transitory. Most of them considered and tried other alternatives – the United States, Israel, France, Germany, and Eastern Europe – and are prepared to make a quick exit, if the need arises. Matti Bunzl writes that "in the context of an explicitly anti-Semitic social field" Jewish narratives emerge as "active forms of resistance. While they ultimately reify – and thereby reproduce – the structured dichotomy between 'Jews' and 'Austrians' from which they emerge, they do so by destabilizing the constitutive valuations underlying the nationalizing fiction of genuine Austrianness. Neither the latter element nor the tensions arising from a sense of threat and instability underlying the works of Jewish-identified authors characterizes the works of Austrian Gentile authors, even those profoundly critical of their native country, Bernhard, Handke, Haslinger, and Mitterer.

Schindel's novel is an exception in that it thematizes a Jewish man's attempt to overcome his alienation, both on the protagonist's level and in terms of the narrative scope. Like Menasse's protagonist in *Schubumkehr*, Schindel's main character also ventures into rural Austria. In Menasse this move engenders an extreme narrowing of the narrator's perspective, but Schindel remains in command of his numerous plots and a complex cast of characters. Moreover, the successful romance between a Jew and a Gentile suggests that it is possible for a Jew to overcome the legacy of the past. Danny enters into his lover's world, her culture and her family. He is accepted by Christine's children and he accepts them. Other encounters in Schindel's narrative lead to similar results: former Nazis learn to interact with Holocaust survivors, and the children of both groups with one another. These contacts occur without ending in near-catastrophes such as the rape in Seelich's *Kieselsteine*. Nor do they lead to the radical individualism and the isolation implied in the endings of Seelich's and Beckermann's films. Schindel suggests that it is possible to overcome the Nazi legacy, first on the level of sexual attraction, then by personal commitment and love. These prove stronger than history, tradition, and politics. To be sure, his solution is personal and private.

In *Gebürtig* the relationship between Jews and Gentiles is in constant flux and the characters multifaceted. They are made up of many characteristics, among them cultural and national identity. These are, however, not the most important facets of Schindel's protagonists. Thus it is possible for the son of a Nazi henchman to suddenly face up to his past, and for the children of Jewish victims to leave their urban coffee houses, restaurants, and party circles. The Austria Schindel shows is open to Jews and Gentiles, a country where a complex multicultural society has the chance to evolve. The options open to Schindel's protagonists run the gamut from assimilation to Jewish separatism, from a religious to a secular existence. Jews who overcome their fears of Gentile society can, in the context of Schindel's novel, live everywhere. This includes not only Austria, but the entire European spectrum that unfolds in his novel, and the world.

The intertextualities with turn-of-the-century and interwar authors that are also present in the themes and issues taken up in Schindel's work suggest a continuity of Austrian Jewish life which in actuality does not exist.[36] Although contemporary Jewish writers write about similar ways of defining and situating themselves within their environment as did authors of earlier generations, their mindset is separated from that of their models by the history of the Shoah. Superficially it may appear that Schindel, and for that matter, Seelich and Beckermann, ponder the same options that Egon Schwarz identifies in conjunction with Schnitzler's *Der Weg ins Freie* (*The Open Road*). Schwarz summarizes the attitudes among turn of the century Viennese Jews: the "successful businessman's clinging to his Judaism in the face of his family's embarrassment," the "son who flirts with an aristocratic lifestyle and conversion," "the Jew who joins the Social Democrats," "the upright Jews without illusions." "But in the end," Schwarz states, "it all boils down to a clash of ideas between those who would emigrate in order to establish a Jewish national home in Palestine and those who would stay where they are, namely in their beloved Vienna." [37] Schwarz also mentions Jewish self-hatred and self-denial, both of which were already explored and discussed during the pre-Nazi era.

All of these approaches to configure Jewish identity are reflected in contemporary literature and films by Jewish authors, and the presence of these themes suggests a continuity between yesterday's and today's Jewish culture. There is, indeed, such a continuity, but it is text-based rather being the expression of a multi-generational community experience. Neither the bookburnings and the continued suppression of Jewish literature prevented persons in search of their Jewish background from searching for the lost tradition and identifying themselves through Austrian Jewish writings of the past. Connecting to the disrupted and defamed legacy enabled them to express their sense of alienation and to formulate their oppositional points of view, thereby validating on their own terms the dissimilation process that evolved from racist anti-Semitism.

After Nazism had put an end to the soon-to-be completed Austrian-Jewish symbiosis, it was to take more than a generation to acknowledge, comprehend, and articulate the finality of the destruction. For the most part, the prewar generations did not succeed in making an intellectual and emotional break from the past because those who continued to maintain relations with Austria were incapable or unwilling to face the full extent of the destruction. Those who did often disassociated themselves from their native culture and often language. Paul Celan, Jean Améry, and Bruno Bettelheim, who tried to live with the full knowledge and awareness of the disasters of the Shoah, ended up committing suicide. Others, refusing to relinquish the values of their younger years, tried to transpose those values and philosophies into postwar reality, or they looked back in mourning, doubting that a new beginning was possible for them.

Only the post-Shoah generation was in a position to forge a new cultural tradition which reflects the past without being paralyzed by guilt and mourning. Both aggressive and introspective, their works convey the experience of a small exclusive community and the subjective insights of individuals. Their texts participate in the larger literary production and shape it as well. At the same time, these authors are and want to remain distinct, autonomous, and unassimilated. Works such as Schindel's novel, however, as well as Menasse's fiction and, most recently, Doron Rabinovici's cosmopolitan post-Shoah detective novel *Suche nach M. (Search for M.)* reveal the many levels on which Jewish and non-Jewish reality intersect on a global as well as on an Austrian scale,[38] thereby suggesting not only the necessity, but also the likelihood that the children of the victims and those of the perpetrators must and will continue to communicate: Both of them participate in the culture of the present and shape the culture of the future.

University of Illinois at Chicago

Notes

1. Marsha L. Rozenblit, *The Jews of Vienna 1867-1914. Assimilation and Identity* (Albany: State University of New York Press, 1983), 14, 194-195.
2. Elias Canetti, *Die gerettete Zunge. Geschichte einer Jugend* (Frankfurt am Main: Fischer, 1984), 31.
3. Egon Schwarz, "Jews and Anti-Semitism in Fin-de-Siècle Vienna," *Insiders and Outsiders. Jewish and Gentile Culture in Germany and Austria*, eds. Dagmar C. G. Lorenz and Gabriele Weinberger (Detroit: Wayne State University Press, 1994), 47-66. Here, 64.
4. Ruth Beckermann, *Unzugehörig: Österreicher und Juden nach 1945* (Wien: Löcker, 1989), 65. "In Österreich durften die Juden, wenn sie brav und still waren, vielleicht wieder leben – allerdings, wie Bundeskanzler Figl betonte, als Österreicher, nicht als Juden."
5. Sander L. Gilman, *Jews in Today's German Culture* (Bloomington and Indianapolis: Indiana University Press, 1993), 69.
6. For example Hilde Spiel comments on her experience with anti-Semitic aggression on the part of Austrian intellectuals in "Ich lebe gern in Österreich." *In meinem Garten schlendernd* (München: Nymphenburger Verlagsanstalt, 1981), 17-21. Here, 20.
7. This is the case in Elisabeth Freundlich, *Der Seelenvogel* (Wien: Paul Zsolnay, 1986) as well as in Benedikt Kautsky's much earlier *Teufel und Verdammte: Erfahrungen und Erkenntnisse aus sieben Jahren in deutschen Konzentrationslagern* (Zürich: Büchergilde Gutenberg, 1946).
8. Hans Weigel, *Man kann nicht ruhig darüber reden* (Graz: Styria, 1986), 117-141.
9. Simon Wiesenthal. "The Waldheim Case." *Justice not Vengeance*. Translated by Ewald Osers (London: Weidenfeld and Nicolson, 1989), 310-322.
10. *Kieselsteine*, script Nadja Seelich, dir. Lukas Stepanik. cinéart, Filmverleih Hans Peter Hofmann, 1982.
11. Ruth Beckermann, *Unzugehörig. Österreicher und Juden nach 1945* (Wien: Löcker, 1989), 17ff.
12. Robert Schindel, *Gebürtig* (Frankfurt: Shrkamp, 1992).
13. Matti Bunzl, "The city and the Self: Narratives of Spatial Belonging Among Austrian Jews," *City and Society* (1996), 50-81. Here, 77.

14. One character, Emanuel Katz, the son of an Auschwitz survivor, has served for years as the "overflow tank" for his family's melancholy. He joins Vienna's intelligentsia, studies Holocaust literature, shaves off his beard, becomes a writer, and begins to date blonde women, denying, however that "... he wanted to bleach himself blonde by keeping company with such women" (Schindel, 29). In turn blonde Käthe, Katz's lover, considers his nose a racial characteristic, and he points out "... while kissing her ... that this was no racial characteristic and that Jews were not a race, etc. She had heard this from her grandmother, she explained thereupon" (137).

15. Robert Schindel, *Born – Where*. Translated by Michael Roloff (Riverside: Ariadne Press, 1992).

16. Herman Wouk, director, *War and Remembrance*. New York: ABC Video 1988.

17. Hugo Bettauer, *Die Stadt ohne Juden: Ein Roman von Übermorgen* (Frankfurt am Main: Ullstein, 1988).

18. Hugo Bettauer, *Die Stadt ohne Juden* was first published in 1925; Friedrich Torberg, *Die Tante Jolesch oder Der Untergang des Abendlandes in Anekdoten* (München: dtv, 1977), 80.

19. Sander Gilman and Karen Remmler, eds. *Reemerging Jewish Culture in Germany: Life and Literature since 1989* (New York and London: New York University Press, 1994) convincingly discuss the reemergence of a Jewish literature in Germany. The same applies to Austria.

20. Ruth Beckermann, director *Die papierene Brücke*. (Wien: filmladen, 1987).

21. Megan Huber, "Peter and the Wolves," *The Jerusalem Report*, November 28, 1996, 24-27.

22. Hans Thalberg, *Von der Kunst, Österreicher zu sein* (Wien: Böhlau, 1984), 460.

23. Sander L. Gilman, *Jewish Self-Hatred. Anti-Semitism and the Hidden Language of the Jews* (Baltimore & London: Johns Hopkins University Press, 1986).

24. "In the words of one student of German attitudes during the Nazi period, 'to be an anti-Semite in Hitler's Germany was so commonplace as to go practically unnoticed.' Notions fundamental to the dominant worldview and operation of a society, precisely because they are taken for granted, often are not expressed in a manner commensurate

with their prominence and significance or, when uttered, seen as worthy by others to be noted and recorded." Daniel Jonah Goldhagen, *Hitler's Willing Executioners. Ordinary Germans and the Holocaust* (New York: Alfred A. Knopf, 1966), 32.

25. Sander Gilman, "Jüdische Literaten und deutsche Literatur. Antisemitismus und die verborgene Sprache der Juden am Beispiel von Jurek Becker und Edgar Hilsenrath," *Zeitschrift für deutsche Philologie*, 107/2 (1988), 269-294, applies the designation "Jewish author" to anyone who, labeled as Jewish, responds to this definition in his or her literary production. Steven Beller considers assimilation and conversion as a part of Jewish history, even if the goal of the assimilationists is to become non-Jews. According to Beller, Hofmannsthal and Wittgenstein – neither one Jewish by religion and by origin only in part – belong to an identifiable group with special social characteristics. He mentions that until 1909 all psychoanalysts were Jewish and that Renner was the only non-Jewish Austromarxist. Steven Beller, "Class Culture and the Jews of Vienna, 1900," *Jews, Antisemitism and Culture in Vienna*, ed. Oxaal, Pollak, Botz (London: Methuen, 1987), 42. According to Clara Pomeranz Carmely, those who distanced themselves from Judaism and those who did not share one fact in common: the Gentile environment identifies them as Jewish – assimilation is ultimately not a matter of an individual decision. Klara Pomeranz Carmely, *Das Identitätsproblem jüdischer Autoren im deutschen Sprachraum. Von der Jahrhundertwende bis zu Hitler* (Königstein: Scriptor, 1981).

26. Ilse Aichinger, "Ortsanfang," *Verschenkter Rat* (Frankfurt: Fischer, 1978), 42. "I have no confidence in the piece, / in the neighbors, the rose hedges, / the whispered word. // I heard that they put skins against the sling, / that they overturn benches before the start of winter, / that their hoorays fill the air . . ." (translation by D. Lorenz).

27. Klaus Khittl, "Warum ich Wien verlasse," *Wochenpresse* 51 (1982), 39.

28. As in Aichinger's poem "Winter, gemalt": "Und in den weißen Röcken im Schnee die Österreicher . . ." *Verschenkter Rat*, 39, and Beckermann's chapter "Juden und Österreicher," *Unzugehörig*, 17.

29. Barbara Frischmuth, *Die Frau im Mond* (Salzburg: Residenz, 1982), 110.

30. Robert Menasse, *Schubumkehr* (Salzburg: Residenz, 1995).

31. Translation by Neil Jacobs.

32. Elfriede Jelinek, *Die Kinder der Toten* (Reinbek: Rowohlt, 1995), 7.

33. Barbara Frischmuth, *Kai und die Liebe zu Modellen* (Salzburg: Residenz: 1979).

34. Elfriede Jelinek, *Die Ausgesperrten* (Reinbek: Rowohlt, 1985).

35. Ruth Beckermann, "Jean Améry and Austria," *Insiders and Outsiders: Jewish and Gentile Culture in Germany and Austria* (Detroit: Wayne State University Press, 1993), 73-88. Here, 73-74.

36. Marsha Rozenblit, *The Jews of Vienna, 1867-1914: Assimilation and Identity* (Albany: State University of New York Press, 1983), 1, writes: "Vienna has also become a symbol of the ability of Jews to participate in German culture, and to play a leading role in its avant-garde."

37. Theodor Lessing, *Der jüdische Selbsthaß* (Berlin: Jüdischer Verlag, 1930). Egon Schwarz, "Jews and Anti-Semitism in Fin-de-Siècle Vienna," *Insiders and Outsiders. Jewish and Gentile Culture in Germany and Austria*, 60-61.

38. Doron Rabinovici, *Suche nach M.* (Frankfurt am Main: Suhrkamp, 1997).

Robert Menasse's Concept of Anti-*Heimat* Literature

Michael P. Olson

Few other Austrians in the 1990s have led the cultural and historical discussion about Austria in as sustained and compelling a fashion as Robert Menasse. When Austria featured its national book trade at the Frankfurt Book Fair in October 1995, Menasse opened the Fair as the keynote speaker.[1] A recent piece in the Austrian magazine *Profil* (Profile) identified the movers and shakers in Austria today; under the rubric for literature was none other than Robert Menasse. Menasse is, the article stated, "the right man for important matters."[2] And readers of the Viennese weekly *Falter* (Butterfly) and other Austrian newspapers already recognize Menasse as a regular commentator on national and regional affairs, or as an increasingly frequent subject for discussion.[3]

For Robert Menasse, what it is to *be Austrian* is decidedly unique, and it is his singular description of an indigenous form of Austrian literature known as *Anti-Heimat-Literatur* (anti-provincial literature) which I shall address in this paper. Menasse returns again and again to the geopolitical aspect of literature in his theoretical works by referring to concepts such as *Heimat*, *Nationalliteratur* (national literature), and *Stadtroman* (city novel). Partly because the Second Republic was so late in developing in contrast to its peer nation-states in the West, according to Menasse, an understanding of what it is to *be Austrian* and what it is to *write Austrian literature* is difficult to describe in purely theoretical terms. However, representations of the terms just mentioned are possible to determine if concrete examples are provided. In Menasse's novels, the self-described trilogy consisting of *Sinnliche Gewißheit* (Sensual Certainty, 1988), *Selige Zeiten, brüchige Welt* (Blissful Times, Fragile World, 1991), and *Schubumkehr* (Implosion, 1995), Menasse weighs in with his own notion of what literature can offer in the present age.[4] This article focuses on Menasse's theoretical essays rather than on his novels and combines an analysis of these works with discussions I had with Menasse in Vienna in October 1996 and in New York City in January 1997.

The working definition of *Heimat* for this paper is taken from a composite of meanings. According to Karl-Heinz Hillmann's *Wörterbuch der Soziologie* (Dictionary of Sociology, 1994), the term signifies "a territorial unit to which a person feels especially attached."[5] Similarly, in the *Soziologie-Lexikon* (Encyclopedia of Sociology, 1991), edited by Gerd Reinhold and others, it is defined as "a geographical area, usually identified with a nation-state, to which someone feels especially attached."[6] The one source to whom we might best turn is Donald Daviau, who introduces a recent issue of *Modern Austrian Literature*, a special issue on *Heimat*, with the following:

> The term "Heimat" remains one of those concepts that are difficult to define precisely because it involves emotional rather than logical concepts. . . . In simplest terms "Heimat" means the place where one feels most comfortable, relaxed, and at home. It might be the locale where one was born, but it can also be another adopted place. The choice can be quite arbitrary since it is based totally on feeling rather than on reason.[7]

The more one tries to define *Heimat*, the more one gets into trouble. For this reason my own definition is very simple: *Heimat* is *a person's attachment to a specific area*. As frequently as the term *Heimat* is bandied about, it is worth noting that everyone does not agree on any one definition, and of course the term has many subtle nuances depending on context – for example, the differentiated use of *Heimat* by Austrian politicians during the 1994 federal election.[8]

The first point to be made about Menasse's preoccupation with the term *Heimat* is that Austrians, in his opinion, have shown little attachment to the Second Republic. "Austria is a nation but not a *Heimat*," he says in leading off Chapter 8 of *Das Land ohne Eigenschaften* (The Country Without Characteristics), his most central discussion regarding *Heimat*.[9] Menasse continues:

> Nation without *Heimat*.
> Certainly it's not an accident that the so-called anti-*Heimat* literature was created in Austria as an indepen-

dent, new, literary genre, without an international equivalent. Austria is the anti-*Heimat* par excellence. Yet anti-*Heimat* literature isn't only an independent Austrian genre; above all, it's also the most important, dominant form of literature in the Second Republic.¹⁰

Menasse then cites nineteen Austrian authors ("to mention just a few"), all practitioners of anti-*Heimat* literature who comprise a veritable Who's Who of Modern Austrian Literature: Hans Lebert, Gerhard Fritsch, Peter Handke, Thomas Bernhard, Gert Jonke, Alfred Kolleritsch, Alois Brandstetter, Gernot Wolfgruber, Max Maetz, Peter Turrini, Elfriede Jelinek, Marie-Thérèse Kerschbaumer, Wilhelm Pevny, Michael Scharang, Franz Innerhofer, Klaus Hoffer, Josef Winkler, Marianne Gruber, and Norbert Gstrein.¹¹

Menasse fundamentally agrees with Sigrid Löffler about the current obsession with the development of the negation of *Heimat* in Austrian literature. It began, according to Löffler, in H. C. Artmann's Viennese dialect poetry and continued with the anti-*Heimat* novels of Thomas Bernhard, Elfriede Jelinek, Franz Innerhofer, and Menasse himself. In these examples *Heimat* represents an alien nation; it is a metaphor for what Löffler calls "the dark atavism and backwardness of rural, lower middle-class Austria."¹² According to Menasse, the Austrian authors' collective conflict with *Heimat* – their hatred of *Heimat* and their impatient criticism of its image – is unique. This specific form of *Heimat* in Austrian literature is a symptom, according to Menasse, of the societal makeup of Austria today – a makeup which, in political terms, works its way down from the Haiders and the Waldheims, and also from the Vranitzkys and Klimas, down to communal politicians of far lesser renown.

Part of that societal makeup is also literary, of course, and has to do with the fact that Austrian authors writing immediately after 1945 lacked role models or beneficent mentors. Menasse notes that few writers of any standing remained in Austria at the conclusion of World War II. Richard Beer-Hofmann, Robert Musil, and Franz Werfel died in exile. Hermann Broch, Elias Canetti, Johannes Urzidil, Albert Ehrenstein, and Erich Fried never returned to Austria from England or America. The one grand man of letters who remained, Alexander Lernet-Holenia, alone constituted the world of contemporary Austrian literature. In short, as Hans Weigel said in 1948: "Austrian literature at present consists of two authors: Lernet and

Holenia."[13] Indeed, recent studies have reconfirmed the point made by Gerhard Fritsch: Austria had no Wolfgang Borchert and no Gruppe 47.[14] Austrian writers who looked to the Gruppe 47 for encouragement were sometimes viewed with suspicion by the German literary establishment as expatriates seduced by the prospect of success in Germany (Ingeborg Bachmann, Ilse Aichinger, Herbert Eisenreich) or provocateurs (Milo Dor, Reinhard Federmann). Working on their own, then, Austrian writers turned to topics other than fascism and war as they affected Austria during the Second World War. According to Menasse, "No country has publicly questioned itself and fundamentally reflected upon itself as little as Austria's Second Republic."[15]

Many of these writers turned to treatments of what Menasse derisively calls *das flache Land* (the flat countryside). In another phenomenon that is not at all coincidental with the phenomenon of *das flache Land*, Menasse states that another type of fiction, the Austrian city novel, has not been written since Heimito von Doderer[16] – at least not a city novel such as Tom Wolfe's *The Bonfire of the Vanities* in which Wolfe's New Yorkers glide effortlessly within their own social class and from one class to another. Such a novel not only takes place in an identifiable city. It evokes New York as a key conditioning factor in the protagonists' varying behavior. Since Doderer, Menasse argues, there has been no true Vienna novel, no true Graz or Klagenfurt novel, not even, he adds mischievously, a true Bludenz novel. Menasse certainly knows the works of his colleagues well enough to know that, for example, Elfriede Jelinek's novels, in a literal sense, are Vienna novels, and that much of Thomas Bernhard's work treats Austrian cities and towns (sometimes in excruciating detail). These examples are not, however, city novels as Menasse defines them: they feature neither the city nor its urban life, nor the city's various societal levels – as the primary focus of the work. To take just one example, Bernhard's Salzburg, according to Menasse, deals less with an encompassing description of the city than with a protagonist's very personal problems with Salzburg.

Menasse is clear when talking about the requisites for exemplary literature: it must be different and it must be natural. First, difference: Change is an essential requirement of any decent writer, according to Menasse – change both in narrative technique and literary content. He mocks authors such as Peter Handke who cannot, or choose not to, change and develop their craft. As much as Handke's first five or six works impressed Menasse (because they were so varied), Menasse stopped reading Handke as soon as Handke stopped being original. Menasse distinguishes Handke's later work from that of Thomas Bernhard. Bernhard's œuvre is essentially one and the same book, according to Menasse, yet Bernhard develops his œuvre by increasingly radicalizing each successive work. Bernhard's œuvre is therefore continually dialectic, while Handke's remained static after his first half-dozen books.

Second, naturalness: Menasse does not try to determine whether a national literature is more "national" or less "national" than the literature of another nation. His question is always whether any work of literature is sufficiently transcendental to qualify as world literature. James Joyce's *Ulysses* is an example of both Irish literature and world literature, according to Menasse: national literature for the Irish, world literature for the non-Irish who frankly do not care to what extent the novel is "typically Irish." *Ulysses* has retained the status of world literature because it continues to interest a sufficient number of international readers. However, one may fairly ask the following, as Joseph O'Connor did: to what extent is the "Irish national literature" still purchased in Ireland? Sales from a recent twelve-month period, such as they were, from one of the largest bookstores in Dublin showed that twenty copies of Joyce's *Ulysses* were sold; *A Portrait of a Young Artist*, twelve copies sold; *Dubliners*, seven; *Finnegans Wake*, zero (!).[17] Presumably Menasse would rather write (and see colleagues he favors write) transcendental literature that sells, internationally and domestically.

To take another example of natural literature: when Menasse reads Philip Roth's *Portnoy's Complaint*, he does not ask "To what extent is this work typical of American literature?" What concerns him are the work's moments of connection, such as the parents talking to each other in *Portnoy's Complaint*, which reminds Menasse of his own grandparents talking to each other. A writer's remaining true to his or her own identity is a crucial component of many examples of world literature, as the naturalness contained therein allows for the best chance of evoking the human, universal attributes that attract an international readership.

Thus follows Menasse's contention that the best Austrian literature written in the Second Republic is comprised of anti-*Heimat* literature, literature both innovative and depicting accurately what it attempts to depict (even if that depiction skewers, often in the most acerbic manner, what is believed to be the cliché-ridden conceits of earlier *Heimat* literature). The worst Austrian literature would be the dozens of novels written by authors who live in the country and provinces, like Bludenz – and yet who do not write about Bludenz. This last point is important. For Menasse, Bludenz symbolizes Austria as much as any other area of Austria, except Vienna. Vienna is the lone metropolis; all other cities, towns, and villages fall under the rubric of *das flache Land*. Specimens of *Heimat* literature are inauthentic and all too similar to each other, thus Menasse and other practitioners of anti-*Heimat* literature counter, as the name obviously implies, with a contrary literary mode.

Menasse's theoretical likes and dislikes coincide with his own practice. Since he theoretically dislikes repetitive literature, he avoids writing it himself. His three novels – *Sinnliche Gewißheit*, *Selige Zeiten, brüchige Welt*, and *Schubumkehr* – are three independent parts of a whole, each differentiated from the other two in form and content. His trilogy is meant to be read as volumes independent of each other, as if each novel were a self-contained episode of a TV soap opera. Menasse practices what he preaches in his most recent novel, *Schubumkehr*. Since Renate Posthofen has presented a detailed analysis of *Schubumkehr*,[18] I do not want to provide another interpretation but only to redirect attention to the term "Schubumkehr." Menasse appropriated the term from Niki Lauda, applying a specific technical term from aviation to a general historical moment. "Schubumkehr" occurs during an airplane catastrophe when the plane implodes because of conflicting directional forces. Menasse uses the term in his novel as a metaphor of simultaneous forward and backward motion in the period since 1989. For Menasse, the opening of the Iron Curtain and the fall of communism in many parts of Europe were forward-moving historical moments. During the same period we have seen an increase in nationalism, chauvinism, and religious wars in the same region; these are regressive moments. The simultaneity of progress and regression, then, is at the root of *Schubumkehr*. The novel is at once highly contemporary but also timeless, evoking tropes of literature with which we are all familiar as Menasse situates them anew. It is worth noting that the term "Schubumkehr" has not only been used by Menasse to represent Europe since 1989, but also by Wendelin Schmidt-Dengler, Menasse's Ph.D. dissertation supervisor, to describe contemporary Austrian literature.[19] The best and most interesting Austrian writers of today (writers of anti-*Heimat* literature, it goes almost without saying) all practice their own literary implosion: they challenge existing forms and content, and in so doing ask the reader to reassess received and conventional wisdom. If, in the process, its own type of implosion occurs due to the antidirectional forces of writer and reader imbued in the reader's misunderstanding the writer's intent, so be it. However, the process from (1) a writer taking an idea and crafting it into a finished, published work of fiction, to (2) another person reading the fiction and – ideally, at least – acting on what has been read, can be doubly dialectic: both the writer and the reader have become significantly changed, presumably better selves. And this dialectical process is exactly what Menasse and, I would suggest, many practioners of anti-*Heimat* literature strive for.

Menasse is neither disingenuous nor does he intentionally misread fundamental and crucial aspects of contemporary Austrian literature. Rather, Menasse's comments – about literary theory, his own work, and the work of his peers – all need to be understood for what they are: comments interwoven with recent political developments at federal and local levels of government. Conflict between writers and politicians is a natural process in Austria, according to Menasse. If there were no conflicts, the writers would be no more and no less than court poets. Menasse is, in Vienna if not in all of Austria, an outstanding recent example of an engaged writer, one willing to spar publicly, in print and face to face, with the powers that be. He is a descendant of Karl Kraus's *Nörgler* (grumbler) and Thomas Bernhard's *Störenfried* (troublemaker). Menasse is not only in favor of literary contrariness; he is also a contrary voice in politics, when the moments are right. A "right moment" occurred in Vienna in the autumn of 1996, when Menasse and other writers protested the tax rate imposed on writers who received literary prizes and stipends. This example again showed Menasse practicing what he preaches – being politically engaged, finding possibilities and opportunities to enter into constructive dialog with opposing forces. If, as the president of Germany, Roman Herzog, maintained recently,[20] Germanists need to become more politically engaged, Menasse would maintain that writers also need to be politically engaged, but only if they pick the spots where action has a real chance of effecting progress. If the protest cannot result in any change, then Menasse would rather not participate. He cites two examples where he would rather opt out: one facetious (asking him to participate in a would-be debate on bicycle paths), the other more serious (his unwillingness to help solve the problem of the German spelling reform; many other writers have participated in this debate).[21] Contrariness is for Menasse, as it has been for so many other artists, a prerequisite for becoming and remaining an artist.

The political arena comes right back around to anti-*Heimat* literature. A few quotations bring Menasse's ultimate concern into greater relief. First, in Thomas Bernhard's *Wittgensteins Neffe* (Wittgenstein's Nephew) there is an amusing, if slightly unsettling passage where the narrator, a quasi-autobiographical protagonist, sits unobserved in the middle of the audience as he awaits the presentation of the Grillparzer Prize to himself. The Grillparzer Prizewinner sits and sits without saying a thing, while the dignitaries and the audience become increasingly impatient. Finally, a cultural minister asks: "So where is the writer?"[22] (If the minister had said *Dichter* for "writer," this would have been offensive enough, but he says the even more condescending *Dichterling*.) The second quote is by Alfred A. Knopf, Thomas Mann's American publisher, who once said to Mann with some exacerbation: "You're a Dichter, so dicht!"[23] Menasse, like Bernhard, wants to be a *Dichter*, not a neutralized, patronized *Dichterling*. And like Mann, Menasse wants to be a *Dichter*, and also "dicht"; Menasse needs to be politically engaged.

So, in Menasse's view, how does a *Dichter* do more than "dicht?" If the writer resides in Austria, he or she writes anti-*Heimat* literature, which by definition is intended both to challenge and provoke literary conventions, and to thumb one's nose at the governing bureaucrats and apparatchiks. In other words, that writer is a constructive contrarian – contrary, when it serves a purpose, both with respect to literary matters and to politics in Austria today. Menasse's view of engaged intellectuals, including producers of literature, is that they are meant to comprehend the time and place in which they live. Without naming names, Menasse disparages unengaged authors who, living in the country, write about Barcelona as if they lived in the nineteenth century, writers of altogether different mentalities and different temperaments than practicioners of anti-*Heimat* literature.

Menasse takes a dialectician's tack and not an obstructionist's. It is worth emphasizing that he is not an unrepentant grouch. In his view, for example, Austrians had every right to celebrate "1000 Years of Austria" in 1996, even if the manner of celebration formally decided upon at governmental levels displeased him. His suggestion for an ideal celebration would have been to stage a massive parade on the Ringstraße, which would have included the national dress of every nation in the world. In this way, Menasse suggested, Austrians would have utilized the opportunity to increase their tolerance toward, and indeed love for, non-nationals. Thoughts by Dagmar Lorenz are very apt in this regard. In an article entitled "Austrian Authors and the Dilemma of Identity," she reckoned with the beneficial possibilities of anti-*Heimat* literature, a body of work which (ostensibly, at least) is both negative and negating. She stated that "many of the currently discredited and repressed Austrian discourses do offer alternatives to the confining paradigms associated with *Heimat, Volk* (people), and *Vaterland* (fatherland). Austria's cosmopolitan and multinational tradition, based on enlightened thought and critical intelligence, is waiting to be rediscovered."[24] To be critical is to acknowledge the historical realities; to be uncritical is to hang on to history's clichés. The problem in 1996, according to Menasse, was that short-sighted bureaucrats worried not about how best to celebrate the Austrian millennium amid the post-1989 historical realities (or those of post-1955, post-1945, post-1938, etc.), but about how best to cultivate the image of the chocolate delicacies known as *Mozartkugeln*. One is reminded of the lecture series held in Vienna on 21 March 1994 which concentrated on the then-current image of Austria. The title of the event also expressed the concern: *Sind wir alle Mozartkugeln?* (Are we all *Mozartkugeln?*)[25]

Menasse is impatient with leading Austrian politicians who seem not to acknowledge the diversity of Austria in the 1990s. It is frankly easy to understand his sentiment. In the summer of 1997 Jörg Haider attended a six-week seminar organized by the Institute for International Development at Harvard University. Many of the fifty students came from developing countries such as Zimbabwe and Ghana; several wore sandals and dashikis. Haider, for his part at the seminar, chose neither to adapt the African clothing, nor did he wear a formal suit as he typically would as the head of the Austrian Freedom Party. Instead, Haider appropriated American culture: eating lunch (hamburger and french fries) from a styrofoam take-away container; waving an American flag twice his size; modeling two different Harvard T-shirts; and wearing shorts and Nike running shoes.[26] Haider's remarks on Austria and the difference between Austria and the United States were telling. Austria, according to Haider, is an "underdeveloped democracy." Moreover, "in Austria essentially everything is forbidden which is not explicitly permitted; in America essentially everything is permitted which is not explicitly forbidden."[27] In light of Haider's opinions it is no wonder that he chose to reject his own culture in favor of another. With Austrians like Haider, who needs Americans?

Mozartkugeln, college T-shirts, Nike gear, burgers and fries – like it or not, modern life in much of the world is reduced to such clichés. However, constantly griping about these and other supposed woes, without positing solutions to them, is an exercise which does not interest Menasse in the least. In this sense, his embracement of anti-*Heimat* literature is not an endorsement of what may be called *Jammerliteratur* (literature of complaint). An example of what I mean begins with a joke by the soccer coach Max Merkel, who was once asked about Austria:

> *Interviewer*: What's the matter with Austria?
> *Merkel*: A person could talk about that for a week. Instead you should ask what's good about Austria.
> *Interviewer*: What's good about Austria?
> *Merkel*: Absolutely nothing.[28]

Menasse would claim that contemporary Austrian literature is more than merely a literature of complaint without alternatives. Rather, it is above all analytical literature, basing itself on the fact that, in Menasse's words, *Heimat* has been taken away from (or in Haider's case at Harvard, rejected by) Austrians. Menasse quotes a sentence of Cheryl Berard and Edith Schlaffer: "Austria is a developing country with a few modern big cities."[29] Menasse would agree to a point, but he would rather maintain that Austria is a Disneyland, a country where tourism creates an inauthentic environment and dubious marketing schemes flourish. *Heimat* has become nothing more than another façade. Austria's problem, Menasse summarizes, is ultimately the complete destruction of its authenticity. The project of Menasse and like-minded Austrians is to render and reflect these realities, all the while striving for *Sein* (reality) and not *Schein* (appearance), for naturalness and not façade – in short, to bring Austria back into Austrian literature and in so doing, to depict protagonists and experiences with which readers everywhere can empathize.

Harvard University

Notes

1. The speech is located in Robert Menasse, *Hysterien und andere historische Irrtümer* (Wien: Sonderzahl, 1996), 21-36.
2. *Profil* 1-2 (7 January 1997), 74-79.
3. Robert Menasse, "Ein verrücktes Land," *Falter* 41 (1995), 14-15; Armin Thurnher, "Ich habe das überlebt," *Falter* 4 (1997), 14-16.
4. Menasse's theoretical work, as monographs, include: *Hysterien und andere historische Irrtümer* (1996); *Das Land ohne Eigenschaften. Essay zur österreichischen Identität*, rev. ed. (Frankfurt am Main: Suhrkamp, 1995); *Phänomenologie der Entgeisterung: Geschichte des verschwindenden Wissens* (Frankfurt am Main: Suhrkamp, 1995); *Überbau und Underground: Die sozialpartnerschaftliche Ästhetik: Essays zum österreichischen Geist*, rev. ed. (Frankfurt am Main: Suhrkamp, 1997). His novels are *Schubumkehr* (Salzburg: Residenz, 1995); *Selige Zeiten, brüchige Welt* (Salzburg: Residenz, 1991); and *Sinnliche Gewißheit*, rev. ed. (Frankfurt am Main: Suhrkamp, 1996).
5. Karl-Heinz Hillmann, *Wörterbuch der Soziologie*, 4th ed. (Stuttgart: Alfred Kröner, 1994), 327.
6. *Soziologie-Lexikon*, ed. Gerd Reinhold et al. (München: R. Oldenborg, 1991), 231. Surprisingly, the term is not found in *Lexikon zur Soziologie*, ed. Werner Fuchs-Heinritz et al., 3rd ed. (Opladen: Westdeutscher Verlag, 1994); or in *Wörterbuch der Soziologie*, ed. Günter Endruweit and Gisela Trommsdorff, 3 vols. (Stuttgart: Ferdinand Enke, 1989).
7. [Donald G. Daviau], "Preface," *Modern Austrian Literature*, vol. 29, nos. 3/4 (1996), ii. For an overview of the term in connection with recent Austrian history, see Susanne Breuss et al., *Inszenierungen: Stichwörter zu Österreich*, 2nd ed. (Wien: Sonderzahl, 1995), 142-149. An excellent review of the secondary literature on *Heimatliteratur* is provided by Andrea Kunne, *Heimat im Roman: Last oder Lust? Transformation eines Genres in der österreichischen Nachkriegsliteratur*, Amsterdamer Publikationen zur Sprache und Literatur 95 (Amsterdam: Rodopi, 1991), 1-20.
8. See *Profil* 25.2 (10 January 1994), 10-15.
9. *Das Land ohne Eigenschaften*, 103.
10. Ibid., 112-113.
11. Ibid., 113.

12. Sigrid Löffler, "Den Mythos von der österreichischen Literatur analytisch demontieren," *Börsenblatt für den Deutschen Buchhandel* 162.68 (25 August 1995), 11.

13. *Überbau und Underground*, 31.

14. Joseph G. McVeigh, "Lifting the Paper Curtain: The Opening of Austrian Literary Culture to Germany after 1945," *German Studies Review* 19.3 (October 1996), 479-499; see also *Überbau und Underground*, 33 and 67.

15. *Das Land ohne Eigenschaften*, 13.

16. Ibid., 114.

17. Joseph O'Connor, "Warum mir Joyce & Konsorten wurscht sind," *ZEITmagazin* 41 (4 October 1996), 26.

18. Renate S. Posthofen, "'Es sind poetische Wälder – Gefallen findet, wer sie gefällt': Robert Menasses Roman *Schubumkehr*," *Modern Austrian Literature*, vol. 29, nos. 3/4 (1996), 131-156.

19. Wendelin Schmidt-Dengler, "Schubumkehr," *Börsenblatt für den Deutschen Buchhandel* 162.79 (4 October 1995), 32-43.

20. Roman Herzog, "Rede aus Anlaß der Feier '150 Jahre erste Germanistenversammlung in Frankfurt' am 24. September 1996 in der Paulskirche in Frankfurt."

21. "Murks mit Majonäse," *Der Spiegel* (14 October 1996), 262.

22. Thomas Bernhard, *Wittgensteins Neffe. Eine Freundschaft* (Frankfurt am Main: Suhrkamp, 1982), 113.

23. Anthony Heilbut, *Thomas Mann: Eros and Literature* (Berkeley: University of California Press, 1997), 459.

24. Dagmar C. G. Lorenz, "Austrian Authors and the Dilemma of National and Regional Identity at the End of the Twentieth Century," *Modern Austrian Literature*, vol. 29, nos. 3/4 (1996), 24. The title of Lorenz' article applies even to Menasse, who spent time reading newspapers at coffeehouses (an Austrian stereotype) during the early stages of writing about Austrian identity (*Das Land ohne Eigenschaften*, 7). And on the front door of Menasse's New York apartment in 1997 rested a sign saying not "Menasse" but "Haslinger" (Josef Haslinger had preceded Menasse as a writer in residence at New York University).

25. *Inszenierungen*, 200.

26. See Jacob Heilbrunn, "Heil Harvard," *New Republic* (1 September 1997), 15-17; and Ernst Schmiederer, "Jenseits von Gute und Böse," *Profil* (4 August 1997), 24-26.

27. "Jenseits von Gute und Böse," 24.

28. Stefanie Holzer and Walter Klier, "'Ich sehe viele, die nicht hier sind.' Abservieren bis Zola. Lexikon zur österreichischen Literatur. Erste Lieferung," *Gegenwart* 27 (October-December 1995), 1.

29. *Überbau und Underground*, 24.

Gerhard Roth's *Der See* and Josef Haslinger's *Opernball:* A Comparative Treatment of Contemporary Austria

Karl E. Webb

When Gerhard Roth published his novel *Der See* (The Lake) and Josef Haslinger his *Opernball* (Opera Ball) in 1955, it was no surprise to their readers that both authors had apparently again taken the opportunity to critique their native Austria; their works were again preceded by press reports in all the media about yet two more examples of leftwing *Nestbeschmutzung* (dirtying the nest). Having read some excerpts from *Der See*, which were apparently published in advance, Jörg Haider, the leader of the nationalistic Freedom Party (*Freiheitliche Partei*), lodged a complaint against Gerhard Roth (which was, of course, chronicled in all of the Austrian newspapers) for his having supposedly defamed the politician's character in the book. Much like the current controversy in Washington over the NEA and NEH, Haider sought unsuccessfully as a result to curtail federal funding for all Austrian writers.

Both of these works purport to be detective novels or thrillers and display, in fact, the usual strong and obvious plot line, revealing an appropriate variety of heinous crimes and murders, a modicum of suspense, and, typically, a more or less conclusive "happy" ending. In addition, both Roth and Haslinger employ a variety of the usual, one might even say "classic," clichés describing the negative side of contemporary Austrian society, clichés that are based on the works of several other contemporary Austrian writers as well as in the writings of these two authors themselves.[1] Because of this coupling of cliché and thriller, it is easy for the reader to question the seriousness of the authors' literary intent and to have the sense that what both authors really wanted was a sort of ironic post-modernist romp through contemporary Austrian life and that the situations, the events, and even the criticisms are to be taken in that light.

Having said that though, there is no denying the fact that the social criticism, as black-and-white as it sometimes gets, and as full of clichés as it is, exudes a kind of gritty realism that impacts the reader nevertheless with its sordid description of contemporary life. That these authors seem to want to maintain an ironic distance from modern society, through the clichés, but also to engage in a serious conversation about society's ills should not unduly disturb us, since it is also possible for the reader to appreciate these works on each of its levels. Besides, from the apparent point-of-view of both authors, the thriller itself assures a much wider audience for the topic and thus ultimately a wider sensitivity to the brutality, inhumanity, and superficiality of modern society. Perhaps this wider audience will thus begin to understand the seriousness of the problems they confront. As noted by the sales, both authors may well have succeeded in their intent.[2] It is not the effect of the genre upon a popular audience, however, that interests us here primarily, but rather the portrayal itself of the society in which these two contemporary authors reside.

Der See relates in third-person narrative the events in the protagonist's, Paul's, life as he returns to his childhood haunts in and around the Neusiedler See on a quest for self-understanding à la Daniel Haid in *Der große Horizont*.[3] While working in Triest as a representative for a Swiss pharmaceutical firm, a job that he hates, except for its ready supply of drugs which feed his growing drug dependency, he receives an invitation in the mail from his estranged father who requests that he return to Burgenland to join him for a sailing trip on the Neusiedler See. Eck's father and he are estranged because of the former's abandonment years ago of Eck's mother which, Eck believes, resulted in her eventual suicide. He decides, nevertheless, to accept his father's invitation, partially out of curiosity about why his father would have extended the invitation and partially in a continued effort to find direction and bearing in his life again.

Upon arrival in Burgenland, he finds that his father has turned up missing and is suspected of having either fled before the law or of having fallen prey to some unknown criminal act. Eck himself becomes one of the prime suspects. In a series of scenes often viewed as though through Eck's drug-induced stupor, he is reintroduced to the friends, family, and events of his childhood in the various towns surrounding the lake and in nearby Hungary. He continues his pharmaceutical sales activities (under an assumed name) while stealing prescription pads and stamps from his physician clients, and waits for further news of his father's whereabouts. In the course of these scenes, we are confronted with the tourists who visit the resort towns along the shore, with a marine biologist who worries about the pollution in the lake, with physicians who practice an odd assortment of specialties, with political refugees from the east and the south, and even with bank robbers who have set up camp in the trailer next to the one Eck rents for himself.

Eck is a witness to and then a player in the tensions and suspicions of a borderland society too long involved in the political intrigues of the Iron Curtain and now in the war in the former Yugoslavia. He becomes aware of a crime syndicate involving old-time Nazis and his missing father (who was a gun dealer), and he is subjugated to the harassive and brutal tactics of the local gendarmes who are investigating his father's disappearance. In the course of events, Eck is presented with random body parts that wash up on the shore, with burned out cars and rural sprawl, with threats and ominous predictions about the future, and finally with a resolution of all the crimes. The body parts belong to a murdered German tourist and a soldier, and not his father, the bank robbers get into a drunken squabble with the camp guard and kill each other in a hail of bullets and an explosion, and Eck's father is discovered to have drowned in the lake near his overturned sailboat, his death an accident. As the novel ends, Eck himself, still at a loss regarding his past, present, and future, wanders off, presumably from one chance encounter to another, with little direction or purpose.

In contrast to the uncertainty and the general drift in the plot in *Der See*, *Opernball* begins with the most decisive of events: the massive death by asphyxiation of all of the guests at the annual Opera Ball in Vienna, carried out by terrorists or white supremacists. The protagonist, Kurt Fraser, a famous reporter and TV producer for the private European Television Network, has been covering the event from a control wagon outside the State Opera House and sees his own son, Fred (one of the cameramen inside), keel over and strangle to death. The novel then pursues Fraser's attempts to work through his own mourning and guilt by reconstructing the lives of the participants, both victims and perpetrators, and the events leading up to this terrible act. We also learn about Fraser's own background as the son of a Viennese Jew who had fled the Nazis into exile in London, there to serve as a British officer in World War II and later as a professor of German literature at a British university.

Each of the participants: a member of the terrorist group called the Engineer, a policeman who is stationed in the Karlsplatz Subway Station, the wealthy owner of a well-known bread bakery, and a middle-aged daughter of a retired mathematics professor and former Nazi, relates in his/her own words (supposedly recorded by Fraser) the events leading up to the catastrophe and its immediate aftermath. In clear, precise, and detailed observations, they express their own perspectives on the events and their philosophies of life in general. By this means, we get the typical, contemporary glimpse of contemporary Austrian life, be it in the provincial villages of the Waldviertel, the Viennese working district of Favoriten, the luxurious abodes of upper-middle-class society, or in the immigrant circles of exiled Viennese Jews living in London. In the course of all these narratives, the lives of the participants are tied together, the events clarified, and, as is typical of a detective novel, the intrigues and underlying plots exposed.

In portraying modern Austria, whether urban or rural, these two authors create a rather Freudian distinction between a superficial, "public relations-determined" surface reality à la *The Sound of Music* (which these authors obviously portray as disingenuous and silly) and a perhaps exaggerated but still valid underlying reality with an all-pervasive violence and brutality that is in the process of destroying or, in fact, has already destroyed the fabric of this society.

At the superficial level, there are the pleasantries of the tourist boats full of happy tourists, of the children playing innocently on the beach, and of the young women preparing to "come out" at the opera ball with their silly though rather harmless pretenses. There is, of course, the opera ball itself with its lavish decorations and meaningless traditions, and its continuing, unwarranted reverence for Austria's imperial past: "In the corridor I came upon the Imperial-Dynasty. They were apparently on their way to the Philharmonic-Bar with two princesses. As if pulled by two invisible strings, the crowd formed a path, bowed to the passersby and said: 'Your Majesty.'"[4]

Modern popular culture comes in for some mild criticism as well, as Paul Eck stares in wonderment at the bungee-jumping tower that has been erected in one of the public squares at the lake and at the "Beauty-farm Helena" that has been installed on one of the main squares of his home town, directly across from the used car lot. On his radio he hears: "Die Crash-Test-Dummies," and he is almost run over by a young man careening down the sidewalk on a skateboard.

Despite the above, both authors do concede a certain beauty in the external Austrian environment. For Paul Eck in *Der See*, it is the fields, the water, the reeds, the fowl, and the Neusiedler See itself which evoke these feelings:

> In the morning it began to rain hard. Eck drove over a soft rise and suddenly the Neusiedler See lay before him. The clouds appeared as a gloomy prophesy and clouds of fog lay at the edge of the water ... Below, in front of the band of reeds, the water had flooded the meadows ... Suddenly, with the sound of far-away (Eck thought "flat") thunder, a flock of large birds rose from the reeds. Eck recognized that it was hundreds, if not thousands, of ducks that, flying in morning formation to their feeding place, now covered the sky with an endless carpet of feathers.[5]

For Kurt Fraser in *Opernball* it is his first glimpse of the city of Vienna:

> Colorfully painted baroque-façades, Jugendstil-cafés, street musicians, market stalls with southern business acumen in front of which an urban swarm of people of the most varied faces and clothes. The gloomy hostility that I had always associated with Vienna was nowhere ... to be found. (p. 112)

In both cases, of course, these initial impressions are soon destroyed: in *Der See* by the duck hunters on the lake who massacre the ducks and threaten Eck with their shotguns; in *Opernball* by the dark clouds of dissent and intolerance which Fraser is able to see when he gets to know Vienna better.

However superficial and silly this surface existence may appear, the underlying realities of Austrian life are portrayed as being much more pernicious. Beyond and beneath the surface of the seemingly harmless world of "Tourist-Austria," for example, one discovers an overall seediness, a decay, and the progressive disintegration of both the physical surroundings and society itself. This nether-world is a stagnating, lifeless place without direction or goal. The Jewish cemetery of Eck's childhood has grown full of weeds and junk, for example, the old power plant has fallen into ruin, and the streets are lined with deserted shops. The shore is littered in places with discarded polyurethane cups and containers, and the fish die because of insecticides that have washed from the surrounding vineyards into the lake. The trailer park where Eck rents an old and rotting trailer is full of visual blight, not to mention its acute infestation by silverfish. The old farmhouse in Rappottenstein, a village in the Waldviertel where *die Entschlossenen* (the Committed Ones), as the terrorists call themselves, hold their "death" masses and their orgies, is falling down around them: the roof leaks and has collapsed in places, the windows are smashed, and the surrounding farmland has been sold off to developers. All of the above, of course, are well-worn images of contemporary Austria, but, as stated above, they have a real impact on us nevertheless.

Society seems to have suffered the same fate. In the basement of the apartment building on the Lerchenfelder Gürtel in which *der Geringste* (the Least Important One), as the terrorist leader calls himself, rents a basement cubicle, there are also two Serbs, a Bosnian, a family from Somalia, a Rumanian family, a women from Angola, two Egyptians and an Arab. They all share a toilet and a wash basin (p. 38). These people have nowhere to go, no work (except the most menial and degrading), no dignity, and in the end suffer an ignoble and horrible death when the terrorists, in an act of provocation, set fire to the house. The same conditions prevail in the Opernpassage/Karlsplatz subway station, just a few paces removed from the main tourist haunts of the Opernring and Kärntnerstraße. Here the homeless, the drug addicts, and the drunks gather to find a bit of warmth and to keep each other company, and here they wage a continuous battle with harassive police. For their part, the police record one disgusting scene after another among these societal outcasts. All of the above are events and images well-known from recent newspaper headlines, which gives them all the more currency in the minds of the readers.

Adding to this overall societal decay are the growing problems with the increasing numbers of political and economic refugees who stream across Austria's borders primarily from the former Yugoslavia. These refugees, in the eyes of the various "indigenous" groups described in the novels, threaten not only to take away the jobs and the government housing available to Austrian workers, but also to make these already threatened workers feel ill-at-ease even in their own working districts and in their own pubs and meeting places, for example in the 20th district in Vienna. There are fights on the construction sites and in the bars in *Opernball*, and in *Der See* the Bosnians and Kosovo-Albanians are either openly trucked back to the border, whenever they are caught, or are interred in quarters well out of view of the visiting tourists. In both novels this growing hatred of foreigners is exploited by the political candidates on the right. In *Der See* it is the leader of the right-wing nationalistic party, the *Hoffnungsmann* (the Man of Hope), the caricature at which Jörg Haider took such umbrage, who gives threatening speeches against the foreigners and calls for their expulsion, and in *Opernball* it is the figure, Jup Bärenthal, "the political hope of our country" (p. 95), as he is referred to by the policeman, Fritz Amon, who incites the workers to action against the non-Austrians.

Even the so-called "pillars of society," in this case the physicians, demonstrate underneath the surface their fundamental corruption and devotion only to money. As Eck makes his rounds among these doctors to sell his drugs, we learn of their essential indifference to their patients and of their incompetence in general; they are jealous and petty, and they take up the latest medical fads only in order to make more money. We detect not the slightest trace of medical ethics in them as they proceed to treat their patients while conversing with Eck, a total stranger, about these patients' illnesses. Without knowing who he really is, the physicians readily reveal the facts and details about Eck's own family's medical history: that his mother did not want her pregnancy and had sought an illegal abortion, for example. In addition, we learn that one of these doctors, Dr. Goriupp, continues to be a member of a very profitable weapons smuggling operation between Austria and Serbia and Croatia, along with Eck's own father and a number of other old-time Nazis.

A misguided religious cult adds an additional element to the ominous subterranean tensions of typical Austrian life as depicted in *Opernball*. In this case, it is the terrorist group called the *Entschlossenen* who, under the direction of *der Geringste*, evolve a curious amalgam of religious beliefs derived from Catholicism, Mormonism, Christian Fundamentalism, simplistic medieval mysticism, Satanism and pagan ritual, all of which is mixed with "End of the World" rhetoric, proto-fascism and just plain charlatanism. On the pulpit in front of an altar where the *Geringste* speaks and reads, there is always a copy of *The Bible* on one side and *Mein Kampf* on the other. At the end of each of their "death masses," as they are called, they devour a sacrificial lamb. The specific plan to gas the guests at the Opera Ball is called Armageddon, and the goal of the plan is to usher in "ein tausendjähriges Reich." For all the ominous silliness of their cultist beliefs and behavior, their frame of reference leaves them, as in so many fanatic groups within and without modern Austria and contemporary society, with no basis for determining right from wrong, and thus they are perfectly prepared to kill and be killed for the cause.

Fundamental to all of the above, is a basic element of violence and brutality, which both Roth and Haslinger emphasize throughout their works. Most human interactions are dealt with through violence. Eck's younger step-brother, for example, whom he meets for the first time during this visit to the Neusiedler See, resorts exclusively to physical threats whenever he has an encounter with his older brother. He points his shotgun at Eck when they are alone in a fishing boat and then attacks him in what becomes a life and death struggle between the two (pp. 299-201).

The two men in the trailer next to Eck's argue continually and finally shoot it out with the camp guard as he tries to steal the loot. The two murders in *Der See* are committed in a particularly gruesome manner by cutting up the bodies, throwing parts of them into the lake, and burning the rest in a parked car. *Die Entschlossenen* in *Opernball* dispose of one of their former buddies, Feilböck, in a similar manner. They shoot him between the eyes and then cut his body into pieces which are then strewn among the logs to be burned during the evening's ceremonial bonfire. When three of the homeless vagabonds are being taken away by the police, and one of them falls down, an inconvenienced passerby exclaims: "Open up Mauthausen again and this problem will be alleviated"(p. 102). The soldier who committed the murders in *Der See* explains: "We wanted to see somebody die . . ."(p. 223), and Claudia Röhler, the middle-aged housewife in *Opernball*, is accosted by a gang of young thugs while taking an evening walk in the Kärtnerstraße. Again, we are reminded of recent newspaper headlines and of the currency of such events.

Eck himself is drawn into this violent mood. He purchases a pistol in his father's shop, though he seems not to comprehend just exactly why, and carries it around in his pocket loaded. During the nationalistic political rally and while the crowd goes wild over the speech given by the *Hoffnungsmann*, he senses an overpowering feeling of hatred welling up within him and without really knowing what he is doing, he takes the safety off his revolver, raises it up, aims, and pulls the trigger. But, the revolver misfires.

The few sexual encounters in the works are all infused with a callousness and, with the one exception, an extreme level of violence and brutality. Eck is seduced while still in Italy, for example, by a prostitute and then severely beaten and robbed by her accomplices. The *Entschlossenen* convince a mentally retarded young woman from the village of Rappottenstein to join them at their farmhouse, where they exploit her vulnerability and repeatedly abuse her sexually. Three of the vagabonds are discovered in a rest room in the Karlsplatz subway station engaging in crude, violent sex and are threatened and then beaten by the police.

The police, of course, are invariably portrayed in both novels as being brutal, insensitive, and proto-fascistic. Eck is followed by threatening gendarmes as he travels about the villages in Burgenland. They illegally search his trailer, confiscate his mail, and try to intimidate him into admitting that he has had something to do with his father's disappearance. The police in *Opernball* are characterized by their leader, Reso Dorf (a naturalized Serb). He is crude, calculating, and violent, and the leader, it turns out, of a conspiracy to take control of the government by making common cause with the *Entschlossenen* and then manipulating their plans to the benefit of the police.

Both novels explain the brutality of Austrian life as a result of the abiding fascistic, nationalistic tendencies apparent at all levels of society. The *Hoffnungsmann* in *Der See* incites the gathered crowd to defend themselves at all costs and to retake possession of "their Austria" before they are driven out themselves (pp. 186-187). Jup Bährenthal, in *Opernball*, is known for his similar tactics. The *Entschlossenen*, of course, make these ideas part of their creed. Mixed into the brew are the old-time Nazis who still have influence and play a central role in Austrian society. As we have noted, they smuggle arms to the Serbs and the Croats in *Der See*, and they plot secretly behind the scenes with the leader of the terrorists. In the end, they seem to have prevailed.

Closely intertwined, at least in *Opernball*, with the negative forces mentioned above are the media, which are just as malevolent in intent and effect as the above. On the one hand, they perpetuate the superficial "public relations-view" of Austria by their sugar-coated coverage; on the other, they encourage and then exploit any problem or disaster. The TV network for which Kurt Fraser works not only benefited from the coverage of the ball itself, which it had incidentally programmed from start to finish, it also became the sole beneficiary (besides the police and the neo-fascists) of the opera ball attack. Even Kurt Fraser, who by the death of his son becomes the victim of his own medium, relates the tale of his own earlier "luck" as a television reporter in being in the right spot at the right time to capture on film the explosion of a bomb in the market square of Sarajevo which blew up an old woman beside her vegetable stand. Thus his career was made.

The view we get of contemporary Austria in both *Der See* and

Opernball, then, is a fundamentally negative one, full of clichés to be sure and dramatized and sensationalized as per the detective novel, but based nevertheless on a current sense of reality. What in this society is not superficial and just plain silly, what does not belong to the view of Austria that has been designed by public relations experts to attract the well-healed tourists from abroad, is made out to be sinister and foreboding. Under the shallow and sugar-coated surface and despite the exaggerations typically found in this type of novel, we nevertheless view a society that is coming apart, a society bereft of moral purpose or direction, a society in which fascist tendencies prevail, a society that is at heart a violent and a brutal one.

It is not a pretty picture at any level, but it is a picture that we are familiar with from the works of Thomas Bernhard, Peter Handke, and other modern Austrian writers, including Roth and Haslinger themselves. In these detective novels, however, both Roth and Haslinger, seem to have modified this picture in a couple of important and interesting ways. Elsewhere, the typical invectives against modern Austrian society are usually directed outward toward forces external to the protagonists themselves (since they are rarely a part of this society). In these novels, however, as if to emphasize not only the depth and pervasiveness of the corruption and decay in modern society, but also its seductive force, the main characters themselves, despite some initial resistance on their part, become just as much participants in the evils of society as their compatriots. Paul Eck, for example, is eventually just as caught up in the violence of his surroundings as are the other residents of the Neusiedler See region, and, except for the misfiring of his revolver, could truly have killed the *Hoffnungsmann* at the political rally. Even at the end of the novel he remains fully absorbed by his negative surroundings and feels no discernible remorse for his intentions nor has he any second thoughts about his actual behavior. Despite his humanistic education and his refugee background Kurt Fraser, at least until the death of his son in the attack on the State Opera, has exploited without second thought the misfortune of others, just as the media in general have done. Indeed, he has built his career upon it. He too has manipulated events for the sake of media attention, and he too has revealed precious little integrity or human compassion. Only Fred's death brings him to a realization of his shortcomings.

Secondly, it is clear in both works, that these two authors do not limit their exposé to contemporary Austria alone. Much of the seediness, the decay, and the crime, brutality, and violence that are illustrated here are all too recognizable in our own society and in fact in all of contemporary Western life (a theme that has been prominent in other works by these two authors, particularly as it refers to America[6]). Even the tendencies toward fascism are much in evidence elsewhere. The *Entschlossenen* draw on support and materials from the United States and are in contact by internet with their compatriots throughout the world. When things get too hot for him, the *Geringste* flees to the American Southwest where he has sympathetic friends. He surfaces again later in Vienna disguised as a Mormon missionary named Steven Huff who, however, looks more like the usual 60s hippie than the genuine, clean-cut type. Huff's grammatical formulations and pronunciation, by the way, give a rather realistic and amusing approximation of a typical American doing his best with the German language. As a continuation of the American parody, the reader gets to visit a drug-treatment program in the wilderness of Moab, Utah where Kurt Fraser takes his son for treatment. Austria, then, is only a microcosm, in all its negativity, for the modern world itself.

Finally, and in contrast to other critical works about Austria, mentioned above, both Roth and Haslinger appear to hold out a type of hope, a solution, if one will, to the negativity of this modern world. The hope they portray, however, is probably motivated more by the requirements of the thriller to present a conclusive and a happy ending than out of a genuine conviction on the part of Roth and Haslinger that a hope truly exists, for the solutions they present remain romanticized, sentimentalized, and in the end unconvincing conclusions to the woes of the world. In *Der See*, the hope is connected to the view of nature itself, to the Neusiedler See, which, it soon becomes clear, represents one of the primary forces in the work. Despite the repeated abuse that the lake suffers from an indifferent surrounding society, it continues to maintain and reveal its pristine beauty, its purity, its omnipresence in the lives of the people of the region, and its undiminished force and power. When the storms come, all that is human and corrupted is swept away. When mankind finally self-destructs, the novel implies, the Neusiedler See will remain.

In *Opernball*, the ray of hope appears in the transformation which Kurt Fraser, the at first unrepentant exploiter and insensitive husband, son, and father, undergoes. Through his suffering, he eventually is brought to the point where he realizes just how important the basic human emotions of love and compassion are and how vital his relationships to his family have become. He is eventually able to share his pain with his estranged wife and with his aging parents, and thus he is led to a renewed capacity to feel and to be human. Perhaps it is possible, the novel implies, for even the hardened, brutalized and brutish inhabitants of modern life to be humanized again. These solutions are merely clichés, of course, and can really only be considered at the ironic, distanced level of the novels.

These two novels, then, manage to explore on a couple of levels the fundamental, all-encompassing, truly monumental corruption and decay of modern Austrian society and modern life in general. We are at once impressed by the black-and-white reality and the contemporary currency of what they present, but at the same time we recognize the typical superficiality of the thriller and the highly dramatized, cliché-ridden plots and solutions that appear. On the one hand, all of society seems genuinely caught up in the evils of the time, including the protagonists of the works, and all of modern life, not only Austria, is shown to be truly decayed, corrupt, and violent. Yet at the end, a hope for the future, that nature will persist even if modern society does not and that some of us may yet learn what it means to feel and to be compassionate toward our fellow man, remains unconvincing and probably intentionally so. Roth and Haslinger appear in these works both to have had their cake and to have eaten it too. They converse compellingly with their more serious readers about serious issues in modern life, topics that have continued to interest both of them throughout their careers. They also attract a wider, popular audience by virtue of the genre and its dramatized events and solutions. At the same time, they even maintain their ironic, postmodernist distance. As for the reader, he/she can have it all as well, from a straightforward and relatively easy read to a compelling and gripping analysis of the woes of contemporary life.

Northern Arizona State University

Notes

1. Compare, for example, Gerhard Roth's *Das doppelköpfige Österreich. Essays, Polemiken, Interviews* (Frankfurt am Main: S. Fischer Verlag, 1995) and Josef Haslinger's *Politik der Gefühle. Ein Essay über Österreich* (Darmstadt: Luchterhand, 1987).

2. This, of course, is not to say that Roth or Haslinger did not have a commercial interest in publishing these works. Given their social

engagement of the past, however, it is relatively safe to assume that they have not abandoned this genuine engagement just for the sake of popularity.

3. Gerhard Roth, *Der große Horizont* (Frankfurt am Main: Suhrkamp Verlag, 1974).

4. *Opernball* (Frankfurt am Main: S. Fischer Verlag, 1995), p. 343. Henceforth referred to only by page number in the text.

5. *Der See* (Frankfurt am Main: S. Fischer Verlag, 1995), pp. 20-21. Henceforth referred to only by page number in the text.

6. Compare Gerhard Roth's *Der große Horizont* (see note 3 above) and Josef Haslinger's *Das Elend Amerikas* (Frankfurt am Main: Fischer Taschenbuch Verlag, 1992).

Post-Bernhardian Austria in Lilian Faschinger's *Magdalena Sünderin*

Gerald A. Fetz

Antonio Fian, in his recent collection of essays, *Hölle, verlorenes Paradies. Aufsätze*,[1] takes the majority of his fellow Austrian writers to task for what he perceives as their exaggerated and hypernegative portrayals of Austria and Austrians. In fact, he diagnoses this undeniable tendency in much of contemporary Austrian writing as a symptom of "linguistic decay," "mental incompetence," and "intellectual dishonesty." Ultimately, he accuses such literary colleagues as Gerhard Roth, Peter Turrini, and Robert Menasse of playing apocalyptic games.

No doubt, contemporary Austrian literature displays a remarkable penchant for being very critical of Austria and Austrians, past and present, and for doing so in a language and with images that are intended to provoke, stir up, and even enrage. One example will suffice: at one point, in somewhat representative fashion, Peter Handke termed Austria "the fat which makes me choke."[2] When one looks closely, in fact, there are very few post-1945 Austrian writers who have not engaged in rather strident critiques of their homeland, directing special attention in the process to debunking the clichés and myths of that special Austrian *Gemütlichkeit* which the tourist industry so ubiquitously touts and which sentimental visitors find so appealing. Striking and impressive examples of such self-reflective literary critiques of their Austrian homeland can be found in works from Ilse Aichinger to Josef Haslinger, from Hans Lebert to Gerhard Roth, from Gerhard Fritsch to Franz Innerhofer, from Peter Turrini to Waltraud Anna Mitgutsch.

Starting with the 1960s one could speak convincingly of a new literary genre in Austrian literature: the "Anti-Heimat Novel," a type of novel which turned the traditionally positive "Heimatroman" with its heavily romanticized portrayals of Alpine village life inside out.

Fritsch's novel *Fasching* (1967, Carnival), Innerhofer's *Schöne Tage* (1974; *Beautiful Days*, 1976), or Mitgutsch's *Die Züchtigung* (1985), to name just three examples, offer rather horrifying counter-portrayals to the *heile Welt*, the wholesome world of the traditional "Heimatromane" (Provincial novels) or of the glossy and very effective tourist brochures. In a 1975 article titled "Die Welt als Mordschauplatz"[3] (The World as Murder Site), the journalist and critic Karin Kathrein actually suggested that her title described precisely the way Austria was being depicted in much of contemporary Austrian literature. The hills represented here, one must conclude, are hardly alive with the sound of music.

It should not be implied, however, that it was the post-1945 generation of Austrian writers who first invented this critical tradition. They could draw freely on the tradition of negative portrayals of Austria and its inhabitants found in the works of literary predecessors like Grillparzer and Nestroy, Kraus and Horváth; and they have.

Nonetheless, it was unquestionably Thomas Bernhard who took this tradition of "Österreichbeschimpfung" (Austria-scolding) to new heights (or depths, if you agree with Antonio Fian). Bernhard's uncanny knack for goring just about every Austrian ox imaginable is by now legendary. I have argued elsewhere that it is dangerous to take Bernhard at face value, to take him literally, because he is such an "exaggeration artist," is consistently contradictory, and rarely without irony. But when he claimed that he was essentially a "Märchenzerstörer," a destroyer of fairy tales, I think that we can take him at his word. And, as he stated in one of his literary prize acceptance speeches in 1968, the fairy tale he was most keenly interested in de-storying was "the fairy tale of beautiful Austria.[4]

From his breakthrough novel *Frost* (1963) to his final, scandalous play *Heldenplatz* (1988), Bernhard's works challenge and confront Austria and Austrians, their institutions and illusions, their historical blindspots and ethical hypocrisies. His method is frequently exaggeration, for, as Schmidt-Dengler has pointed out, "only through exaggeration does it become clear how necessary it is to distort the world in order to make it recognizable."[5] Bernhard obviously loved a good scandal, enjoyed being outrageous, and he cultivated the theatrical gesture; but those were not his only motivations for being so willfully irritating and provocative in speech and print. As Matthias Konzett has recently claimed, Bernhard was also genuinely interested in serious social and political criticism. Konzett asserts in fact that Bernhard "extended the criticism of fascism from its institutional suprastructure to the base of society, where it is embedded in various forms of everyday fascist discourse and petty terror."[6] Gerhard Roth suggested something very similar in his eulogy for Bernhard in 1989: "Bernhard recognized early that the roots of the Austrian malaise are to be found in a "mélange" of national socialism, Catholicism, and (later) pinstripe socialism which, in combination, define Austrian politics to the present day."[7]

It would be misleading to leave the impression, however, that Bernhard's Austria-criticism was concentrated exclusively on the continuities between fascist (1934-38)/national socialist (1938-45) Austria and the postwar Second Republic, although that remained right up through his final work *Heldenplatz* (1988) a crucial concern. He was also interested in attacking, sometimes comically, sometimes bitterly, a very wide range of individual Austrian traditions, institutions, and perceived attributes. We will investigate that more closely below in the context of our discussion of Lilian Faschinger. But it should be noted that, in spite of the frequently provocative hyperbole and scathing indictments, Bernhard's relationship to Austria cannot be dismissed as merely one-sided or myopic "Österreich-Besudelung" (Austria defilement), "Nest-Beschmutzung" (nest dirtying), or "Österreich-Verunglimpfung" (Austria denigration), as not just a few commentators and insulted fellow Austrians have asserted over the years. Bernhard's approach, again in line with a very reputable and venerable Austrian tradition, was ambivalent to the core; his purported "hatred," actually a genuine "Haßliebe" (love-hate), much like that of a disappointed lover.

In the fall of 1996 I was fortunate enough to hear Lilian Faschinger read from her 1995 picaresque novel, *Magdalena Sünderin* (*Magdalena the Sinner*, 1997[8]). I was immediately impressed with the work, with its compelling and seductive language, its evocative images, and with its simultaneous humor and seriousness; I was also struck by her indebtedness to and artistically sophisticated adaptations of Bernhard's language, style, and themes. As I have studied her novel further, the "Bernhard tradition – and I think it clearly justified to speak of such already – has become even more evident, but so has Faschinger's uniqueness in taking up with this powerful tradition. That her indebtedness is conscious is directly hinted at near the beginning of the novel when Magdalena describes the books frequently encountered in her fellow Austrians' personal libraries: there next to the *Brockhaus Encyclopedia,* Burton's *Anatomy of Melancholy,* and the *Letters of Maria Theresia to Her Daughter Marie Antoinette* one can inevitably find a dog-eared, oft-read copy of Bernhard's first novel *Frost* (*Magdalena the Sinner,* 17). As will become obvious below, the numerous adoptions and adaptations from Bernhard leave little room for doubt that Faschinger intentionally meant to pay a kind of homage to him with this work.

Since *Magdalena Sünderin* is a relatively recent novel, I assume that many are therefore unfamiliar with it; it might be useful at this point, therefore, to offer a brief synopsis of the plot before attempting to analyze what I have chosen to call "Faschinger's Post-Bernhardian Austria." The story is both simple and quite realistic, if, simultaneously, rather implausible. Magdalena, a very attractive young Austrian woman, has just kidnapped a Catholic priest in the middle of a Pentecost Mass in his church in a small East Tirolian village. She has fled with him into the provincial Austrian countryside, driving him in her Puch 800 motorcycle with side-car to an isolated location where they are unlikely to be discovered. There she has tied him to a tree, gagged him, and, over the course of the next few days, and nights, she unloads on him her confession, that is, the story of her life and sins. During her narrative, which the reader of the novel receives in the priest's later retelling, she relates with thoroughness and visible joy the picaresque adventures she claims to have experienced between her leaving Austria sometime earlier and her recent return to the homeland from which she feels alienated, but also drawn back. Interjected between the long monologue sections of her now retold story, the narrator-priest divulges his own thoughts and development over the course of days and nights during which he listens silently, but attentively, to Magdalena's confession.

Magdalena's travels and adventures have led her to Italy, to Paris, to London, and then back to the continent, where she spends time in Baden-Baden and Garmisch-Partenkirchen before finally being pulled back, somewhat inexplicably, to Austria. At each stage of her journey she becomes involved, usually romantically, with a man, eight in sum, but in all but one case the relationship, begun with such hope and even passion, ends disastrously, at least for the man. Each of these men, in his own way and due to his own peculiar male pathology, becomes impossibly oppressive for Magdalena, and she finds she has no choice but to kill him. Only one of her lovers, the sole Austrian among them, is allowed to escape. As she tells her detailed story of love and murder to the priest, her initial compulsion to seek absolution through confession appears to diminish, as does his compulsion to judge. By the time she concludes her narration, the mere telling, to someone who listens without interruption (most of the time he is gagged), seems to satisfy her, even to provide her with a kind of self-absolution, making any official Church absolution superfluous. The priest as well has clearly succumbed to her narration skills as well as her charm and sensuality; in fact, their relationship has become sexual, and he can hardly wait for the next night to fall so that he may enjoy the world of sensuality which she has opened up to him.

As everyone familiar with Bernhard's work knows, his criticisms and attacks on Austria and his fellow Austrians take numerous forms. The range of this Faschinger novel is narrower, but she picks up on several themes of criticism found in Bernhard and adds a few intriguing twists of her own. To begin with, one finds in Bernhard and here again in Faschinger's novel a wide-ranging indictment of Austria and Austrians in general. We can recall Bernhard's exclamation in one of his prize acceptance speeches from 1968: "You are the cause, strip of land, perverse foundation of my existence,"[9] meaning, of course, Austria. The instances in which his fictional characters curse Austria, in spite of their usual neurotic attachment to it, and the times when he and his characters attack their fellow Austrians for their alleged "Stumpfsinn" (dullness) and destructive provincialism are both numerous and, by now, very well known. These criticisms are most often expressed in clearly exaggerated and absolute terms; but one does not need to be an overly discerning or sophisticated reader to sense the large dose of irony and ambivalence behind them.

On one level, perhaps, Bernhard was at least half-serious when he let Robert in his play *Heldenplatz* exclaim: "Austria is nothing but a stage on which everything is decayed, rotten, and depraved/ a walk-on role for six-and-one-half million abandoned self-haters/ six-and-one-half million who are feeble and raving mad."[10] But he also clearly enjoyed making such ridiculously exaggerated claims and then observing the irate responses of those who felt stung or who were too defensive to smile at such criticism, too literal to recognize the irony, the humor, and the ambiguity of his exaggerations. On one level, though, Bernhard is quite obviously attached to Austria, and his feelings toward her are at center extremely ambivalent: Austria is both "beloved" and "hated" intimacy.[11]

Faschinger lets her heroine Magdalena assert to her captive priest that the only reason she has returned to Austria is her love of Austrian baked goods: "Basically, I returned to Austria only for the pastry.... With the exception of its pastry Austria has nothing that would make it worth returning to, nothing one longs to return to once one has finally left its borders behind. But I missed the pastry. The Austrian pastry I missed ruined the most beautiful places abroad for me" (*Magdalena the Sinner*, 22). The playful humor of this rather absolute and all-encompassing attack is impossible to overlook. Elsewhere in the novel it becomes evident as well, in spite of Magdalena's frequent condemnations of Austria in a similar vein, that her feelings about her homeland and fellow Austrian citizens are extremely ambivalent. Among her several lovers, for instance, it is only the Austrian chauffeur Clemens whom she doesn't kill; in fact, she ends the relationship with him for fear that its continuation would mean his doom. (At this point in the story, one needs to know, she has been infected by a former lover who was a vampire, and she, too, finds herself lusting after Clemens's juicy neck). She claims, for example, when she first arrives at the villa in Baden-Baden: "Except for Clemens, the chauffeur I didn't like because he was Austrian, I found the rest of the staff to be quite pleasant" (227). Yet, over the course of her stay there, she becomes estranged from the "rest of the staff" and actually falls in love with her fellow Austrian, Clemens. During the latter part of her trip on the continent, after she leaves Baden-Baden, she also finds herself, against her conscious will, being pulled back, closer and closer and, finally, to Austria where she kidnaps the priest. One reads Magdalena's frequent protests that Austrians drive her crazy, for instance, because: "People who choose an unencumbered lifestyle, those who move from place to place such as myself, are always in danger in Austria. Austria doesn't like such people, particularly when those people are women.... A nomadic existence is suspect in Austria, in Austria sedentariness is highly valued" (23). Nonetheless, she admits to having returned to Austria, to having chosen an Austrian priest for her confession, even though he is from East Tyrol and not her home province of Carinthia, precisely because a non-Austrian would not understand her:

> I have chosen an Austrian priest to hear my general confession because it is clear to me that only an Austrian priest is in the position to fully understand this general confession. Only an Austrian priest will be entirely able

> to put himself into the twists and turns of an Austrian brain, the cerebral convolutions of which, of course, are arranged differently from the convolutions of those who live in other countries.... (23-24)

At another point in her monologue-narrative Magdalena exclaims: "... I had never felt love of or pride in Austria, Austria never succeeded in filling me with love or pride, rather, it often filled me with anger, disappointment, disdain, and sorrow, or at least with shame" (115). Again, this may be true on one level, but the instances of obvious attachment and perhaps only partially explicable attraction to her irritating and alienating homeland are too numerous to allow us to believe that such an assertion even begins to provide the whole picture.

If we look further at the kinds of things which Faschinger lets Magdalena find worthy of sometimes scathing criticism, we discover many of Bernhard's leitmotifs: their shared criticism of, in this case, Austrian family life, with its insidious methods of repression of the individual members, especially the children; their common attacks on intellectual life in Austria (or lack thereof), claiming that it, too, is stifling and crippling, especially for those who do not fit certain mundane expectations; or in their similar descriptions of what they perceive to be the sorry state of Austrian political life. The following samplings of Magdalena's negative views regarding these three motifs may be regarded as representative, both in style and content, of many of her indictments of Austria. They also illustrate how indebted her prose, again both in style and content, frequently is to Thomas Bernhard. About Austrian families she asserts:

> that of all the family machines of destruction, the Austrian family's machines of destruction are among the most efficient in the Western world, as they take particular aim at the most sensitive, most intelligent, most talented of family members and normally do not take long in destroying this inherent sensitivity, intelligence, and talent. Not for nothing is the family, and in particular the Austrian family, the most common site of acts of violence. (250-251)

Regarding intellectual life in Austria, Magdalena tells the ever-intently-listening priest that she felt suffocated by the "methods of the psychologists, psychotherapists, psychoanalysts, and psychiatrists" (39) which and who are as repressive as the family. She adds that intellectuals in Austria are bores who lack all individuality:

> There is scarcely anything more soporific than the conversation of the so-called educated classes, scarcely anything more deadening to the spirit than the surroundings they have created for themselves. If you've seen one aesthetically furnished apartment, you've seen them all. If you've choked down one aesthetically prepared meal, you've choked them all down. The conversations of aesthetes consist of prefab standard parts, any original word that is interjected completely throws them from their conversational path and is disturbing to them in the extreme. Academics, of course, are the worst. (35-36)

And, finally, at one point in her confession-monologue she complains as follows about the state of Austrian political life: "It would never occur to me to ask for an Austrian newspaper at a kiosk. I was happy not to have to see the miserable or unworthy figures, respectively, that rule Austrian public life and not to experience the lamentable or sinister public events, respectively, of Austrian life" (114-115). With passages like these, can there be any doubt that Bernhard served Faschinger, at least for these and similar aspects of her novel, as model and mentor?

Before suggesting, however, some of the significant ways in which Faschinger liberates herself from this model, from the very compelling "Bernhard tradition," I want to focus briefly on what I take to be the most important and most serious theme or emphasis in the Austria critique of Bernhard, Faschinger, and numerous other contemporary Austrian writers. Near the beginning of my observations above I cited the critic Matthias Konzett as well as the novelist and essayist Gerhard Roth, both of whom have pointed out that it was Bernhard, long before the election of Kurt Waldheim to the Austrian presidency in 1986, who called attention again and again to the continuities in Austrian political and cultural life from the "Ständestaat" period through the Third Reich and into the Second Republic up to the present. It was Bernhard, Robert Menasse suggests in his essay collection *Das Land ohne Eigenschaften*[12] (The Land Without

Qualities), who very early set about to destroy the "fairy tale" and the "lie" which tended to exonerate Austria as the innocent victim of the Nazis, thereby letting her off the hook from confronting and owning up to her own complicity in the terrible crimes of the Nazi period. One need only recall Bernhard's descriptions of the seamless transition from Catholic to national-socialist and back to Catholic administration of his Salzburg boarding school in the autobiographical work *Die Ursache* (1975; *An Indication of the Cause*, 1985) to be able to agree with Roth when he praised Bernhard for being one of the first to point out these disturbing and, therefore, oft-denied or repressed connections. At one point in *An Indication* ... we can read: "Fundamentally there was no difference whatever between the National Socialist system and the Catholic system there. Everything simply had a different veneer and a different name, but in the end the effect was the same."[13] Drawing attention to such a connection, such similarities, such continuities between the two systems remained important to Bernhard to the very end, as is clearly demonstrated in his final play, *Heldenplatz* (1988).

Faschinger, like most of her contemporary Austrian writers in the post-Waldheim period, also condemns the fact that her country refused for so long to confront its own role in and responsibility for the crimes of the Third Reich, for the Holocaust, preferring instead to live what Robert Menasse and others have termed the Austrian "historical lie."[14] And Faschinger, like Bernhard, singles out the Catholic Church for special attention in her criticism of institutions in Austria that have generally refused to confront their past and have continued to support fascist, at least repressive mechanisms, attitudes, and tendencies in society. As Magdalena boldly asserts:

> In order to keep such a large number of people dumb for thousands of years, the dignitaries of the Catholic Church, that is to say, those who determine the policy of the Catholic Church, are obviously very intelligent, above all those higher-ranking dignitaries.... It is not left to true believers of the Catholic Church, whose shepherd, Jesus Christ, so appropriately refers to them as His sheep, to think for themselves, any more than it is left to those who live under a dictatorship.... (80-81)

Before proceeding any further, lest all readers unfamiliar with

Faschinger's compelling and delightful novel gain the impression that she is little more than a Bernhard epigone, I would like to suggest briefly some of the ways in which she has adapted and altered, rather than merely adopted, her mentor's example. Magdalena, with her very evocative name, is not only a woman, but a very sensual woman at that. She is a woman with many sins, whether one takes her story of the seven murdered lovers as truth or as tale, something she and Faschinger leave ambiguously open from the beginning.

With what appears to be a traditional motivation, Magdalena seems intent on giving her confession, having a priest listen to her, and, subsequently, receiving absolution from the Church through him. From the beginning, however, the impetus for kidnapping the priest, tying him to a tree and gagging him for several days while she delivers her monologue-confession, transcends the traditional motivation of the sinning believer. As she tells the priest when she finally gets him settled against and tied to the tree: "I need a public, Reverend, a need you as a priest undoubtedly will understand. The public is the eyewitness, without a public every act is meaningless from the outset, an attentive public is proof of an active existence" (4). And she continues a short time later, significantly: "It's a matter of you listening quietly without interrupting me – I who have been constantly interrupted – and without cutting me off – I who have constantly been cut off" (11). She then relates episodes in her life, episodes in which she has been interrupted, silenced, hushed up, ignored, put down, not listened to. Her mother, her father, her teachers, her professors, even priests in confessionals had interrupted her, continuously, had not let her find her voice or tell her story, state her thoughts and opinions or express her wishes. Appropriately, though, each of the relationships that ended disastrously, for the men in a fashion reminiscent of Dante's *Inferno*, one of Magdalena's favorite books, was characterized by representative male and, therefore, societal strategies to stifle Magdalena, as a woman, to make her dependent, to repress her, to silence her.

This complaint about a kind of repression of women told and retold by hundreds of women, feminists and non-feministst alike, is not an issue in any of Bernhard's works. It is rare, in fact, as Ria Endres pointed out several years ago in her polemical study of Bernhard, that a woman's perspective is almost never found in Bernhard's writing.[15] One is also hard pressed to discover in Bernhard's works a thematicization of sensuality, of eroticism. By contrast, that is one of the most significant features of Faschinger's novel. Magdalena exudes sensuality; for that reason, it is not so far-fetched to believe that so many men find her attractive and that she quickly becomes involved in so many love affairs. Additionally, Magdalena views and enjoys food sensually, she enjoys her surroundings sensually, whether they be the Aegean Sea or the city of Paris, and she clearly loves men, sensually, at least until they begin to smother her. She can't even resist touching and then seducing the priest. Faschinger's descriptions of Magdalena's sensuality and related adventures are provocative not in their explicitness, for they are not explicit at all, but for their innocent quality coupled with their outrageousness. There is nothing pornographic about them; instead, they are portrayed playfully, delightfully, and ironically in a clearly exaggerated way. Perhaps the fact that Faschinger has lived for some time in France has enabled her to deal with sensuality and sexuality in ways not frequently found in most German-language literature.

Magdalena's feminist complaint against those who have attempted in various ways, and often succeeded, to silence her, doesn't end there either. And again Faschinger distances herself from the Bernhardian model, for by finding her voice, by finally getting someone with authority, a Catholic priest, an Austrian, a man, to listen to her, with undivided attention, even though she has to resort to rather extraordinary means to make that happen, she liberates and even absolves herself. The priest, silent to the end, is no longer necessary for her absolution. Telling, and being listened to, are sufficient. And in a delightful ironic twist, in the process the priest is also liberated from his stuffy, celibate institutional and societal confines. By being forced to listen, by allowing himself, very slowly at first, then completely, to be enveloped in Magdalena's story and to become vulnerable to her and his own sensuality, he, too, experiences a life-changing emancipation. That is hardly something one finds in Bernhard's world, unless it is in or through death.

The reviews of *Magdalena Sünderin*, on the occasion of its original publication in German and of the subsequent versions in English, one in Britain (1996) and the most recent in the U.S. (1997), have occasionally pointed out similarities and affinities to Bernhard; but they have also suggested additional comparisons, underscoring a broader range of themes, stylistic features, allusions, and literary characteristics of the novel than the intentionally narrower focus of this essay has made evident. Correctly, intertextual connections to such writers and works as Schnitzler's famous/infamous play *Der Reigen* (*La Ronde*), Cervantes' masterpiece *Don Quixote*, Umberto Eco's *The Name of the Rose*, Patrick Süskind's novel of olfactory sensuality *Parfüm* (*Perfume*), and even Thomas Mann's picaresque novel *Felix Krull* have been alluded to more than once. Convincing comparisons can be drawn, in fact, to all of these works and numerous others.

There are also many important connections between *Magdalena Sünderin* and Faschinger's earlier writings. Contrary to the assertion from a review in *Esquire* magazine, cited on the dust jacket of the American edition (1997) – "Lilian Faschinger's beguiling first novel is a worthy European bestseller . . . ," it is not her first novel, even if one can agree that it is beguiling and a bestseller. Prior to the 1995 publication of the original German version of *Magdalena*, Faschinger had already published a volume of poetry, two novels, and a collection of ten short stories. The threads that connect the first two novels (*Die neue Sheherazade*, 1986; and *Lustspiel*, 1989) as well as the stories (*Frau mit drei Flugzeugen*, 1993) are many, but among the most significant are Faschinger's contemporary adaptations of myths and legends, such as the Sheherazade legend which plays a significant role here in *Magdalena* as well as in the first novel which explicitly lays claim to the connection in its title. In virtually all of Faschinger's fiction, in fact, the situation of the female story-teller, telling tales to save her life, both figuratively and literally, is central. As Faschinger herself asserted in an interview, "telling is deliverance."[16] In all of her works, again in contrast to Bernhard, she works and plays with the themes of sensuality, eroticism, gender conflict, the oppression of women in male-dominated societies, and the serious, yet humorous and self-ironic strategies of her protagonists to rebel, to gain revenge, and to liberate themselves.

Since there seems to be some confusion about Lilian Faschinger's background and writing career, even on the part of her American publisher, perhaps a word or two about her in conclusion is in order. She was born in 1950 in the Austrian province of Carinthia, where she also grew up, and she studied English literature and history in Graz where she earned her doctorate. Her first professional work was as a literary translator, English into German. She has lived in Graz and, more recently, in Vienna, but has spent considerable time as well living in the U.S., in France, and in Britain. Her first novel, *Die neue Sheherazade*, was given an award at the Bachmann competition in the year of its publication, 1986, and her subsequent works have all been received, despite the inevitable critical reviews as well, with a great deal of enthusiasm. *Magdalena Sünderin,* for instance, has been called "clever, witty, and rhetorically sophisticated,"[17] an "insanely humorous book, told in complete seriousness,"[18] and "a sparkling satire."[19] The initial American reception of the novel has been very enthusiastic as well, and Barnes & Noble featured it in its Fall 1997 Newsletter, *Discover Great New Writers,* as "an imaginative and erotic book that is completely irreverent." Yet, even this third Faschinger novel has reaped some criticism: it has been termed "obscene,"[20] a "confusedly overdetermined satire,"[21] and a "tortured entertainment novel."[22] On balance, though, *Magdalena Sünderin* has been enthusiastically received by most critics and reviewers thus far as a refreshing and boldly-told "Schelmenroman," that is, a picaresque novel with something new: a female protagonist with impressive ancestral relations in both the original Maria Magdalena and in Sheherazade.

Lilian Faschinger's novel *Magdalena Sünderin* is also, as I have tried to demonstrate in this essay, another clear example of the fact, corroborated by many, that Thomas Bernhard has altered profoundly the landscape of contemporary Austrian writing, not only with regard to the critical portrayals of Austria that it generally contains, but stylistically and thematically as well. Faschinger has taken the Bernhard influence and consciously appropriated and adapted essential features of his vision, style, and language to great advantage. Her scathing yet ironic criticisms of her homeland and her fellow Austrians are no less noteworthy because she, even more than Bernhard, is playful with serious matters, even with death; and they are no less important because she, in this case, unlike Bernhard, allows for the hope, even the possibility of liberation from stifling repression. And perhaps one of the most significant differences between these two Austrian writers lies in the fact that Bernhard was, in his own words and works, a "Märchenzerstörer" (a destroyer of fairy tales), whereas Faschinger has proven with this novel, and her earlier two, that she is very good at creating them.

University of Montana

Notes

1. Graz: Literaturverlag Droschl, 1996.

2. *Der Tod des Nachsommers* (Munich: Carl Hanser Verlag, 1979), back cover.

3. *Die Presse*, 26 and 27 April 1975.

4. "Zwei Reden," in: *Neues Forum* XV, No. 173 (1968), 348.

5. *Der Übertreibungskünstler* (Wien: Sonderzahl, 1986), 104.

6. *'Publikumsbeschimpfung*. Thomas Bernhard's Provocations of the Austrian Public Sphere," *German Quarterly* Vol. 68, No. 3 (1995), 265.

7. "Der Menschenfeind, der der Alpenkönig war. Nachruf auf Thomas Bernhard," in: Gerhard Roth, *Das doppelköpfige Österreich* (Frankfurt a.M.: Fischer, 1995), 137-138.

8. *Magdalena Sünderin* (Cologne: Kiepenheuer & Witsch, 1995; First American edition: *Magdalena the Sinner* NY: Harper Collins, 1997).

9. "Zwei Reden," 348.

10. *Heldenplatz*. (Frankfurt a.M.: Suhrkamp, 1988), 89.

11. Numerous times in Bernhard's writings one can read similar claims to that which his narrator makes about the protagonist Roithamer in the extraordinary novel *Korrektur* (Frankfurt a.M.: Suhrkamp, 1975): "... for that or the one hand he loved, ... was just as clear as that he hated it ..." (28).

12. *Das Land ohne Eigenschaften* (Frankfurt a.M.: Suhrkamp, 1995).

13. In: *Gathering Evidence*, transl. David McClintock (NY: Alfred Knopf, 1985), 120.

14. *Land ohne Eigenschaften*, 16.

15. *Am Ende angekommen* (Frankfurt a.M.: S. Fischer, 1980).

16. Interview in the London-based *Book News* (6 November 1996).

17. Annette Speck in the *Berliner Morgenpost* (9 June 1996).

18. Kerstin Hensel in *Freitag* (13 October 1995).

19. Margaret Walters in *Sunday Times* of London (3 November 1996).

20. In the Viennese weekly *News* (13 July 1995).

21. Simon Carnell in *Times Literary Supplement* London (13 December 1996).

22. Günter Kaindlstorfer in the ORF EX LIBRIS radio review from 1 October 1995.

'Black Holes' in the Novels of Christoph Ransmayr: An Astronomical Interpretation of Images of Alternative Worlds in his Work

Lynne Cook

Although Christoph Ransmayr's novels range far in terms of topography and time, they reveal alternative worlds that are familiar despite their extremity. The following discussion examines the imagery of these worlds and their symbolic relevance to Austria. As part of ongoing Austrian debate concerning identity and place, and a coming to terms with the past, such a discussion presents an aesthetic perspective rather than an essayistic approach. An image, that of the 'black hole,' is used to draw symbolic parallels between the nature of these fictional alternative worlds and issues concerning not just the familiar world of Austria, but of the Western world in general.

Christoph Ransmayr is going places, in every sense of the expression. Whether he is accepting another literary accolade (in 1996 the EU Aristeion Prize, shared with Salman Rushdie; in 1997 the Solothurner Prize), holding the opening speech for the Salzburg Festival, spending two months with Tibetan nomads or climbing mountains in New Zealand, he is on the move.

But despite life in motion and an apparent driving curiosity for the new, Ransmayr turns his pen in his three novels to sketch creative responses to his homeland, to Austria, and contemporary experience in Europe.[1] As Michael Cerha points out in Vienna's *Der Standard*, Ransmayr, as a traveler to new places, "experiences (when he arrives) a world that he had left behind, one that familiarity had disguised."[2] In fact Cerha (tongue in cheek) sees Ransmayr as some sort of literary budgerigar, who once in flight is driven on by curiosity into possibly inhospitable worlds. However, when flying homewards, a new perspective on what is home has been gained.

Such a new perspective takes creative form in the imagery used in Ransmayr's novels. In examining the imagery of the alternative worlds of Ransmayr's fiction — in what could be seen as a piece of postmodernist borrowing — I would like to use an analogy from the world of science, the 'black hole.' I am intentionally following Cerha's lighthearted lead in this respect. Ransmayr, especially in the reception to his second novel *Die letzte Welt* (*The Last World*),[3] has been seen as a dark poet of the postmodern apocalypse. Perhaps a balance can be struck between text and reader response which, by contrast, reinforces the obvious power of Ransmayr's vision.

The concept of 'black holes' in science has entered common parlance and has become widely popularized, aided by the writings of those such as Stephen Hawking in his *A Brief History of Time*; and while it is obviously not intended here that such a definition will be used, I find that the idea of the 'black hole' is very useful in an interpretative response to Ransmayr's three novels, *Die Schrecken des Eises und der Finsternis*, 1984 (*The Terrors of Ice and Darkness*, 1992), *Die letzte Welt*, 1988 (*The Last World*, 1991) and *Morbus Kitahara*, 1995 (*The Dog King*, 1997). I feel it is possible to draw a link between science and fiction in an examination of Ransmayr's work. While his novels in no way would be classified as belonging to the genre of science fiction, there is a decidedly apocalyptic feel to much of Ransmayr's writing, in particular his second novel, the best-selling *The Last World*. In all three novels the reader is drawn into some sort of alternative time experience, whether in a possible future or past. That the reader is confronted, too, with visions of extreme worlds, worlds on the edge, in a landscape which works as alien on several levels, allows such a popularist science to fiction link to be made.

In keeping with our layman's perception of what a 'black hole' is, Ransmayr's novels (paradoxically) hold at their symbolic centers notions of absence, disappearance, lack or emptiness. Yet a further paradox can be understood when one is aware that the apparent emptiness of a 'black hole' is actually the site of the densest matter in the system, compelling the strongest attraction. In both *The Terrors of Ice and Darkness* and *The Last World* a structural center has physically disappeared which is, in both cases, a pivotal character; a young traveler from Vienna, Josef Mazzini, who disappears into the Polar wastes, and the Roman poet, Ovid, who is lost into the forlorn landscape of exile in the 'last world.' Ironically, the absent Subject compels an intensity of focus. The idea of lack and emptiness is also prominent in varied forms in each novel, in either the world view or direct experience of the characters. In *The Dog King* the whole fabric of the text is permeated by a sense of lack; a lack of understanding, a lack of place, of belonging, and a lack of communication. This lack is intensified around the central character, Bering. The darkness within these novels is often physical, part of the natural landscape, but it is also a darkness of being and of future.

Just as a 'black hole' in scientific terms begins to develop where a star's equilibrium of forces (that of gravitational attraction and the repulsing pressure of burning gases) is upset, the worlds of Ransmayr's novels also are facing collapse, indicating a loss of balance, of equilibrium, revealing stages to a transition or transformation. The extended 'black hole' metaphor of collapse, disappearance, and darkness takes on different forms in each novel.

In *The Terrors of Ice and Darkness* the Arctic landscape is both the site of confrontation and adversarial force for the Imperial Austrian North Pole expedition, where rationalist-imperialist notions of superiority confront the endurance and impenetrability of nature. ("Weyprecht tells them that above all else it is order that keeps them alive; ... Maintenance of law and discipline is, in fact, simply an expression of humanity and the only way to survive in this desolation," TID 97). The same landscape is the focus for the obsessive Mazzini whose quest for identity and authenticity results in his disappearance into the Arctic wastes a century later.

In *The Last World*, the dialectic of rationality and myth is located symbolically in Ransmayr's model of Classical Rome (a totalitarian regime, reminiscent of the Nazi Reich) and in the outpost of exile, Tomi, respectively. It is Cotta's physical journey between the two worlds which symbolizes the changing mindframe from extreme order and control, to chaos and insanity. This novel most graphically of all illustrates a dark and chaotic world in a state of entropic collapse. In *The Dog King* the landscape and mindscape of Moor and its inhabitants progressively decays. The darkness of degeneration and barbarity is linked to a destructive moral vacuum which is shown symbolically in Bering's blindness, his susceptibility to the disease, Morbus Kitahara.

In Ransmayr's alternative worlds we find ourselves poised over the void, threatened with being sucked towards an existential emptiness. The reader finds himself or herself in a position on the theoretical event horizon of a literary 'black hole' observing worlds, both personal and social, in a state of transition and imbalance, sliding towards darkness, emptiness and loss as different forces contend. It is important to note here that a 'black hole' has the potential to expand. Paradoxically, the larger a hole becomes, the emptier it becomes. This concept is relevant when one considers the growing feeling of darkness and emptiness which pervades Ransmayr's work. The alternative worlds in his novels themselves cause an existential 'black hole' to develop, and are simultaneously threatened and overwhelmed by it.

What keeps the reader drawn to the edge of the potential black hole, the gravitational pull that draws Ransmayr's readers into a consideration of worlds on the brink – is the addictive seductiveness of his imagery. Images of both Imperial Austria and contemporary Austria created in *The Terrors of Ice and Darkness* are drawn in response to the great, white antagonist of the Arctic itself. In *The Last World* Naso/Ovid's stadium speech in Rome referring to the birth of the ant people is symbolically powerful in opening to the reader's contemplation life in a totalitarian state. Various reworked transformation stories from the lost *Metamorphoses* text reveal a postmodern/post-industrial last world, a strangely familiar place being overtaken and consumed by a restless and out-of-balance nature. Both worlds have relevance to social, political, and ecological issues facing twentieth-century Austria. The world of Moor and a world beyond are also familiar in *The Dog King*, with its resonances of post-World-War-Two Austria; labor camps, occupation forces, refugees and an issue of moral blindness in the process of being identified and faced.

In beginning a more detailed examination of images of Austria in Ransmayr's novels within the context of this 'black hole' analogy, one is drawn, in a reading of *The Terrors of Ice and Darkness,* to the character of the explorer-painter Payer, who after his return from the Arctic, completes canvas after canvas of ever-increasing dimensions, reproducing his own Arctic drama in paint. The scene of the expeditioners crawling, kneeling, overwhelmed by a physical world of darkness and ice is the key to a major confrontation in the novel; between the forces of nature and of civilization. "More than anything else (the painting) is a glorification of Weyprecht . . . the commander on water and ice stands before his men as they lie or kneel huddled in the snow – a preacher with his Bible in his right hand" (TID 194).

In the narrative strand of the novel which follows the experiences of the Weyprecht-Payer expedition to the North Pole between 1872-1874, the expeditioners' world represents a microcosm of the society of the Austrian Empire for the glory of which they venture northwards. It is a society privileging the scientific, the rational, the ordered, and also the heroic and elitist. The expedition leaders and representatives of Empire, Weyprecht and Payer, seek to conquer an alien polar terrain, but the Arctic exerts its own pressure in return, in the force of its climate and its extreme landscape. In archival documents, primarily the diaries of Weyprecht and Payer, the intention of these two leaders is clear. The Arctic landscape is seen as a tabula rasa upon which they will make their mark. They literally seek to define its boundaries, conquer its North Pole and raise flags of conquest over this alien world. "Payer now wants to set a new latitude record. The rumor spreads in the crew's mess that the first lieutenant not only wants to cross the 82nd parallel, but in fact also hopes to conquer the North Pole" (TID 155). Payer becomes obsessive. He becomes a tyrant on his dogsled expeditions, in his need to stamp his imprint on the Arctic landcape. His men "measure and baptize and suffer. Only Payer appears to bear these renewed tortures with enthusiasm" (TID 155-6). Weyprecht, a man of science, of reason, observes and records in the pursuit of knowledge. He conducts experiments to expand the boundaries of the known, not in terms of physical space, as did Payer, but in the realms of science. He compels his men by force of personality to trust him. He will be the center of their universe, their savior – "Weyprecht tells them they should not trust in miracles, but in him" (TID 70). This role is immortalized in Payer's final painting.

The mastery of man over nature and, further, man over men reveals a hierarchy dear to Enlightenment philosophy. The desire for order and rationality, for control and domination is seen in the image of expeditioners, as their ship is held fast in the Arctic winter, attempting to create cities of ice; building walls, houses, towers, even forts and palaces to impose their presence on the landscape (TID 71). Although the sailors see this as some sort of game, the activity is a potent symbol of the colonizing spirit of nineteenth-century Europe. However the movement of the ice causes the crew's man-made structures to collapse and sink. The power of nature is too strong and men's efforts are for nought. The expedition is drawn into the white hugeness of space, the 'white hole' of nature![4] The natural world transforms the men who seek to conquer it. The "Chronicle of Failure" (TID 56) tells of explorers, heroes, adventurers who are transformed into corpses and cannibals, their ships are damaged or sunk, when nature with all of its extreme means confronts the onward march of civilization.

The negative transformative power of this confrontation takes yet another form, which increasingly concerns Weyprecht. He sees the darkness revealed when the veneer of civilization is peeled back. This is the essential wolfishness of man, man's reversion to a natural brutishness, (an idea further examined in *The Last World[5]*). The physical darkness of Arctic winter is paralleled by a darkness of human behavior in the face of extremity and hardship, when codes of honor and decency slide toward the edge. As the narrator paraphrases, "No, an Imperial North Pole expedition could not ... *dared* not deteriorate into a pack of emaciated wolves" (TID 182). The physical darkness of the Arctic winter parallels the darkness of human behavior when confronted with extreme deprivation and fear. Civilized conventions of honor and decency disappear. Payer comes particularly to the reader's attention here. His treatment of the expedition crew becomes irresponsible, to the extent of putting them in unnecessary physical danger (TID 161). Weyprecht reports about Payer's threat to shoot him, should Payer be unable to return home (TID 183). This dark transformation can be seen as the effect of the confrontation between two worlds, the reemergence of a more primitive inner nature opposing that of the so-called civilization of humankind.

However, even after the expedition has survived unbelievable hardship to return home, confrontation between two opposing worlds is not yet at an end. The two expedition leaders must, despite an initial jubilation at their return, face questioning of the value of their achievements. The delirium of Weyprecht's final illness six years after his return from the Arctic parallels the dreamlike euphoria of their triumphal parade through Vienna. But Weyprecht comes to understand that "Arctic research has degenerated ... into a game for martyrs and was exhausting itself in the current ruthless pursuit of new latitude records for the sake of national vanity" (TID 188). Weyprecht and Payer must realize the transience, even uselessness of their almost superhuman efforts. Payer suffers the ridicule of cynics who have never left Vienna, when they reject his scientific findings. Vienna in fact becomes for Payer his own personal 'black hole,' symbolized as it is by petty jealousies, ignorance and doubt (TID 192). He is drained of integrity and rationality by it when he returns. So great is Payer's disappointment that he adds a footnote to his expedition report, "As to the discovery of a land unknown before ... I personally place no value on it today" (TID 193); and this from a man who had believed that "returning home with nothing to show, without a land: that would be more shameful than death" (TID 73).

The Weyprecht-Payer expedition occurred on what was virtually the cusp of two ages. The men were Enlightenment heroes, educated, confident and accomplished explorers. They survived the might of nature in their explorations and attempted to impose an order of maps, experiments and observations on that same unpredictable nature. But they both also experienced the darkness of doubt and eventual loss of certainty which became the experience of Austria and the rest of the modern world in the early twentieth century. The 'black hole' becomes a symbol for the modern condition. The disintegration of the world of Weyprecht and Payer and the questioning of the Enlightenment myth also anticipates the wider displacement and questioning of identity and place for Austria after the collapse of the Hapsburg Empire and a confrontation with the Hapsburg myth after the first World War.

The second narrative strand of *The Terrors of Ice and Darkness* concerns the disappearance of the young traveler, Josef Mazzini. He has physically vanished in the North Polar Circle and the novel is structured around his disappearance. Mazzini intends following in the footsteps of Weyprecht and Payer, but despite this act he is still seen by the reader as the antithesis of the heroic earlier leaders. Yet Mazzini is just as much a representative of *his* age, as were they. He is an isolated man, with no fixed identity or social place. From his childhood on, in his mother's home-town of Triest, he lived in the fantasy world of great adventurers and heroes. After his escape from the parental home to Vienna, he discovers how he can make his fantasies concrete: he writes stories. To his acquaintances he says that "he was redesigning the past ... He would think up stories, invent a plot or a course of events, write them down, then check whether there ever had been *real* precursors of his imaginary figures in the distant or recent past ... he was traveling back in time" (TID 11).

Mazzini first seeks to find his own authenticity through the creative imagination and writing. His explorations take place for many years in his head or in the archives. His adventures are an effort to reinvent reality and to pit himself against a society that he feels denies him credibility and challenge. Later he believes he is mounting his own struggle against forces of society that substitute real experience with simulation or a gratuitous enjoyment of extreme experiences through second-hand reading about them in travel books or watching films. As the narrator in the preface *Above All* expresses it: We were not content simply to go adventuring. We also made our adventures public . . . above all in reports and accounts, profusely illustrated and secretly fostering an illusion: that even the most remote and distant spot is as accessible as an amusement park, a twinkling Coney Island (TID 1).

While the technological twentieth century provides Mazzini with international plane flights and ice breakers to approach the North Pole in a way that negated the adventure and of course the hardship of an earlier age, he does act to refind an identity and a place, his own reality, away from the emptiness of his life in Vienna. In an ironic movement, Mazzini has pulled away from the 'black hole' of inauthenticity, dislocation and isolation, symbolized by his empty room in Vienna, for a voluntary and authentic movement into the white void of the Arctic. Ironically, shortly before he disappears, Mazzini appears to find an identity and a place. He stops writing in his journal, for, as the narrator comments, "A man who has found his place keeps no more travel diaries" (TID 172).

For Mazzini, the Northern Polar Circle is a further stage upon which a dark struggle occurs: the confrontation between the individual's need for authenticity and the impulse to the act of simulation in (post)modern society. Although the reader wishes to applaud Mazzini's attempt to escape the draining alienation of twentieth-century existence, to flee a life of second-hand experiences, one realizes that by wanting to recreate the Weyprecht-Payer expedition, to follow in its footsteps, Mazzini is simply carrying through another simulation, his own twentieth-century version of Nietzsche's eternal recurrence.[6]

The irony continues. Mazzini has wanted to become a hero. But in Longyearbyen in the Arctic Circle he is dismissed as a "spindly carnival fool" (TID 49). He is referred to by the locals as the "vacation boy" and "little one" (TID 87). Mazzini puts his own identity into question. He introduces himself as Antonio Scarpa (his ancestor who had traveled on the Weyprecht-Payer expedition) and is addressed in fun as "Weyprecht" by the eccentric Flaherty (TID 88)

Mazzini's achievements remain primarily cerebral, even after his journey to the Arctic Circle. However, after a failed effort to get to Franz Joseph Land by ship, he is taught how to dogsled by Kjetil Fyrand. It was his desire to emulate Commander Julius Payer, a dogsled expert. In this attempt Mazzini disappears with the dogs and sled into the ice and darkness. He leaves behind no sign, no remains on the tabula rasa of the Arctic landscape. In this act he erases his identity and place. This result can be seen as some sort of existential answer to the internal struggle between two worlds; the failure of Mazzini's attempt to find an authenticity of existence, a place and a name. The issues that Mazzini faces are universal in the post-industrial age. Issues of identity and place are also of particular relevance to Austrian generations, slowly confronting the myriad changes in geography, identity, truths and values over the past decades.

In Ransmayr's widely acclaimed second novel *The Last World*, the poet Ovid (Naso, in the novel) is reported as having died in exile. He has disapppeared, is absent from the life of the text but remains its focus. The Author is dead, but the text *Metamorphoses* lives on in the experience of his acolyte, Cotta, in the last world. Cotta, searching for the absent Ovid and his text, is subject to twin forces in contest. On one side is the repressive rationality of Augustus' Rome – represented as the center; on the other, the world of myth, literature and fantasy – on the edge, the outpost of exile, Tomi. However Cotta arrives in a 'last world' of transformation, which possesses characteristics of both worlds; the brutality, repression, passivity, violence of totalitarian Rome – and the chaos, craziness, and euphoria of myth and phantasia. The last world of Tomi is literally a 'black hole,' a dump at the end of the world, in which nothing and nobody retain their form. The transformations of Tomi spread only an existential darkness. In spite of the image of a reemerging Olympus, the end of the novel remains pessimistic. In the last world everything is other than is expected. Olympus can become a monster rising, sweeping the landscape free of humankind.[7]

In the novel Rome is drawn as a totalitarian state, a model of an ultra-rationalist Enlightenment society of the type critiqued by Adorno and Horkheimer.[8] Augustus is dictator, and an apparatus of state extends surveillance into all aspects of life. Ovid/Naso in Rome attempts to exert his individual voice and place but has been denied. Naso's play *Midas* is banned after violent protests by the moneyed classes (LW32). His exile is pronounced, based on a bureaucratic interpretation of a lazy wave of Augustus' hand (LW 42).

Naso's speech at the dedication of Augustus' Stadium of the Seven Refuges serves not only to evoke but to provoke. It is an address to the masses, telling of the birth of a new race, born of ants, after the plague on the island of Aegina. As Kiedaisch and Bornemann point out,[9] the language used to describe this birth is evocative of the Third Reich mentality. Naso describes the people born of ants so: "They were docile and asked no questions and followed their new leaders ... without complaint ... In times of war they were a nation of warriors. In times of defeat, they were slaves, and in victory, masters" (LW 36).

It is also highly provocative that Naso directly addresses the Roman citizens – and not their emperor. His speech contains subversive concepts such as transformation, change and the power of the masses. But the transformation that Naso anticipates is ambiguous. The malleability of the ant-people is such that would be manipulated by a totalitarian state.

From Naso's Book of Stones, Echo tells Cotta of the birth of a new race after the downfall of "wolfish humankind" (LW 96). They were a "brood of mineral-like hardness, with hearts of basalt ... without feelings, without a language of love" (LW 100). Ransmayr's adaption of this story of Deucalion and Pyrrha and Naso's Stadium speech are linked by the implied strength and hope of a new race, but it is a race which ultimately proves to have no individual power or will. These stories provide the reader with images of rebirth and transformation which are essentially pessimistic. The mythical and the real are connected in an analogy formed by the historical consciousness of the reader, where a reworked story of antiquity becomes a creative evocation of contemporary experience, with particular reference to the Nazi period in Austria.

The central image in *The Last World* that spans the totalitarian repression of Rome and the frightening chaos of metamorphosing Tomi is the saying of Thies, the German grave digger, "Man is a wolf to man" (LW 161). The brutish nature of mankind, revealed in a world of extremes is a central concern in Ransmayr's work. Thies is German, a moral refugee, the man with the unprotected heart (LW 160). He walks the paths of the last world, ministering to the sick and burying the dead. Thies had fled from Europe, but has found, like the reader, familiar horror in this world on the periphery. More than any other character, Thies' memories lift the reader out of the novel's atemporality to connect the last world with the horror of mass suffering of war and the Holocaust in our twentieth-century world. His comment, "They were all capable of anything" (LW 160), presents an essential pessimism concerning human nature in any age.

Time and place collapse in Ransmayr's last world. The collapse and transformation of the last world is potently communicated in the imagery of a chaotic imbalance in the landscape of exile. Tomi, the town of iron, is being eaten away by rust. The natural world actively overwhelms the man-made landscape (LW 165). Vegetation and animals overrun the buildings. Unpredictable and abnormal climate changes (LW 71), the beaching of fish (LW 71), the blooming of trees in midwinter (LW 6) not only reveal a world which cannot be interpreted logically, but a world whose phenomena seem to be extreme versions of environmental abnormalities that have developed in the Western world in the late twentieth century (for example global warming [10] and chemical pollution.).

Although he believes he left Rome as a personal protest, on the Black Sea Cotta remains a product of Rome. In Tomi he grasps desperately at notions of rationality and order, but he is overwhelmed by the darkness of the last world and succumbs to its chaos and confusion. He accepts the petrification of Battus (LW 132-134) and later symbolically takes his place on the epileptic's stool in Fama's shop. He becomes one of them.

One of Cotta's last rational thoughts brings him the realization that transformation is the existential condition between the two worlds. He understands that "nothing retains its form" (LW 6). Fantasy becomes reality, literature comes to life in the characters of the last world.

What the reader notes most clearly is that these metamorphoses in the last world do not create a positive new world. The transformations are signs of a material and symbolic condition of imbalance and darkness, of space where entropy reigns, a world in collapse. The massive landscape assumes new forms in the rolling convulsion of avalanches and earthquakes. Naso's columns do not survive in the expected form – and with that, Naso's claim to immortality engraved upon them (LW 28-9). The stone columns are almost always covered by a slimy carpet of slime, primeval sludge. In the final earthquake they are overturned. The words are lost to sight, but the truth of the *Metamorphoses* text lives on in life itself.

The 'black hole' of the last world seems to swallow any perception of form or identity. Cotta believes several times he has found Naso. The first time it was a carnival figure (Battus with the cardboard nose, LW 55), then later a trunk of a pine tree, stripped of its bark (LW 146). Other last world characters are transformed into stone (Battus), sound (Echo), birds (Tereus, Procne and Philomela) or other animals (Lycaon). Even Cotta seeks his place, his own name (LW 176). But his search for his own identity ends in a form of disintegration, a disappearance into emptiness, a transformation into the imbalance and chaos of the last world as he seeks the echo of his name.

The search for a universal truth, and an identity among the structure and artifacts of the past; the interpreting of myths of a bygone era, and the rejection of the brutalities of a recent past, places the experience of Cotta and the cast of the last world on one level in a particularly Austrian context. However the dialectic developed in *The Last World* is of universal as well as specific significance.

In Ransmayr's third novel *The Dog King*, the author has responded yet again to an historical moment and redrawn the history of that time. This world of the text is one which at major points diverges from what we accept as the history of post-World War Two Europe. The first set of worlds which contend in this novel exist in the receptive critical consciousness of the educated, historically aware reader. We know the essential facts of the Allied victory over the Nazi powers, the occupation of Germany and Austria – and also the political, economic and social policies followed by the Allies for the postwar period. It is the fictive world of Moor in Ransmayr's text that shakes us into a renewed contemplation of that postwar period, rewriting as it does the history of reindustrialisation and re-assimilation, reassessing the moral response of the occupied and occupying populations, and the inheritance of defeat in Germany and Austria. The complexity of the confrontation of these two worlds, that of the actual and that of the once-possible, is that there are seen to be many points where one shifts into the other. At these points of divergence the reader is jolted into a new alertness.

The fictive world of the text is also seen to be a dialectic composite. The world of occupied Moor is set against the world beyond the mountain barrier, the town of Brand and the lowlands. Another site of conflict is to be found within the character of Bering as he enters the town of Brand, literally the city of consumer bright lights and plenty, after a lifetime trapped in the dark exterior and interior world of Moor. The following discussion confines itself to this site of conflict in the text itself – the existential place between the worlds of light and darkness, 'black hole' of bitterness and despair into which Bering is drawn. Bering's almost dumb suffering strangely does not lift the flatness, almost indifference that permeates the text and chills the reader. The cast of Moor is frozen into inaction, both physically and morally in confrontation with a psychological and physical brutality that lives on after the end of the war.

The dark world of Moor is familiar to Ransmayr's readers. It is a variation of his 'last world' vision. Moor's inhabitants live an increasingly brutalized and primitive existence as a result of the Stellamour Plan, introduced by the occupying victors after the Oranienburg Peace at the cessation of European hostilities in the Second World War (DK 29). The Stellamour Plan follows the policy of deindustrializing the defeated, and returning the area to a harmless, self-sufficient, agrarian state. This policy forcibly re-primitivizes Moor and returns the area to a new barbarism. The area is isolated by the dismantling of transport and trade links. There is no electricity or fuel and Moor is progressively abandoned and forgotten as the occupying forces withdraw.

The darkness of Moor's physical landscape is paralleled by the effect of the Stellamour policy-makers on the mindscape of the inhabitants. Responses vary from the roaming bands of skinheads terrorizing the defenseless community, through the secret meetings of war veterans muttering impotent threats, to the ragged columns of pilgrims chanting slogans of atonement as they go from one memorial site to another.

The notorious occupation commander Major Elliot undertakes singlehandedly the moral re-education of the population, beginning with his Stellamour Parties (DK 34-5). At these, the villagers are forced to reenact scenes from the forced labor camp at the granite quarry. This undertaking is overtly theatrical. The villagers as newly recruited prisoners are allowed to carry cardboard cutout granite blocks, and blankets are provided for waiting extras on cold days as photographic shoots are set up: "But Elliot was not cruel. He did not insist that his supernumeraries stand half-naked in the snow like the figures in his mildewed snapshots, but provided them with blankets ... ; children and old people were allowed to wait in the tents during the set-up" (DK 35).

Such acts only establish the obvious impossibility of comprehending the horror of the original labor camp experience. The central image of such an attempt to force the Moor population into atonement is the memorial built into the quarry face, each letter being the size of a person. Its ironic message:

> Here
> Eleven Thousand nine Hundred and Seventy-
> Three People Lie Dead
> Slain by the Inhabitants of this Land
> Welcome to Moor. (DK 24)

This quarry is symbolically part of the barrier between Moor and the world beyond. It backs onto the Stony Sea, a natural barrier of mountains, glaciers, labyrinths of stone, a forbidden no man's land. The inhumanity of the events which took place in the quarry also separate this barbaric place from what is generally seen as the world of civilization.

Bering, the central character (despite the emphasis given by the translated title of the novel)[11] is a child of the peace, born on the last night of bombing. He appears as a man without a place. Even as a baby Bering seeks an escape, a place beyond the grasp of the pain and noisy suffering of the world around him. He swings aloft in his cradle like a bird and imitates the squawking of the chickens to blot out the painful sounds of the world his sensitive ears pick up (DK 12-13).

A member of the postwar generation, Bering symbolically rejects his place and his past. From the first he tries to escape the embrace of his newly returned soldier father, who drops the struggling child to earth. ("he cries, *Bleeds*!/ he cries/ *Stinks*! and squirms in the arms of the thin man . . . he begins to cackle! to cackle like a crazed, panicked chicken . . . so that the thin man can finally hold onto it no longer" DK 19-20). Bering inherits his father's role as blacksmith (and to an extent his father's blindness) but leaves the family home to link his fate with a new family, the representatives of the postwar era. His new master is Ambras, an ex-labor camp inmate in Moor, now the granite quarry's new manager, also known as the Dog King. The trio is completed by Lily, the blackmarket trader and border crosser, the daughter of an SS officer, who seeks a new life in Brazil.

As Ambras' chauffeur, Bering's early affinity with birds and flying itself is further symbolically strengthened. He drives Ambras' repaired and restructured limousine, which he christens the Crow (DK 76). The elegant vehicle with its shining claws is Bering's work of art. What he experiences as he drives is a form of flight. When the limousine is burned by the villagers of Moor, Bering mourns more over this loss than over the death of his mother.

It is in the world of rock and stone that Bering experiences the moment of truth that links the failure of flight, the failure of sight and the failure of his humanity. He is journeying through the Stony Sea between Moor and Brand with Lily, taking his delusional father to Brand, when he coldbloodedly shoots a chicken thief. Reawakened are his connections with the world of birds (DK 249-50), when the two thieves are seen carrying braces of living hens around their neck and heads, a seeming cloak of feathers (DK 247). Bering loses control, and on killing the defenseless thief also loses any possibility of connection with Lily. The perpetrator/victim relationship is also symbolically extended when Bering believes he sees Ambras in his rifle sights and asks himself whether "if it had been Ambras who was hit, he would have flung his arms that high above his head" (DK 251). Bering precipitates the death of his own humanity when he shoots the chicken thief, who is described as a "bird man" (DK 252), just as Bering himself had been described earlier.

Bering feels the power of the killer, and when Lily recognizes herself in him the moment separates them completely. Bering loses the object of his constant desire but discovers the invulnerability a weapon gives. Bering's capacity for unnecessary violence, including murder, is employed to a tragic extent later in the novel (DK 352).

The most powerful irony and inversion of the text occurs when Bering enters Brand. Brand is only in physical terms a city of light. Bering undergoes an existential enlightenment in Brand, but any sort of extended and enduring moral illumination does not occur. In fact, while Bering is given an explanation for his growing physical blindness and his disease is diagnosed as temporary, a greater moral darkness ultimately results.

Here Bering is given the answer to the black holes in his sight (DK 281-2). He has suffered a progressive darkening of his sight from the time he held Lily in his arms for the first time, his first and only kiss. Bering has become increasingly fixated on Lily. This fixed focus is apparently the cause of Bering's growing blindness. As Morrison, the eye medico of Brand explains it, Bering has stared too closely at one point for too long. ("What is it you can't get out of your head? . . . What have you been staring at? . . . some enemy . . . or some girl?" DK 280-81). Ironically the black holes in Bering's sight gradually disappear after Morrison's diagnosis. Yet while Bering's feelings for Lily alter,[12] a blackness of vision remains as a direct response to the second moment of illumination he undergoes in Brand.

Upon Bering's arrival Brand is literally an exploding ball of fireworks. The atomic bomb has been dropped on Nagoya, Japan bringing to an end the war in the Pacific (twenty-five years after the European peace). The Allied soldiers occupying Brand are celebrating, roasting chicken over fires, drinking (DK 260), the lights of the full shop windows and cinema screens making the scene almost as bright as day (DK 261). Bering's sense of alienation amid all this light and plenty is reinforced. Drunk and in the "wolf hours" (DK 264) after midnight, he sees for the first time the reality of life in his occupied country. His vision promotes an intense bitterness – "All a hoax!" (DK 268). His sense of injustice and unfairness bursts forth:

> Cars, tracks, runways! High-tension lines, department stores! Garbage cans full of delicacies, whole kettles full of punch! ... Was that the penitence, the punishment the great Bringer of Peace had prescribed for the lowlands? Was that their punishment? ... Shit, goddam bullshit ...
> Had there been no camps or barracks in the lowlands? No lime pits full of corpses?" (DK 267)

Bering's outburst suggests the ambivalence of Austria's moral response to past atrocities. The granite quarry, the symbolic heart of Moor stands as a memorial, that the shameful past should never be forgotten. But where are the monuments, shrines, memorial plaques, "temples of remembrance" in Brand? (DK 268): "The lowlands sparkled and shone like a huge amusement park, while ... in Moor ... black flags were raised on anniversaries, banners unrolled: *Never forget ... Thou shalt not kill"* (DK 269).

An overt consumerism clouds the lessons of the past. Remorse appears skin deep. The experience of Bering; his rejection of the past, fear of his darkening sight, his delayed attempt to understand the gaps in his vision and a residual moral blindness are emblematic of a wider debate in contemporary Austria. The delayed and partial attempt to come to terms with the past, a rejection of complicity, has great relevance to the society's confrontation with issues of Austria's role in the Third Reich. Such a confrontation can, however, only be portrayed in shades of gray.

Bering's response becomes frozen on the level of perceived injustice, and his bitterness and frustration increase upon his return to Moor, upon his discovery that his townsfolk had burned his beloved Crow, Ambras' Studebaker. An ever increasing series of inversions, repetitions and parallels grow from this point on in the text.

The population of Moor themselves prepare to become evacuees, refugees, the new dislocated. Their town is abandoned, to be used as an army practice ground. Bering becomes brutal and violent in overseeing the dismantling of the quarry's machinery. His power is backed up by a steel claw he has fashioned from the remains of Ambras' limousine. Bering assumes the ferocity of a dedicated Kapo, the forced labor this time is undertaken by the once masters of the quarry, the citizens of Moor.

The cycle continues. Ambras, Bering and Lily set sail for Brazil to set up a new granite quarry in Pantano ("Moor" in Portugese). Ambras suffers increasing torment from his shoulder joints, caused by his torture while in the Moor camp. The sexual ministrations of Lily open a door into the past, where once again Ambras is in the arms of his Jewish love, then again sentenced to the labor camp in Moor. The Dog King refinds his earlier fate by visiting the old prison ruins in Dog Island off the coast of Pantano.

The fateful expedition of Ambras, Lily, Bering and their Brazilian hostess Muyra to Dog Island suggests the futility of breaking the cycle. The past is alive and unavoidable. It becomes the present. Bering destroys almost by default the one person capable of giving him human warmth and an end to his isolation. His act shows the ever present darkness of violence and inhumanity that has blossomed from the dark inheritance of his life in Moor. And again he seeks to deny culpability.

Bering's ineffective attempts to escape the horror of his past and of his world; his desire for flight from his moral and physical entrapment in the world of darkness and stone, are capped symbolically by his final flight from the collapsing battlements on Dog Island. Linked by rope to his master Ambras, the two are irrevocably connected by the umbilical cord of history that has joined the master/ servant, perpetrator/victim over the centuries. Bering is dragged into the air by Ambras' step into nothingness as Ambras steps back in time to join the floating ash of his labor camp companions, as the bushfires on Dog Island send up their plumes of smoke.

On first examination, the world of occupied Moor is a 'black hole' in itself, a place delineated by the negatives of human experience. Isolation, brutality, inhumanity and ignorance continue to exist under a new postwar hierarchy of power. The darkness of bitterness and violence dominates even as Bering physically regains his sight. His blindness has been evidence of his emotional paralysis, his lack of real contact and communication. But there is no relief or brightening of existential vision. The site of conflict between worlds of darkness and light serves to deepen a black hole of despair and violence in Bering.

The dark holes in Bering's physical vision gradually disappear while a deeper moral blindness grows.

The final vision of *Morbus Kitahara* is one of futility and inevitability. One cannot escape the draining black hole of the past. Humankind exists on the brink, isolated and blinded. Of the three main characters in the novel, it is only Lily who is able to break the cycle. The motion of her life has always to break through barriers and to push into new space.

It appears it would take a strong dose of humor and lightheartedness to lift the reader's mood after an examination of Ransmayr's work. Consistently observed in his novels are the perception of alternative worlds existing in opposition, and a tension between the forces ruling these. This results in a draining negativity, a 'black hole' which symbolizes simultaneously the emptiness of human existence and the heavy threat the human race poses to itself in a postmodern future, not just in Austria but in the Western world in general.

University of New South Wales

Notes

1. It is, however, not the intention of this article to examine Ransmayr purely as an Austrian author or his novels simply as Austrian novels, as Robert Menasse suggests in his book *Das Land Ohne Eigenschaften* (*The Land Without Qualities*) (Frankfurt am Main: Suhrkamp, 1995), 142.

2. Ransmayr, "having arrived experiences a world which he left behind, which concealed its self-evidentness. . . ." Michael Cerha," Aufmerksamer Verfolger des Uneinholbaren," *der Standard*, 'Kopf des Tages,' Vienna , October, 1996.

3. The Ransmayr texts referred to in this article are: Christoph Ransmayr, *The Terrors of Ice and Darkness* (translated by John E. Woods) (London: Paladin, 1992), identified in the article as TID: Christoph Ransmayr, *The Last World* (translated by John E. Woods) (London: Paladin, 1991), identified in the article as LW: Christoph Ransmayr, *The Dog King* (translated by John E. Woods) (London: Chatto and Windus, 1997), identified in the article as DK.

4. The purity of nature in all her original power and cold-hearted beauty can be seen here as a contrast to an expanding 'black hole' of

civilization, where in the Ransmayr context an existential desperation is growing.

5. This idea is located primarily in the character of Thies and his comments on humankind's brutality, for example,"Man is a wolf to man," LW 161)

6. "... haven't we all been here before? ... mustn't we all not return for eternity?" in Friedrich Nietzsche, *Werke in Zwei Bänden (Works in Two Volumes)*, Volume 1, ed. Karl Schlechta (München: Carl Hanser, 1962), *Also Sprach Zarathustra (Thus Spake Zarathustra)*, Part 3 (Munich: C. Hanser), 653.

7. Ransmayr says: "The world emptied of homo sapiens does not have to be an apocalyptic, nuclear contaminated desert. What is so dreadful about a growing, blossoming wilderness without us?": Translated from Renate Just's article; *Christoph Ransmayr: Erfolg Macht Müde (Success is Exhausting)* in *Zeitmagazin*, N. 51 (16 December 1988), 50.

8. Theodore Adorno and Max Horkheimer, *Dialectic of Enlightenment* (translated by John Cumming) (London: Verso edition, 1979), 3-42.

9. As discussed in the article by Petra Keidaisch and Christiane Bornemann, 'Der Mensch ist dem Menschen ein Wolf' ("Man is a Wolf to Man') in Helmut Keise and Georg Wöhrle, "Keinem bleibt seine Gestalt: Ovid's *Metamorphosen* und Christoph Ransmayrs *Letzte Welt*' ("Nothing Retains its Form, Ovid's *Metamorphoses* and Christoph Ransmayr's *The Last World*'), *Fußnoten zur neuen deutschen Literatur* (University of Bamberg), Vol. 20, (1990), 14.

10. Peter G. Christensen examines this in his article, "The Metamorphosis of Ovid in Christoph Ransmayr's *Die letzte Welt*," *Classical and Modern Literature* (1992, Winter), Vol. 2/2, 148.

11. *Morbus Kitahara*, the original title, directs the reader's focus to Bering and specifically to Bering's disease, his partial blindness. This disease has, of course, a highly important symbolic role in commenting on the Austrian moral response to events in the time of the Third Reich and after.

12. For Bering the association between Lily and 'black holes' in his vision never quite ends. In the final chapter we find, "Where Lily is, there are always spots" (DK 351).

Underground Austria

Pamela S. Saur

The literary element known as place or setting looms large in much of Austria's literary history. Rural settings are prominent in *Volk* (popular), *Heimat* (provincial) and *anti-Heimat* (anti-provincial) literature of various genres, as is Vienna, in her various guises as intellectual coffeehouse society, kitschy tourist attraction, theatrical-operatic hub, cosmopolitan or proletarian city or multinational imperial capital. Interactions between rural and urban environments are common too, not only in literary works, but also in literary history; think, for example, of the uneasy union that occurs when *Volk* dramas are performed in the stately Burgtheater. In Austrian literature, too, East and West collide and interact; in Joseph Roth's Trotta family history in his novel *Radetzkymarsch* (Radetzky March), for example, the grand totality of the Austro-Hungarian Empire includes a moody Eastern realm that offers Carl Joseph von Trotta an alternative family root and a mental and physical retreat from the pressures exerted on him by his father and his military position, both representing the urban-centered Austro-Hungarian Empire. Looking beyond the literary territories of city and country, whether real or imaginary, what happens if we journey past the surface of the Austrian land and consider what lies below; what do we find, or what is conjured up in our imaginations, by the notion of another place: Underground Austria?

The phrase is likely to suggest immediately Freud's concept of the subconscious mind. Such an association is encouraged by Freud's statement, "I have an overwhelming affection for Vienna and Austria, even though I'm familiar with their underground territories."[1] Or, the phrase Underground Austria might evoke thoughts of a nightmarish Kafkaesque labyrinth reminiscent of the alleys of Prague's ghetto and appropriated as a cosmic home for modern anti-heroes alienated from everywhere real. The extraordinary influences of Freud and Kafka can justify thinking of Underground Austria as representing the subconscious mind and the existential nightmares of the entire Western world. On another level, Underground Austria is a real place, a counter-city existing beneath the streets and buildings of Vienna. Vienna Underground contains a modern subway system displaying ancient Roman artifacts unearthed when it was constructed in the late twentieth century. It contains catacombs and graves, deep storage and treasure rooms, wine cellars tinged with echoes of Turkish invasions, all steeped in history and tradition, memory and mood. This underground is full of cultural meanings, significant to religion and art, to monarchy, empire, ancient wisdom, and buried secrets, even to banal tourist enjoyment of Viennese coffee as a legacy of the Turks or new wine sipped in an ancient cellar. It is a landscape equally suited to Baroque visions of death as to buried guilt over Nazi collaboration or ancient anti-Semitism, as to any number of societal or individual fixations on the past or attempts to probe the reality (*Sein*) underneath the surface (*Schein*) of life. Austria aboveground, a thousand-year-old complex of real and literary *Heimaten* (homelands) is reflected, contrasted, and deepened by its counter-world below.

In the many definitions of typical Austrian literature, an enduring influence of the Baroque is frequently mentioned; a feature taken for granted despite the oddness that a movement that supposedly died out in 1690 in Germany should persist into the modern and postmodern ages in Austria. Also odd is the fact that the Baroque is sometimes defined as religiously earnest, primarily Catholic, although sometimes Protestant. In Austria, the label can just as easily be applied to Jewish writers and to writings that are quite secular. Some of the features of the Baroque are subtle and rather hard to measure; it would be a challenge to prove that Austrian literature, compared to other traditions, has more of the Baroque qualities of fluidity of form, tension, imbalance, or interaction of opposites. More easily identified are theatricality, contrasts and shifts between illusion and reality, and the emphasis on death and the transitoriness of life. The slogan "*Schein und Sein*" is identified with both Austrian and Baroque literature, along with its corollaries "life is a dream," "the world's a stage," and "the transience of all things." Life is a play or a dream; nothing is what it seems; we are all wearing masks and acting roles; everything around us, even life itself, is an illusion.[2] The cliché *Schein und Sein* may point to ironies, confusions, tricks, and deceptions found in human interactions, to levels of truth, complex communication, illusions, dreams, and artistic constructions that are somehow truer than reality. Behind our masks and underneath our costumes we may sometimes find dark and hidden secrets, other times death itself. Behind the beauty of the most perfect human body and the most sophisticated human behavior, however adorned and dressed up, is ugliness: whether in the form of ugly, even evil secrets of the human heart, or in the ugliness of the end of life, the hideous rotting corpse. The surface of Austrian literature – and of life as portrayed therein – must have a dimension behind it; if Austrian literature is Baroque, it must have created an ornamental surface in order to drive underground the truth of human life: the truth that much of our lives are governed by illusion, and the ultimate truth that life is short and transitory and death is eternal, the same truth that haunted the medieval as well as the Baroque age. Underground Austria represents death and the grave, hidden truth, eternal time, and a cultural past that will not die.

Another Underground Austria is the world of the suffering proletariat hidden behind Austrian culture of the wealthy and educated. Behind the surface of Vienna's artistic gaiety is a world of poverty and privation, a reminder that wealth and leisure are prerequisites for much art and many concerns of aesthetics, philosophy, and lifestyle. The socialist writer Alfons Petzold paints a grim picture of a Vienna of poverty and privation in his autobiographical novel of 1920, *Das rauhe Leben* (Raw Life). Among the countless ill-paid and insecure jobs held by Petzold as a teenager and young man in Vienna were writing cabaret songs and making plaster statues, but these artistic stints were only marginally less demeaning than the various types of dangerous and strenuous physical labor he had to perform to survive, interrupted by periods of unemployment and homelessness.

Writing about a particularly bad winter, Petzold draws a sharp contrast between the worlds of the rich and poor in Vienna:

> During the winter we were as hungry as dogs ... Unemployment rates in every trade were terrible, and the suffering of the lower classes kept getting worse ... The daily papers were full of reports of deaths from hunger and cold. Hordes of wretched people swarmed over buildings trying to get warm, and bloody fights broke out at the homeless shelters. At the same time other crowds of Viennese attended gay balls and enjoyed the spread of the festive mood of the carnival season ... At the sight of a poster proclaiming, "Singing and dancing all night long," I suddenly remembered a brief article in the paper with the headline, "Homeless man found frozen on manure pile."[3]

Among other harsh and unjust conditions, the novel chronicles a history of inhumane and demeaning treatment by doctors and hospitals in Vienna, suffered by both Petzold and his parents. In a particularly ringing indictment of the city, an unusually compassionate physician, Dr. Stein, tells his young patient, "Dear friend, . . . you have a bad infection in both sides of your lungs. But your real sickness is Vienna! Vienna with its air full of dust and particles of granite, is the cause of your tuberculosis."[4]

The author of *The Viennese: Splendor, Twilight and Exile*, Paul Hofmann, titles his introduction "The Roots of Ambivalence." His first sentence refers to a two-layered city, as he begins, "Like most clichés, those of Viennese charm and of merry Vienna are both true and false."[5] Hofmann suggests that the gay surface of Viennese life hides a dark reality behind: a reality of despair and suicide. He also sees a good deal of deception in Vienna, claiming that truth is often obscured by what he refers to as "the old Viennese art of '*Schmäh*' ("blarney, Viennese style")." He asks, "What is *Schmäh* and what is truth?" and gives a sobering example, asking if the [real feelings of the Viennese] were revealed when they passionately welcomed Hitler in 1938 or when they tearfully applauded the signing of the 1955 peace treaty, or whether both reactions were genuine.[6]

Hofmann also states in this introduction, "Burial pomp satisfies the Baroque city's enduring passion for theater,"[7] and claims that the Viennese "have always been fascinated by the macabre. An elaborate funeral is in the local vernacular called '*a schöne Leiche*' (literally: 'a beautiful corpse'). Members of the State Opera chorus will pick up a few extra schillings by singing at the graveside." He quotes Mozart as follows, "As death . . . is the true goal of our existence, I have formed during the last few years such close relations with this best and truest friend of humankind, that his image is not only no longer terrifying to me, but is indeed very soothing and consoling!"[8] Hofmann says further: "The city that inspired Mozart, Beethoven, and Schubert, the capital of Gemütlichkeit, of hand-kissing and the waltz, of . . . whipped cream and the annual opera ball, has long had one of the highest suicide rates in the world. When Sigmund Freud started investigating hysteria and other neuroses, . . . he found an ominous welter of cases."[9] He asks, "Is it surprising that in the city of imperial and plebian suicide and 'beautiful' corpses Freud discovered the death wish?"[10]

The view that literary and real Austrians are fascinated with death is also advanced by William M. Johnston in *The Austrian Mind*. He too comments on the high suicide rate, particularly among well-known Viennese, and adds, "Well into the twentieth century, Austrian Catholics believed that the dead live on in the souls of their relatives and friends. Grillparzer's *Die Ahnfrau* (1818) dramatized the legend of the 'poor soul' that wanders on earth until it has been avenged.... Exaggerated reverence for the dead encouraged indifference to the living. During the mid-nineteenth century Vienna's physicians seemed to prize the results of postmortem autopsies more highly than saving a patient."[11] Johnston also sees the preoccupation with death in more recent literary schools as well as in the Baroque movement, asserting, "Fascination with the transitory justifies classifying writers such as Hofmannsthal, Schnitzler, Beer-Hofmann, Schaukal, and Altenberg under the rubric of Impressionism."[12]

Impressionism focuses on savoring the sensory experiences of each moment, so it presents more of a materialistic, even hedonistic rebellion against transitoriness than the type of serious religious awareness of transitoriness that would warn the sinner to discount the surface of mortal life and look to the eternal. Hofmannsthal claimed that the Austrian sense of time differed from the German. Donald Daviau has written, "One major difference is the German lack of any sense of the present, according to Hofmannsthal, whereas Austrians live in the present: 'They (the Germans) struggle to attain a sense of the present; to us it is simply given.' Hofmannsthal adds that this is the source of the 'Glücksgefühl' (feeling of happiness) that comes from the music of Haydn, Mozart, Schubert and Strauss."[13] Time and space are needed to conceive of the Viennese surface that covers Vienna Underground. The surface consists of notes of music which can be heard only in the present, in visual life, celebrated in *Wie ich es sehe* (As I See Things), Peter Altenberg's first book; in the surface of masks and roles in the opera and theaters and in the hurly-burly carnival of Viennese cultural life. One might say that such a surface is all the more beautiful and celebrated because of what it covers up; or one might say that the Austrian culture's devotion to the beautiful surface causes the repression of ugly realities and the awareness of hideous threatening death. According to Johnston, Austrian fetishism about death "casts its spell most conspicuously in the crypt of Vienna's Capuchin Church (*Kapuzinergruft*), where since 1633 deceased Habsburg rulers have lain in bronze caskets ... In the crypt a visitor – even today – cannot help but tremble before the dead, as they molder side by side in sarcophagi sculpted with emblems of life yet enveloped in an odor of dust."[14]

Hofmann also remarks on the same attraction. He describes the double sarcophagus of Empress Maria Theresa and her husband as "almost frivolous in its Rococo playfulness: the imperial couple are shown sitting up in their matrimonial bed with a cherub benignly looking on." Commenting on the number of corpses there and the skulls of rulers wearing imperial crowns, Hofmann says, "The Capuchin crypt seems designed to inspire odd and morbid sentiments rather than reverence."[15]

The word *Kapuzinergruft* was given special meaning in literary history by Joseph Roth, in a novel so titled. The novel is a sequel to the more famous and better loved *Radetzkymarsch*, a poignant portrayal of a family whose history is infused with the history and values, glories and flaws, as well as the geographical and ethnic breadth of the Habsburg Empire; the family's waning and dying out parallels that of the Empire as well. The fact that there is a sequel does not mean that the Empire in the first book does not live on in the present day as a contribution to the enduring "Habsburg myth" of tourism and literary imagination. In the sequel, another member of the Trotta family struggles with personal, familial and national identity crises after returning from service and Russian imprisonment in World War I. This Trotta, Franz Ferdinand, comes home only to be deserted by his wife and become lost in alienation. The announcement of the Anschluss, in the final pages of the book, completes the process of his utter disorientation in the world. In a pitiful and ridiculous gesture, he makes a pilgrimage to the *Kapuzinergruft*, which is not even open for visitors, telling the monk on duty, "I want to visit the coffin of my Emperor, Franz Joseph." The monk blesses him, and the novel concludes with the question, "Where can I, a Trotta, go now?"[16] Franz Ferdinand is not allowed to complete his pilgrimage underground and into the past, but the *Kapuzinergruft* is here accorded the historical and cultural meaning ascribed to it by commentators Hofmann and Johnston. The book ends at the dawn of the Nazi era, to which Roth gives no underground associations; Joseph Roth did not live long enough to see Austria freed and labeled the "first victim of Nazi aggression," or to assess the ensuing fifty years of complex Austrian reactions to the Nazi period.

Particularly in the English-speaking world, popular images of Vienna above and below ground have been influenced by the classic British mystery film of 1949, "The Third Man," starring Orson Welles.[17] Filming took place in postwar Vienna, still divided into four zones by the occupying powers. Mood, characters, and plot all depend heavily on the realities of that decade-long historical period, namely, a thriving black market, strict controlling authorities, and widespread mistrust between authorities and citizens, foreigners and natives. Nevertheless the film has contributed to a lasting image of Vienna as a double-dealing and mysterious place, where nothing is what it seems. The traditional dichotomy of *Schein und Sein* is put to particular use, both in the context of a mystery movie and in the historical context of the postwar period. The shadowy city, still filled with wartime rubble, is an eerie enough setting, but the violent denouement of the story takes place underground, as the characters chase each other through Vienna's dark and echoing labyrinth of underground sewers and canals. So haunting are these scenes that they are included, in association with Freud's theories on Oedipus and the subconscious mind, in an educational film on modern influences of Greek mythology.[18] According to a 1997 booklet on Austrian film by Gertraud Steiner, the film had this lasting effect: "Vienna's sewers, where Orson Welles met his end, have remained a major tourist attraction to this day."[19]

The enduring influence of this film is also seen in the sub-title of Berndt Anwander's 1994 tourist-oriented guidebook, *Unterirdisches Wien: Ein Führer in den Untergrund Wiens. Die Katakomben, der Dritte Mann und vieles mehr* (Underground Vienna: A Guidebook: The Catacombs, The Third Man, etc.) The many chapters and photographs in this book provide a guide through underground Vienna, concluding with "Sagen und Legenden" relating various chilling stories about strange underground creatures, lost wayfarers, and amazing underground connections. The book ends with a discussion of the interest in Underground Vienna stimulated by the film "The Third Man." Among the rumors and speculation is the belief that Orson Welles had the canal walls perfumed and that he used a "double" for some underground scenes, a Viennese butcher. The book ends with this question, "Is the 'real' 'Third Man' actually Viennese after all?"[20]

The postwar author, Herbert Zand, published *Erben des Feuers* (Legacy of Fire) in 1961, a novel that uses underground cellars and ruins to emphasize Vienna's dark and violent underside. One event mentioned repeatedly in the book is an experience that haunts one of the female characters. She was raped by a soldier in a cellar, and she bore a son as a result. The city is also haunted by the escapades of violence and vandalism of a rich industrialist's son, whose disturbed condition is at least partly a result of wartime trauma. However, his powerful father covers up his crimes, just as Vienna's postwar veneer of prosperity and apparent well-being seems to cover over the repressed Nazi past and the horrors of war. When the industrialist is compelled to go underground to chase his errant son, he feels claustrophobic. He and several others confront the son in his underground hideaway, which was built by the invading Turks and used by the German army during World War II. After the ensuing cover-up, the comment is made, "There wasn't even a scandal," followed by these words: "The whole city is a scandal. But if you take a closer look, you find only honorable ladies and gentlemen."[21]

Franz Ferdinand Trotta's modern homelessness, like the literal exile of Joseph Roth and so many other authors who fled the Hitler regime, is a persistent theme of modernist literature of the Western world. Thus, instead of being a real place, the underground can also serve as a metaphor for alienation. In 1973 the American critic Edward F. Abood published a book called *Underground Man*. Beginning with Dostoevsky's character in *Notes from Underground*, he proceeds to identify a gallery of European literary characters as archetypal underground men, alienated outsiders who view human society as strangers. The viewpoint and assumptions of the book are now rather out of date, as is the prefeminist exclusion of female experience and the cold-war chapter "Underground Man and Communism." Among the now quaint features of the book is the fact that it is virtually lacking in consideration of the idea of the underground as a place at all. Rather, the territories from which these characters view the world are clearly psychological or philosophical, not underneath any geographical or physical space. In contrast to such a notion of the underground are the richly concrete and specific associations evoked by the phrase "Underground Austria."

In addition to the other darlings of the American sixties and seventies, Sartre, Camus, and Hesse, Abood not unexpectedly claims Franz Kafka as one of his Underground Men, deciding to categorize him under "Underground Men and God," not "Underground Man and the Void," where he probably also could have been made to fit. While most of the discussion concerns Kafka's *The Castle*, despite its towering above-ground height, Abood does refer to a notable underground story of Austrian tradition. He writes, "The humanlike animal in 'The Burrow,' who has spent most of his life constructing an under-the-ground fortress against his enemies, suddenly begins to hear noises which grow progressively louder and which portend his imminent destruction."[22] This story describes an underground dwelling-place in very physical terms. The protagonist calls it a "fortress," using these words, "my fortress . . . which I have torn away from the unyielding soil by scratching and biting, shoving and pounding...."[23] The rooms and passageways are also described, as is the mossy cover supposed to hide the burrow from enemies.

Physical as the burrow is, the story concentrates a good deal on the psychological meaning of the burrow to its inhabitant. He is protective of his food and constantly in fear of enemies and death, as animals in the wild may well be. However, animals in the wild do not verbalize their thoughts as this one does, so it is hard not to think of this animal as representing human psychology in some way, whether that of Kafka or so-called "modern man." The burrow-dweller says that his camouflaged moss-door is "the actual entrance to the burrow," and continues, "It is secure, if anything in the world can be called secure."[24] This could be an expression of insecurity experienced by animals; however, other statements express masochistic feelings animals are less likely to have. The animal says he threw himself deliberately against a thorn bush, "to punish myself for a guilt that I can't identify,"[25] and he reproaches himself for taking too many breaks in his burrow-building work. Despite the fact that the burrow, its inhabitant, and the meat it eats and hordes, are described in concrete physical terms, the reality of the burrow seems more psychological and imaginative than geological or biological. The setting of the story is underground, but we are not told under what nation or neighborhood it lies. While we might presume that it is beneath the Austro-Hungarian Empire, Kafka's status as a world author would make it safer to suggest that it lies beneath the Western world, or human society in general.

The haunting cultural icons of Kafka and Freud are present in both the empty placeless psychological dwelling of Abood's Underground Man and in the overly full and physically real territories of Underground Austria. In the book, *Eine Reise in das Innere von Wien* (A Journey into the Interior of Vienna) Gerhard Roth includes an essay on underground Vienna called "The Second City." He remarks there, "The thought comes to mind that Sigmund Freud could have made his discoveries only in Vienna, where such truths are not out in the open, but buried underground, seemingly 'vanished,' but still there."[26] Despite this somewhat fanciful association of underground Vienna and the subconscious, the essay it introduces attempts to be scrupulously factual and statistical. Marshaling facts about numbers of people buried and items stored underground, interviews conducted, smells and sights of dust, Roth also emphasizes his emotional reactions to exploring Underground Vienna. He says dramatically, "Vienna is a great necropolis, a city of the dead."[27]

Roth notes that the idea of an elaborate underground network under inner Vienna is something of a legend, and asserts, "This legendary labyrinth actually existed."[28] At the time of the Turkish invasions of 1529 and 1683, enormous rooms were constructed, and cellars as deep as seven levels underground. These cellars were used as air raid shelters during World War II, and largely closed up again thereafter. Roth next describes the underground storage system beneath the National Library, containing 2.6 million volumes, and growing every year. He adds that this system was also used during the war to protect treasures, and he adds that people can easily get lost in the system, and books are sometimes lost for years. Many volumes carry another sign of the not-so-distant but haunting Nazi past, bearing a mark of censorship, the stamp "*Gesperrt*," crossed off. Other eerie underground regions are former Imperial wine cellars under the Hofburg castle, now containing hundreds of plaster statues of Emperors, writers, even a washerwoman, dusty and randomly mixed together.

Roth continues, "An additional depository of stage props for nightmares is found in the cellar of the Natural History Museum." Here are stored thousands of scientific specimens of fish, some poorly preserved and disintegrating, some several hundred years old. Roth comments, that they make one think "of the terrifying childhood memory of being confronted with death for the first time." Next Roth reassures us, "Less bizarre is the mausoleum for paintings under the art history museum."[29] and then turns to the *Kapuzinergruft*, pointing out in particular that the hearts, brains, eyes, and bowels of many rulers were buried in separate containers. After cataloging how many thousands of graves lie beneath the *Michaelerkirche* (St. Michael's Church) and the *Stephansdom* (St. Stephan's Cathedral) in central Vienna, Roth mentions the Roman graves, ruins, and 90,000 artifacts unearthed by the 1973 subway excavation; he describes enormous storage vaults of wine, and ends with descriptions of rain water and waste sewers.

We arrive at the notion that, when the truth comes out, Vienna, and perhaps Austria and the world itself, is a foul-smelling sewer, if a perfumed one. Accompanying the traditional cliché of beautiful Austria and the traditional cliché that beautiful Austria covers up an ugly underneath, is the tradition of asserting that the ugly underneath is the real thing. Thomas Bernhard, for example, writes in his autobiographical books about the misery of his childhood and his longing to commit suicide: "My grandfather saw the world correctly, as a sewer."[30] His hometown, not Vienna, but Salzburg, is world-renowned as a beautiful tourist attraction; this beauty makes him all the more eager to expose the dark side. Bernhard writes:

> Everything in this city stifles creativity ... The city is built on a foundation of hypocrisy ... Salzburg is a perfidious facade, used by the world to portray its falseness, ... My hometown is in reality a fatal disease ... and if [its inhabitants] don't leave at the decisive moment, then directly or indirectly, sooner or later, they kill themselves or are destroyed ... slowly and miserably by Salzburg, with its archbishops and fine architecture, an anti-human slow-witted Nazi Catholic cemetery. This city is ... a burial ground for fantasies and wishes, beautiful on the surface, but all the more hideous underneath.[31]

If Austria is a beautiful proud land and a disgusting sewer of misery and self-hatred, then it must still be a tense Baroque union of opposites. The idea of Underground Austria brings together fantasy and reality, serious literature and history, popular film and anecdote, and cultural materials ranging from the most scholarly to the most popular and tourist-oriented. Of course, all lands are lands of contrast, all literary traditions confront death and deception; all lives and societies have their dark sides and their peculiarities; nevertheless, the real and imaginary territories of Underground Austria do seem to be peculiarly Austrian.

Lamar University

Notes

1. Quoted by William M. Johnston, *The Austrian Mind: An Intellectual and Social History 1848-1938* (Berkeley: University of California Press, 1972), 444.
2. The source for this discussion is *German Baroque Literature: The European Perspective*, Gerhart Hoffmeister, ed. (New York: Ungar, 1983).
3. Alfons Petzold, *Das rauhe Leben* (Berlin and Weimar: Aufbau Verlag, 1985), 153.
4. Ibid., 368.

5. Paul Hofmann, *The Viennese: Splendor, Twilight, and Exile* (New York: Anchor Press, Doubleday, 1988), 1.
6. Ibid., 6.
7. Ibid., 5.
8. Ibid., 4.
9. Ibid., 1.
10. Ibid., 4.
11. William M. Johnston, *The Austrian Mind: An Intellectual and Social History 1848-1938*, 166-168.
12. Ibid., 169.
13. Donald G. Daviau, "The Reception of Franz Grillparzer by Turn-of-the-Century Writers," *Modern Austrian Literature*, Volume 28, Nos. 3/4 (1995), 215.
14. Johnston, 167-168
15. Hofmann, 4.
16. Joseph Roth, *Werke* II (Köln: Kiepenheuer & Witsch, 1976), 982.
17. *The Third Man*. Producers Carol Reed and Hugh Perceval. Screenplay Graham Greene. British Lion Films. 1949.
18. *Greek Fire: Source and Myth*. Producer Reed Guest. Consultant Oliver Taplin. Mystic Fire Video. Transatlantic Films Productions. 1989.
19. Gertraud Steiner, *Film Book Austria: The History of the Austrian Film from Its Beginnings to the Present Day* (Vienna: Medium Owner, Federal Chancellery, Federal Press Service, second edition, 1997), 34.
20. Berndt Anwander, *Unterirdisches Wien: Ein Führer in den Untergrund Wiens. Die Katakomben, der Dritte Mann und vieles mehr.* Mit 160 Fotos von Thomas Reinagl (Wien: Falter Verlag, 1994), 342.
21. Herbert Zand, *Erben des Feuers* (Wien: Europa Verlag, 1972), 236.
22. Edward F. Abood, *Underground Man* (San Francisco: Chandler & Sharp, 1973), 33.
23. Franz Kafka, "Der Bau," *Beschreibung eines Kampfes: Novellen, Skizzen, Aphorismen aus dem Nachlaß* (New York: Schocken Books, 1946), 191.
24. Ibid., 172.
25. Ibid., 186.
26. Gerhard Roth, "Die zweite Stadt," *Eine Reise in das Innere von*

Wien (Frankfurt am Main: Fischer Taschenbuch Verlag, 1994), 14.

27. Ibid., 26.

28. Ibid., 15

29. Ibid., 21

30. Thomas Bernhard, *Die Kälte: Eine Isolation* (Munich: Deutscher Taschenbuch Verlag, 1991), 68.

31. Thomas Bernhard, *Die Ursache: Eine Andeutung* (Munich: Deutscher Taschenbuch Verlag, 1977), 9-10.

American Writers and Austria in the 1930s

Horst Jarka

Even when Austria was still one of the countries "much less trodden by English travelers"[1] its scenery and art did not blind visitors to its social problems, and in 1837 John Murray in the standard English-language guide book of the time felt obliged to defend Metternich's Austria against its critics "who have not even done justice to the beauties of the country." American Romantic writers like Washington Irving and Longfellow still found the Austria they had expected from their reading, a country of picturesque scenery, of legends and folksy charm, but with the advent of Realism in American literature, criticism in travel writing increased. The most widely read critic of Austria in the nineteenth century was, of course, Mark Twain; no matter how much this dyed-in-the-wool democratic American enjoyed being lionized by Viennese high society and how much he praised Vienna's cultural richness, his sharp perception of social and political reality was never bribed by glamour or by aesthetics.[2] He was the first of many subsequent travelers to condemn Austrian anti-Semitism. Only the New England patrician Henry Adams shared the prejudice: he found both Vienna and Salzburg to be "Americanized and Judasized."[3] Twain was aware of just how wobbly the Monarchy was; the Italophile antimonarchist Adams would have liked to see the Austro-Hungarian Empire "wiped out"; he died a few months before his wish was fulfilled.

The American involvement on the Italian front in World War I came late and was very limited, so in American war fiction Austria did not figure at all except as the unqualified enemy in Hemingway's *Farewell to Arms* (1929), and the glorious winters of 1924/26 that he spent in Vorarlberg[4] made him forget that his skiing buddies had ever been soldiers on the other side. Anti-Austrian polemics only surfaced in the Cantos of the Italophile Ezra Pound in which he repeatedly debunked Franz Joseph, the "old bewhiskered sonovabitch Francois Guiseppe of whom nothing good is recorded."[5] He blamed him for World War I and was delighted at the Austrians' loss of Südtirol.

Other American writers in the twenties were more friendly, that is, the few who visited or wrote about Austria at all. The expatriates of the Lost Generation had made Paris their base camp. Austria was still off the beaten track and suffering from the aftermath of the war and the peace. In 1919 T.S. Eliot found "the destitution, especially the starvation in Vienna unspeakable."[6] In his *Waste Land* (1922) of Europe, Vienna was one the unreal cities threatened by Bolschewism, the "hooded hordes swarming over endless plains" speeding the *Untergang des Abendlandes* (Decline of the West). In July 1927, when the police massacre foreshadowed the decline of Austrian democracy, the left-wing writer Sinclair Lewis wired home three newspaper reports on the theme "Gay Vienna is no longer Gay."[7] For Thomas Wolfe who a few weeks later visited Vienna as a culture tourist the city's traditional image reasserted itself: "There was a revolution here three weeks ago in which four hundred people lost their lives, but you could not tell it from the gaiety of the city's life [which] is un-Teutonic as anything [and] more spontaneous than that of the Parisians."[8] Only when a year later he accidentally found himself in a district beyond the *Gürtel*, did he realize that Vienna could be as dreary as the slums of England or America.

So much for minimal pointers to back up my focus on Americans' reflections on Austrian socio-politics in the 1930s when they were inescapable to even the most devoted pilgrim to Alpine beauty and Vienna's glory – which was the first to fade.[9] Although all of the works I am going to present strongly reflect Austrian politics, my focal reduction cannot do justice to all facets of these often very complex literary works.

With the onset of the thirties the myth of "Gay Vienna" could only be evoked ironically as in Robert E. Sherwood's play *Reunion in Vienna* (1931). Lynn Fontanne and Alfred Lunt delighted 280 audiences with this hilarious satire on a decrepit nobility, the Habsburg laws, and psychoanalysis, "Austria's last remaining industry,"[10] all succumbing to the irresistible charm of some archduke Rudolf, who in defiance of Mayerling and all that, conjures up a happy-go-lucky Habsburg myth. Sherwood wrote the play as a conscious escape from his pessimistic view of the future. "It is relieving," he wrote in his preface, "for an American writer to contemplate people who can recreate the semblance of gaiety in the face of lamentably inappropriate circumstances."

How inappropriate the circumstances were for the semblance of gaiety in Austria, American readers could discern from Brunngraber's devastating *Karl und das 20. Jahrhundert* (*Karl and the 20th Century*) whose translation in 1932 Dorothy Thompson had urged because of its relevance for America (*Books*, 1933). It was this international context in which the tragedy of February 1934 attracted world-wide attention. There was, however, no International Brigade to help the *Schutzbündler* who were the first to defend democracy against European fascism, but there were some British and American writers who passionately took sides with their pens after the bloodshed. In fact, February 1934 evoked the sympathies of more American writers than any other event in Austrian history before 1938 and put an end to the myth of Gay Vienna. In the American image of Austria in the twenties sympathy had prevailed. In the Great Depression Austria shared the crisis well known to American writers, and in their image of Austria sympathy deepened into empathy – an empathy with the Austrians of a shared ideology – and this empathy was expressed with an emotional engagement unheard of in any accounts before. In 1934 Boris Todrin, a nineteen-year-old student in New York, wrote: "Although the fire was raging in Austria, I felt its hot flames here in America."[11] His forty-page poem *Five Days* describes the details of fight and defeat, contrasting the achievement of Red Vienna with the destruction and suffering.

Heroics turned into accusation in a poem that Alfred Hayes published in the *Partisan Review* (April-May, 1934). Following the Communist Party line he blamed the Social Democratic leader Otto Bauer for the debacle. Of all such damnations of the "traitor" Bauer, that of Hayes was one of the most vicious. Much better known than Todrin or Hayes was Vincent Stephen Benét who in 1936 published his "Ode to the Austrian Socialists." He destroyed the cliché of "the laughing city of tunes and wine," contrasted the "city of *Schlagobers*" to that of "starved children," and mourned the progressive image of Red Vienna, the ordinary life of the peaceful people "who believed in parks and elections," and city apartments "built by people for people, not to make one man rich."[12] On his travels through Europe Paul Engle changed from an applauded American patriot to a "disappointing" left-winger and was horrified by Vienna's tragedy: "Here, Europe laughed and then the jaw was broken,"[13] and with Whitmanesque pathos Engle eulogized the dead workers. Benét's, Todrin's, and Engle's long poems are the American examples of what the Austrian historian Adam Wandruschka called "a kind of Karl-Marx-Hof-Mystik"[14] which, however, unlike other mysticisms, was based on brick and mortar and low rent. These three young authors said poetically what the journalist John Gunther was to say in 1938 in his widely read *Inside Europe*: "The workers of the world will never forget the February heroism of the Vienna proletariat."[15] Gunther at least did not forget it. Thirty years later in his novel *The Lost City* (1964), Gunther reaffirmed his sympathies with the Viennese Socialists and, in his highly fictionalized autobiography, he himself, as an American journalist, fights with the *Schutzbund* in Floridsdorf.

The extensive treatment that the complex February issue demanded was attempted by Hilde Abel in her novel *Victory Was Slain* (1941), based on newspaper accounts and ideologically, it seems, on Friedrich Wolf's play *Floridsdorf. The Vienna Workers in Revolt* (American translation 1935) and possibly on Franz Hoellering's *The Defenders* (1940). According to *Books*, 26 October 1941 "the book presupposes a sound knowledge of events in Central Europe or the reader will hardly be able to follow her story." The reader who has such knowledge is not much better off; he recognizes the main events, but when Abel fictionalizes them, the weaknesses of a first novel become glaring. Abel divides the characters into the bad Blacks and Greens, and the good Reds and the doubtful Pinks who eventually turn red and fight. She psychologizes the tensions between the workers and the intellectuals in the Socialist leadership, reduces the enemies to caricatures, and loses her readers in the fighting scenes. Abel spins too many threads, some of them promising, but leaves many knots. Clear is Abel's conviction that the Socialist defeat prepared the way for the Nazi-takeover four years later. The book was published a few weeks before the United States entered the war in 1941, and the account of the *Schutzbund*-martyrdom implied a plea for American intervention: "May the readers heed Abel's plea that democracy must never again act too late" (*Books*, 26 October 1941).

Christopher Isherwood (1904-1986) offered a completely different point of view. His novelette *Prater Violet* (1946) was not about the battle of February 1934 but the reactions to it in far-away London, those of a Viennese Jew, and of the Londoners in the film studio for which he works. Isherwood juxtaposes the intense political awareness and worries of the Austrian who was robbed of his livelihood in Berlin by Hitler and whose family is still in Vienna, to the insular indifference around him, the emotionality of the Austrian to the coolheadedness of the English and their coolheartedness out of ignorance. To this contrast of hetero- and auto-images (Isherwood was an Englishman who had become a U.S. citizen in 1939) is added the irony between the operetta-Vienna of the "Prater Violet," the movie the Austrian has to direct, and the reality of the February disaster. In another ironic twist, the reactionary movie is a success, even in post-February Vienna. This skillful interplay of images of Vienna gains human concreteness in the character of the fervent Socialist film director, Isherwood's loving portrait of his friend Berthold Viertel.

The critical months after February 1934 were the background of the work of Kay Boyle (1909-1992), who did not depend on secondary sources but supposedly wrote from first-hand experience. Her controversial and contradictory works demand some background: Boyle was a twenty-two-year-old, rebellious writer with leftist sympathies when she joined the expatriates in France, and was one of the very few who went on to Austria. The Boyles arrived in Vienna in September 1933. Kay, depressed by the poverty in the Vienna streets, the rain, and a flu, moved to Kitzbühel and lived there until April 1935. i.e. she was in Austria during the worst of the Depression, the February tragedy, and the murder of Dollfuss. Boyle was, however, not aware of Austrian politics when she arrived. She had just published a sensitive novel about homosexuality, and her first Austrian character (in *Count Lothar's Heart*, 1935) was an officer who returned from a P.O.W. camp in Siberia and revealed to his fiancé his true sexual preference. In her sympathy with the ostracized, Boyle also added another nuance to the image of Gay Vienna: in one of her Viennese scenes a gay and lesbian bar is vandalized with tear gas.[16] It is not clear whether the scene was factual or fictitious and whether there were any political implications. Boyle's defense of homosexuality was unequivocal. Still, for herself she believed in motherhood and, only after three disappointing girls, was blessed with the wished-for boy.

Politics were still avoided in *Maiden, Maiden* (1934), another early story which, however, introduced the Austrian male type that Boyle favored: the tough, tanned mountain man with gleaming white teeth, an Aryan sexual ideal à la Louis Trenker, the movie hero. In this story he is a mountain guide irresistible to a frustrated American woman. Such men are obviously not found in Vienna, where it was usually the beautiful women who attracted foreigners. Now Boyle's Austro-American focus shifted from the capital to the western provinces and thus to the rise of Nazism so strong there. The Alpine scenery of traditional mountaineering, travel and tourist writing was no longer a relaxing playground but a battlefield, still beautiful but charged with tensions. The romanticism of "mountain gloom and mountain glory" [Marjorie Nicholson] blended with the romanticism of a political mythology. Every night the mountain slopes blazed with swastikas, and one of the men who lighted them was the sympathetically portrayed protagonist in Boyle's much anthologized short story "The White Horses of Vienna." This clean-cut, blond, and athletic mountain village doctor has been injured on one of his nightly climbs, and a Jewish assistant from Vienna, filling in for him, lives in the same house. The doctor, not overtly anti-Semitic, tolerates him because he needs him; the doctor's wife sees in him an incarnation of all the anti-Semitic and anti-city clichés so prevalent in rural Austria. The Jewish doctor, for a Viennese intellectual of the time incredibly unpolitical and naive, approaches others on a purely human level and even wants to help when the doctor is arrested for his Nazi activities. Devoted to art, the Jew talks enthusiastically about the Lipizzan stallions as a symbol of beauty and grace, and an Austrian tradition and culture whose power he still feels although its glory is gone – a culture, though Boyle does not explicitly say so, in which the Jew could still feel at home. Boyle, the American, succeeds in preserving as a valid symbol of the Habsburg myth the White Horses which already at that time had been reduced to a patriotic tourism cliché. In the story the graceful dance of the horses is contrasted to the artistry of the Nazi doctor's grotesque marionette play in which a "monstrous grasshopper" (Hitler) outdoes a pitiful clown (Dollfuss). Boyle's color symbolism, which ties the story together, shows the cultural deterioration: the whiteness of the horses has been superseded by the whiteness of the "savagely clean" doctor's and other Nazis' shirts and knee-socks, and the inhuman, alienating snowfields and glaciers.

Boyle's story was awarded the O'Henry Prize in 1935. The one dissenting vote on the jury seemed justified by Boyle's approach in her next work, in which one becomes aware of the dividing line between works written before and after 1938, between lack of foresight and the benefit of hindsight. Boyle's novel *Death of a Man* (1936) is set in the months preceding the assassination of Dollfuss in July 1934. After the Socialist defeat in February, the battle rages between the two kinds of fascism, the Nazis and the homemade variety, the *Heimwehr*. In the novel another Nazi doctor in Tyrol is portrayed with even more empathy than the one in the story. He is a conscientious doctor, loving to the children under his care, he is sporty, loves the mountains, and is, of course, handsome. The novel starts out with a romance between this doctor and a holidaying American who sends her weak husband packing. But the time is summer 1934, and the love story turns political. The American's infatuation even makes her light swastikas with the other Nazis and swear at the *Heimwehr* who puts them out – in a scene that recalls the camaraderie of Leni Riefenstahl and Trenker in their nationalistic mountain movies in the 1930s. Finally she, who had once lost her identity in her own American, i.e. Middle Western, male-dominated family, is afraid of losing it again and deserts the doctor for having lost his free will by becoming a cog in the Nazi machine. After Hitler has Röhm murdered on 1 July 1934, the doctor realizes that the Nazis and he himself are "in a delirium of faith, reeling completely drunk towards death."[17] Looking for his lover, he goes to Vienna at the time of the murder of Dollfuss in which he is not involved. The lovers never meet again. Their trains cross. The doctor, the "man who died," since he had given up his self, disappears over the German border to escape arrest for something he, we are led to think, no longer believes in. But this realization comes very late, i.e. after three hundred pages of what critics in 1936 called a "Nazi idyll" (Time, 12 October 1936) and "mysticism and kraut" (*The New Republic*, 12 October 1936).

Though the end shows that Boyle did not want to write a pro-Nazi book, she got fascinated with her main character's fascination with Nazism to a degree that made her critics wonder whether Boyle had joined those who like G. B. Shaw and Pound sympathized with fascism. Joan Mellen in her thoroughly researched biography *Kay Boyle* (1994), persuasively subtitled *Author of Herself*, shows that Boyle's novel offers insights not only into the Nazi mentality, but also into Boyle's own personality. She traces Boyle's empathy with the Nazi doctor to her youthful emotionalism, her own political insecurity, her lack of any systematic sense of history which made her extend her sympathies for the suppressed to Nazis under Austrofascism,[18] and her distrust of Roosevelt and the New Deal. The unfavorable auto-image (i.e. Boyle's negative image of her own country) facilitated her ambivalent hetero-image. Boyle sees the economic depression as the sole and justified reason for the gains of the Nazis in the western provinces, where Hitler was seen as their "liberator" from poverty and the "persecution" by the Dollfuss government which made them "victims"[19] – an example of the first "victim theory." Probably in 1945 the same Austrians considered themselves "victims" of German aggression.

Nevertheless, Boyle's images of Austria are complex. One of her special concerns is women; she corrects the cliché of the yodeling maidens bursting with health and beauty, and she shows Austrian country women's varying relation to politics. They glorify their Nazi lovers or reproach as irresponsible their Nazi husbands in jail, and they all hate the Dollfuss government which put them there. She shows the political eroticism of women who worship Hitler like a movie star and take his photo to bed with them – a mild anticipation of Ernst Jandl's poem "Heldenplatz." There is the aging, crippled Catholic nun who worships the doctor and, when she finds out about his American lover, informs on him for listening illegally to the German radio (significantly, the head of the clinic does not hold against him what he by implication does himself). There is a woman who questions the blissful reports from Hitler's Germany, and one who counters the queries with what Boyle ridicules as propaganda fairy tales. And there is the innkeeper's wife who, quite unnecessarily, fears for her business because of the politics of her husband, a Nazi macho party boss who tyrannizes the women working at the inn and the party men under his command. But besides these critical insights there are pages in which the doctor fervently defends his creed to the skeptical American who, being the rootless product of an American patriarchal family, admires his strong conviction only to realize at last the same pattern of domination in the Nazi movement.

Boyle limits the point of view almost completely to that of the Nazis who feel persecuted by the Dollfuss government and never mentions the German boycott of tourism that caused the economic hardship in the Western provinces. She herself witnessed the Nazi terrorism described in the book (an explosion in the beer garden of the Innsbruck inn where she was staying) but never reminds the reader of the constant criminal Nazi violence that caused the reintroduction of the death penalty, never raises the question of Austrian independence. When the book was published in 1936 it was already outdated; in that year Schuschnigg amnestied all Nazis and signed the fateful agreement with Hitler. And one cannot help wondering whether the doctor, "the man who died," was not resurrected when the Nazis were on top.

Boyle's novel could never have been written after 1938. She did write a kind of lame postscript to it: the story "Anschluss" (*Harper's*, 1939) which again traces the romance between a holidaying American girl and an Austrian lover before and after 1938.[20] Boyle again added the attraction of political heroics. Toni is an unemployed Nazi rebelling against the Schuschnigg government, but when the girl returns in the summer of 1938 he has become a Nazi Puritan and ends the romance by telling her to get rid of her lipstick and nail polish, and to put on a decent swimsuit, because times have changed. The Austrian "bronzed Apollo" returned in Boyle's work and life. She had an affair with an apolitical Austrian skiing instructor in France, where she also met, on the ski slope, the anti-Nazi refugee Joseph von Franckenstein[21] whom she later married; Boyle made both of these Austrians, so different in their outlook, into characters in her work.[22] Her ties with Austria went far beyond her interest in the country's political drama as a subject for fiction.

In spite of the political tragedy in the 1930s, Austria's image as an island of peace survived – as a treasured memory – in the work of Frederic Prokosch (1906-1980), son of the distinguished Professor of Germanic Languages at Yale. Frederic, born in Madison, had spent two years as a schoolboy in Austria and Munich. As an adult he often returned to Europe, and finally he became one of the cosmopolitan expatriates. His books reflect his experiences in several countries, and his impressions of Austria are all the more interesting because they allow comparisons within an international setting. The characters in his *The Seven Who Fled* (1937, Harper Prize) – not a political but a poet's novel of outer and inner adventure and spirituality – "were fragments of Europe that imprint their [poetic] 'meanings' on the deserts of Asia."[23] One of them is an Austrian, and, in positive contrast to that of his fascistoid German fellow traveler, his 'meaning' is the gentlest of the seven: a dream vision of childhood and youth in a picture-book Austria of village life in the Salzkammergut, very idyllic, yet also moving in its emotional intensity. Apart from one reference to the dancers in a village as the "handsome children sprung out of the sorrows of war," (303) there is hardly any indication of history. Prokosch invokes the sublimating powers of memory: "It is the years, the saddening, exhausting years, that have designed this tender resonance" (304). Indeed, tenderness, an absence of harshness, softens all of Prokosch's impressions of Austria, even when they are more realistic. Of the Austrian in his novel he says: "Two longings had, all his life long, lain warm within him: that for a home and that for a distant land, in other words, that for the gentle past, and that for the exciting future" (312). Prokosch's poetic fiction of 1937 cannot be compared with any of the other works discussed here; read along with them, the young Austrian's "exciting future" turns into bitter irony.

Political reality invades Prokosch's *The Skies of Europe* (1941), again a novel with an international setting, describing the hero's friendships and love affairs in a time of impending war. Compared to Munich, where the hero witnesses the disintegration of a family because one of the sons is a Nazi, a village in the Salzkammergut before 1938 seems to be a haven of peace. The topos of city-versus-country is extended to one of Germany-versus-Austria and resolved in favor of the latter. The Austrian idyll of Prokosch's previous book still softens the scenes, and in contrast to the hero's experiences in Paris and Spain, his two visits to the Austrian village take on the personal warmth of a return to one's home. The chapters dealing with Austria are more lyrical than the rest of the book. Prokosch's own background and memories made him view Austria with obvious affection.[24] Philip, the protagonist, has relatives there, and the innkeeper is his uncle whose business concerns date Philip's first visit some time after Germany, in order to cripple Austrian tourist trade, imposed a 1000 Mark exit fee in 1933. There are only a few foreign guests "and the Viennese Jews . . ." (98). Family harmony is threatened. (The young generation hates the Dollfuss government; the old uncle, unlike Kay Boyle's innkeeper, is not a Nazi but a good patriot.) But the conflict does not lead to a tragic break as in the Munich family. As in Kay Boyles's Tyrol, the popularity of the Nazis in Salzburg is due to economic hopes. Even the Count of the local castle is willing to accept the Germans, while the monarchist Margravine adamantly rejects them.[25]

Philip's return to the same village some time after the Anschluss is one of elegiac leavetaking. With his uncle old Austria has died. The old monarchist links the political malaise to the Austrian national character: "Ever since the war, life here has been quite dull and aimless, without bones, so to speak. It's the Austrian blood. We need an Emperor once more. We're a weak people, to be quite truthful about it: weak, easily disheartened, lazy. And nowadays – well, what have we to live for? Our darling Austria is a ghost" (450).

In contrast to Boyle's Anschluss, in Prokosch's Austria after 1938 even the young Nazis are disappointed: "None of the young fellows got the positions they'd been promised . . . [Franzl] lost his head . . . with the German officials . . . Got into a fight with one of the Stormtroopers down in Salzburg. He's at Buchenwald now" (432) – There is no mention of Jews or others there. But the reaction to Franzl's plight ("Served him right . . . The good of one's country must always come first" [433]) indicates no sympathy with anyone in a camp. The general political mood Prokosch paints varies; it is partly that of the letdown after the jublant Anschluss, partly the relief over "full employment" (in the armament works Linz!), partly fatalism: "No one wants war. But you know, no one here would really care. No one really cares about anything any more. It almost feels as though . . ." (436). Prokosch's diagnosis of the public temper may have been accurate for parts of the population, but his selection of characters excludes fervent Nazis as well as all those who were persecuted. Prokosch retains his limited point of view of the outside observer and does not judge. As a "neo-romantic"[26] he holds on to an image of Austria that could not stand scrutiny, it is one of sympathy and understanding, of a helpless country, victim of doom, remembered with melancholy. Prokosch's image of Austria confirms the Spenglerian pessimism concerning the inevitable decline of Europe. Today it strikes us as an unpolitical American's uncritical support of the "victim-theory" held by many Austrians after the war.

In his comparisons of national characters Prokosch followed Romantic myths: "Each landscape nourished and tolerated only its own native philosophy of life . . . Everywhere the spirit of man sank its roots into the landscape . . . In Paris life was dry, ironical, precise; in Austria it seemed mellow and easygoing, troubled by an undercurrent of music." Even love is better in Austria: "With Maria [who had shared a passionate hour with Philip in the Austrian hay] all life had appeared simple; with Saskia [in France] bright with treachery and suspense" (316). Maria is a national type: "She breathed warmth, sweetness, womanliness: but peculiarities, none. A slight impatience, perhaps? A touch of ironic sentimentality? But even those were not her own, they were as Austrian as the village laughter" (100).

What Kay Boyle had missed in her perception of Austria in 1936 and what Prokosch's aesthetic premises had excluded became the subject of Catherine Hutter's novel *The Outnumbered* (1944),[27] also set in the provinces, a small town in Lower Austria and a nearby TB sanatorium. For the *Weekly Book Review* (19 March 1944) "the setting and atmosphere evoke[d] Thomas Mann's *The Magic Mountain*" – a very Austrian Magic Mountain, not only in elevation – one has to add, and a Lower Austrian *Zauberberg*. The sanatorium with its patients and visitors of various class and national backgrounds, including a fervent German Nazi aristocrat, is contrasted to the primitive provinciality of the town with its innkeeper and Nazi cronies and anti-Semitic priest. In this environment of racism and bigotry, coexistent with rational humanism, Hutter places her true heroine, a poor orphaned Jewish girl, moving in her suffering and her survival. The assimilated Jewish director of the sanatorium gives her asylum by making her part of the staff. A German Protestant nurse introduces the rootless girl to Christianity, and the doctor's Catholic wife wins her over to Catholicism.

The unsuccessful ideological counterpart to these converters is a Socialist schoolteacher who befriends the girl when she gives an English TB patient German lessons. She explains to him, and through him the American reader, the political history of the First Republic and the turmoil of Austrian politics from the Social Democratic point of view. She does not convince the Englishman, who rejects any ideology and insists on ethical individualism. The Jewish-Catholic girl only believes in God and rejects all politics as godless. Hutter's presentation of alternatives makes it clear that she put her own conviction into the girl's mind. The Socialist teacher is, however, drawn sympathetically in her conflicts; her Socialist love of humanity is constantly questioned by the village children: she sees in them savages that cannot be made human and can only be controlled by projects that make practical sense to them. She organizes a Christmas play which unites the village community for an evening but, as Hutter emphasizes, does not transcend the commercialism of innkeepers and the village priest. And a village Nazi praises the teacher because he confuses the *Reich Gottes* (kingdom of God) in the play with the Reich of Hitler. A short time before, the village had witnessed the "teutonic," "New German" wedding glorifying the pseudo-mystics of the Nazi ersatz religion with its mustachioed "God." And the anti-fascists in the book? In February 1934 the teacher's brother, a member of the Social Democratic Defense League is killed; she is arrested, escapes but dies in Spain, like her brother, "for a lost cause."

In this deeply religious book, the most religious by any of the writers under discussion, the only cause against the barbarism is Christianity, not the church which is seen very negatively, but the spirit incarnate in Fehge for whom "service is the perfect freedom" (not the Socialist ideal of freedom nor that "liberation" of the "Ostmark" promised by Hitler). Shortly after the Anschluss Fehge demonstrates the power of the spirit in what the doctor diagnoses as hysteria but everybody else accepts as a miracle: she displays stigmata which save her from the Nazi thugs; their gangleader hangs himself. The "miracle" is followed by an even more perplexing political fantasy: a Social Democratic leader implores Fehge to lead the thousands of pilgrims that have come to see her in a crusade to stop the German invasion. But the girl refuses the role of a Jeanne d'Arc, and the sober Englishman takes her with him to England because in Austria "the kind are outnumbered" (122, the book's title anticipates Erika Weinzierl's study of Austria under Nazi rule, *Zu wenig Gerechte*, 1969). Hutter's book ends with a Nazi hunt for the Social Democratic leader and the Jewish doctor.

Hutter draws special attention to the atrocities of Austrian Nazis: the Jewish doctor's prayer: "When they come, dear God, let it be the Germans, not the Austrians" is not answered; "S.A. men, rowdies from the suburbs of Vienna . . . made him do a series of unmentionable things before he died" (398, 402). Hutter radically corrects the positive image of Austrian Nazis not only in Boyle's work; in Phyllis Bottome's novel, *The Mortal Storm* (1938), widely read in the U.S., a Bavarian helping anti-Nazis escape to Tyrol before 1938, says: "They have Nazis there, but of a less severe kind. The Church also is able to prevent crimes – perhaps it is nearer to the Pope – here [in Germany] he can do nothing for us" (259).

Hutter's novel about a rural community in a part of Austria unknown to most Americans is a powerful negation of Prokosch's idyllic village, an indictment of the oppressive and brutal savagery that was to erupt in 1938, a *Vor-Alpensaga* foreshadowing Peter Turrini's six-part television series.

What reads like a religious tour de force at the end, incongruous with the realistic tenor of the whole, actually follows from the novel's ideological premise. Fehge is a symbol of simple saintly goodness living the gospel, triumphing over the evil personified in some of the characters. Most of them, however, are shown in their conflicting natures, even the "good" Englishman cannot silence the inner voices protesting his absolute individualism. Hutter's unsentimental portrayal of the Austrian social reality is all the more compelling for being based on her own experiences.[28]

Catherine Hutter (1907-1997) was born in Berlin. At the outbreak of World War I the family settled in New York. In 1922 her parents divorced, and Catherine and her mother went to Europe. All her life she went back and forth between the U.S. and Europe spending many years in each; she became literally a double expatriate. In this she was an exception among the writers under discussion. Since she only wrote in English and was a U.S. citizen throughout her adult life, her inclusion among American writers seems justified.

As a child, Catherine's son was cured of tuberculosis at the Sanatorium Wienerwald in Pernitz, Lower Austria, and she lived there and in Vienna for three years. Her close friendship with Sophie Lazarsfeld and her husband, both very active Austromarxist intellectuals, explains her sympathetic characterization of the school teacher in the novel, though it did not influence the religious tenor of the whole in spite of the criticism of the Church which Hutter shared with the Austrian Left. She also witnessed the Nazi wedding described in the novel, and at that time people did talk about a case of stigmatization in the area. Hutter was in Austria during the Nazi takeover in 1938. When her son "came in one afternoon from the playground and heiled her" she decided to leave and arrived in New York in October 1938. Her aunt stayed and died in a death camp.

The Jewish girl's conversion to Catholicism may also have been autobiographically motivated. The Hutters (Catherine assumed her maiden name again after her divorce) were a family of "thoroughly assimilated Jews in whose lives their heritage had long since ceased to be a factor," and with whom baptism of their children had been not uncommon. How much Catherine was attracted to Catholicism when she wrote the novel cannot be ascertained – the novel certainly suggests such an attraction. After the war she did become a practicing Catholic. In the mid-1950s Hutter began her annual visits to Vienna and stayed there from 1979 to 1987. During these years she became a close friend of the Austrian poet Erika Mitterer, a devout Catholic who revived Hutter's at times faltering Catholicism which, however, "remained more of an intellectual exercise." After her return to the States she did not pursue it with any fervor. Hutter's association with Austria was long, intense, and varied. *The Outnumbered* reflects the most dramatic phase in it. She did not write about Austria again.

The works I have discussed deal with a phase in Austrian history charged with tension, ideological drama, and heated emotions. Their American authors (with the exception of Prokosch) have responded in kind, taking sides just as passionately. One could have expected that, as outsiders, they would have observed the scene with irony, even satire. There was none of that, no Mark Twain to cut through the Austrian miasma with the knife of his wit, maybe because none of the writers could afford such distance. The battles they witnessed were fought not only in Austria and, in the long run, decided more than her future.

Today, these works may be of interest only to historians of

Austro-American cultural relations. We must remember, however, that they disclosed dark, social truths that Austrian writers did not touch until after the war. For "foreign onlookers," that alone is no small achievement. How "their Austria" compares with that of the many Austrian writers in exile only a separate study could show. We can assume that most of these writers confirmed Hutter's condemnation and that Prokosch's nostalgia was known to many of them.

If the politics outdated most of the works I have discussed, it also caused the revival of at least two of them when in the 1980s some of the publishers' reprint-interest in Austria's "dirty thirties" returned. *The Outnumbered* (1944) was available again for some time after 1981, and in 1989 New Directions republished Kay Boyle's controversial *Death of a Man* as a "Revived [not revised] Modern Classic."[29] Boyle had developed into an outstanding progressive, had been investigated during McCarthyism, had become an important figure in the civil-rights and anti-war movement, and was even put in jail briefly. The reproaches of her critics in 1936 were now considered unfair. While Alfred Kazin in 1936 had praised Boyle's insight into "the impulses that have driven so many plain folk to Hitlerism" but nevertheless found that the book was "built on sand" (*NY Times Book Review*, 11 October 1936), Burton Hatlen in his introduction to the edition of 1989 (i.e. before Mullen's biography was published) praised the author for "never making the mistake of assuming that a human being can be summed up under a single rubric such as 'Nazi.'" He lauded the book for its political and psychological perception and its feminist disclosure of patriarchal power structures. He also concluded that, after February 1934, Nazism was the only alternative open to Austrians. Like Kay Boyle, Hatlen completely disregarded all those who did not accept that alternative and risked their lives fighting against it.

It was another American woman, Muriel Gardiner, who not only remembered them but was also one of them. In 1988 Yale University Press published her memoir *Code Name Mary*, a beautifully written work of literature. In Muriel Gardiner's life the cliché of the American going to Vienna to be psychoanalyzed became reality. Her treatment and subsequent study of medicine soon were allied with ethical engagement; Gardiner's Vienna was the city of Freud *and* of Austromarxism. What makes her book so moving is the image of Vienna of the 1930s reflected in the many concise biographies and psychograms of real people who desperately needed help. It is the Vienna of the anti-fascist underground, and Gardiner used her considerable financial resources to help people threatened by Austrian fascism and later by the Gestapo to escape, not in the sensational manner of Lilian Hellman's story and film "Julia"[30] but quietly, persistently, courageously. The professional writers I have discussed made their first- or second-hand impressions of Austria, their criticism, their empathy, into literature; Muriel Gardiner, the scientist, turned them into action.

The University of Montana

Notes

1. *Handbook for Travellers in Southern Germany; Being a Guide to Bavaria, Austria, Tyrol, Salzburg, Styria etc.* (London: John Murray, 1837), 3.

2. Cf. the comprehensive study by Carl Dolmetsch, *Our Famous Guest. Mark Twain in Vienna* (Athens and London: University of Georgia Press, 1992).

3. *Letters of Henry Adams*, W.C. Ford, ed. 2 vols. (Boston: Houghton Mifflin, 1930, 1938), vol. 2, 178.

4. Described in "There Is Never Any End to Paris," in: Ernest Hemingway, *A Movable Feast* (New York: Scribner's, 1964, 197-211.

5. *The Cantos of Ezra Pound* (New York: New Directions, 1948), Canto XXXV, 22. See also XVI, 71; XXXVIII, 38; L, 41.

6. See Stan Smith, "Unreal Cities and Numinous Maps: T.S. Eliot and W.H. Auden as Observers of Central Europe," in: Waldemar Zacharasiewitz, ed. *Images of Central Europe in Travelogues and Fiction by North American Writers* (Tübingen: Stauffenberg, 1995), 166-181. Cited passages on 166, 168.

7. *New York Evening Post*, July 19, 20, 21, 1927.

8. Elizabeth Nowell, ed. *The Letters of Thomas Wolfe* (New York: Scribner's, 1956), 127, 149.

9. Apart from what Americans learned about Austria in the 1930s from the radio and print media, their literary images of the country were formed not only by the works discussed here. The books on Austrian themes by British authors, and they were much more numerous than those by Americans, were often read in the U.S., most of them in American editions. For a discussion of works by John Lehmann, Stephen Spender, and Christopher Isherwood see Horst Jarka, "British Writers and the Austria of the Thirties," in: Otto Hietsch, ed., *Österreich und die angelsächsische Welt*, Vol. 2 (Wien: Braumüller, 1968), 439-481.

10. Robert Emmet Sherwood, *Reunion in Vienna* (New York: Scribner's, 1932), 126.

11. Boris Todrin, *5 Days. Austria: February 12th to 17th, 1934* (Chicago: The Black Cat Press, 1936). Todrin's statement is from a letter quoted in the introduction to the German translation (1948): see Ernst Glaser, "Der Februar 1934 in fremdsprachigen Dichtungen," in: *Das Pult*, Vol. 16, No. 71 (1984), 57.

12. *Selected Works of Stephen Vincent Benét. Volume One: Poetry* (New York: Farrar & Rinehardt, 1942), 432-435, quoted passages on p. 432 f.

13. Paul Engle, *Break the Heart's Anger* (Garden City, New York: Doubleday, 1936), 111-118, quoted passage on p. 132.

14. *Geschichte der Republik Österreich*, Heinrich Benedikt, ed. (Wien: Verlag für Geschichte und Politik, 1954), 461.

15. John Gunther, *Inside Europe* (New York: Harper's, 1938) 331.

16. *305 Days*, Kay Boyle, Laurence Vail, Nina Conarain eds. (New York: Harcourt Brace, 1936), 369 f.

17. Kay Boyle, *Death of a Man* (New York: New Directions, 1989), 298.

18. In "February 20" in: *305 Days* (see note 16!), 57, Boyle sympathizes with pupils demonstrating against the dismissal of their Nazi teacher.

19. In this respect Boyle's point of view parallels that of the Austrian Nazi writers at the same time; cf. "Die Verbotszeit in der Ostmark 1933-1938," in: Heinz Kindermann, ed. *Heimkehr ins Reich. Großdeutsche Dichtung aus Ostmark und Sudetenland* (Reclam: Leipzig, 1939), 147-368.

20. The frustrated Anglo-Saxon woman who falls for the irresistible mountain man is a stock character in mountaineering/ skiing fiction of the time.

21. Cousin of Georg von Franckenstein, Austrian Ambassador in London before March 1938.

22. The skiing instructor in *The Diplomat's Wife* (1940); the Baron in *Men* (1941), and both in *Primer for Combat* (New York: Simon and Schuster, 1942).

23. Frederic Prokosch, *The Seven Who Fled* (New York: Farrar Straus Giroux, 1984 [1937]), x.

24. Autobiography blends with fiction. "When I first set foot in Austria as a boy of five, I was convinced that I had been there before, long ago. And years later . . . for a moment it seemed . . . that at last I

was returning to the warm, kindly home of my peasant and soldier grandfathers" (316 f.). Prokosch had gone first to Austria when he was eight years old and visited his grandfather in Eger. In his memoir *Voices* (1983) his later visits to Austria are hardly mentioned at all.

25. The portrayal of Austrian aristocrats in American fiction of the 1930s follows the authors' point of view: it is humorously satiric in Sherwood's play, adamantly negative in Abel's novel and the works of the left-wing poets, positive in Boyle's autobiographically colored work. In Hutter's novel (see below) a Count breaks up a Nazi meeting and bitterly resents his Nazi son.

26. Robert H. O'Connor, "Fredric Prokosch," in: *Dictionary of Literary Biography*, vol. 48, 346. For an introduction to Prokosch, the highly regarded author of fifteen novels, several volumes of poetry and translations, see Radcliffe Squires, *Frederic Prokosch* (New York: Twayne, 1964).

27. I am indebted to Dr. Ernst Glaser, Vienna, for drawing my attention to Catherine Hutter, cf. his article cited in note 11!

28. Catherine Hutter (1907-1997) published four novels, several translations from the German, including Goethe's *Die Leiden des jungen Werthers*, and Schnitzler's *Jugend in Wien*. She left no autobiographical accounts. For the following information I am greatly indebted to Margaret Hutter, Catherine's daughter-in-law. She very kindly sent me two extensive letters (dated May 7 and June 28, 1997) from which the following quotes are taken.

29. It was not widely but positively reviewed as in *The San Francisco Chronicle* (14 September 1989): "Putting all this bubbly emotion into a historical moment at which we look back with horror may ask a lot of a reader, but Boyle's accomplishment is to make this jump relatively easy."

30. Cf. "Publishing: New Memoir Stirs 'Julia' Controversy," in: *The New York Times*, 29 April 1983, C 30, and Muriel Gardiner, *Code Name 'Mary.' Memoirs of an American Woman in the Austrian Underground* (New Haven: Yale University Press, 1983).

Austria in the American Short Story

Rita Terras

John Irving's intense involvement with Vienna and Austrian culture has long been recognized. It grew out of a year of study in Vienna when Irving was an undergraduate at the University of New Hampshire in 1963/1964 and a subsequent three-year stay in the city as writer of a screenplay which was never produced (1969-1971). Vienna, the Viennese, Austria's fate in the middle of the twentieth century appear again and again as autobiographical elements in his novels.[1] Yet, the essence of Irving's conception of Austria and Austrians is encapsulated in two short stories, "Interior space" (first published in 1980) and "The Pension Grillparzer" (first published in 1976). Both stories were republished in his most recent book, a collection of short texts entitled *Trying to Save Piggy Snead* (1996).[2]

It so happened that Ray Bradbury – best known for his science fiction, in particular his novels *Fahrenheit 451* and the *Martian Chronicles* – also published a new volume of short stories *Quicker Than the Eye* in 1996 which includes an Austrian-American narrative called "The Unterderseaboat Doctor" (first published in 1994).[3] In addition, an earlier volume of Bradbury short stories *The Toynbee Convector* (1988) contains a minor reference to Austria in the story *On the Orient, North.*"[4] Contrary to John Irving, Ray Bradbury apparently never lived in Vienna, does not speak German, and is not personally involved with Austria.

Bradbury and Irving represent two entirely different approaches to Austrian subject matter, with Bradbury's embedded in a fairly longstanding American tradition and Irving's entirely his own. Bradbury's view of Austria and Austrians, as represented in his stories, simply continues a cliché, while Irving makes a serious attempt to disregard the traditional, superficial view and to recreate the contemporary Austrian scene as truthfully as possible. Excepting Irving, one may say that, if Austria and Austrians are mentioned at all, the country and its populace appear in the American short story of recent and of older vintage in one of two molds, both invented by writers only superficially familiar with and superficially interested in Austrian subjects. In these stories Austria and Austrians are either totally romanticized – in the popular understanding of the word – or, Austrians are shown as somewhat suspect stock characters of questionable background with long and – for an English speaking reader – altogether unpronounceable names.

The romantic Austrian in his romantic home country appears early on in Mark Twain's long short story *"The Mysterious Stranger,"* written between 1897 and 1900 and first published posthumously in 1916.[5] Years later, the romantic image resurfaces in Kay Boyle's Austrian stories (1933-1938)[6] and in Leo Rosten's "Romance in Vienna,"[7] as well as in Bradbury's "On the Orient, North." Mark Twain uses the model of a romantic Austria for a serious purpose. He chose a sixteenth-century Austrian setting to confess to his agnosticism. In *The Mysterious Stranger* Austria serves to obscure and to lessen the impact of the author's controversial attempt to explain his unchristian position. Twain traveled in Europe and to Vienna in the late 1890s. He began to write the first of three versions of his story in Austria, changed the locale in his second version, and restored the Austrian motif in version number three, thus indicating how important it was to his purpose. On 13 May 1899, Twain explained himself in a letter to William Dean Howells:

> What I have been wanting was a chance to write a book without reserves – a book which should take account of no one's feelings, no one's prejudices, opinions, beliefs, hopes, illusions, delusions; a book which should say my say, right out of my heart, in the plainest language and without limitations of any sort.[8]

At the turn of the century such a book could hardly be set in Hannibal, Missouri, or, for that matter, in Connecticut. It had to be dressed up as an allegory taking place in medieval *Eseldorf,* Austria, with Austrian actors. Its main characters are three young boys, Nikolaus Baumann, Seppi Wohlmeyer, and Theodor Fischer. They are visited by a mysterious stranger named Satan – a nephew of *the* Satan. The story begins:

> It was in 1590 – winter. Austria was far from the world and asleep; it was still the Middle Ages in Austria and promised to remain so forever.... It drowsed in peace in the deep privacy of a hilly and wooded solitude where news from the world hardly ever came to disturb its dreams, and was infinitely content. At its front flowed the tranquil river ... from the top of the precipice frowned a vast castle, its long stretch of towers and bastions mailed in vines.[9]

It is notable that Mark Twain as well as later Leo Rosten and John Irving, in writing about the "baroque museum," as Leo Rosten called Vienna and Austria, infuse their language with baroque word accumulations and florid descriptions.

Kay Boyle's Austrian stories are told with the same fairy-tale overtones that are to be found in Mark Twain's "The Mysterious Stranger" and John Irving's novel *The Hotel New Hampshire*.[10] The fairy-tale atmosphere is not so much the result of imitating the language of the Brothers Grimm through a careful choice of words and phrases, as it is created through the evocation of a Central European landscape filled with shadowy and – to the American mind – strange characters. Mark Twain's boys live in a dark forest and are visited by priests and Satan. The weird characters in Irving's novel permanently inhabit a run-down, back-street hotel which is void of ordinary guests. Kay Boyle prefers the rugged Tirolean mountaineer, a stereotype known to her pre-World-War-II generation through Louis Trenker's film portrayals of such men. These mountain people are one with their landscape. They know every nook and cranny of the dangerous terrain. Their life is an everlasting confrontation with the elements which finally will overwhelm them. In "Maiden Maiden" Johannisöl of Heiligenblut is felled by the Grossglockner which previously claimed the life of his grandfather. He is described as having "thin cheeks" and wearing a "smart little velvet coat that had been washed many times over," as well as a "green felt hat." Johannisöl is a guide and "with a rope around the thin part of his being, he guided climbers up the mountains and guided others down."[11]

In "White Horses of Vienna" the village doctor suffers a painfully sprained knee while climbing. "The agony that he would not mention was marked upon his face." After studying in several cities, the doctor had come back and bought a piece of land in the Tirol, with a pine forest sloping down it. The accident sets the scene for a fairy tale centered around the doctor's Jewish replacement from Vienna – named Doktor Hein – who tells the story of the Viennese Lipizzaner horses, unaware of the fact that he arouses violent anti-Semitism in one of his listeners and becomes involved in political upheaval.[12]

In Bradbury's Orient Express story a ghost, traveling as a passenger on the train, speaks of his former undisturbed 200-year existence in the Vienna Woods. His somewhat regretful comment is, that in the latter half of our century Austria has entered the modern world forcing friendly ghosts to move to Scotland, the only backward place left in Europe. Bradbury thus confirms what Mark Twain had shown earlier, namely, that Austria served in American literature as a romantic backwater, known to both writers and readers but not well enough known to demand a precise and accurate description. Mark Twain, Kay Boyle, and Ray Bradbury show Austria as a distant – in both time and locale – sealed and uncanny venue where mysterious events take place. Leo Rosten, on the other hand, tells his insipid love story of Sheldon (London born, but with a Viennese mother) and Marianne, a "not really beautiful" Austrian baroness, against the background of post-World-War-II Vienna, as observed through the keen eye of a journalist, Rosten himself:

> I said I had first seen Vienna in my college days, entranced by its history, thinking of imperial Rome, the Ottomans, the Magyars, the Habsburgs, churning with romanticism about Mozart and Beethoven, awed by the quite beautiful but moribund city, trying to be frivolous, but sad. Oh, it was *gemütlich* enough, all froth and bowings and I-kiss-your-hand Madame, but I had never been able to shake off a sense of something cynical behind the courtesy, something contemptuous beneath the charm...

Rosten goes on to say that later he thought of Vienna:

> as a shell of splendor, a husk of glory gone to dust, a baroque museum, all flowing curves and arching domes, ornate cupolas and statues – so many statues, parading across the rooftop balustrades: kings, prophets, princes, angels, each caught in midgesture, pointing, praying,

turning, kneeling, rising in a sea of swirling robes and rearing horses, a surge of scornful figures in the sky, monarchs, prelates, schemers, saints – transfixed celebrants of Catholicism and Empire.[13]

Missing in Mark Twain's and Kay Boyle's stories is the note of regret that the old romantic and positive image of Austria and Vienna can no longer be sustained, a note that is common to all post-World-War-II American writers on Austria. It also is present in the British author Graham Greene's story and film script *The Third Man*. Speaking in the same regretful tone of voice which is to be found in Rosten, Bradbury's "Orient, North" and in Irving, Greene has his narrator state at the beginning of the first chapter:

> If you are to understand this strange, rather sad story you must have an impression at least of the background – the smashed dreary city of Vienna divided up in zones among the four Powers.... I never knew Vienna between the wars, and I am too young to remember old Vienna with its Strauss music and its bogus easy charm; to me it is simply a city of undignified ruins.... I haven't enough imagination to picture it as it once had been.[14]

In other words, World War II destroyed the romantic image of Austria in American literature.[15]

The war, however, did not eliminate the stock Austrian figure that early in the twentieth century appears in one of Edith Wharton's stories. This stereotype, always male, emerged as an object of interest to American women looking to Europe for prestige by marrying into the nobility. Edith Wharton's short story "The Last Asset" (1908) exemplifies this type of characterization, albeit with the author's own individualized twist. The American woman, who associates with the Austrian Baron von Schenkelderff, is interested in his money, which she needs to facilitate her daughter's marriage to a French nobleman. Mrs. Newell has existed on the fringes of moneyed American society for many years and has used up whatever credit she could muster. Her association with the Baron is an indication of how low she has sunk. Von Schenkelderff is described "as so glossy and ancient that he gave one the effect of having been embalmed and then enameled." We are also told that "his connection with a race as ancient as his appearance" was obvious.[16] However, the Baron has money. He also speaks six or seven languages, two facts which compensate for his arrogance and his not quite comme-il-faut behavior. He is a very recent and certainly not yet fully accepted aristocrat of unknown Central European heritage. The Baron plays no more than a minor role in the story. A most astute writer, Wharton usually draws piercing portraits of her players and relies on stock characters for lesser roles only.

In the second half of this century the Austrian stock figure of American literature was reshaped into the often mad psychoanalyst with a thick German accent and bizarre behavior patterns. That characterization was possibly invented by University of Chicago students and comedians Elaine May and Mike Nichols during their 1950s radio show. In the 1960s Sid Ceasar brought the character to TV. It is quite likely that Bruno Bettelheim, the then director of the Orthogenic School for autistic children at the University of Chicago, contributed to the development of this peculiar stereotype of literary as well as cinematic fame. Richard Pollak, Bettelheim's latest biographer, remarks:

> By 1944, Bettelheim had developed a growing reputation at the University of Chicago.... As with other émigrés who had begun attracting attention at American colleges and universities, his thick accent and intellectual exoticism gave him star potential in a secure land where Europe equaled better.... It didn't hurt if ... learning had been acquired on the Ringstrasse and carried the aura of psychoanalysis.[17]

Writers of fiction or of film scripts never bothered to develop a more realistic conception of Austria and its population. They simply inserted the stock characters into their texts – usually in a minor role, serving as a foil to the main character.

Ray Bradbury's "Unterderseaboat Doctor" stays well within the limits of the popular image of Austrians but constitutes an exception to the rule in that the stock character is also the main character of this action-packed satire. The events of the story are told from the point of view of a patient who is the narrator. As such he begins with the words: "The incredible event occurred during my third visit to Gustav von Seyfertitz, my foreign psychoanalyst." The author himself provides the reader with a clue to the origin of his invention by having his narrator tell us: "Gustav von Seyfertitz stood pretending not to notice me .... Very calmly, in the fashion of Conrad Veit in *Casablanca* or Erich von Stroheim, the manservant in *Sunset Boulevard*." Curiously, a similar reference to Erich von Stroheim is to be found in Pollak's biography of Bruno Bettelheim. He describes Bettelheim as "half Viennese uncle" and "half Erich von Stroheim." Bradbury's narrator reveals his analyst's full name as Gustav Mannerheim [surprisingly close to Bettelheim] Auschlitz von Seyfertitz, Baron Woldstein." In his final words the patient/narrator muses: "What, I often wonder, ever happened to Gustav von Seyfertitz? Did he move to Vienna to take up residence, perhaps, in or near dear Sigmund's very own address?"[18] The point of the story is, of course, that Seyfertitz, the psychiatrist, is rather more severely mentally ill than his patient. He wavers between being an analyst and imagining that he is a submarine commander. Instead of a periscope he now owns and uses the "first psychological kaleidoscope in history" which permits him to observe – with Jungian overtones – the collective nightmares of his patients.

John Irving has said of his short stories "The Pension Grillparzer" and "Interior Space" that they are his number one and number two favorites. They are also the only two among his short stories that involve Austria and Austrians. "Interior Space" is, in many ways, an ordinary short story told in the typical Irvingean manner: stylistically ornate and overwritten, structurally based on a great deal of chatty dialogue which attempts but does not quite succeed in giving depth to the story's characters. These include Herr Kessler, an Austrian gentleman living in the United States, and Kessler's black walnut tree. In true Irvingean style, neither of them survive. Irving is known for his predilection for finishing off his characters in some bizarre manner. The tree is being dismantled and killed in part by three bungling tree pruners and, in part, by the evil intentions of a neighbor whom Kessler calls "der pest Bardelong." Kessler, no longer young and a widower with lung disease, suffers a heart attack and demands "noch ein Bier," when he is momentarily shocked back to life. The German words are, of course, meaningless to the attending cardiologist whose new revival machine is out of order, sealing Kessler's fate. Kessler wears Lederhosen and an Austrian straw hat. He is further characterized by his strange use of the English language. Irving seems to be intrigued by German word order, particularly dependent clauses with the verb at the end. He is also interested in verbs with separable prefixes. It amuses him to assume that German speakers of English translate word by word from their native language, retaining the peculiar German word order. Kessler, thus, comes up with sentences such as: "You are going this wall to down-take, yes? ... well ... what will the ceiling uphold?"[19]

It is noteworthy that Irving's linguistic acrobatics are the same that Mark Twain features in his essay "The Awful German Language."[20] He made up sentences such as "in the Night, the Tavern called 'The Wagoner' was downburnt" or "when he, upon the street, the (in-satin-and-silk-covered-now-very unconstrainedly-after-the-newest-fashion dressed) government counselor's wife met, ..." The latter absolutely nonsensical construction with the verb far removed from its subject, is Twain's word by word translation of a sentence from a novel by Mrs. Marlitt. As Twain recorded it, Marlitt wrote: "Wenn er auf der Strasse der in Samt und Seide gehüllten jetz [sic] ungenirt [sic] nach der neuesten Mode gekleideten Regierungsrathin [sic] begegnete, ..."[21] Unfortunately, this kind of convoluted and unrealistic speech pattern is just about the only characterization of Herr Kessler which the reader gets. Beyond it, one learns very little about the Austrian. Irving's weakness as a writer is his inability to create characters of consequence. His literary inventions consistently remain superficial whether they are of Austrian or any other nationality. Kessler could be called the prototype of such Austrian characters as Grandmother Johanna in "Grillparzer" or the hotel owner Freud in *The Hotel New Hampshire*. Irving himself mentions in the postscript to his story that he worked first on "Interior Space" in 1974 before he began to write *Garp* and "Grillparzer," and long before he thought of *The Hotel New Hampshire*. "Interior Space" rested in a drawer for six years before it was published.[22]

"The Pension Grillparzer" is unusual in that it is not only a story within a story but that it appears in the novel *The World According to Garp* in two parts. Irving's editor decided that Garp, at age nineteen, could not possibly have been the author of such a perfect story written in only one sitting. Consequently, it was presented in two parts in the novel after it had been previously published in *Anteus* in 1976 and had won a prestigious Pushcart Prize. "Grillparzer" is also unusual in that it is a completely Austrian story written by an American author. It takes place in Vienna and all of its characters are Austrian, including the narrator and Irving's inevitable bear. If, at one point in the story, the narrator compares American and Austrian hotels and their toilets as if the story were written from an American point of view, this is inadvertent. On the other hand, his consistent use of the term WC for toilet, a known but rarely employed word in American English, is most likely an attempt to authenticate the narrator's Austrian background.

"The Pension Grillparzer" could be classified as a water closet story since the action revolves primarily around the common toilet in the grade C hotel. An Austrian family – parents, two sons, grandmother, and pater familias who grades hotels for the Austrian Tourist Bureau – stays overnight in the "Pension" which has applied for an upgrading to B status. The rumor, that a bear is living in the hotel, turns out to be true. Part of the hotel is permanently occupied – somewhat similar to the situation in *The Hotel New Hampshire* – by a group of performers from the Circus Szolnok which includes a bear. Acquaintance with most of these permanent hotel guests comes during trips to the WC by various members of the family. At one time the toilet is occupied by a man who walks and uses the toilet on his hands. At another time the brown-pawed bear uses it after riding his unicycle up and down the hotel corridors. The rather undesirable permanent hotel guests are relatives by marriage to the hotel's proprietor Herr Theobald. His sister, who owns the bear Duna, is or has been married to at least two members of the group. The story ends with most of the main characters neatly dispatched to heaven or hell. Irving never specifies which. As Grandmother Johanna says: "They have fallen past 'z' . . . . They have disappeared from the human alphabet." The author elucidates further in his postscript to the story:

> What made the "Pension Grillparzer" special to me . . . was both the grandmother's dream and the epilogue – everything does connect. The ludicrous and doomed effort at reclassification is a foreshadow of the "terminal cases" theme . . . . The younger brother blown up in a history class, the innkeeper is [literally] frightened to death by the bear "unicycling in the lunatic's left behind clothes" – the bear himself is "embarrassed to death" – and especially the man who could only walk on his hands, strangled by his necktie on an escalator . . . these calamities foreshadow . . . the unlikely disasters that many book reviewers have called my penchant for the bizarre.[23]

Irving sees Austria, a reflection of our world, as an amoral place where people, culpable or not, come to a sudden and unexpected end. The terminal cases theme is present also in "Interior Space," but it is much more pronounced in "The Pension Grillparzer." Of the family, only the narrator remains at the end of the story. His brother has been killed, his grandmother and parents have died of natural causes. Of the Circus Szolnok, only the sister of Herr Theobald is still around with all others literally dead or figuratively so. The so-called dream man is in a mental institution, and the Hungarian singer has gone away in the wake of yet "another woman thrilled by his voice."

One puzzling fact about "The Pension Grillparzer" is the Pension's name. It has meaningful literary connotations for speakers of German but is meaningless for the English-speaking American reader. We know that Irving is often intrigued by names and likes to use them to establish connections. A key figure in *The Hotel New Hampshire* is called Freud and the character's bizarre behavior and, later, heroic death permit us to assume that Irving wanted to show a certain amount of respect for the signature Austrian, Sigmund Freud. In the same novel the author uses such appellations as *Schwanger*, *Fehlgeburt*, and *Arbeiter* because, I assume, they allow him to make fun of the group of bumbling would-be revolutionaries who inhabit the hotel. The name of the title character in Irving's novel *A Prayer for Owen Meaney* (1989) is meant to point the attentive reader to Günter Grass' novels *Cat and Mouse* and *The Tin Drum*. Little Owen Meaney – O.M. – and his friends could be seen as the American cousins of little Oskar Matzerath – another O.M. – and the boys of *Cat and Mouse*.[24]

A closer look at the name Garp, the fictitious author of *The Pension Grillparzer*, reveals two curious facts. First, read backwards, the name Garp means Prag, in its German spelling, and second, the name Garp is contained in the name Grillparzer. Could it be said that the fictional author of the story Garp, who is the child of an unusual union between a strong woman and a mere supplier of sperm, has found his real father in Franz Grillparzer, an Austrian antecedent of literary fame? As is not unusual in a father-son relationship both Garp and Irving are highly critical of their mentor Grillparzer. For Garp, who in the novel reads Grillparzer's *The Poor Fiddler* in an edition by Ivar Ivask and quotes from Ivask's introduction, Grillparzer is a model "for what a writer should *not* be doing." He calls Grillparzer's *Spielmann* "baldly sentimental" and "ludicrously melodramatic." "Dostoevsky," he writes "could compel you to be interested in such a wretch;

Grillparzer bores you with tearful trivia."[25] Thus the Pension is named Grillparzer to designate it as a place of trivial and melodramatic events that, in the skillful hands of a gifted writer, reveal a great deal more about Austria than is obvious.

With the neat division into two camps – the Austrian family and the Empire circus – and based on the grandmother's recurrent, nightmarish dream which, after her death, is inherited by her daughter, "The Pension Grillparzer" may be read as an allegory on the demise of the Austrian and Austro-Hungarian empire. Proper Austrians and representatives of the empire exist side by side in a tenuous relationship. The bear Duna (Hungarian for Danube) remains alienated from all of them – an innocent bystander caught in the whirl of events. The scene for the decline of Austria is set with grandmother Johanna's dream. Her nightmare concerns Charlemagne and his knights who gather nightly in the courtyard of her dream castle and are slowly diminished until "the horse looked gaunt ... and the men looked more like unoccupied suits of armor balanced delicately in the saddles."[26] In this last sentence the reader will detect echos of a theme that permeates most of the recent American stories concerned with Austria: Austria's glorious past and its present state of decline. Irving enhances his vague account of Austria's history by staging a multicultural clash around a WC in a third-rate Pension in Vienna. His is a sad commentary on his host city and host country but doesn't carry quite as much weight as it seems to, once the reader is familiar with Irving's pessimistic evaluation of any culture, be it Austrian, American, or of some other nationality.

Connecticut College

Notes

1. *Setting Free the Bears* (New York: Random House, 1968). *The 158-pound Marriage* (New York: Random House, 1974). *The World According to Garp* (New York: E.P. Dutton, 1978). *The Hotel New Hampshire* (New York: E.P. Dutton, 1981). *The World According to Garp* was awarded the 1979 American Book Award as best paperback of the year. In 1982 the novel was made into a film. Critics such as Gabriel Miller, *John Irving* (New York: Frederick Ungar Publishing Co., 1982) have shown parallels between Austrian developments and events in

Irving's life.

2. *John Irving, Trying to Save Piggy Snead* (New York: Arcade Publishing Co., 1996).

3. *Ray Bradbury, Quicker Than the Eye* (New York: Avon Books, 1996).

4. Ray Bradbury, *The Toynbee Convector.* Stories (New York: Alfred Knopf, 1988).

5. *The Portable Mark Twain*, ed. by Bernhard de Voto (New York: Penguin, 1977), 631-744.

6. Kay Boyle, *Fifty Stories*. Introduced by Louise Erdrich (New York: New Direction Publishing Corp., 1992). I was not aware of Boyle's Austrian stories until Professor Horst Jarka (University of Montana) mentioned them in his paper given at the 1997 Symposium on Austrian Literature at the University of California, Riverside.

7. Leo Rosten, *People I Have Loved, Known or Admired* (New York: McGraw-Hill Book Co., 1970).

8. Quoted in: John C. Gerber, *Mark Twain*. Twayne's U.S. Author Series (Boston: Twayne Publishers, 1988). Gerber also addresses the complicated history of the publication of this particular Mark Twain story, 152/153.

9. *The Portable Mark Twain*, 631.

10. Gabriel Miller calls the novel a fairy tale and explains it in terms of Bruno Bettelheim's *The Uses of Enchantment.*

11. *Fifty Stories*, 136 and 130.

12. *Fifty Stories*, 151. Kay Boyle covered Europe for *The New Yorker* until the editors withdrew her accreditation at the onset of a three-day hearing by the McCarthy Commission. She had lived in Vienna and Kitzbühl (1933-35) and was married to Joseph Franckenstein, an Austrian who later became an American citizen. The story "The White Horses of Vienna" won the 1935 O'Henry Prize.

13. *People I Have Loved, Known or Admired*, 336.

14. Graham Greene, *The Third Man and The Fallen Idol* (London: Penguin Books, 1971), 14.

15. Orson Welles who played Harry Lime in the film *The Third Man* tried to soften Greene's harsh condemnation of post-World-War II Vienna by adding the following – by now famous – words to the author's script: "After all, it's not that awful – you know what the fellow said ... In Italy for thirty years under the Borgias they had war-

fare, terror, murder, bloodshed – they produced Michaelangelo, Leonardo da Vinci and the Renaissance. In Switzerland they had brotherly love, five hundred years of democracy and peace, and what did they produce? ... The Cuckoo clock." Quoted in: David Thomson, *Rosebud*. The Story of Orson Welles (New York: Alfred A. Knopf, 1996), 297.

16. *The Stories of Edith Wharton*. Selected and Introduced by Anita Brookner (New York: Simon & Schuster, 1980), p. 74. "The Last Asset" first appeared in 1908. The action of the story takes place in the 1890s.

17. Richard Pollak, *The Creation of Dr. B.* A Biography of Bruno Bettelheim (New York: Simon & Schuster, 1997), 126/127.

18. *Quicker Than the Eye*, 2 and 15.

19. *Trying to Save Piggy Snead*, 176.

20. In: Mark Twain, *A Tramp Abroad* (New York: The Heritage Press, 1966), appendix D, 373-385.

21. *A Tramp Abroad*, 374/375.

22. *Trying to Save Piggy Snead*, 217.

23. 261 & 267.

24. 420.

25. *The Poor Fiddler by Franz Grillparzer*, Introduction by Ivar Ivask (New York: Frederick Ungar Publishing Co., 1967).

26. *Trying to Save Piggy Snead*, 246.

The Idea of Austria in Djuna Barnes' *Nightwood*

Geoffrey C. Howes

The American author Djuna Barnes's novel *Nightwood*, published in 1936 in England and in 1937 in the United States, opens with a joyless, decadent representation of Austria in the form of the genealogy and character of Felix Volkbein, one of the book's five main figures. The other four are Americans, and Felix represents a past-ridden Europe that contrasts with their world: half Jewish, saddled with a false pedigree, he is, paradoxically, entrapped by history yet unable to draw from it a meaningful identity. The Americans, three lesbian or bisexual women and a homosexual man, have no history or context for their eccentric identities, and so they seek new surroundings in Europe. They do not really succeed, for expatriation simply removes them from a troublesome old identity; it does not supply a new one. The lack of a positive identity is what Felix shares with his American counterparts. This essay will argue that certain aspects of Austria at the end of the Habsburg empire – its decadence, morbidity, and mixing of cultures – provide ideal motifs for the theme of estrangement that stands at the center of the text, and that it was no accident that Barnes chose to make Felix Volkbein a Viennese.

Nightwood has been called a "poetic" novel, and indeed one rarely encounters a work of fiction with such densely composed prose or such vivid and original expression.[1] Barnes accomplishes this on the one hand through the melody and richness of her narrator's diction, and on the other by a remarkable set of characters who speak with unusual imaginativeness, chief among them a certain Matthew O'Connor. Clifton Fadiman, reviewing the novel for the *New Yorker* in 1937, numbered it among those books that "approach the non-representative condition of pure music, in that they defy description in other terms. Everything that they are is immovably contained in and identical with the original phrasing of the author."[2] Even if this phrasing is sometimes nearly incomprehensible, and even if the narrative seems to run in place while the words get done, *Nightwood* is nothing if not a work of literary art, creating its own reality in language.

Another illustrious reviewer cautions, however, that the poetry of *Nightwood* is not gratuitous, but tightly bound to its sources in experience. Dylan Thomas wrote: "It isn't a lah-de-dah prose poem, because it's about what some very real human people feel, think and do."[3] The themes and content are nearly as remarkable as the form, not only because the novel is one of the most important works of literature about homosexuals. The extremes of passion and pessimism that enthrall its characters are nearly unbearable. The novel also confronts the old decadence of Europe with the young cynicism of America in a singularly bleak fashion. It tells of four people connected by their relationship to Robin Vote, an American woman who lives passionately and recklessly, drawing others in with her beauty and vitality, yet unable to maintain stable relationships with any of them. Three people come under her influence, or draw her into theirs: Felix Volkbein, the pseudo-aristocratic Austrian who marries Robin and has a child with her; Nora Flood, an American who abandons her salon for the spiritually wayward and follows Robin to Europe; and Jenny Petherbridge, an emotional opportunist who lures Robin away from Nora. Acquainted with all of these figures is the already mentioned Matthew O'Connor, a homosexual quack doctor, an expatriate in Paris who listens to Felix's and Nora's woes with Robin and indulges at length in witty, cynical, and sometimes brilliant disquisitions about their troubles, his troubles, and the troubles of modern culture generally. Although Robin stands in the middle of the book, O'Connor, as the others' confidant and as the chief commentator on their affairs, is its protagonist. His wry and vitriolic wit, according to one critic, could have made Matthew O'Connor a role for Groucho Marx.[4]

The plot, at times barely coherent, consists of tiny bricks of action cemented with the vast mortar of O'Connor's comments, and to a lesser extent those of the narrator and other figures. O'Connor helps Felix and Nora contend with the loss of Robin, though this "help" is ultimately an apology for desperation. He tells Felix, for example: "Man was born damned and innocent from the start, and wretchedly – as he must – on those two themes – whistles his tune" (121). Experience leads neither to redemption nor to wisdom, only to wretchedness, as he says to Nora: "Be humble like the dust, as God intended, and crawl, and finally you'll crawl to the end of the gutter and not be missed and not much remembered" (147). After Robin has left Felix for Nora and Nora for Jenny and Jenny for who knows what, the novel ends back in the United States. Nora, unseen, watches Robin, alone and broken, in a small chapel in the woods, caught between spirituality (innocence) in the form of an improvised altar to the Madonna, and bestiality (damnation) as she descends to the level of her dog, barking and whimpering.

Considering the wealth of controversial themes and the richness of the poetical medium of *Nightwood*, the study of one motif – Austria – might seem trivial. But in a book marked by modern decadence, anti-Semitism, neurosis, and the meeting of the Old World with the New, Barnes's choice of Austria as a representative of Europe was not capricious. As Jane Marcus has written, "*Nightwood*, like modernism itself, begins in Vienna in the 1880s. Freud, fascism, Hitler, 'high art,' and the lumpen proletariat haunt the text as a potent 'political unconscious.'"[5] And Meryl Altman writes: "Felix's appearance in *Nightwood*'s opening pages embeds all the novel's deviants deeply in twentieth-century European social history, yes, but more specifically in a semiscientific, highly ideological discourse about racial origins and racial destinies."[6] I will expand on these observations that place *Nightwood* in the context of *fin-de-siècle* Austria by arguing that Austria provides the text not only with a modernist "political unconscious" and a sociohistorical and ideological context, but also with a central ethical motif, which is the source of the book's tragic sense. The idea of Austria in *Nightwood* is the idea that history and culture forge the general conditions of identity, an identity we are thus born with (innocence), but each single manifestation of this identity must be discovered and invented, and here history and culture provide little help (damnation). The past creates us, but there is no foothold in the past for selfhood. Finding oneself in the majority culture, even if one can do so, is actually a loss of individual contour, and hence a procuring of identity at the cost of a loss of self. Some people (Jews and homosexuals, for instance) do not have the choice to thus lose themselves, and so they cannot even have the illusion of a positive identity, they are always the Other. The paradox of identity, that it is at once a necessity and an illusion, a reality and a dream, is at the center of *Nightwood*, and it is a paradox that is especially pronounced in Austrian culture.[7] It is the idea that history washes us up and then retreats like a spent breaker.

Felix strives for the illusion of historical identity; it is his motive for marriage and fatherhood. O'Connor has abandoned the quest, though he is fascinated by what it does to others, and his stereotyping of nationalities is a satire of the quest for historical or "racial" identity rather than some witless bias that sounds incorrect to disingenuous postmodern ears.[8] Robin tries to fill the space of non-identity with love, but since what others love in her is just this negative space of possibility, they cannot fulfill her, and she moves on to the next lover. Nora tries to fix identity in a stable (if not clinging) relationship, which Robin cannot offer her. Only Jenny operates on the surface of illusion, with no deeper need of fulfillment. But even this cynical acceptance of superficiality does not protect her. O'Connor remarks, with a crude and brilliant simile: "Jenny is one of those who nip like a bird and void like an ox – the poor and lightly damned! That can be a torture also" (138). Later, Milan Kundera would recognize this torture and call it the "unbearable lightness of being," which makes us "only half real," and our "movements as free as they are insignificant."[9]

Though Robin Vote is a central character in the novel, she actually appears in only four of the eight chapters, and one of those is the very brief concluding chapter. O'Connor, as has been noted, is the real protagonist, and he spends much more time with Nora and Felix than with Robin. Thus Barnes is as interested in Robin's effect on others as in Robin herself. Indeed, the novel recognizes that a crucial, elusive, and painful component of identity is the self as it exists in others' minds. It is a part of identity that we strongly depend on yet have little control over. It is the source of most of the pain in this novel of anguish, as Felix and Nora yearn to mean something to Robin that they cannot mean to her, and Robin, wishing to have people mean something to her, ends up using them. The fascination with Robin's sway over others has autobiographical roots: the novel is in large part Barnes's attempt to come to terms with her thwarted love for a woman named Thelma Wood (whose name is probably also one allusion of the title). O'Connor functions almost like a chorus to the dramas around Robin, for his tragic situation in the world is this: as a homosexual charlatan he is absolutely something other than the world will accept, yet he is unable and unwilling to adapt to the world, whose cruelty and hypocrisy seem to him much more vicious than his own "perversions." He has nothing to lose, and so he sees with ruthless clarity, and although his unfailing detection of baseness, selfishness, and irrationality in others is clouded by bitterness, it is supported by sympathy. In the parlance of childhood banter, "it takes one to know one."

We meet Robin Vote's first lover, Baron Felix Volkbein, in the first chapter, "Bow Down," the main chapter that develops the idea of Austria. The book begins "[e]arly in 1880" with the scene of Felix's birth. His mother is "a Viennese woman of great strength and military beauty." She gives birth on a bed bearing both the "bifurcated wings of the House of Hapsburg" and the coat of arms of the Volkbein family (1).[10] Hedvig Volkbein looks at the heraldic symbols, names her newborn son "Felix," pushes him away, and dies. Felix is thus born an orphan, for his father Guido Volkbein, "a Jew of Italian descent," had died six months before. Guido was "both a gourmet and a dandy," "small, rotund, and haughtily timid," with a bulging stomach "produced by heavy rounds of burgundy, schlagsahne, and beer" (1). In *Vienna and Its Jews* George E. Berkley writes that such staidness was sought after in Vienna as part of a "mania for stability" that glorified age and denigrated youth and "even made it fashionable to cultivate some portliness, a goal that the heavy, rich Viennese diet certainly facilitated."[11] Guido is thus a stereotype of the Viennese bourgeois at the end of the century: corpulent, hedonistic, and both arrogant and fearful.

He is also an impostor: the Volkbein coat of arms, as we discover, is a fraud. Guido, a Jew cut off from his people, wished to be accepted by the Christian world. "In life he had done everything to span the impossible gap; the saddest and most futile gesture of all had been his pretence to a barony. He had adopted the sign of the cross; he had said that he was an Austrian of an old, almost extinct line, producing, to uphold his story, the most amazing and inaccurate proofs: a coat of arms that he had no right to and a list of progenitors (including their Christian names) who had never existed" (3). As pathetic as Guido's aspirations are, they are nonetheless historically recognizable as part of a Viennese veneration for all things aristocratic. By emulating the nobility, Guido is actually carrying to an absurd degree the general bourgeois-Viennese imitation of aristocracy. Paul Hofmann writes: "The Viennese populace, which lived so long in close contact with the imperial family and the aristocracy, serving and observing them, inevitably and imperceptibly took on something of the court manner and no one more so than the bourgeoisie that emerged at the end of the eighteenth century. Enduring Viennese characteristics can thus be explained: ceremoniousness, a love of gossip, a propensity for intrigue, adeptness at maneuvering for preferment, and the dogged pursuit of patronage."[12] Thus Barnes has prepared a historical background for her idiosyncratic literary figure. This wedding of excess in fact with excess in fiction lends Barnes's hyperbole much of its improbable verisimilitude.

Guido tries to enhance his Christianity and his Germanness by marrying Hedvig, who enters the marriage because she too admires aristocracy: "The thing that she had stalked, though she herself had not been conscious of it, was Guido's assurance that he was a Baron. She had believed it as a soldier 'believes' a command" (5). Here again the undue Viennese adulation of nobility draws this unlikely pair together. Guido, for his part, tries "to be one with her by adoring her, by imitating her goose-step of a stride, a step that by him adopted became dislocated and comic" (3). What is ridiculous in a gentile is pitiable in the Jew Guido, who believes he is able to assimilate by imitating an imitation. He is twice removed from a delusion, for Hedvig's devotion to soldierly virtues itself has the exaggerated features of a mask.

There also is a historical context for Guido and Hedvig's overweening admiration for the Germanic. The unification of Germany and its newfound political and economic power spurred German sentiment in Austria as well (Berkley 49-50). Furthermore, in the wake of industrialization and urbanization in the late nineteenth century, which increased the migration of non-Germans to Vienna, the Viennese, especially the lower middle class, feared dilution of "true" German Austrians by these migrants from the Crown Lands, and were hence susceptible to Pan-German ideas such as those championed by the nationalist anti-Semite Georg von Schönerer, who organized a powerful, radical "German People's Party" in 1882. This helps explain Hedvig's character, which with its rather Prussian military esprit does not seem to fit the stereotype of the Viennese. She is a sort of gentile alrightnik,[13] whose Germanic and aristocratic ambitions go hand-in-hand, and are a denial of what Austria and Vienna were becoming in 1880: increasingly middle-class, increasingly non-German, and increasingly untraditional. These new energies are, of course, impulses to the modernism that Jane Marcus finds at the root of *Nightwood*.

Nor is it unusual that Guido is also pro-German. George E. Berkley writes: "Among those who succumbed to the spirit of Germanism were the integrationist Jews," and Guido certainly fits this category (50). His conversion to Catholicism is also not particularly anomalous, for even in the wake of the *Kulturkampf* Austrian Catholics were drawn to Protestant Germany (Berkley 49). Thus both Guido and Hedvig are reactionaries of historically distinct types, who try to become more upper-class, more German, and more history-bound. The ironies of their using each other to do this are manifest: Guido falls into the arms of someone who, at the time of the publication of *Nightwood* in 1936, would probably support the Nazis and their Nuremberg Laws, and Hedvig willfully ignores the fact that the man she steps on in her social climb is a Jewish commoner.

Let us look closer at this irony. We have several clichés of late-nineteenth-century Austria: two bourgeois who emulate the aristocracy rather than cultivating a proper middle-class culture; a Jew with origins outside of Vienna who wishes to assimilate to Christian culture; an effete, non-German epicure; and a Germanic, military type. Aestheticism and militarism coexist in an uneasy union, made possible only by shared self-delusion. While the elements of this typology are familiar enough in the prewar multicultural state that was half-heartedly trying to shift from a dynastic power to a modern polity, Barnes transcends the clichés by bending and blending them: Germanic Hedvig is willing to overlook Guido's Jewish Italianness to gain access to his supposed aristocracy. Guido is willing to abandon his Jewishness, but this gains him not admission to society, but a substitute past. Barnes makes it clear that this flight from one identity to another is ultimately futile: "When a Jew dies on a Christian bosom he dies impaled" (3).

Another curious feature of this weird marriage, which is also a marriage across years, since Guido is fifty-nine and Hedvig is forty-five, is the partial reversal of gender roles: Hedvig is the strong, masculine one and Guido is the effeminate, submissive one, reminiscent, perhaps, of Otto Weininger's identification of Jewishness and femininity. United in marriage, these warped stereotypes produce an allegory of Austrian paradoxes at the end of the nineteenth century: Austria, especially in its capital Vienna, was a middle-class aristocratic multinational German Christian Jewish masculine feminine refined artistic militarist state whose main claim to a continued existence in the future was a long, ever more imaginary existence in the past.

This inordinately representative Viennese existence – representative at the level of the "political unconscious" (Jane Marcus) – is embodied in Guido's house in the Inner City, overlooking the Prater, "a house that, large, dark and imposing, became a fantastic museum of their encounter" (5). In this city of museums that Broch called a museum of itself,[14] Guido and Hedvig live in a museum. The description of this house shows how Barnes is able to combine description, narration, historical allusion, and characterization in a fascinating lyrical style:

> The great salon was of walnut. Over the fireplace hung impressive copies of the Medici shield and, beside them, the Austrian bird.
> Three massive pianos (Hedvig had played the waltzes of her time with the masterly stroke of a man, in the tempo of her blood, rapid and rising – that quick mannerliness of touch associated with the playing of the Viennese, who, though pricked with the love of rhythm, execute its demands in the duelling manner) sprawled over the thick dragon's-blood pile of rugs from Madrid. The study harboured two rambling desks in rich and bloody wood. Hedvig had liked things in twos and threes.... The full length windows (a French touch that Guido thought handsome) overlooking the park were curtained in native velvets and stuffs from Tunis, and the Venetian blinds were of that peculiarly sombre shade of red so loved by the Austrians. (5-6)

Dominating the great salon are two life-sized portraits of Guido's putative parents, who are actually strangers, their likenesses bought for the purpose of establishing a lineage.[15] This scene shows at once the character and a caricature of *fin-de-siècle* Vienna, exaggerated by the pretensions of these would-be nobles. I could continue my list of incongruities: virile daintiness, calculated passion, soldierly art, restrained excess, and insular worldliness are all suggested by this passage. One might even speak of "modernist Biedermeier."

His parents' Austrianness, their false obeisance to history and rank, furnishes the character of Felix Volkbein: he inherits the legacy of a borrowed glory and a purloined past. Thus Felix is doubly removed from a historical identity, cut off from his past not only personally, through the deaths of his parents, but also historically, because this past is a lie. Barnes writes: "At this point exact history stopped for Felix who, thirty years later, turned up in the world with these facts, the two portraits and nothing more" (7). Thirty years later is 1910, and this representative of *felix Austria* with the ironically appropriate name is hardly happy. He is cosmopolitan but alone, monocled with no place to go, and so concerned with always appearing proper that he never looks appropriate, for he "was tailored in part for the evening and in part for the day" (8). Felix is compelled to construct an identity, but it is a monstrous one: "From the mingled passions that made up his past, out of a diversity of bloods, from the crux of a thousand impossible situations, Felix had become the accumulated and single – the embarrassed" (9). He tries to compensate for this embarrassment with his excessive admiration for "Old Europe": "aristocracy, nobility, royalty" (9). "He felt that the great past might mend a little if he bowed low enough, if he succumbed and gave homage" (9).

Hence the chapter's title, "Bow Down," and hence Felix's peculiar mishmash of pride and shame. His necessarily superficial relationship to nobility leads him to a fascination with the pageantry of the theater and the circus (10-11), and of the church (12), and the main action of the first chapter takes place when he is forty and consorting with circus people in Berlin. Through his circus connections he meets Matthew O'Connor and Nora Flood.

The doctor appeals to Felix because he promises to be a "valuable liar," and his "manner was that of a servant of a defunct noble family" (30), a discarded servant for an abandoned house. O'Connor will also take Felix's lying seriously – he won't believe him, but he will understand his need to invent an outrageous identity. They frequent cafés in Paris together, discussing national and ethnic characters in often stereotypical, but entertaining and sometimes even illuminating, terms. This is the "semiscientific, highly ideological discourse about racial origins and racial destinies" that Meryl Altman describes (163), and the doctor is the "voice of sexual (and racial) theory in the novel" (166). According to O'Connor, the Irish are common but have imagination and "creative misery" (31). The Irish lie and Jews meddle, he says, and he explains his obsession with nationality thus: "'No man needs curing of his individual sickness; his universal malady is what he should look to'" (32).

We must consider the source of such pronouncements. O'Connor is a character in a work of literature, not the author of a tract, and so ideology is the background of his discourse, not the foreground. What should we make of his statements? On what level of universality is he speaking? Individual variations on historical themes are mere quirks. Our national and historical backgrounds determine, sometimes grimly, who we are. Even if we take O'Connor to be a race theorist, which he undoubtedly is, among other things, the sources of his ideas are less important than their implications. For him, whatever determines national character, race, biology, history, or self-definition, it is not a positive attribute, but a malady. He is not a race theorist in order to aggrandize his or any other "race," rather he is a student, if you will, of comparative culturopathy. In this vision of original sin without prospect of redemption, Jewishness and homosexuality are particularly difficult versions of a certain general difficulty: it is impossible to combine passion and justice. This tragedy is played out throughout the novel. Desire is never commensurate with its object, neither for Guido and Hedvig, nor for Felix and Robin, nor for Nora and Robin, nor for Robin and Jenny. The states of "otherness" are not essentially troublesome; they are the victims on the level of culture of this imbalance of wish and reality. The Christian, European, heterosexual culture is no happier than its subcultures, but its suffering can take the form of power, while the Other in Barnes's novel works out its malady by cultivating suffering, by developing ever more exquisite forms of misery. Without the identity of power, the most available source of identity for the Other, rightly or wrongly, is suffering.

Felix adds to this discussion with a theory of beverages. He tells the story of the Turks bringing coffee to Vienna, and "from that day Vienna, like a woman, had one impatience, something she liked. You know, of course, that Pitt the younger was refused alliance because he was foolish enough to proffer tea; Austria and tea could never go together. All cities have a particular and special beverage suited to them. As for God and the Father – in Austria they were the Emperor" (33). This flighty and incongruous explanation of Austrian character is not so interesting for its content, though such witty generalities often have a kernel of truth, as for how it further shows Felix's motivations in thinking about life, his proud orientation to the past, his making a religion of nation, aristocracy, and history. He is fatherless, and so he adopts the Emperor. He is motherless, and so he adopts the empire. Differing taste is the strongest mark of nationhood. He is without history, and so he adopts history itself as his reality. The fact that the Emperor and the Empire exist only in history makes his situation as poignant as that of Franz Ferdinand Trotta in Joseph Roth's *Kapuzinergruft*.

Although inextricable from his Jewishness, it is primarily Felix's Austrianness that defines him. In the post-Holocaust world, we need reminding that in many prewar Jews' minds at least, Jewishness was a secondary characteristic. Steven Beller writes, "The attitude to Judaism among the assimilated bourgeoisie was generally one of indifference."[16] One was in the first place Austrian, bourgeois, cultured, a participant in the best of German-language culture from Goethe to Hofmannsthal. The Jews "wanted to identify with Western civilization, and Western civilization in the Austrian Empire seemed to have reached its zenith among the Austro-Germans" (Berkley 50). This tendency supplies an answer to Meryl Altman's question whether the "Volkbein plight" is a "result of oppression or of their attempts to hide who they are, to 'bow down' and thus to rise" (161). This is not an either-or question. Oppression made assimilation desirable for Austrian Jews who wanted to improve their material condition, and the Revolution of 1848 and the Emancipation of 1867 made such assimilation possible.[17] Bourgeois Jews of Felix's generation were generally cut off from their Jewish past and pursued the dream of becoming European, that is, cultured, civilized, and Western. In secularized modern society the abandonment of religious Jewishness was mainly a formal matter (Beller 84). Thus it makes sense that Felix, who was not raised as a Jew, in his quest for a past pursues not a Jewish identity, but an "old Austrian" identity. Barnes is remarkably attuned to this Austrian Jewish rootlessness, and to the dangers it presents in Christian society. However far he is from being a Jew, Felix cannot stop being one, for his environment will not permit him to assimilate fully. Since he has no sense of Jewish culture, he can only try more furiously to become Austrian, German, and Christian. Because he sees this combination idealized in the old empire, which is dead, he must paradoxically seek the past in the future, and for him the future of the past is embodied in Robin Vote.

Felix meets Robin when he joins "Doctor" O'Connor on an emergency call to help a woman who has fainted. The woman is Robin, and Felix is immediately fascinated, both in a direct way, by the "mysterious and shocking blue" (37) of her eyes, and indirectly by a sense that she is an "infected carrier of the past" (37). Although "racially incapable of abandon, he felt that he was looking upon a figurehead in a museum" (38). He admits his fascination to O'Connor and states that he wants a son who will feel as he does about the past. And curiously, it is with an American that he thinks he should have this son: "'With an American anything can be done'" (39). As his parents in some sense completed the Austrian past by wedding the German and the Jewish, so Felix hopes by marrying the Austrian past to the American future he can complete his plan for a future in which the past has some meaning. "'To pay homage to our past is the only gesture that also includes the future'" he tells O'Connor (39). And so he pursues and marries Robin.

Taking Robin to Vienna, hoping to establish a connection between her and his past, Felix himself is revealed as an exile, a tourist in the world he cherishes most: "To reassure himself he showed her all the historic buildings. He kept saying to himself that sooner or later, in this garden or that palace, she would suddenly be moved as he was moved. Yet it seemed to him that he too was a sightseer" (43). His memory is only second-hand: "he found himself repeating what he had read, for it was what he knew best" (43). The foray into past glory is reduced to a tour, and longed-for glory is substituted by the homely Viennese cuisine. After reminding Robin that she is now a baroness (a sad lie), Felix watches her eat. "He spoke to her in German as she ate the heavy *Schnitzel* and dumplings, clasping her hand about the thick handle of the beer mug" (43). The way to the Austrian past is through the *Backhendlfriedhof*, not through higher culture, for the imperial palace at Schönbrunn, the Gloriette, and the memory of Francis Joseph only make Felix aware of the futility of trying to convert Robin to Imperial Austria. It would take something neither he nor Vienna can offer, namely authenticity, "someone of that old régime" (44). He gives up after ten days (about the length of Djuna Barnes's only trip to Vienna[18]) and he takes her back to Paris, where he takes comfort in "the discovery that she was an enigma" (44), possibly harboring greatness.

Robin herself, the American in voluntary European exile, also seeks in this union some sort of identity: she imagines her pregnancy even before it is a fact as "some lost land within herself" (45). She gradually prepares for the act of giving a future to the past by converting to Catholicism, and by wandering from church to church in Paris: "She tried to think of the consequence to which her son was to be born and dedicated. She thought of the Emperor Francis Joseph" (47). She thinks about other women of destiny in history and literature, "and now there was this woman Austria" (47). But these thoughts gain no substance, and her attempt to connect herself to history has failed even before the child is born.

Ahmed Nimeiri has interpreted the breakdown of this marriage to mean that "outside America, the American is doomed to share the perpetual alienation of the outcast and never become a part of a meaningful experience."[19] He further states that "Felix only offers her a travesty of the values that make life meaningful" (107). For Nimeiri, only the parallel between the Jew and the American can explain why the first chapter is even included: the "pathetic situation of the Jew" provides "an appropriate explanation and a frame of reference for the predicament of the American innocent, who strives to transcend his innocence and achieve a human identity" (103). "Meaningful experience" and "human identity" apparently consist in the acknowledgment of "dark realities" that Europe "accommodates and regards ... as an integral part of man's being" (107). But thus celebrating Europe for its hard-nosed sophistication narrows Barnes's focus too much, for it is not only the Jew and the American who cannot find such values; Hedvig is as pathetic as Guido, and the circus people, who are European, are themselves a travesty, also in the literal sense, of the historical continental values of aristocracy and pomp. Hence Nimeiri's view, which seems to be warped by a lens of anti-American and anti-Jewish bias, is too simplistic, for it ignores the fact that not only America is in a "time of crisis after the old certainties and values have been tested and proved inadequate" (Nimeiri 111), but Europe is too, and nowhere more than in Austria.

The night of Robin's labor is the night she begins to detach herself from Felix and their son Guido. She disappears, and is next heard of in the company of Nora Flood, who, as a fellow American and a fellow woman, is about as different from Felix as you can get. Their offspring turns out to be a sickly boy, a ghost not a hope. Felix's longings are ruined. Barnes writes that the child had been "born to holy decay. Mentally deficient and emotionally excessive, an addict to death; at ten barely as tall as a child of six, wearing spectacles, stumbling when he tried to run, with cold hands and anxious face, he followed his father" (107). The boy Guido wants to enter the church, and this is a turn away from life: "in accepting his son the Baron saw that he must accept a demolition of his own life. The child would obviously never be able to cope with it" (108). This is Felix's great sacrifice, of his imagined past for a real but hopeless future in his son, and it is almost a redemption.

Thinking that his son will probably not be able to become a monk in France, Felix decides to return to Austria. Before he leaves he meets O'Connor and reflects on his relationship with Robin: "I find that I never did have a really clear idea of her at any time. I had an image of her, but that is not the same thing. An image is a stop the mind makes between uncertainties" (111). His image was that she shared his devotion to history, but her devotion was, in the words of O'Connor, fundamentally different from Felix's. Whereas Felix's devotion to the past is "perhaps like a child's drawing," his familial memory being preserved as a simple figure on the same scale with the present, Robin was seeking not security and certainty, but freedom in a past of her choice. O'Connor says: "our faulty racial memory is fathered by fear. Destiny and history are untidy; we fear memory of that disorder. Robin did not" (118).

At one level, this is a confrontation of an American attitude with a European one. The American's lack of a past in the European sense, in which self and culture coincide, instills the search for one; but the very fact that one can seek out a past reveals this as an act of freedom, of adventure, of self-invention. The European is given a past whether he wants it or not, and so seeking it out is not self-invention, but a discovery of the limitations of the self (what O'Connor calls "racial memory"). The European seeks order, the American seeks freedom. Barnes makes use of these stereotypical cultural patterns, but they take on unique and extreme forms in her characters Felix and Robin. Felix is given a caricature for a past, a simple-minded lie, but it is all he has. Robin cannot endure the moment in which the present becomes the past, which is every moment. In seeking disorder, because it is vital, she abandons anything that limits her: a husband, a child, a lover. Felix cannot endure the moment in which the past becomes the present, which is likewise every moment. He seeks order and finds only disorder. For different reasons, both Felix and Robin are cut off from their present by their past, but they are also cut off from their past by the present, and so they are anchored in neither. This is the basis for their otherwise inexplicable attraction and marriage.

O'Connor points out to Felix that his son Guido is actually what he has been looking for: "'Guido . . . is blessed – he is peace of mind – he is what you have always been looking for – Aristocracy,' he said, smiling, 'is a condition in the mind of the people when they try to think of something else and better," (121). What Felix has actually been looking for is this "addict to death," and his dedication to the past is a flight from life. What Robin is looking for – something to fill the space of identity that always seems to empty itself again – is life, but it is impossible to make a past into a present, it is impossible to live life always in the present, no matter how often you run away.

A note on the novel's creation might help put the issues of history and identity in perspective. Djuna Barnes got her impressions of

Vienna on a brief visit there in 1931. She was traveling with the writer Charles Henri Ford, one of her acquaintances in Paris, and they spent five days in Munich, eleven days in Vienna, and a week in Budapest (Herring 176). In Paris she knew a left-bank character named Daniel A. Mahoney, who is the model for Matthew O'Connor (Herring 210). Felix Volkbein is based on a real-life figure, her one-time publisher Guido Bruno of Greenwich Village, and a Felix Paul Greve, who sometimes signed himself Baron Volkbein, seems to have supplied the name (Herring 215-216).[20] As already noted, Nora Flood is basically an autobiographical figure, while Robin Vote is Barnes's former lover Thelma Wood. *Nightwood* is a caustic but brilliant act of revenge for Thelma's having abandoned Djuna. But we would be misled if we tried to explain *Nightwood* by overemphasizing the autobiographical. Instead we must concentrate on the artistic transformations of this substance. One important transformation is its embedding in the historical context of Old Austria.

Barnes's accurate, if exaggerated, image of Old Austria is remarkable considering her brief stay there, but like Felix's knowledge of his country, it is bolstered by book learning. Indeed, the core of the book was originally the Felix material, whose origins precede the 1931 visit to Vienna, and which is apparently based on research that Barnes describes in a Guggenheim application of 1930: she planned to "'research the relationship of the Jew and the court for a book in progress whose chief figure is an Austrian Jew.'"[21] The thematic fundament of the novel thus seems to be Felix's problematical relationship to the past, which is subsequently mirrored in the figures of O'Connor and Robin. Barnes's accomplishment is portraying the link between these seekers within a dense poetical reality.

Barnes's translation of the idea of Austria into a literary motif, although in some respects a stereotype, conveys a sense of lived experience in the detailed impressions that she must somehow have absorbed during her visit. Austria stands for the end of the old Europe and the pathological persistence of aristocracy, a functionless pageantry that has the same social status as the circus, while it imagines itself cultured, tasteful, and refined. This travesty of past values is not peculiarly Jewish, as Ahmed Nimieri seems to maintain, but one of many general European reactions to the malady of loss after World War One. The distress was especially acute for those who idealized the empire like Joseph Roth (or with more ironic distance Robert Musil). It was also painful for Austrian Jews who saw Francis Joseph as an emancipator and emulated aristocratic cultural values, and thus felt less comfortable in a German-Austrian republic than in a multinational monarchy. Precisely this discomfort is what Barnes seizes upon, and those familiar with Austria's social and cultural conflicts in the 1920s and 30s, when she was writing, can recognize her perceptiveness even in its grotesque overstatement.

The idea of Austria, which opens and grounds *Nightwood*, is a tragic idea. T. S. Eliot wrote of this novel: "What I would leave the reader prepared to find is the great achievement of a style, the beauty of phrasing, the brilliance of wit and characterisation, and a quality of horror and doom very nearly related to that of Elizabethan tragedy" (*Nightwood*, "Introduction" xvi). What is tragic about *Nightwood* is the modern compulsion to construct an identity while neither personal nor national history supplies enough material to do so. Robin tries to turn history in the form of Felix Volkbein into a personal sense of significance; she tries to gain a past, but she is incapable of settling for what she has chosen when it turns out wrong, and so she seeks a perpetual present. Felix tries to turn his past into a future through marriage to Robin Vote and his child Guido, but his devotion to history turns out to be a devotion to a dead, counterfeit past. It can have no future. The two pass each other briefly in their futile pursuits.

Meryl Altman worries that Felix's condition, his embrace of Christian history as a "wet nurse whose milk was his being but which could never be his birthright" (10), indicates that he "will never be able to write his own story or even remember his own history, that Jewish culture is doomed to be sold and resold, and that assimilation – which will never really work – is nonetheless the best the Jew can hope for"; and she suspects that Barnes does not disapprove of this (168). What is wrong with Altman's concern, however, is just this assumption that Barnes is being prescriptive, that she is writing a "a Christian discourse" (168) dominated by "an approving God" (168). Even in the passage cited, Barnes does not make Christianity look very attractive, with its "traffic in retribution that has made the Jew's history a commodity" (10). Barnes is being descriptive, and the historical alternatives available to European Jews in the 1930s bear out her pessimism.

Another error is Altman's assumption that Felix Volkbein is representative. Barnes's language makes it clear that he is an example of what the Austrian-Jewish predicament meant, just *one* example of what the stew pot of the late empire was capable of producing. The more general problem, which obtains regardless of religious, cultural, or sexual arrangement, is a modern dilemma, the simultaneous surfeit and lack of history.

Is this dilemma not our dilemma as students of culture? We too struggle with the historical nature of individual phenomena. But we must not get the imperative of cultural studies backward by making texts and their contents stand for more than themselves. The idea of Austria in *Nightwood* does not primarily help us understand Austria; the Jewish figure in *Nightwood* does not primarily help us understand "the Jewish situation." Rather, our study of Austria and the Jewish situation can help us understand *Nightwood*. Marsha Rozenblit tells us of the tremendous diversity just within Viennese Jewry (13), and while Barnes's narrator speaks often of "the Jew," Felix is clearly "one Jew," with a very specific background that has produced, in fiction, a singular person. According to the narrator, he is "the accumulated and single – the embarrassed" (10). The presence of three very different lesbians in the text similarly attests to Barnes's lack of interest in generalizing about "the lesbian experience." Nora (the "Djuna Barnes" figure) does not stand for all lesbians, and to make Felix stand for all Jews, and to make his fate into a vicarious judgment on all Jews, is to load more upon Felix than he can bear, and to do an injustice to Barnes's text as literature. It is unreasonable to expect *Nightwood* to give the Jews "an authentic discourse of their own" (Altman 168). How could it? Rather, against the background of Austria that has been developed here, we can recognize the verisimilitude (not the representativeness) of Felix Volkbein. Given Austrian history, it is likely that a character like Felix could exist. History accounts for Felix; it would be too much to ask him to account for history.

Likewise, history and culture can account for Djuna Barnes, but we should not demand that she account for history and culture. Literature is more modest than cultural studies, and hence it is more supple. In *Nightwood*, Austria is a background, the birthplace of the modern, the scene of a particularly fierce struggle between tradition and novelty, between the past and the future. Both in the characters' minds and in the metaphorical economy of the narrative, Austria and Vienna are places where the inaccessibility of the past is poignant because of the omnipresence of the past. Thus Austria contrasts with America, where the need for history stems, if you will, from its omni-absence. But both crave history; hence Robin converts to Catholicism, marries an Austrian and gives birth to another one, and shuttles between Europe and America, all without finding peace. Neither Old Austria nor young

America is complete; each lacks what the other offers, a future and a past respectively, but the offers are merely tantalizing. In *Nightwood*, the idea of America is the idea of a place without a past, so open and restless that it has no substance. The idea of Austria is the idea of a place without a present, so refined and depleted that it too has no substance. The notion, pursued by every expatriate, that the old world and the new world could complement each other and produce something of substance is, for Djuna Barnes at least, a tragic delusion.

Bowling Green State University

Notes

1. For example, James B. Scott titles a chapter in his monograph *Djuna Barnes* (Boston: Twayne, 1976) "*Nightwood*: The Poetic Novel" (86-119).

2. Clifton Fadiman, review of *Nightwood* in the *New Yorker* (13 March 1937), quoted in Jane Marcus, "Mousemeat: Contemporary Reviews of *Nightwood*," *Silence and Power: A Reevaluation of Djuna Barnes*, ed. Mary Lynn Bore, with an afterword by Catharine Simpson (Carbondale and Edwardsville: Southern Illinois University Press, 1991), 203.

3. Dylan Thomas, review of *Nightwood* in *Light and Dark* (Oxford and Cambridge, March 1937), quoted in Marcus, 200.

4. Roger Shattuck, review of Nightwood in the *Village Voice* (22 May 1962), quoted in Marcus, 196.

5. Jane Marcus, "Laughing at Leviticus: *Nightwood* as Woman's Circus Epic," in Bore, 222.

6. Meryl Altman, "A Book of Repulsive Jews? Rereading *Nightwood*" *Review of Contemporary Fiction* 13, 3 (Fall 1993), 163.

7. The pair "dream and reality" has often been associated with the cultural contradictions of Austria and Vienna around the turn of the century. It supplied the title of a major exhibition in 1985: *Traum und Wirklichkeit: Wien 1880-1930*.

8. Meryl Altman, for instance, is troubled by the racial theorizing of O'Connor, whom she regards as the "voice of sexual (and racial) theory in the novel" (166). But even a character like O'Connor does not speak "for" the novel; he is a character, whose appearance in a text does not imply the author's sponsorship of his ideas any more than Oedipus imparts Sophocles' approval of patricide and incest.

9. Milan Kundera, *The Unbearable Lightness of Being*. Translated by Michael Henry Heim (New York: Harper & Row, 1984), 5.

10. Djuna Barnes, *Nightwood* (New York: New Directions, 1946), 1. Further citations in text by page number.

11. George E. Berkley, *Vienna and Its Jews: The Tragedy of Success 1880s-1980s* (Cambridge, MA: Abt Books; Lanham, MD: Madison Books, 1988), 19.

12. Paul Hofmann, *The Viennese: Splendor, Twilight and Exile* (New York: Doubleday, 1988; Anchor paperback edition 1989), 26.

13. Not finding "alrightnik" in a standard dictionary, it perhaps behooves me to explain the word. Leo Rosten defines it thus: "1. One who has succeeded, i.e. done 'all right,' and shows it by boasting, ostentation, crude manners. 2. *Nouveau riche*, with trimmings," And further: "As it is true of many Yiddishisms, the pungent suffix '-nik' is enlisted in the service of scorn. . . *Alrightniks* may be envied, but are not admired; for they have succeeded whether or not they have taste, breeding, or spiritual values. Above all, they are not learned, nor devoted to learning – hence cannot be really respected." *The Joys of Yiddish* (New York: McGraw-Hill, 1968; Pocket Book edition 1970), 12.

14. Hermann Broch, *Hofmannnsthal und seine Zeit* (Frankfurt am Main: Suhrkamp, 1974), 43.

15. An interesting parallel to this genealogical ruse can be found in Robert Musil's *Mann ohne Eigenschaften*. The description of the Tuzzis' salon, where the first great meeting of the *Parallelaktion* is to take place, includes a portrait of a "Woman with an hourglass figure which Mr. Tuzzi while serving as Consul had once brought home from someplace, althought it might just as well have been the picture of an ancestress." *Gesammelte Werke*, vol. 1 (Reinbek: Rowohlt, 1978), 163. While not as flagrantly devious as Volkbein, the Tuzzis do nothing to correct the assumption that the portrait represents an admirable lineage.

16. Steven Beller, *Vienna and the Jews 1867-1938* (Cambridge: Cambridge University Press, 1989), 84.

17. See Marsha L. Rozenblit, *The Jews of Vienna 1867-1914: Assimilation and Identity* (Albany: State University of New York Press, 1983), 13.

18. Philip Herring, *Djuna: The Life and Work of Djuna Barnes* (New York: Viking, 1995), 176.

19. Ahmed Nimieri, "Djuna Barnes's *Nightwood* and 'the Experience of America,'" *Critique* 34, 2 (Winter 1993), 107.

20. Lynn DeVore notes that Felix Paul Greve was a Canadian novelist who published under the name Frederick Phillip Grove. "The Backgrounds of *Nightwood*: Robin, Felix, and Nora," *Journal of Modern Literature* 10, 1 (March 1983), 79.

21. Quoted in Cheryl J. Plumb, "Introduction," Djuna Barnes, *Nightwood: The Original Version and Related Drafts*, edited and with an introduction by Cheryl J. Plumb (Normal, IL: Dalkey Archive Press, 1995), ix - x.

Schlagobers and Blood: Vienna in John Irving's Novel *The Hotel New Hampshire*[1]

Jörg Thunecke

> "Life is serious but art is fun."
> King of the Mice[2]

From the beginning, Vienna has figured prominently in the fiction of American novelist John Irving (*1942). Both his first novel *Setting Free the Bears* (1968),[3] and his fourth novel *The World According to Garp*[4] contain numerous references to the Austrian capital,[5] and as in those earlier works, Vienna, in *The Hotel New Hampshire*, his fifth novel, conforms to the author's familiar rites of passage formula: "separation – initiation – return."[6] However, *Hotel* is a far more hermetic work than *Bears* or *Garp* ever were:[7] for it is primarily the novel's narrated time, with its "museumlike" quality (Miller) of Vienna's *fin-de-siècle* era, which emphasizes Irving's thematic concern, and far less so its narrative time, which, only to a very limited extent, reveals minutiae of the Vienna during the years 1957-1964.[8]

Fin-de-siècle Vienna was a city in the midst of social and cultural disintegration,[9] and, as pointed out by Gabriel Miller, John Irving seems to have deliberately exploited parallels between late nineteenth-century decadence,[10] and those of his own era. It is not surprising therefore that in *Hotel*, too, one encounters the recurring motif of "the maturing or formative experience of the American protagonists . . . as the result of an extended stay in Europe, in Vienna,"[11] confirmed by Irving himself in an interview during the early 1980s:[12] "And, of course, in the case of *The Hotel New Hampshire*, the *foreign country* those children *really* go to is the place we all go [to] when we're forced to grow up too soon. Growing up is a *foreign country*; you leave home in a sense [my emphasis]."[13]

In *Hotel*, the "Gasthaus Freud," later renamed "Hotel New

Hampshire," is merely one in "a series of hotels, each one progressively less ... real,"[14] representing more "a state of mind"[15] than an actual building, a "phase somewhere between childhood and getting to be grown-up,"[16] and is a *locus* which supposedly "requires the least amount of understanding of the so-called *real* and outside world ...."[17] Consequently, critics have on the whole been in agreement that Vienna, in the fiction of John Irving, generally reflects the "classic light-dark-light, America-Europe-America scheme"[18] of earlier US writers (like Henry James[19]), "the dark, the decadent, the incorrigible but necessary interruption of innocence by bleak experience;"[20] that the obligatory trip to the Austrian capital is part of the protagonists' initiation rites;[21] and that in the specific case of *Hotel* it amounts to a trip "from the relatively pristine world of New England ... to the utterly incorrigible realm of *fin-de-siècle* Vienna, a city in the last stages of spiritual, political, and cultural entropy,"[22] whose "foreignness" (285) frightens the American juveniles.

*

In principle, *any* foreign place would have served the author's scheme of a modern fairy tale,[23] thwarting Win Berry's American dream abroad, as well as that of his surviving children: Frank, Franny, John and Lilly, whose future has already been very severely affected by the fact that they arrive motherless in Austria;[24] and consequently the *historical* Vienna of the late 1950s and early 1960s was of relatively *little* importance, as emphasized by the author himself. However, Irving, during an extended stay in Europe, had lived himself for a couple of years in the Austrian capital (1963-1964 and 1969-1972),[25] and consequently was in a good position to draw this town in *Hotel* as a distinct geographic entity,[26] recognizable as a place, emerging from wounds inflicted during the Second World War (200) and the occupation period (234-235).[27] The Berrys' "American dream" of a world inhabited by blissful innocence would therefore have turned into a nightmare just about *anywhere else* abroad; however, Irving – as in the plot of his previous novels – chose to inextricably link this "dream" – and its violent conclusion – to the decadence of the *Austrian* capital's *fin-de-siècle* era, which resurfaced in the children's imagination as so-called "plums" of a once great city's past (201) – though only "ossified" features of this historical period actually survived the horrors of two world wars.

Understanding *Hotel* therefore assumes a certain knowledge of Vienna's cultural heritage, particularly of the decadence of its *fin-de-siècle* era, partially echoed in the novel's narrative time, lasting from 1957 to 1964, a world of the past, aesthetically encapsulated in a symbol like "Schlagobers" (whipped cream), representative of the city's grand architecture,[28] its coffeehouses and theatres, and above all its world-famous State Opera House.

"Schlagobers" is therefore without doubt one of the key symbols in Irving's novel, linked, from a certain point in the narrative, to that of "blood," the other main symbol of *Hotel*, representative of revolutionary forces hellbent on the use of violence as a way of freeing contemporary Austrian society of all latent forms of decadence, past and present.[29] Consequently, the Berry family, and particularly its children, being totally preoccupied with certain aspects of Viennese history at the turn of the century, become – almost of necessity – embroiled with anarchic forces determined to rid Austria of its decadent past.[30] The terrorists, by planning on blowing up – in exemplary fashion – the State Opera House during a live performance of Donizetti's *Lucia di Lammermoor* (1835) – like all so-called serious operas considered to be "Schlagobers and blood" music (337)[31] – aim their attack at the heart of the capital's cultural industry, and – despite its ultimate failure – succeeded in destroying the American family's dreamlike innocence.

The decadent side of Austria's past, for which Irving consulted books like *Fin-de-Siècle Vienna. Politics and Culture* by Carl E. Schorske[32] and *A Nervous Splendor. Vienna 1888/1899* by Frederic Morton,[33] an indebtedness which he acknowledged in the credits of *Hotel*, is first introduced in the opening section of the novel, particularly in Chapter 7, entitled "Sorrow Strikes Again,"[34] some time prior to the Berry family's departure from the provincial New England town of Dairy to metropolitan Vienna. It is foreshadowed by the way the "Gasthaus Freud" is surrounded by various confectioneries, whose signs read: "BONBONS, KONDITOREI, ZUCKERWAREN, SCHOKOLADEN" (277), and their arrival in the autumn of 1957 coincides with liquid candy and the smell of burned chocolate filling the lobby of the hotel as the result of a fire in one of the adjacent shops (236).

The "'plums' of Viennese history" (201), as Frank, the eldest of the five Berry children, labeled certain "outstanding" historical events of the Austro-Hungarian Empire's *fin-de-siècle* era, included features like the circumstances surrounding Crown Prince Rudolf's murder of his mistress Maria Vetsera, and his subsequent suicide at Mayerling in

1889 (202-203);[35] the fact that the writer Arthur Schnitzler (1862-1931) made love 464 times to his "sweet girl" Jeanette Heger in just over one year in the late 1880s (203);[36] that Anton Bruckner (1824-1896), on the occasion of the exhumation of fellow composer Franz Schubert in 1888, could not restrain himself from grabbing the dead man's skull and hugging it until being asked to let it go;[37] right down to trivialities like the information that in 1900, at the Paris World Fair, Austria won the Most Beautiful Uniform Prize (204): "... it was no wonder that the *fin de siècle* in Vienna appealed to Frank. It was only alarming that the *fin de siècle* was the only period Frank really learned and taught to us. All the rest of it was not as interesting to him" (204). Consequently, it was the supposedly "good old time" of Vienna's past the Berry children learned about, of which Bratfisch, Crown Prince Rudolf's personal horse-cab driver, allegedly sang at the Fiacre Ball: "Wo bleibt die alte Zeit / und die Gemütlichkeit?" (206),[38] although, even prior to their departure from the United States, there are ominous historical references that appearances may be deceptive: when e.g., during such an "excursion" into Viennese history, it is pointed out to them that a section of the capital's Ringstrasse was named after an infamous anti-Semite, former mayor Dr. Karl Lueger (1844-1910), and that at about the same time Sigmund Freud (1856-1939) had postulated that all Vienna was merely "an elaborate job of concealing sexual reality" (207),[39] two items of information which do feature prominently again in the middle section of *Hotel*, set primarily at the second "Hotel New Hampshire" on Krugerstrasse in the first District. On the one hand, Freud's – that is Win Berry's blind old mentor, and not the famous psychoanalyst – tour of the former Jewish quarters of Vienna is a sinister reminder of the city's unholy past, which immediately succeeded that of the *fin-de-siècle* era:

> "At Judengasse, turn right!" Freud would instruct. And we would follow Jews' Lane to the church of St. Ruprecht.
> "The eleventh century," Frank would murmur. The older the better for Frank.
> And down to the Danube Canal; at the foot of the slope, on Franz Josefs-Kai, was the monument Freud led us to rather often; the marble plaque memorializing those murdered by the Gestapo, whose headquarters had been on that spot.

> "Right here!" Freud screamed, stamping and whacking with the baseball bat. "Describe the plaque to me!" he cried. "I've never seen it."
> Of course: because it was in one of the camps that he went blind. They had performed some failed experiment on his eyes in the camp.
> . . .
> "Not *summer* camp, Lilly," Frank said. "Freud was in a *death* camp."
> "But Herr Tod never found me," Freud said to Lilly. "Mr. Death never found me at home when he called."
> . . .
> Franny and I got gloomiest when Freud directed us along Wipplingergasse to Füttergasse.
> "Turn!" he'd cry, the baseball bat trembling.
> We were in the Judenplatz, the old Jewish quarter of the city. It had been a kind of ghetto as long ago as the thirteenth century; the first expulsion of the Jews, there, had been in 1421. We knew only slightly more about the recent expulsion.
> What was hard about being there with Freud was that this tour was not so visibly historical. Freud would call out to apartments that were no longer apartments. He would identify whole buildings that were no longer there. And the *people* he used to know there – they weren't there, either. It was a tour of things we couldn't see, but Freud saw them still; he saw 1939, and before, when he'd last been in the Judenplatz with a working pair of eyes (289-290).

On the other hand, the citation of Sigmund Freud's famous remark is reminiscent of the fact that the Berrys effectively lived in a whorehouse for the whole seven years of their stay in Vienna, prostitution being another aspect of the link between late nineteenth century and mid-twentieth century decadence; for on the same tour of Vienna, under the guidance of the other Freud, the children, for example, discover the following historical details, relating back to the eighteenth century:

It was Freud who explained to us that the nudes in the fountain at the Neuer Markt, the Providence Fountain – or the Donner Fountain, after its creator – were actually copies of the original. The originals were in Lower Belvedere. Designed to portray water as the source of life, the nudes had been condemned by Maria Theresa.
"She was a bitch," Freud said. "She founded a Chastity Commission," he told us.
"What did they do?" Franny asked. "The *Chastity* Commission?"
"What *could* they do?" Freud asked. "What can those people *ever* do? They couldn't do anything to stop the sex, so they fucked around with a few fountains."
Even the Vienna of Freud – the *old* Freud – was notorious for being unable to do anything to stop the sex, though this didn't stop the Victorian counterparts of Maria Theresa's Chastity Commission from trying. "In those days," Freud pointed out, admiringly, "whores were allowed to make arrangements in the aisles of the Opera."
"At intermissions," Frank added, in case we didn't know (289-290).

And on another occasion, more up-to-date information on prostitution during the 1950s and 1960s is conveyed to the reader, as a further reminder of the prevailing decadence of the city:

We learned from the whores that, outside the Inner City, the Mariahilfer Strasse was the most promising hunting-ground for ladies of the night. And every whore spoke of getting out of the business if she was ever demoted to the district past the Westbahnhof, to the Kaffee Eden, to the one-hundred-Schilling standing fuck in the Gaudenzdorfer Gürtel. We learned from the radicals that prostitution wasn't even officially *legal* – as we had thought – that there were registered whores who played by the rules, got their medical checkups, trafficked in the right districts, and that there were "pirates" who never registered, or who turned in a *Büchl* (a license) but continued to practice the profession: that there were almost a thousand registered whores in the city in the early 1960s; that decadence was increasing at the necessary rate for revolution (308).

When Fehlgeburt (Miss Miscarriage), one of the female radicals, confesses to the narrator that the revolutionaries, the so-called "Symposium on East-West Relations," occupying the fifth floor of the second "Hotel New Hampshire," are planning to blow up the Vienna State Opera House at the beginning of the new season (i.e. in late summer of 1964), the main reason given for such a horrific act of terrorism is the decadent state of contemporary Austrian society:[40]

> Everything. *Schlagobers*, the erotic, the State Opera, the Hotel New Hampshire – everything had to go. It was all decadent. I could hear them intoning. It was full of disgust. They would litter the Ringstrasse with *art*-lovers, with old fashioned idealists silly and irrelevant enough to like *opera*. They would make some point or other by this kind of everything-bombing (312).

*

As commonly known, the *fin-de-siècle* era achieved a particularly negative distinction because of its overt cultural decadence, characterized by over-sophistication of taste, "Weltschmerz," day-dreaming, pessimism, and the cult of beauty (aestheticism), as well as a preference for complicated psychological conditions, morbidity, eroticism and perversion.[41] In John Irving's novel *The Hotel New Hampshire* such decadent tendencies are inextricably linked to revolutionary activities, as pointed out by the leader of the terrorist group intent on blowing up the Vienna Opera House with a car bomb:

> "Decadence enhances the revolutionary position," Ernst [Mr. Serious] told [Franny].... "Everything that is decadent speeds up the process, the inevitable revolution. At this stage it is necessary to generate disgust. Political disgust, economic disgust; disgust at our inhuman institutions, and moral disgust – disgust at ourselves, as we've allowed ourselves to become" (267).

Symptomatic for this kind of nostalgia and decadence is the Viennese coffeehouse culture of places like the former Café Griensteidl (which was demolished in 1897),[42] or the Café Central (which exists to this day), and finding aesthetic expression in a symbol like "Schlagobers," the whipped cream used to "decorate" various kinds of *café au lait*.[43] This, at least, seems to be the essential point made by Ernst, who – apart from being a part-time lecturer on erotic literature at the local university, and making a living as a professional pornographer – is the "brain" of the revolutionaries, exuding "that cocksure quality, the touch of evil, that hint of destruction, that icy leadership" (269), which the narrator later learns to equate with terrorist traits: "'... *personally* I am an aesthete: I reflect upon the erotic. If Schwanger [Miss Pregnant, the other female terrorist] mourns for her coffee-house – if she is sad about her *Schlagobers*, which the revolution must also consume – I mourn for the erotic, for it must be lost, too'" (268).

From a certain point onward in the novel, decadence, as represented by the coffeehouse culture, and revolution, characterized by terrorist activities, therefore become linked in the symbols of "Schlagobers" and "blood," in precisely the way Arbeiter (Mr. Worker), another of the revolutionaries, juxtaposed them during a fierce argument with fellow anarchist, Old Billig (Mr. Cheap), and Schwanger:

> "You want *Schlagobers*?" Arbeiter roared at her. "*I want Schlagobers* running all over the Kärntnerstrasse," he said crazily. "I want *Schlagobers* and blood," he said. "That's what you'll see: over everything. Oozing over the streets!" said Arbeiter. "*Schlagobers* and blood." (292)

In fact, the whole central section of Irving's novel is devoted to this symbolic connection, expressed even in a chapter heading entitled "A Night at the Opera: *Schlagobers* and Blood,"[44] and given further emphasis, when the terrorists finally proceed to execute their long drawn-up plan on blowing up the Vienna Opera House, which, they believe, will in itself be quite an aesthetic spectacle: "'Everyone on-stage will die, and probably most of the orchestra, and most of the audience in the first few rows of seats. And to those sitting safely back from the stage it will be truly *operatic*,' Ernst said. 'It will provide a very definite spectacle,' said Ernst" (350).

As John Berry, the narrator in Irving's novel, wanders back in a state of shock from Fehlgeburt's apartment near the university to the "Hotel New Hampshire" on Krugerstrasse, having just been told the news of the intended car-bombing of the Opera, he stops for a "Kaffee mit Schlagobers" at Hawelka's on Dorotheergasse,[45] the twentieth-century equivalent of the Café Griensteidl,[46] only to overhear a conversation – symptomatic for the plot of the narrative at this junction – between a Trotzkyite and his girl friend, in which the young man announces the imminent demise of modern culture and society: the death of representational art, of rhyme and metre in poetry, of plot and characterization in fiction, of democracy and socialism (316); and, for the first time, it occurs to the narrator what revolutionaries, claiming to be true humanists, really stand for:

> "Your country, if you'll forgive me," said one of the other radicals – the one they called simply Arbeiter ... , "your country is really a *criminal* place," Arbeiter said. "If you'll forgive me," he added, "your country is the ultimate triumph of corporate creativity, which means it is a country controlled by the *group*-thinking of corporations. These corporations are without humanity because there is no one personally responsible for their use of power; a corporation is like a computer with a profit as its source of energy – a profit as its necessary fuel. The United States is – you'll forgive me – quite the worst country in the world for a humanist to live in, I think." (262)

Circumstances therefore force John Berry to accept the notion that the revolutionaries of the so-called "Symposium on East-West Relations" are in fact terrorists, and that "it was people they wanted to blow up," since "people are more easily destroyed than buildings" (319). When subsequently walking across Heldenplatz, where thousands of cheering fascists had once greeted Hitler in 1938, it suddenly dawns on him that "fanatics would always have an audience," and that "all one might hope to influence was the *size* of the audience" (314); and, while still standing on the Plaza of Heroes, it also dawns on him "how Hitler had made so many people seem *expendable* to such a mob of true believers [my emphasis]" (315):

> In the quiet evening I could almost hear the mindless din of "*Sieg Heil!*" I could see the absolute self-serious-

ness of Schraubenschlüssel's face [Wrench, (431) another revolutionary] when he tightened down the nut and washer on an engine-block bolt. And what else had he been tightening down? I could see the dull glaze of devotion in Arbeiter's eyes, making statements to the press upon his triumphant arrest – and our motherlike Schwanger sipping her *Kaffee mit Schlagobers* . . . (315-316).

For the radicals – it occurs to the narrator – the spectacle of a major terrorist attack,[47] and an international audience, are the true goals of their intended action, as Ernst, their leader, expanded to his American captives:

". . . after we blow up the Opera," Ernst said, "after we destroy an institution that the Viennese worship to the *disgusting* extreme they worship the *past* – well . . . after we blow up the Opera, we'll have possession of an American family. We'll have an American family as hostage. And a *tragic* American family . . ."
"We demand nothing," said Ernst, patiently – ever patiently. "We'll already have what we want," Ernst said. "An international audience. Not just a European audience, not just the *Schlagobers* and blood audience, but an *American* audience, too. The whole world will listen to what we have to say." . . .
"Most terrorists fail," Ernst reasoned, "because they take the hostages and *threaten* violence. But we're beginning with the violence. It is already established that we are capable of it. *Then* we take the hostages. That way everybody listens" (351).

After such a lengthy explanation of the "Symposium's" terrorist ideology, John Berry, all of a sudden, realizes that revolutionaries like Ernst are in fact willing to maim and murder, *not* for a cause, but for an audience (351). It furthermore dawns on him what such terrorists' aims actually are, and that their claim that "[t]he ends *do* justify the means" (346) amounts to no more than self-righteous justification of their evil deeds:

> I realized what a terrorist is. A terrorist, I think, is simply another kind of pornographer. The pornographer pretends he is disgusted by his work; the terrorist pretends he is uninterested in the *means*. The *ends*, they say, are what they care about. But they are both lying. Ernst loved his pornography; Ernst worshiped the means. It is never the end that matters – it is *only* the means that matter. The terrorist and the pornographer are in it *for* the means. The means is everything to them. The blast of the bomb, the elephant position, the *Schlagobers* and blood – they love it all. Their intellectual detachment is a fraud; their indifference is feigned. They both tell lies about having "higher purposes." A terrorist *is* a pornographer (354).

*

The Berry family's, and particularly the children's, grotesque experience in the Austrian capital[48] therefore becomes a shaping force in their lives, which contributes to thwart their "American dream" that goodness ultimately prevails over evil. As far as they are concerned, Vienna turns out to be "emblematic of the decadent culture which has no potential,"[49] and for them the second "Hotel New Hampshire" (the former "Gasthaus Freud") is synonymous with the death of sympathy. As such it is also closely connected to the demise of all innocence, on a macrocosmic scale,[50] the way this process had already been set in motion on a microcosmic scale during their stay in the first "Hotel New Hampshire," back in the United States in the mid-1950s.[51] For in the world of John Irving, *no one* is ever truly safe, least of all abroad![52] The external world constantly threatens the individual, setting off learning processes dominated by sex and violence.[53] As a consequence, in Vienna, the Berry children become marooned in "a landscape of sad history, violent politics, and serious sexuality,"[54] a world of chaos from which none of them can hope to escape unscathed. It is not surprising therefore that Irving himself equated this period of the Berry children's childhood with "that sort of nightmare time you have to go through, where you meet the demons in the world and either come out on top or run away or deal with them however you can."[55] In the case of *The Hotel New Hampshire* the Berry children's place of "initiation," their maturing and formative experience, happens to be Vienna, in Irving's fiction a place of violence and degradation (265),[56] of "antilife" and "antilove."[57] Despite misgivings prior to their departure for Europe,[58] none of the Berry children could have foreseen though that Vienna, their home for the next seven years, would turn out to be the very location where "an Old World kind of decadence," found its perfect expression, and where, as Irving once put it himself, "... the great New World form, the great contemporary form of it" first manifested itself in "the willfulness of terrorism," in "the belief in an idea to the extent that human beings caught outside or on the other side of that idea are simply *expendable* ... [my emphasis]." The ultimate triumph of a system based on "*Schlagobers* and blood" therefore demonstrates that it is "fascistic in method but vaguely mystical in justification,"[59] in which someone like the younger Freud "survive[d], only ... to suffer the contemporary Nazi, ... the terrorist, as the contemporary fascist spirit, a kind of born-again Nazism ...."[60] However, despite their horrific experience in Vienna, most of the Berry children emerged from this "adventure" abroad, each in his or her own way, considerably strengthened to deal with the rigors of life facing them on their return to the US in the mid-1960s. In fact, they resurfaced, after a seven year stay in Vienna, the way the eldest daughter anticipated this encounter with Europe in 1957:

> I suddenly felt [says John, the narrator] we couldn't get to Vienna soon enough.... It suddenly occurred to me that Franny might have been thinking of Vienna in somewhat the same way: of *using* it – to make herself smarter and tougher and (somehow) grown-up *enough* for the world that neither of us understood (220).

Consequently, Vienna, in John Irving's novel *The Hotel New Hampshire*, turns out to be a motif in a contemporary *Bildungsroman*,[61] being the location where the protagonists' "initiation period" takes place: for after their return to New York in 1964, and as a result of their experience abroad, the Berry children – or at least three of them, Lilly, the novelist being the exception[62] – seem better prepared for the hostile US world of the mid-1960s, the third stage of the rites of passage formula.[63]

The second of the Berry girls, who stayed a dwarf, is a notable exception to this rule: for following the success of her bestseller *Trying to*

Grow (369-370) Lilly felt unable to write a novel aesthetically on a par with *The Great Gatsby* (1925) by her favorite author Scott Fitzgerald (1896-1940). As a result, she ultimately committed suicide by jumping from a window of her apartment in the Stanhope Hotel in Manhattan (425-426) with a verse from a *Heurigen* song on her lips, reminiscent of a similar song by the King of Mice,[64] and quite obviously a flashback to the Berrys' Vienna days:

> Verkauft's mei Gewand, I [f]ahr in Himmel.
> Sell my old clothes, I'm off to heaven (425).

Lilly's failure was the result of setting herself too high a standard as a writer: "Just not big enough," as she herself put it rather ambiguously in her suicide note (426). As it turned out, she was *the only one* of the surviving four Berry children, who still had a dream after returning from abroad, similar to Gatsby, at the end of Fitzgerald's novel – which Fehlgeburt, back in Vienna, had read to the youngsters over and over again – who still believed in an "orgiastic future," despite the fact that it receded year by year before him (256). Lilly was good at writing a "screenplay" for exacting revenge on Chipper Dove, the guy who had once raped her sister Franny a decade earlier, an "opera" "in the grand tradition of *Schlagobers* and blood" (422); however, she was dissatisfied with her second novel *Evening of the Mind*, which did not live up to her own high artistic expectations, and she altogether failed to come to terms with her third book *Everything After Childhood*. Consequently, it was literary quality – or the lack of it – that killed Lilly, as both Frank and John Berry later agreed: "it was the end of *The Great Gatsby*, ... which was *not* an ending in her grasp [my emphasis]" (422-423). For deep down she was more like her father, himself an inveterate dreamer,"[65] whom Lilly equated with Fitzgerald's hero: "'Father is a Gatsby, ... I know he is!,'" she at one point exclaimed, a sentiment echoed by Win Berry's admission, after his daughter's suicide: "'... Lilly just dreamed more than she should *do*. ... She *inherited* the damn dreams. ... From me'" (431).

Unlike the notorious Viennese street artist, the King of Birds – in the novel he is called King of Mice – who failed to "keep passing the open window," and – mindful of his own maxim: "Life is serious but art is fun" (205)[66] – committed suicide,[67] Frank, Franny and John Berry did *not* succumb to the pressures of modern life, each in their own way becoming successful agents, film stars,[68] and hotel owners.

As mentioned earlier, John Irving's novel *The Hotel New Hampshire* is a modern-type of fairy tale, "the only literary form that has ever satisfactorily tamed the horrible".[69] As pointed out by Bruno Bettelheim, the message that fairy tales usually get across to the child is "that a struggle against severe difficulties in life is unavoidable, is an intrinsic part of human existence . . . ,"[70] and many fairy tales therefore begin with the death of a mother or father.[71] "Contrary to what takes place in many modern children's stories," according to Bettelheim, "in fairy tales evil is as omnipresent as virtue."[72] As a consequence, and as explicitly carried out by John Irving in the middle section of *Hotel*,

> [o]nly by going out into the world can the fairy-tale hero (child) find himself there; and as he does, he will also find others with whom he will be able to live happily ever after; that is, without ever again having to experience separation anxiety. The fairy tale is future-oriented and guides the child . . . to relinquish his infantile dependency wishes and achieve a more satisfying independent existence.[73]

As Edward C. Reilly concluded in his study of those of the author's novels with a clearly detectable link to Austria: ". . . Irving's protagonists must learn from Vienna's violent history so that they will not be victimized by life's forces":[74]

> Despite the unhappy endings, doom, and sorrow, the Berrys discover what and how to make life meaningful. Each one has . . . a *bearish* tenacity to put meaning into life despite the various shapes of sorrow and doom that plague and haunt [them].[75]

Nottingham Trent University

Notes

1. New York: E. P. Dutton, 1981; all citations in this article refer to the reprint edition of 1982 (New York: Pocket Books).

2. In *The Hotel New Hampshire*, 205. According to Gabriel Miller (in: *John Irving* [New York: Frederick Ungar, 1982], 157), this is Irving's aesthetic credo, borrowed from Schiller's play *Wallensteins Lager* (1798); cf. also note 58.

3. New York: Random House, 1968, reprint New York: Pocket Books, 1979.

4. New York: E. P. Dutton, 1979, reprint New York: Pocket Book, 1979 (cf. Chapters 5 and 6: "In the City Where Marcus Aurelius Died" and "The Pension Grillparzer"); T. S. Garp's first short story was initially published in *Antaeus* (Winter 1976, 7-27), but as Irving himself commented in an "Afterword" (267) to a reprint version published in a collection of short stories entitled *Trying to Save Piggy Snead* (New York: Arcade Publishing, 1996, 233-265), most readers probably saw it first in *Garp*, "in its divided form." Another story of Irving's referring to Vienna: "Interior Space," first published in *Fiction* (6 [1980], 2, 26-58), was also reissued in *Trying to Save Piggy Snead* (173-216).

5. Vienna also is a secondary but important setting in *The Water-Method Man* (1972) and *The 158-Pound Marriage* (1974).

6. Miller, 133; cf. also Joseph Campbell, *The Hero with a Thousand Faces* (Princeton: Princeton University Press, ²1973; 1949), 30.

7. Miller, 193.

8. Ibid., 154.

9. Ibid.

10. Edward C. Reilly ("The *Anschluss* and the World According to Irving," in: *Research Studies* 51 [June 1983], 2, 107) mistakingly links postwar Austria to the effects of the Anschluß: "The effects of the *Anschluss* and its aftermath are evident everywhere in Vienna.... While also symbolizing Vienna's inner decay, the German [*sic*] radicals' extremist ideologies and actions are more representative of the effects of the *Anschluss* and World War II on modern Vienna."

11. Ibid., 178.

12. An interview with John Irving conducted by Gabriel Miller at Bread Loaf, Vermont, on August 17, 1981 (ibid., 175 ff.).

13. Ibid., 180-181.

14. Ibid., 194.

15. Ibid.

16. Ibid., 195.

17. Ibid., 193.

18. Carol C. Harter/James R. Thompson, *John Irving* (Boston: Twayne, 1986), 105.
19. Cf. e.g. James's novels *The Europeans* (1878 f.) and *The Portrait of a Lady* (1881).
20. Cf. Harter et al., 105.
21. Edward C. Reilly, *John Irving* (Columbia: University of South Carolina Press, 1991), 81.
22. Harter et al., 109.
23. Cf. Gabriel Miller's assessment of the middle section of *The Hotel New Hampshire* (*John Irving*, 129), based on Bruno Bettelheim's study *The Uses of Enchantment. The Meaning and Importance of Fairy Tales* (New York: Vintage, 1977; ¹1976); cf. also Edith Milton's review of *Hotel* in "Fables for our Times: Six Novels" (*The Yale Review* 71 [Winter 1982], 262), who claims that Irving's novel is the "antithesis of a fairy tale."
24. Mary Berry, the mother, and Egg, the youngest son, die in a plane crash on the way to Europe (230-231).
25. Cf. Harter et al., 4 and Reilly, 1-2.
26. Miller's assessment of Irving's picture of Vienna in *Hotel* as being "sketchy" is misleading (129).
27. According to James Atlas in a review of *Hotel* entitled "John Irving's World" (in: *The New York Times Book Review* [September 13, 1981], 40), "[t]he Vienna chapters evoke the city with impressive clarity."
28. Cf. E. Borsi/E.Godoli, *Wiener Bauten der Jahrhundertwende – Das alte Wien und seine Bauten. Die Architektur der Habsburgischen Metropole zwischen Historismus und Moderne* (Hamburg: Nikol Verlagsgesellschaft o.D.; ¹1985).
29. Benjamin DeMott, in a review of *The Hotel New Hampshire* entitled "Domesticated Madness" (in: *The Atlantic Monthly* 248 [October 1981], 104), argues that these symbols – the "sunshine" and "nightmare" side of Irving's novel – occur simultaneously, adding: "A fair question about this pairing is: What's it for? Does juxtaposing the quotidian and the melodramatic – the normative and the eccentric, the healthy and the sadistic – offer much besides shock value?" Howard Jacobson, in a recent report on Vienna entitled "The Sugar Club" (in *The Sunday Times*, [March 23, 1997], Section 6, 1), even more aptly equates these two symbols with "schmaltz and gloom."

30. The choice in *Hotel* of Vienna as a foreign city associated with terrorism is arbitrary and coincidental, and neither Irving nor the author of this article are suggesting that the Austrian capital was a center of violence in the late 1950s and early 1960s, although the location of a film like the "The Third Man" (1949), based on Graham Greene's novel, with Orson Welles in the lead role, did contribute to give postwar Vienna that particular *film noir* flavor, of a "frontier" town just behind the Iron Curtain, closely linked to espionage and counterespionage, as well as all kinds of communist and left-wing activities.

31. As the result of their experience, the Berry family asked for a particularly farcical opera to be played in their honor at the Vienna Opera House: "We didn't want to sit through any *Schlagobers* and blood. We'd already seen *that* opera. That was the opera that played in the Hotel New Hampshire for seven years" (360).

32. New York: Alfred Knopf 1980; cf. especially Chapter II: "The Ringstrasse, Its Critics, and the Birth of Urban Modernism" (24-115).

33. Boston/Toronto: Atlantic/Little Brown, 1979.

34. Cf. 193-232.

35. Cf. Morton, 227-235.

36. Ibid., 185-186.

37. Ibid., 97-98.

38. Ibid., 298-299.

39. Ibid., 140.

40. According to Edward C. Reilly ("The *Anschluss*," 100) terrorism is a phenomenon which links the Anschluss of Austria to the postmodern world: "For Irving, the *Anschluss* ... not only establishes the precedent for the brutal, chaotic fury of World War II, but also for the random, irrational violence which, in his literary vision, lurks threateningly in the post-modern world."

41. Cf. Gero von Wilpert, *Sachwörterbuch der Literatur* (Stuttgart: Kröner, [7]1989), 171-172; cf. also Karl Johann Müller, *Das Dekadenzproblem in der österreichischen Literatur um die Jahrhundertwende* (Stuttgart: Akademischer Verlag H.-D. Heinz, 1977) and R. Bauer et al., eds. *Fin de siècle. Zu Literatur und Kunst der Jahrhundertwende* (Frankfurt am Main: Vittorio Klostermann, 1977), esp. Chapter A, "Begriff und Intentionen," 3-39.

42. Cf. the chapter "'Eine Schale Gold.' Die Wiener Kaffeehaustradition," in: Klaus Thiele-Dohrmann's study: *Europäische Kaffee-*

hauskultur (Düsseldorf/Zürich: Artemis & Winkler, 1997), 107; cf. also Gustav Gugitz, *Das Wiener Kaffeehaus. Ein Stück Kultur- und Lokalgeschichte* (Wien: Deutscher Verlag für Jugend und Volk, 1940), especially Chapter VII, 182-211; Ulla Heise, *Kaffee und Kaffeehaus. Eine Bohne macht Kulturgeschichte* (Leipzig: Gustav Kiepenheuer, 1996); Holger Hasenkamp/Katerina Vastella, eds. *Das Wiener Café* (Zürich: Jacobs Suchard Museum, 1989).

43. Cf. Thiele-Dohrmann, 113.
44. Cf. e.g. Chapter 10 (322).
45. Cf. Franz Hubmann, ed. *Café Hawelka. Ein Wiener Mythos* (Wien: Brandstätter, 1982).
46. Cf. Thiele-Dohrmann, 114-115.
47. Cf. a similar theme developed by Josef Haslinger in his novel *Opernball* (Frankfurt am Main: S. Fischer, 1995).
48. Cf. Gene Lyons, in a generally negative review of *Hotel* ("Something New in Theme Parks," in: *The Nation* [September 26, 1981], 277-280), states: "one quality I like in Irving is his ability to create children who act like children" (277).
49. Cf. Harter et al., 109.
50. Cf. Reilly, 93.
51. Ibid., 92.
52. Miller, 146.
53. Ibid., 147.
54. Ibid., 165.
55. Ibid., 195.
56. According to a character in the novel called Susie the Bear.
57. Miller, 160.
58. Franny, the eldest daughter, keeps maintaining: "'Don't you see? Vienna isn't *like* that anymore'" (205).
59. Miller, 184.
60. Ibid, 198.
61. Reilly, 97.
62. Cf. Eric Korn, "Trying to Grow the Freudian Way," in: *The Times Literary Supplement* (November 6, 1981), 1302.
63. Miller, 133.
64. Cf. Morton, 298-299; Johann Pfeiffer, the historical "King of the Birds," "reminded the Viennese of one of his specialities: the art of making life unserious" (299).

65. This theme was also developed in Steven Millhauser's recent Pulitzer-Prize-Winner novel *Martin Dressler. The Tale of an American Dreamer* (New York: Vintage Books, 1996).

66. According to James Wolcott in a review of *Hotel* entitled "House of Mirrors" (in: *Esquire* 96 [September 1981], 21), this "isn't a joshing sentiment – *The Hotel New Hampshire* really does try to turn life's sorrows and miseries into pink wisps of cotton candy...."

67. Cf. endnote 2.

68. In a final reminder of the Berrys' Vienna years, Franny's association with Junior Jones, her erstwhile rescuer, is being likened to the fact that "[t]he Black Arm of the Law and Hollywood had, at least, *Schlagobers* and blood in common" (433).

69. DeMott, 104; according to James Atlas, 1: "Irving reminds us with tireless zeal that his novel *is* a fairy tale – 'The Hotel New Hampshire' is both fanciful and cruel."

70. Ibid., 8.

71. Cf. endnote 23.

72. Bettelheim, 8.

73. Ibid., 11.

74. Reilly, "The *Anschluss*," 100.

75. Edward C. Reilly, "John Irving's *The Hotel New Hampshire* and the Allegory of Sorrow," in: *Publications of the Arkansas Philosophical Association* 9 (Spring 1983), 82.

"I wept while I was dreaming"
How to Survive the Holocaust after the Holocaust
in Jon Marans' Play *Old Wicked Songs*

Gerd K. Schneider

In his play *Old Wicked Songs* Jan Marens treats the question of how one can live in Vienna after having experienced the Holocaust. He presents this theme by masterfully integrating Schumann's song-cycle *Dichterliebe* (A Poet's Love) into his text, thereby achieving an effect which Nietzsche called dramatic music. In the process, Marans shows some of the cultural differences between Austria and the United States and criticizes 1986 Austrian politics.

The Sunday edition of the *New York Times* on 23 February 1997 carried in its Off Broadway section of the *Arts and Leisure Guide* the following brief commentary about *Old Wicked Songs*:

> A drama by Jon Marans about a young American piano virtuoso who reluctantly agrees to study with a Viennese music professor. Directed by Seth Barrish. "Deeply satisfying, remarkably assured." With its deft, intelligent use of a Schumann song cycle, the production "never cheats on the rules of the neatly tailored, mainstream play," but it also incorporates "a greater spirit of ambiguity." Justin Kirk and Hal Robinson are excellent. (H 42)

Old Wicked Songs,[1] a two-character drama by Jon Marans, premiered at the Walnut Street Theater in Philadelphia in 1995 and in New York at Playhouse 91 in 1996. Subsequently it was performed at the New York Jewish Repertory Theater in November 1996, and then moved to the Promenade Theatre in New York, where it ran before sold-out houses until March 1997. The majority of the reviews were very favorable, including the one in London's Gielgud Theatre in November 1996.[2] It does not surprise, then, that *Old Wicked Songs* was nominated for Best Play by the Drama League and the covetous 1996 Pulitzer-Award in the category *Drama* for a distinguished play by an American author dealing with American Life. This prize, however, was awarded to *Rent* by the late Jonathan Larson, which had not only received more publicity, but also deals to a greater extent with American life than *Old Wicked Songs*.

The title of Marans' play derives from Heinrich Heine's "Lyrisches Intermezzo" in his *Buch der Lieder (Book of Songs)*. In this work Heine describes the imperfections and disappointments of life, mixing joy, pain, nostalgia, and melancholy, often in the form of self-preserving irony. Robert Schumann found in Heine's poems a vehicle to express his own feelings. In 1835 the twenty-five-year-old composer fell in love with the beautiful and brilliant pianist Clara Wieck. Her father opposed a marriage at first and Clara subsequently became estranged from Schumann, which made him desperate. The two reconciled, however, and in 1840 they married. In that year Schumann wrote 140 songs, among them the sixteen tone-poems of *Dichterliebe*, in which he tells the story of his love for Clara in the past, with all its agonizing pain and suffering. This combination of sadness and joy which characterizes Heine's cycle and Schumann's musical rendering is also the basis of Marans' creation.

Old Wicked Songs is a two-act drama, not a musical, although almost one third of the play contains music. The play takes place in Vienna in the spring of 1986, the year Kurt Waldheim was running for president of the Austrian Republic despite his Nazi past. Stephen Hoffmann, a burned-out piano prodigy, is sent to Vienna by his family in order to take classes from the renowned music professor Schiller so that he can accompany singers. It is not Schiller, however, whom he meets in the studio, but Josef Mashkan, a voice coach, who instructs him in the art of singing, so that he can learn how a singer feels. Both protagonists have little in common at first. Stephen is an arrogant twenty-five-year-old Californian whose philosophy of life is based on either-or decisions, while Mashkan is given to the as-well-as approach to life. In the course of the play these two different personalities with different backgrounds approach and get to know each other as human beings. We find out that Mashkan is Jewish, that he was born in Vienna, and that he was transported to Dachau in 1943. He survived and is now struggling through his second survival: how to keep on living after the concentration camp. Stephen's initial arrogance and self-righteousness give way to tenderness and compassion toward his wise teacher; he reveals to Mashkan that he is also Jewish and that he had to promise his parents to visit Dachau in exchange for their paying his expenses in the Old World.

The answers to the many problems raised are not one-sided, but they are steeped in ambiguity and force the viewers to reflect upon them and provide their own answers. This technique is typically Brechtian, and it does not surprise that a quotation by Brecht appears as a motto to this didactic play: "A man's stature is shown by what he mourns and in what way [sic][3] he mourns it."

While the central problem of the play is the survival of the Holocaust after the Holocaust, the American theater public is informed about the differences between the American and Austrian mentality, Austrian architecture, Austrian politics, and Austrian culture with a small c. A substantial part of the dialogue is rendered in Austrian-flavored German, since the setting of this play is Vienna, or actually two Viennas: one around 1900 and the other of 1986. The Vienna of 1900 is shown in the stage set of Mashkan's habitat, decorated with paintings of Klimt, Kokoschka, Makart, and Hampel; "the paintings," so the stage directions read, "reflect the glitter of early twentieth-century Vienna, rather than its darker side" (9), a euphemistic phase meaning the political skeletons nobody talks about publicly.

This ambiguity is also carried into the customs of the Viennese and the Americans who, according to Mashkans' perspective, are quite different. One of the small differences is the way in which food, especially pastry, is offered and appreciated in Austria. Mashkan explains this custom to his American visitor who is not acquainted with this convention:

> In Vienna, if you offer something just once, the other person is supposed to say 'no'! Only if the giver persists two more times do you really know he wants you to have it! If I could, I would rip that pastry from you[,] but you've already stuffed half of it down your throat! All Americans devour food! You take no time to appreciate anything! (28)

Taking no time for appreciation also characterizes Stephen's attitude toward music. Feeling unobserved by Mashkan, he kicks the piano and plays the first song of *Dichterliebe* in a technically perfect manner but lacking any emotion. To Mashkan this is just like rape, because for him "there is a direct correlation between making love to a woman and making love to a piano" (14). The condition for a successful union, be it with a woman or with the piano, is tenderness, trust, and the ability to wait for this courtship to blossom. A piano, according to him,

> must be flirted with, not pounced on. Let her know that she is safe in your arms. Once that is established, *then* you can be wild and passionate. Come. Stand here. Let me show you how a seduction is done. First admire her smooth, shiny skin. See her warm, bright smile.... Flirt with her. Run your hand through her strings.... Slower. (14-15)

In addition to patience and empathy which Stephen lacks and Mashkan has in abundance, there are other behavioral patterns which may be termed typically Viennese or Austrian. Typically Viennese, for instance, is the *Grüss Gott* with which Mashkan greets his new student; Mashkan's addiction to coffee which he consumes constantly; the craving for the previously mentioned Viennese pastry which Mashkan offers on various occasions to Stephen and for which he demands payment afterward: "Have a pastry. On me. Only eighteen schillings" (41). Later on he offers the pastry-on-him for twenty schillings, a price which Stephen finds exhorbitant because he gets his pastry for sixteen schillings from Tabir's pastry shop (33).

Even architecture offers a clue to the differences between the American and Austrian mentality. Americans love clear-cut lines, without ambiguities. Stephen exemplifies these traits; he is very pragmatic and not given to sentimental attitudes: "I guess I've been spoiled by modern architecture," he tells Mashkan, "you know, simple beauty. Clean lines. Nothing gaudy. I grew up in California" (11-12). What he lacks is the wisdom which comes from the experience that life does not always proceed along straight lines. Life is not that simple. Austrian architecture, especially buildings in Vienna, reflect this insight, as Mashkan explains to his student:

> Look at our city when you stroll about. See the firm old buildings, the thick solid walls. But notice the flourishes

– the statues, the arches, the molding, the cornices, the façades, each different from the next. Each building eventually rising to a peak, but so many choices for the eye to find its way to the top. Not like your modern American box buildings which lead the eye straight up. (23)

When Stephen replies that "modern architecture is just a streamlining of your buildings" (23), Mashkan replies:

Ah, streamlining. A very evocative sounding word, but what does it mean? Stripping art of all its beauty until it is reduced to science. Just as modern composers streamline music, remove the emotion, reduce music to mathematical theory. Give me too much passion to none at all!!... Stefan, stop thinking like your simplistic modern American music and architecture. Life is not always so clear-cut. (23)

Later Mashkan comes back to this contradiction, but this time in a political framework. Prior to the election Stephen had asked Mashkan if he believed that Waldheim was a Nazi and received the following reply: "Well, *ja*, we are the ones electing him president . . . It's 1986. Who cares?" (12). A little later he quips: "I am sure Waldheim will win. And when he does, the Viennese can make bets on which countries will refuse to greet him" (49-51). After Waldheim's election his sarcastic reaction is: "That doesn't mean I believed it!... Even Waldheim's opponents didn't bring up his past. They thought it might lose him votes. And I thought life was so complicated. It is very clear-cut" (60).

Present attitudes are rooted in the past, and those "firm old buildings, the thick solid walls" (23) in Vienna are also a metaphor for the conservative attitudes of the Viennese. For example, one of the old buildings is the *Staatsoper* which was destroyed during the war but later on rebuilt exactly as it was. To the pragmatic American Stephen, this is incomprehensible: "All that effort – why didn't they just put up a new one?" Mashkan responds: "Ah yes, that was foolish of them. But I suppose some people prefer to live in the past.... Or maybe, perhaps, the original represented the heart of Vienna – and we needed to get it back" (35). This statement, "and we needed to get it back," in this specific context refers to the realm of architecture. It is part of Marans' technique, however, to lift ideas out of the original context and put them into another one where they acquire a totally different meaning. In the above case, the message turns political. Just as the *Staatsoper* was rebuilt exactly like the original building, so the Austrians tended to elect someone with a past history. While the preservation of the blueprint was good for the rebuilding of the *Staatsoper*, it was embarrassing when applied to the election of the *Staatsoberhaupt*, or Head of State.

Mashkan refers to the past activities of the president when he asks Stephen if he knew the latest joke going around in Vienna. When Stephen says no, Mashkan tells him:

> You know of Alzheimer's disease, *ja*?
> Stephen: *Ja.*
> Mashkan: Apparently, there is a new disease called Waldheimer's. You get old – and forget you were a Nazi! (65)

Mashkan informs him that the election of Waldheim was not an isolated case in Austria because other known Nazis also held influential positions:

> Mashkan (*Speaking very casually, half-amused.*) I do not know what all the fuss is over Waldheim. When the government was run by Kreisky – who wouldn't even admit he was a Jew – he recruited politicians with as much of a past as Waldheim. At least four ex-Nazis and one S.S. Officer. You can't run a country so heavily Nazi without hiring a few. So what's the fuss with Waldheim?! (49)

The mentioning of Austria being "so heavily Nazi" brings up the suffering of the Jewish population, which, paradoxically, is rejected by Mashkan. When Stephen remarks: "The Jews have certainly suffered," Mashkan says laconically: "I don't think so" (27). When Stephen points out that the Jewish population in Vienna decreased from 300,000 before the Anschluss to a mere 10,000 today, Mashkan retorts: "Why does everyone harp on the Jews?! They are not the only ones who suffered" (36). When Stephen sets out on a trip to Dachau, Mashkan informs him that it will be a sad experience for him. He appears to be highly prejudiced when he adds: "Besides, Dachau is just a bunch of dead Jews"(41), a statement which, according to Stephen, could get him fired as a teacher. Later Mashkan explains why he made the nonchalant statement about the Jews: "And do you know," Mashkan informs Stephen, "how many times I have heard it said by intelligent Viennese men and women? ... this is why I say anti-Jewish comments first – before anyone else has the chance. My words sting, but not quite as sharply as theirs ..." (50). Maybe some of Mr. Marans' personal experiences in Vienna are incorporated here. The critic Tommasini suggests this when he writes in his review: "And Mr. Marans, who is Jewish, experienced anti-Semitism first-hand in Vienna. 'It's so blatant you can't believe what you are hearing,' he said" (5).[4]

What Stephen sees in Dachau, however, is not a bunch of dead Jews, but a bunch of forgotten Jews. When he left for Dachau, he had anticipated seeing

> the *Arbeit macht frei*[5] sign, the barbed wire fences, the guard posts. I wasn't prepared for how beautifully Dachau had been fixed up. No, covered over. Most of the buildings – gone. Those that were left – whitewashed. The grass – so green. A stream near the side of the camp had a quaint little bridge. If I hadn't known better, I'd never suspect these few acres of land had been crowned with thousands of emaciated, tortured bodies. (47-48)

Leaving this site, he does not "stroll through the lovely town of Dachau" (48), as the brochure recommends. The 'hidden' side of Dachau is for Stephen just an attempt of the former perpetrators to forget this period in their own personal and their country's past. He now sees this same cover-up in Vienna, where everything is different from the way it appears, as he points out:

> I walked around Vienna these last two weeks. It's all a lie. The Blue Danube isn't blue, it's brown! And it doesn't even run through the city. The Wien river does. The *Ringstraße* running around the center of Vienna isn't a ring, but three quarters of a circle at most. St. Mary's on the Banks doesn't even lie on a bank! Your history

books say you were forcibly invaded by the Germans, but in 1938 there were about half a million Austrian Nazis – proportionally more Nazis than in Germany. (*Music continues.*) And only a few months ago Kurt Waldheim's campaign slogan was "A man whom the world trusts!" (44)

Stephen's experiences in Dachau have taught him to look through the Viennese veneer and discern now the unspeakable behind the beautiful surface or, in Nietzschean terms, the terrifying Dionysian behind the beautiful Apollinian. He sees his surroundings with other eyes, piercing through the external to get a glimpse of the covered-up material. The following quote shows how Marans takes the well-known command "end of the line," which was the signal for the Jews to get off the train, out of the Holocaust-context and inserts it into the Apollonian description of beautiful Vienna: "And every time I turned and saw a beautiful bridge or a quaint babbling brook, I broke into a sweat. And every time I got off the U-Bahn and heard that recorded message 'End of the line, everybody off', I felt sick to my stomach. And thought of a man I had once respected. Once" (49).

This respected man is Mashkan who has now also become as suspect to Stephen as everything else. Mashkan does not like this overgeneralization which condemns everything and everyone, and he replies curtly: "I listened to your story! Please, do not turn this into some kind of overly tragic Viennese melodrama" (49).

It has been observed by many critics that the Schumann song cycle threads itself almost seamlessly into the dramatic plot. These songs provide a commentary, just like the Greek chorus. These songs are, as David Spencer pointed out in his review of the Promenade-Theater-production, *source music*, "that is, music that is acknowledged as such on the stage, as opposed to underscoring. It comments on the action in a way that manages to be obvious while avoiding heavy-handedness – an amazing balancing act."[6] This technique brings together the past and the present, as Hal Drucker comments in *New York Now*: "It seems that with this play ... classical music is weaving its way into the fiber of current theater pieces, like a Bach counterpoint,"[7] and Anthony Tommasini from the *New York Times* considers the interweaving technique an excellent "example of how music can be tellingly incorporated into drama" (5). And this is exactly the intention of the author who remarked in the Author's Note:

> At the end of the Scene 1, and at the end of every scene throughout the play, different songs from the *Dichterliebe* are heard. These very specific songs choices serve two vital purposes. They are integral to the drama of the play, heightening the lead-out of scenes and emotionally aiding the lead-ins to the next scene. Also, they allow the audience the chance to hear these songs in order, thus helping them more deeply absorb the emotional impact of Schumann's song cycle. Therefore, the songs listed should not be altered. Consider them as much a part of the text as the dialogue. (17)

This total integration of music and poetry is reminiscent of Nietzsche's concept of 'dramatic music': "Dramatic music becomes possible only when the tonal art has conquered an enormous domain of symbolic means, through song, opera and a hundred experiments in tone-painting."[8]

It is, however, not only Schumann, whose music weaves itself into the text, but also the reference to *Bajazzo*. Mashkan had recommended that Stephen go to the Staatsoper and hear *Cavalleria Rusticana* and *Der Bajazzo*, because listening to opera is vital for someone who wants to be trained as a singer, and going for the first time "to the *Staatsoper*, seeing that hall, hearing that music, it is always a thrill!" (28). Stephen agrees reluctantly but returns overwhelmed by this experience: "I've never been a great fan of opera – since there aren't many piano solos, but tonight, hearing *Pagliacci* . . . for me the best part of the evening was at the end. The clown, his life in shambles, cries *La comedia est finita!*" (32-33). This short reference to *Bajazzo* underscores again the play's main idea, which Mashkan summarizes as: "Sadness and comedy all in one moment" (33).

This *leitmotiv* of sadness and joy runs through the entire play, either explicitly or by way of word association. While playing and singing the first song in the cycle, "Im wunderschönen Monat Mai," Mashkan explains:

> This combination of joy and sadness – this is the core of truly beautiful music. Just as it it is the core of drama. Of life. . . . Sadness and joy. When a composer finds both, the result is Mozart. Beethoven. And how do you

> acquire this perfect combination? Why do some countries give us great composers, while others [do] not? Take England. Good composers, like Benjamin Britten, but no musical geniuses. And few great singers. Why? Because England has no prolonged national suffering. Since the days of the Romans they have not been invaded. And having never lived through great sadness, they have little comprehension of great joy. However, here in Austria and in Germany, our soil has been ravaged by two world wars. Before that, invaded many times. And we have Schubert, Brahms, Schumann. And great singers like Leonie Rysaneck....(26)

The notion that sadness and joy are conditions for greatness is not new. It reminds one of Nietzsche, who stated this idea numerous times, as for instance in his *Genealogy of Morals*: "Whoever has at some time built a 'new heaven' has found the power to do so in his *own hell*."[9] A more popularized version of the same idea we find in Carol Reed's film *The Third Man*, the suspense-mystery-drama, set in 1949 postwar Vienna. Here we have Orson Welles's famous speech at the Great Wheel, a speech Wells added to Graham Greene's script: "In Italy for thirty years under the Borgias they had warfare, terror, murder, bloodshed – they produced Michelangelo, Leonardo da Vinci and the Renaissance. In Switzerland they had brotherly love, five hundred years of democracy and peace, and what did they produce ... ? The cuckoo clock."[10]

The dramatic high point of Marans' play comes when Mashkan feels psychologically ready to tell Stephen about his Viennese experience in 1940 and subsequently about his life in Dachau. The precipitating cause for this release is the song "Ich hab' im Traum geweinet" ("I wept while I was dreaming") which, according to Mashkan, is the most difficult song in the cycle. While Stephen sings every line of this song, Mashkan stops playing the piano and speaks instead so that his words are just like a running commentary to the Heine-Schumann creations. The words all of a sudden become translucent and call back experiences which Mashkan had repressed for a long time. When Stephen sings the first line of second stanza: "I wept while I was dreaming," Mashkan tells his story: "You asked me why I was muttering 43, 44, and 45? Those are the years I remember almost nothing" (62). While Stephen continues singing "I dreamed you were leaving me," Mashkan goes on: "Who wants to remember a starving bunkmate pleading for bread? I turn away. He must not have a face. I do not want a friend. If he dies – I must face the loss, not him. (*Lightly*) Who needs more depression? I am already in a concentration camp" (62). To Stephen's line "When I awoke," we hear Mashkan's commentary: "And so I survive. Not because of my courage or compassion, but because I think only of myself" (63).

With Stephen intonating "I was crying" in the background, Mashkan then tells him about his apparent immortality: "Perhaps I will never die. For after each attempted suicide, I become more like that boiling coffee on the stove – growing stronger and stronger – and more and more bitter" (63). His bitterness started in 1940, the year when "we were told to pack whatever we could fit into a suitcase . . . It was spring – in the loveliest of months – May. (*Sarcastic.*) 'Im wunderschönen Monat Mai' – (*Recorded music of 'Im wunderschönen Monat Mai' is softly heard.*)" (63). The stage directions of this scene then read:

> "*As Mashkan leans into Stephen, the lights dim. Mashkan speaks, but no words are heard coming from his mouth. Instead we only hear the music of the* Dichterliebe *growing in volume. Stephen nods, listening carefully to what Mashkan says. As the lights continue to dim, a single beam of light – just like the one described in the Israeli Memorial at Dachau – a single beam of light surrounded by darkness – shines on Stephen. Stephen stands – nodding and listening. Stephen starts to tear up. He tries not to cry. But does. Then sobs.*" (64)

While the song "Im wunderschönen Monat Mai" opens the cycle, "Die alten bösen Lieder," or "The Bad Old Songs," conclude it in Schumann's rendering and also in Marans' play. In the final short segment of this play, called *Coda*, Mashkan plays this song while Stephen sings the last two stanzas:

> Die sollen den Sarg fortragen
> Und senken ins Meer hinab!
> Denn solchem großem Sarge
> Gebührt ein großes Grab!

> Wisst ihr, warum der Sarg wohl
> So gross und schwer mag sein?
> Ich senkt' auch meine Liebe
> Und meinen Schmerz hinein. (64-65)

The significance of this song is emphasized by also singing it in English, the first stanza by Mashkan, and the second stanza by Stephen:

> Mashkan:
> They are to bear the coffin away
> and sink it into the deep sea!
> Such a large coffin
> needs a large grave.
> Stephen:
> Do you know why this coffin
> should be so huge, so heavy?
> I am burying in it all my love . . .
> (*Stephen truly sees Mashkan*)
> and all my pain. (66-67)

The importance of this song was recognized by Tommasini, when he remarks that "[t]eaching Stephen these songs becomes the means through which Mashkan breaks down the pianist's rigidity while encouraging him to accept the imperfections of life, its constant mix of 'joy and sadness'" (5). Equally important, however, is that Mashkan also is characterized by rigidity, not stemming from intellectual insight but from emotional linkage to the past. It is at this point that he breaks down and relates his experiences which have been haunting him.

The solution for Mashkan is to try accepting the past with all its suffering and pain and considering it as a necessary element not only in experiencing joy, but also in the creative process, similar to Nietzsche's conviction that all great culture is born out of conflict. Stephen also finds a way to overcome his hatred. After Dachau he hates the Germans and the Austrians so much that he vows not to speak German any more. Singing "Ich grolle nicht," his translation is: "I hate – you not" (45). When Mashkan points out "The translation is *I bear no grudge*. These are the words" Stephen replies: "But not the feelings" (45). At the end, Stephen has learned how to overcome his hatred; he speaks German again, and he realizes that life is not always so clearcut and simplistic as he imagined it. Transcending the personal level, this play seems to say that the experiences of the past should be buried, just like the coffin in the final song, so that a new beginning can be made. "It is your responsibility during this solo," Mashkan instructs Stephen at the end, "to release us from the sadness we have heard – make us remember the Poet's suffering, but give us a glimmer of hope that this experience will not completely destroy his life. Who knows, perhaps he will learn from it and move to a higher plane. *Verstehst du, Stefan?* Understand?" (67).

Learning from the past and moving to a higher plane also extends to Austria and the Viennese. The symbol for this spiritual re-birth is the rococo-clock, the biggest piece of furniture in Mashkan's room next to the piano. The clock has no functional value; it does not show the correct time of day since it has stopped at 5:35. As a *Dingsymbol*, however, it serves its purpose well. To Stephen it means loss of strength, or as he says to Mashkan: "It looks like both hands have drooped just about as low as possible, without the energy or strength of character to pull themselves back up" (44), to which he then adds: "You might say it represents Vienna. Trapped in a moment of time. But is it right before sunrise or the last gasp before sunset?" (44). This is a rhetorical question which is reminiscent of the German word *Dämmerung*, indicating either dusk or dawn. The author does not provide an answer; in a typically Brechtian mode, the audience is encouraged to draw its own conclusion. One interpretation suggested by the play is that only a person who has endured great suffering can also experience great joy and that the union of suffering and joy is the indispensable condition for creating great art.

Syracuse University

Notes

1. Jon Marans, *Old Wicked Songs*, (New York, New York: Dramatist's Play Service, Inc.: 1990, 1996). All quotations referring to this play are taken from this edition and cited in the text by page number. The first public printing appeared under the title *Old Wicked Songs* (Garden City, N.Y.: Fireside Theatre, 1996).

2. For reviews of the performance at the Jewish Repertory Theater see Lawrence van Gelder, "A Piano Student, His Teacher, Passion, Loss and the Holocaust," *New York Times*, 11 November 1995, Sec. A, 19; Clive Barnes, "Writer, Actors give Perfect Pitch to Songs," *New York Post*, 14 November 1995, 40; Amy Reiter, "Old Wicked Songs," *Backstage*, 17 November 1995, 19. For reviews of the production at the Promenade Theater see Anthony Tommasini, "When the Music Plays a Starring Role," *New York Times*, 1 September 1996, Sec. H, 5; Donald Lyons, "Theater: Rescuing Tennessee," *Wall Street Journal*, 6 September 1996, Sec. A, 12; Ben Brantley, "Clashes, Lies and Always, Always Music," *New York Times*, 6 September 1996, Sec. C, 1, 21; Howard Kissel, "Pianist's Dilemma a Grand Tale," *Daily News*, 17 November 1966, 45; Ed Siegel, "On NY Stage, Moral Questions Take Dramatic Shape;" *Boston Globe*, 6 October 1996, Sec. N, 2. For the performance at the Gielgud Theatre in London see Michael Billington, "It's Schumann on the Line," *Guardian*, 19 November 1996, Sec. A, 9.

3. A more accurate translation is: "A man's stature is shown by what he mourns and by the way he mourns it."

4. Anthony Tommasini, "When the Music Plays a Starring Role," *New York Times*, 1 September 1996, Sec. H, 5.

5. Literal translation: Work liberates. Slogan at the entrance gate of German concentration camps.

6. David Spencer,"Old Wicked Songs," *Aisle Say New York*, http://www. escape.com/~theanet/Old-Wicked.html

7. Hal Drucker, "Old Wicked Songs," http://www.nynow.com/cgi-bin/nynow .theater_page/old_wicked_songs.html

8. Friedrich Nietzsche, Human – *All Too Human. A Book for Free Spirits*. Translated by R. J. Hollingdale. Introduction by Richard Schacht (Cambridge: Cambridge University Press, 1996), Paragraph 215, 99.

9. Friedrich Nietzsche, *On the Genealogy of Morals and Ecce Homo*. Translated by Walter Kaufmann and R. J. Hollingdale. Section "What is the Meaning of Ascetic Ideals?", Paragraph 10 (New York: Vintage Books, 1969), 115.

10. Andrew Sinclair, ed. *The Third Man*. A Film by Graham Greene and Carol Reed (New York: Simon and Schuster, 1968; Modern Film Scripts), 114.

The Image of Austria in Literary Readings from American Textbooks

Susan C. Anderson

The works of well-known Austrian literary figures, such as Hugo von Hofmannsthal, Arthur Schnitzler, Ingeborg Bachmann, and Peter Handke, are almost always included in courses for majors and graduate students in American departments of German. Yet institutional constraints often hinder departments from offering full-fledged courses on Austrian culture and society. Austrian texts are usually represented as examples of "German" literary culture. At the lower level, however, most textbooks incorporate excerpts of Austrian literature into their reading selections. Indeed, the vast majority of students exposed to Austrian literature are those fulfilling a foreign-language requirement by completing one to three years of German language courses. Such students comprise the broadest American readership for Austrian writing. What exactly are they learning?

In order to formulate a suitable response to that question, I have investigated literary passages in leading American textbooks of German to ascertain how they represent Austria.[1] My focus has been on textbooks intended for use in the second and third years of language study, that is, when the students have achieved at least an intermediate level of reading proficiency. An investigation of the texts themselves, almost all of which were written in the twentieth century, reveals the literary images of Austria offered to the language students.[2] An analysis of the pre- and post-reading exercises and activities shows how they contribute to the textual imagery. I have also considered the information provided about the writers as well as the chapters containing the readings. On the basis of that material this essay demonstrates how textbooks use Austrian literature to transmit certain ideas about "German" culture. Such "guided" readings may be the only exposure students ever have to Austrian literature. Thus the Austria they read about plays a prominent role in their intellectual encounter with Austrian culture.

I have confined my study to twelve second and third-year textbooks, books which are prominent in the market for intermediate German-language instruction and which include texts dealing with Austria. Two of the second-year textbooks, *Spiralen* (Spirals) and *Wendepunkt* (Turning Point), contain little material on Austria, yet each has a reproduction of a Hundertwasser painting on the cover.[3] That in itself indicates the manner in which most textbooks present Austria, that is, as a minor province of the Federal Republic of Germany.

In a special issue on Austria in the journal *Unterrichtspraxis: Teaching German*, the Austrian literary scholar Klaus Zeyringer pleads for a more differentiated approach to the teaching of Austrian literature by contextualizing it within the Austrian cultural sphere and history. His critique concentrates on the international field of "Deutsch als Fremdsprache" (German as a Foreign Language). In his studies of anthologies of German literature, Zeyringer has discovered books with such titles as *Deutschland erzählt: Von Rilke bis Handke* (Germany Narrates: From Rilke to Handke) and noticed that in such anthologies Austria and Switzerland have been absorbed into the concept of "West-German Literature."[4] In addition, while the latest young German writers are swiftly accepted into the contemporary canon, newer Austrian talents, including such names as Joseph Haslinger, Marie Thérèse Kerschbaumer, Anna Mitgutsch, and Werner Kofler, go unmentioned. Such neglect follows a long tradition in the German press. Hugo von Hofmannsthal, Peter Handke, Ingeborg Bachmann, Thomas Bernhard, and Ernst Jandl have crossed over into the German canon, but their works are presented as no different from German texts. Zeyringer asserts, "To put it bluntly, the discipline of German in Germany pays hardly any attention to the Austrian context."[5] He insists on a reevaluation of the treatment of Austrian literature, so that readers can approach it in its cultural, historical, and political difference. In his view, this means not just writing the Austrian myth but analyzing it instead.

Zeyringer addresses general difficulties with the cultural Germanization of Austria. His findings also find resonance in the American textbook industry, which likewise tends to present all German-speaking cultures from a Federal Republican perspective. There are differences, however, which will become apparent in this analysis.

Before delving into the stories, it is important to know how they have been packaged, that is, into which chapter they have been embedded and with which materials they have been combined. The mixture of visual and written texts is also significant. The Austrian stories and poems in the second-year textbooks that I have surveyed are contained within chapters dealing with such general topics as "einander kennenlernen" (getting to know one another), "Freizeit" (free time), "unheimliche Begegnungen" (uncanny encounters), or "lustiges Leben" (funny life).

For instance, Aurelia Bundschuh's story "Das Alibi," which depicts a man seeking the help of a lonely woman in a park to support his contention that he did not murder his former girlfriend, is part of the chapter "Unheimliche Begegnungen" in *Palette* (1995).[6] The pre- and post-reading activities all focus on different aspects of the text, asking students, for instance, to speculate about the man's and woman's motivations, or whether the man really could be a murderer. They are even encouraged to enact a meeting between the couple after the man has confessed to murder. Aside from Bundschuh being identified as an Austrian, there is nothing about the text or exercises dealing specifically with Austria.

There is, however, a scenic photograph embedded within that part of the chapter. It depicts a group of people hiking on a mountain with the explanation: "Germans traditionally have a close relationship to nature."[7] The chapter focuses on unexpected meetings that turn into romance, and the vocabulary and grammar exercises reiterate that theme. The accompanying photo of Germans hiking in the mountains represents a rather uncanny encounter of Austrian text with German subtext. The contrast of a story about a mysterious, potentially dangerous man attracting a lonely woman in an Austrian park with a picture of a group of Germans smilingly ascending a mountain is striking. The narrative problematizes the fear of being alone by representing partnership as threatening. The woman prefers a future of shared walks in the park with the stranger to her previous solo perambulations. But at what cost does she enter into the new relationship? The photo, whether appended inadvertently or not, adds a twist to that question with its view of happy wanderers exploring a mountain together. Unlike the misguided Austrian woman, the Germans have found camaraderie in the great outdoors, enjoying the company of others, yet maintaining their self-determination. They are together because of common interest, the picture suggests, rather than fear of loneliness. Thus the German way, which intrudes into Bundschuh's romantic tale, appears more fulfilling.

Another chapter in the same textbook revolves around Elfriede

Jelinek's "Aufforderung zur Unfreundlichkeit" (Invitation for Unfriendliness), a warning against stereotypical gender roles. The chapter effectively integrates the themes into a larger German context by inserting brief excerpts from the magazine *Stern* on bodybuilding and notions of beauty. For instance, one woman asserts, "I like my hair, my skin, and my hard muscles. That's why I work out every day for half an hour. I find myself really beautiful."[8] Jelinek's story criticizes just such sentiments. Yet, aside from mentioning the fact that the author is Austrian, the textbook does not connect the narrative to an Austrian context. In a similar move to annex culturally Austrian intellectuals, the third-year textbook *Stimmen eines Jahrhunderts* (Voices of a Century) contains a chapter on Gustav Mahler's "Briefe aus Leipzig" (Letters from Leipzig).[9] They reveal his renown within the greater Germanic world, thereby lending his significance more "legitimacy." The same book presents a brief autobiographical excerpt by Elias Canetti, with no explanation as to who he was or where he grew up. Yet it tries to make amends for such omissions with a section on Christiane von Hofmannsthal's diary, "Wiener Tagebuch" (Viennese Diary). Those excerpts from the period after 1918 provide a solid historical background to events in Vienna right after the war.

In fact, Vienna is the preferred site of Austrian cultural tidbits. Out of thirteen literary excerpts which I found to have direct or strongly implied reference to Austria, eight had Vienna as a setting, portrayed as a site of cultural, social, and linguistic diversity. The other excerpts emphasized the natural beauty of the Alps, praise of the republic and its traditions, or childhood in the country. Yet out of the thirty-seven Austrian literary texts which I was able to locate in the twelve textbooks, only those thirteen had any identifiable connection to Austria at all. The majority of readings are presented as having universal themes, which American college students can easily connect to their own experiences.

That in itself is a necessary component of any didacticization of reading material. Yet intellectual sparks can also be ignited when delving into cultural differences. Texts by such writers as Ilse Aichinger, Alfred Polgar, Thomas Bernhard, and Hugo von Hofmannsthal contribute to textbook discussions of the consequences of lying, hypocrisy, faith in technology, and passion. But only the description of the author betrays the Austrian connection. Some textbooks omit the nationality of the author entirely. For instance, Ingeborg Bachmann in *Alles in allem* (All in All), Ernst Jandl in *Kaleidoskop* (Kaleidoscope), Maria von Ebner-Eschenbach in *Blickwechsel* (Change of Perspective), and Elias Canetti in *Stimmen eines Jahrhunderts* are entirely absorbed into the German cultural sphere.[10] The students must depend on the instructor for enlightenment.

One example of the need for further explanation is the inclusion, in a section entitled "Erinnerungen an die Weimarer Republik" (Memories of the Weimar Republic) from *Stimmen eines Jahrhunderts*, of Maria Gaberschek's memories of growing up in the southern Tyrolean Alps in the early part of the twentieth century. Gaberschek later moved over the border to Austria. While the facts find mention in the introduction to her recollection, its juxtaposition with texts by German actor Paul Wegener, Hamburg student Heinrich Kelb, and writer Ernst Toller gives the impression that Austria, too, was part of the Weimar Republic. The historical chronologies at the beginning of each section do nothing to dispel that assumption, for Austrian events are barely acknowledged.

What image of Austria do the obviously Austrian texts present to the students? For one thing, the alpine landscape is breathtakingly beautiful, inspiring patriotic sentiments in Wolfgang Bauer's poem "Österreich" (Austria) and H. C. Artmann's "Mein Vaterland Österreich" (My Fatherland Austria). If one tires of nature, the obvious choice of urban action is Vienna, a city in which young men try to pick up young women as they go home from work, elderly ladies insist on renting apartments to only certain types of people, women artists take advantage of lonely men to help them exhibit their works, and the overweight go to fitness clubs. Another reason why Austrian texts do not figure more prominently is the vernacular. The Viennese use Austriacisms, and such texts need extra glosses to explain terms like *Karenzjahr* or *Gassenkabinett*.

On the other hand, the lack of historical context for the readings overemphasizes the role of the author in determining the cultural context for understanding the narratives and poems. For Austrian writers do not deal only with Austrian themes. One wonders how significant it is to know the national identity of the author, if that is the only cultural information provided about the text. What other means of contextualization could the textbooks offer?

One piece that differs from the others is an historical comparison of Germany and Austria since 1871. *Deutsch – immer besser* (Increasingly Better German) devotes twenty-five pages to political events affecting Germany and Austria.[11] It even includes Austrian jokes critical of the Anschluss (German annexation of Austria in 1938). Students receive a solid overview of the interrelation of the two countries and the problematic concept of Germanness for Austrians. Yet that book, too, portrays the relationship from a West German perspective, neatly summing up the present situation by stating that Austrians no longer have a problem with their *Deutschtum* (Germanness), as they did during the Anschluss, because of the positive changes in both countries since 1945. The passage ends by asserting, "The Austrians know that language and culture bind them to the Germans, but they do not have to draw any political consequences from that fact: friendship, yes – Anschluss, no."[12] That statement obviously ignores the cultural annexation of Austria into German language textbooks.

After reading Zeyringer's critique of West German publishing practices and publishers' virtual neglect of new Austrian talent, it is refreshing to see the variety of contemporary Austrian literature, whether identified as such or not, introduced to American language students. Aside from the well-known writers mentioned above, there are short pieces by Alexander Roda-Roda, Marianne Gruber, Barbara Gappmeier, and Clemens Hausmann. Other less common names, to which birth dates are not appended, are Helmut Zenker, Martin Rombach, Wolfgang Bauer, Manfred Richter, Herbert Eisenreich, and Ernst Ekker. The only writers not born in the twentieth-century whose work is deemed of interest to people around twenty years of age are Alfred Polgar, Maria von Ebner-Eschenbach, and Hugo von Hofmannsthal.

A sampling of the narratives and poems of those writers reveals a stimulating response to middle-class virtues and anxieties. Maintaining appearances or failing to see through them is a recurrent theme in several textbooks. Ilse Aichinger's "Seegeister" (Lake Spirits), in *Allerlei zum Lesen* (All Kinds of Things to Read), depicts a man who eventually turns into a ghost after he cannot make his motorboat stop, but is too embarrassed to admit his powerlessness.[13] Her story "Das Fenster-Theater," in *Blickwechsel*, focuses on a nosy neighbor who is convinced, erroneously, that the man across from her is committing a crime on the basis of his antics at the window. And Peter Handke's "Lebensbeschreibung" (Description of a Life) in *Rückblick* (Retrospective) can still provoke lively discussion for its unorthodox depiction of the life of Jesus Christ.[14]

Other stories confront stereotypes and prejudices. Marianne Gruber's narrative "Der Mongo" (Mongo) centers on discrimination against the handicapped; Christine Nöstlinger's and Ernst Ekker's "Ohne Vorurteile" (Without Prejudices), two different stories with the same title, both criticize gender bias at the workplace; and Clemens Hausmann's narrative "Sonntagnachmittag" (Sunday Afternoon) grapples with coming to terms with the Nazi past. Ingeborg Bachmann's poem "Reklame" (Advertisement) parodies the false cheer propagated in advertisements.

Humor plays a role as well in many of the excerpts. Certainly, Ernst Jandl's "Die Zeit vergeht" (Time Passes), "Bibliothek" (Library), and "A Love-Story dringend" (A Love Story – Urgent) have enticed many a student to probe their imagery. Canetti's memory of sticking out his tongue in "Die Zunge" (The Tongue) or Martin Rombach's recounting of the consequences of a wild horse ride into the center of town from the "Tagebuch des Försters Rombach" (Forester Rombach's Diary) provide a humorous touch to problems arising from spontaneous deeds.

The same story or poem can evoke various images, depending on how it is integrated into the textbook. Bernhard's "Eine Maschine" (A Machine) for example, is in the middle of a chapter in *Spiralen* entitled "Modernes Leben: Überlegen und Überleben" (Modern Life: Reflecting and Surviving) which highlights environmental issues, questions the advantage of technological advances, and suggests alternative modes of transportation. Two stills of the *Roboterfrau* (robot woman) from Fritz Lang's "Metropolis" accompany the story. While only three of forty chapter pages are devoted to the narrative, the photo of the Weißensee in Kärnten on the first page of the chapter signals the presence of something Austrian within the following pages, although it is not clear what. The pristine lake in Kärnten turns out to represent an environmental ideal. Further Austrian images include two pictures of recycling containers, a Hundertwasser "nature" painting, and a chart representing industrial nations' expenditures for the environment in 1991 – Austria spent the most. Indeed, Bernhard's critique of technology fits well with the general depiction of Austrian concerns about protecting the natural world. By integrating these representations of Austria with images of Berlin, the Elbe, and "Metropolis," the chapter then subsumes the Austrian issues under a more general discussion of the interaction of humans with nature. The few questions following "Eine Maschine" focus on comprehension.

In *Mosaik*'s (Mosaic) presentation of Bernhard's account, on the other hand, seven out of eighteen pages revolve around the text.[15]

This time, however, the chapter, "Der Mensch als Arbeitswesen" (The Human Being as Working Person) is introduced by a photo of a woman Lufthansa pilot, and another picture, of apprentices standing by a machine in a factory, expands the topic of the German workplace. The pre- and post-reading activities provoke students to view the events from the perspectives of various workers, from any country. The "horror story" is embedded in a series of questions and activities about one's dream profession, innovations in the 1980s, and the role of technology in the workplace. *Mosaik* allows more engagement with the text, while *Spiralen* emphasizes understanding the plot. Both employ Bernhard's tale for discussions about work in Germany and the U.S.

Polgar's "Geschichte ohne Moral" (Story without a Moral) is an integral part of the *Kaleidoskop* chapter on "Freizeit," yet in a general way. "Freizeit" is the very first chapter and begins with a photo of a snowboarder in the Austrian Alps, gleefully ushering the students into a presentation of leisure activities and holidays in the German-speaking countries. Four pages of color photos of German locations interrupt a subsequent section on bungy-jumping. Polgar's narrative follows a report on the Wartburg and the Bertolt Brecht poem "Vergnügungen" (Amusements). Jandl's poem "Die Zeit vergeht," a pyramid constructed from the repetition of the word "lustig," appears after the vocabulary list for the Polgar story. The questions focus on the humor of the reading selection. "Geschichte ohne Moral" introduces an ironic perspective on the activity of spending free time with one's family, a perspective that privileges more individualist activities and relates the narrative to the pictures of bungy-jumping and snowboarding. Austria thus appears as a site of exhilaration, populated by young people who refuse to allow familial obligations to hinder their pursuit of fun. The other texts accompanying the Polgar and Jandl pieces incorporate the Austrian experiences into the idea of a greater Germanic culture with multifarious forms of play. Polgar's text recurs in the reader *Mitlesen-Mitteilen* (Read Along-Communicate), but this time only as a listening-comprehension text.[16] The latter textbook, however, hints at its Austrian connection by glossing the term "gnädige Frau" as a very polite Austrian form of address.

These examples reveal that students do indeed encounter Austrian writing in their lower-division courses. But what do they really learn about Austria? Obviously, the answer depends on which textbook the instructor happens to have chosen for the course. Some textbooks, such as *Impulse* (Impulses), *Weiter! Lesen, Reden und Schreiben* (Further! Reading, Speaking, and Writing), or *Prisma* (Prism) have no Austrian components.[17] *Deutsch: immer besser, Kaleidoskop, Mosaik, Palette, Rückblick, Spiralen,* and *Wendepunkt* present only one or two reading pieces with an Austrian connection. *Allerlei zum Lesen, Alles in allem, Mitlesen-Mitteilen,* and the third-year *Blickwechsel* and *Stimmen eines Jahrhunderts* have four or more textual examples. Yet quantity does not mean increased cultural awareness of Austria, for *Alles in allem* provides very little information about the texts or even the authors. The third-year textbooks and the reader *Mitlesen-Mitteilen*, which is directed at either second or third-year students, allow more intellectual space for debating the ideas within the stories, but only Christiane von Hofmannsthal's "Wiener Tagebuch" deals specifically with Austrian concerns. Indeed, the most overtly informative text is the comparative German/Austrian historical overview in *Deutsch: immer besser*. Yet despite the paucity of overtly Austrian themes, the students are still obtaining exposure to Austrian culture albeit indirectly. They also have the opportunity to become familiar with a wider variety of narratives than they would in upper-division or graduate courses, in which writers like Marianne Gruber or Christine Nöstlinger or Anneliese Meinert are underrepresented. They just do not have much chance to relate those texts to specific issues in Austrian culture and society.

Instead, American students are guided to interpret the texts, by means of the pre- and post-reading activities, as dealing mainly with problems they all confront: unrequited love, discrimination, greed, and hypocrisy. They also learn of the intellectual joys of wordplay, childhood memories, pride in one's country, and compassion. Aside from Barbara Gappmeier's "Der gute Mann" (The Good Man), reduced in *Mitlesen-Mitteilen* to a listening-comprehension text, and the historical overview, the Nazi past goes unmentioned, a past that could evoke explorations into historical contrasts. The visual texts are soothing and stress the tourist's view of the country as a picturesque mountain retreat or a series of Hundertwasser paintings, an approach favoring West German ideas of Austrian vacations. Except in a few cases, cultural differences are deemphasized in favor of a universalizing approach meant to help American college students identify with the topics. The idea is to provoke conversation and develop reading and writing skills in German, that is, to serve the greater cause of increasing students' level of language proficiency.

Austria appears thus as a province of Germany, with textbook space for it decreasing as more varied samples of German (by writers living most or all of their life in Germany) writing are included. Yet as it shrinks within the greater German conglomerate, the idea of Austria becomes part of an even more insidious Americanization of European culture. For the German writings also lack much context. Learning German from the current crop of textbooks means, more often than not, realizing that Germans, Swiss, and Austrians are basically the same or even just like us. History and socio-political particularities become irrelevant in the timelessness of the textbook world. If we want our students to learn to question stereotypes of Austria, then the textbooks need to provide more context. Language courses offer the opportunity to provide cultural knowledge as well, and the textbook notion of Austria plays a significant role in forming cultural awareness. It would therefore behoove us to examine more closely the impressions our language students are absorbing.

University of Oregon

Notes

1. See also Jürgen Koppensteiner's essay, in which he found that the major Austrian themes in American textbooks of German were "Gemütlichkeit," Grinzing, and "Gugelhupf" (21): "'Land der Berge, Land der Seen': Zum Österreichbild in amerikanischen Deutsch-Lehrbüchern," *Unterrichtspraxis* vol. 11, no. 2 (1978), 20-26.

2. For a detailed list of Austrian literature in readers and anthologies for American undergraduate students as of 1973, see Horst Jarka, "Austrian Literature in Editions for American Undergraduate Students," *Modern Austrian Literature* vol. 8, nos. 3/4 (1975), 151-167. I am grateful to Professor Jarka for sending me a copy of his essay. To learn which Austrian authors were represented in German courses for Americans as of the early 1980s see Jorun Johns, "Survey of Courses on Austrian Literature and Culture Offered in the United States," *Österreich in amerikanischer Sicht: Das Österreichbild im amerikanischen Schulunterricht,* vol. 3, ed. Herbert Lederer and Maria Luise Caputo-Mayr (New York: Austrian Institute, 1984), 13-21. See also

Koppensteiner, "Innerhofer, Wolfgruber, Scharung: Literarische Kritiker Österreichs für Unterrichtszwecke?" *Österreich in amerikanischer Sicht: Das Österreichbild im amerikanischen Schulunterricht*, vol. 1, ed. Herbert Lederer and Maria Luise Caputo-Mayr (New York: Austrian Institute, 1980), 27-35; Koppensteiner, "No Worthwhile Poems in Decades? Some Thoughts on the Situation of Austrian Literature in the United States," *Modern Austrian Literature* vol. 20 nos. 3/4 (1987), 17-24; and Joseph P. Strelka, "On the Reception of Austrian Poetry in the United States as Exemplified by Two Recent American Anthologies of Austrian Poetry," *Modern Austrian Literature* vol. 20 nos. 3/4 (1987), 25-31.

3. Heidi Byrnes and Stefan Fink, *Wendepunkt* (Boston: Heinle & Heinle, 1987) [Ingeborg Bachmann, "Reklame," 193; H.C. Artmann, "Mein Vaterland Österreich," 348-349.]; Stefan Fink and Sigrid Berka, *Spiralen* (Boston: Heinle & Heinle, 1994). [Thomas Bernhard, "Eine Maschine," 282-284; Ernst Jandl, "Bibliothek" and "A Love-Story dringend," 333-335.]

4. Klaus Zeyringer, "Kultur-Differenzen und 'Prozesse literarischen Handelns': (Deutscher) Kanon und österreichische Literatur," *Die Unterrichtspraxis* vol. 29 no. 2 (1996), 165-173.

5. Ibid., 168.

6. Jillian S. Haeseler, *Palette* (New York: McGraw-Hill, 1995). [Aurelia Bundschuh, "Das Alibi," 93-102; Elfriede Jelinek, "Aufforderung zur Unfreundlichkeit," 127-145.]

7. Jillian S. Haeseler, 103.

8. Ibid., 128.

9. Andreas Lixl-Purcell, *Stimmen eines Jahrhunderts* (Fort Worth: Holt, Rinehart, and Winston, 1990). [Elias Canetti, "Die Zunge," 11; Gustav Mahler, "Briefe aus Leipzig," 17-23; Christiane von Hofmannsthal, "Wiener Tagebuch," 87-96; Maria Gaberschek, "Kindheit am Land," 133-142.]

10. Jeanine Briggs and Beate Engel-Doyle, *Alles in allem* (New York: McGraw-Hill, 1995) [Roda Roda, "Mein erstes Abenteuer," 45-52; Birgit Kral, "Mißverständnisse," 60-61; Werner Kofler, "Lernprozesse," 70-71; Helmut Zenker, "Schweinegeschichte," 124-135; Martin Rombach, Auszug aus dem "Tagebuch des Försters Rombach," 136-141; Wolfgang Bauer, "Österreich," 141-146; Ingeborg Bachmann, "Reklame," 160-161; Manfred Richter, "Wien-Altenmarkt," 226-234.]; Jack Moeller, Winnifred R. Adolph, Barbara Mabee, and Helmut Liedloff, *Kaleidoskop* (Boston: Houghton Mifflin,

1998). ["Wiener Fitneßclub – Reklame," 8-9; Alfred Polgar, "Geschichte ohne Moral," 21-28; Ernst Jandl, "Die Zeit vergeht," 25; DBG-Handlexikon, "Wolfgang Amadeus Mozart," 105-107; Franz Schubert, 117-119.]; Jacqueline Vansant, *Blickwechsel* (Boston: Houghton Mifflin, 1990). ["TV Österreich," 7-9; Marie von Ebner-Eschenbach, "Die Nachbarn," 41-47; Ilse Aichinger, "Das Fenster-Theater," 88-95; Marianne Gruber, "Der Mongo," 107-116; Ernst A. Ekker, "Ohne Vorurteile," 152-161.]

11. Heimy Taylor, Werner Haas, and Elfe Vallaster-Dona, *Deutsch-immer besser* (New York: John Wiley and Sons, 1996), Chapter 3, 66-91.

12. Ibid., 72.

13. Hermann Teichert and Lovette Teichert, *Allerlei zum Lesen* (Lexington, MA: D. C. Heath, 1992). [Ilse Aichinger, "Seegeister," 115-124; Herbert Eisenreich, "Verlorene Liebesmüh'," 135-143; Alfred Polger, "Sein letzter Irrtum," 165-174.]

14. Lixl-Purcell, *Rückblick: Texte und Bilder nach 1945* (Boston: Houghton Mifflin, 1995). ["Steirische Spezialitaeten," 87-88; Peter Handke, "Lebensbeschreibung," 143-149.]

15. Rosemary Delia, James A. Fassold, and Horst M. Rabura, *Mosaik* (New York: McGraw-Hill, 1992). [Thomas Bernhard, "Eine Maschine," 84-91.]

16. Larry D. Wells, *Mitlesen-Mitteilen* (Fort Worth: Holt, Rinehart, and Winston, 1995). [Anneliese Meinert, "Rotkäppchen '65," 63-68; Christine Nöstlinger, "Ohne Vorurteile," 83-88; H. C. Artmann, "Keine Menschenfresser, bitte!" 89-95; Barbara Gappmeier, "Der gute Mann," 141-143; Clemens Hausmann, "Sonntagvormittag," 145-148; Alfred Polgar, "Geschichte ohne Moral," 181-185; Hugo von Hofmannsthal, "Die Beiden," 231-232.]

17. David Crowner and Klaus Ill, *Impulse: Kommunikatives Deutsch für die Mittelstufe* (Boston: Houghton Mifflin, 1995); Isabelle Salaun-Gorrell, *Weiter! Lesen, Reden und Schreiben* (New York: John Wiley and Sons, 1994); Mark Rectanus and Renate Hiller, *Prisma* (Lexington, MA: D. C. Heath, 1992).

Name Index

Abel, Hilde 228, 241
Abgood, Edward F. 219
Adams, Henry 225
Adler, Alfred 98, 99
Aichinger, Ilse 141, 142, 156, 179, 312, 314
Aleichem, Scholem 109
Alexander II 110
Altenberg, Peter 60, 63, 65-72, 216
Altmann, Meryl 264, 271
Améry, Jean 135, 141, 145, 148
Andreas-Salomé, Lou 92
Andrian, Leopold von 61
Anwander, Bernt 218
Aristotle 22
Artmann, H. C. 155, 313
Austen, Jane 82
Bach, Johann Sebastian 302
Bachmann, Ingeborg 141, 142, 156, 190, 309, 310, 312, 315
Bahr, Hermann 61
Bakhtin, M. 82
Barnes, Djuna 256, 259-273
Barrish, Seth 295
Bartsch, Kurt 5
Bauer, Otto 227
Bauer, Wolfgang 313, 314
Beckermann, Ruth 134-139, 142-147
Beer-Hofmann, Paula (born Paula Lissy) 48, 52, 54, 149
Beer-Hofmann, Richard 48-59, 155
Beethoven, Ludwig van 215, 246, 303

Beller, Steven 51, 261, 265
Benét, Stephen Vincent 227
Berard, Cheryl 162
Bernhard, Thomas 145, 155-157, 159, 160, 175, 180, 181-192, 310, 312, 315, 316
Bertschik, Julia 2, 14
Bettauer, Hugo 139
Bettelheim, Bruno 91, 148, 248
Beutin, Heide 19
Bismarck, Otto von 14, 15, 18
Bleibtreu, Karl 60
Boltzmann, Ludwig 79
Bottome, Phyllis 236
Borchert, Wolfgang 156
Boyle, Kay 229-232, 234, 235, 238, 239, 241, 242, 244-247
Bradbury, Ray 243, 246-248
Brandstetter, Alois 155
Brecht, Bertolt 297, 316
Breuer, Josef 92, 93, 100
Broch, Hermann 140, 155, 262
Bruckner, Anton 279
Brunngraber, Rudolf 226
Bundschuh, Aurelia 311
Bunzl, Matti 136, 141, 145
Burgess, Anthony 90, 98, 99
Caesar, Sid 248
Camus, Albert 145, 219
Canetti, Elias 133, 155, 313, 315
Canetti, Veza 140
Celan, Paul 141, 148
Cerha, Michael 193, 194
Cervantes, Miguel de 6, 190
Charlemagne 253
Conrad, Joseph 2, 10, 11

Cowart, David 74
Critchfield, Richard 49
Csokor, Franz 121
Dante 188
Denker, Henry 90, 96
Denkler, Horst 9
Docker, Ulrike 33
Doderer, Heimito von 61, 140, 143, 156
Dollfuss, Engelbert 230, 231, 234
Dor, Milo 156
Dostoevsky, Fyodor 219, 252
Drucker, Hal 302
Ebner-Eschenbach, Marie von 313, 314
Eco, Umberto 190
Ehalt, Hubert 62
Ehrenstein, Albert 155
Eichmann, Adolf 140
Einstein, Albert 76
Eisenreich, Herbert 156, 314
Ekker, Ernst 314, 315
Eliot, T. S. 226, 271
Elisabeth, Empress 91
Endres, Ria 188
Engels, Friedrich 25
Engle, Paul 227
Eugenie, Empress 37
Fadiman, Clifton 256
Faschinger, Lilian 179-191
Federmann, Reinhard 156
Fian, Antonio 179, 180
Figl, Julius 133
Fitzgerald, F. Scott 288
Fliess, Wilhelm 92, 96, 97
Fontane, Oskar Maurus 79
Ford, Charles Henri 270
Franckenstein, Joseph von 232

Franz Ferdinand 217
Franz Joseph, Emperor 91, 103, 106, 110, 111, 115, 116, 121, 123, 124, 127, 142, 217, 225, 267
Fontanne, Lynn 226
Freud, Martin 91
Freud, Sigmund 49, 79, 86, 88, 89-100, 169, 212, 215, 216, 218, 220, 239, 252, 278, 279, 280, 287
Fried, Erich 134, 135, 155
Friedländer, Otto 64
Frischmuth, Barbara 143, 144
Fritsch, Gerhard 155, 156, 179, 180
Fry, Varian 105
Fuchs, Eduard 41
Gaberschek, Maria 313
Galileo 87
Gappmeier, Barbara 314, 317
Gardiner, Murial 239
Gay, Peter 88-90
Gelber, Mark 49
Gilman, Sander 133, 140
Goethe, Johann Wolfgang von 97, 242
Goldhagen, Daniel 140
Grass, Günter 252
Greene, Graham 247, 292, 304
Grillparzer, Franz 4, 5, 24, 25, 126, 160, 180, 250, 252, 253
Grimm brothers 245
Gruber, Marianne 155, 314, 317
Gstrein, Norbert 155
Günther, John 227, 228
Haider, Jörg 140, 145, 155, 161, 162, 166

Hallberger, Eduard 13
Handke, Peter 146, 155-157, 175, 179, 309, 310, 314
Hannibal 100
Haslinger, Josef 146, 166, 175, 176, 179, 310
Hatlan, Burton 239
Hauptmann, Gerhart 60
Hausmann, Clemens 314, 315
Haydn, Joseph 216
Hayes, Alfred 227
Heger, Jeanette 279
Heine, Heinrich 104, 296, 304
Heisenberg, Werner 76, 77
Hellman, Lillian 240
Hemingway, Ernest 225
Henisch, Peter 143, 144
Henrich, Friedhelm 15
Herzog, Roman 159
Hesse, Hermann 219
Hillmann, Karl-Heinz 154
Hitler, Adolf 104, 105, 127, 133, 215, 228, 230-232, 236
Hoellering, Franz 228
Hoffer, Klaus 155
Hofmann, Paul 215, 216, 260
Hofmannsthal, Christiane von 312, 317
Hofmannsthal, Hugo von 49, 61, 216, 309, 310, 312, 314
Hollander, Anne 32
Holz, Arno 60
Horch, Hans Otto 6, 7
Horváth, Ödön von 180
Howells, William Dean 244
Hundertwasser 317
Huston, John
Hutcheon, Linda 88

Hutter, Catherine 235-238, 241, 242
Innerhofer, Franz 155, 179, 180
Irving, John 243, 245, 249, 250, 252, 276-278, 282, 283, 286, 289
Irving, Washington 225
Isherwood, Christopher 228, 229
Ivask, Ivar 252
Jandl, Ernst 231, 310, 312, 315, 316
Jean Paul 4
Jelinek, Elfriede 142, 144, 145, 155, 156, 312
Johnston, William 215-217
Jones, Ernest 89, 91
Jonke, Gert 155
Joyce, James 157
Jung, Carl 98, 99
Kafka, Franz 92, 212, 219, 220
Kalb, Heinrich 313
Kallir, Otto 49
Kant, Immanuel 76
Karl, Emperor 124
Kathrein, Karin 180
Katz, Friedel 105
Katz, Henry William 103-119
Kazin, Alfred 238
Keats, John 90
Kermode, Frank 75, 81, 83
Kerschbaumer, Marie-Thérèse 155, 310
King, Rene 31, 32
Kirk, Justin 295
Klein, Johannes 10
Kleinschmidt, Erich 49
Klima, Viktor 155
Klimt, Gustav 66, 297

Kluger, Ruth 142
Knigge, Adolph 41
Knopf, Alfred A.
Kofler, Werner 310
Kohn, Salomon 109
Kokoschka, Oskar 297
Koll, Rolf-Dieter 7
Kolleritsch, Alfred 155
Kompert, Leopold 109
König, Rene 31
Konzett, Matthias 180, 186
Kraus, Karl 60, 63-74, 139, 140, 159, 180
Kreisky, Bruno 300
Kreisler, Georg 13
Kretzer, Max 60
Kundera, Milan 259
Lang, Fritz 315
Lang, Marie 37
Larson, Jonathan 296
Lauda, Niki 158
Lazarsfeld, Sophie 238
Lebert, Hans 155, 179
Lernet-Holenia, Alexander 155
Lessing, Gotthold Ephraim 109
Lewis, Sinclair 226
Lind, Jakov 134, 142
Longfellow, Henry Wadsworth 225
Lorenz, Dagmar 161
Lueger, Karl 92, 279
Lunt, Alfred 226
Mach, Ernst 79
Magris, Claudio 5, 121
Mahler, Gustav 49, 312
Mahoney, Daniel A. 270
Makart, Hans 297

Mann, Thomas 89, 100, 160, 190, 210, 235
Marans, Jon 295
Marcus, Jane 258
Maria Theresia, Empress 217
Marx, Groucho 257
Marx, Karl 227
May, Elaine 248
Mayreder, Rosa 31, 34-47
McClintock, Anne 22
Meinert, Anneliese 317
Menasse, Robert 134, 137, 142, 143, 148, 153-165, 179, 186, 187
Merkl, Max 162
Metternich, Klemens von 37, 225
Meyer, Nicholas 90, 94, 96
Meynert, Theodor 96
Michelangelo 255, 304
Miller, Gabriel 276
Millhauser, Steven 294
Mitgutsch, Anna 144, 179, 180, 310
Mitterer, Erika 140, 238
Mitterer, Felix 146
Morgan, Lewis Henry 25
Morton, Frederic 278
Mozart, Wolfgang Amadeus 215, 216, 246, 303
Murray, John 225
Musil, Robert 5, 75, 78, 155, 270, 274
Naetz, Max 155
Nestroy, Johann 180
Nichols, Mike 248
Nietzsche, Friedrich 92, 93, 100, 137, 295, 304, 306
Nora, Pierre 56

Nöstlinger, Christiane 315, 317
O'Conner, James 157
O Henry 230
Ovid 201
Palacky, Frantisek 23
Palencia-Roth, Michael 90
Petzold, Alfons 60, 63, 70-72, 214, 215
Pevny, Wilhelm 155
Polgar, Alfred 312, 314, 316
Pollak, Richard 248
Posthofen, Renate 158
Pound, Ezra 225, 231
Preisendanz, Wolfgang 4
Prokosch, Frederic 233-238, 241
Raabe, Wilhelm 1-18
Rabinovici, Doron 148
Ransmayr, Christoph 193-195, 210
Rauchensteiner, Manfried 84
Reed, Carol 304
Reilly, Edward C. 289
Reinold, Gerd 154
Renan, Ernest 22
Richter, Manfred 314
Riefenstahl, Leni 230
Robinson, Hal 295
Roda-Roda, Alexander 314
Rombach, Martin 314, 315
Roosevelt, Franklin Delano 231
Rosegger, Peter 140
Rosten, Leo 244-246, 274
Roth, Gerhard 166-178, 179, 181, 186, 220, 221
Roth, Joseph 104, 114-117, 120-131, 135, 141, 142, 212, 217, 219, 265, 270
Roth, Philip 157

Rottger, Friedrich 12
Rozenblit, Marsha 133, 272
Rudolf, Crown Prince 91, 226, 278, 279
Rudolph II, Emperor 4
Rushdie, Salman 193
Said, Edward 81, 82
Sammons, Jeffrey 14
Sartre, Jean Paul 90, 93, 96-98, 145, 219
Scharang, Michael 155
Schaukal, Richard von 216
Sherwood, Robert 241
Schiller, Friedrich 109, 290
Schindel, Robert 134, 136-139, 142, 144, 146-148
Schlaffer, Edith 162
Schmidt-Dengler, Wendelin 158, 180
Schnitzler, Arthur 49, 61, 135, 140, 144, 147, 190, 216, 242, 279, 309
Schnitzler, Olga 56
Schönerer, Georg von 261
Schorske, Carl 278
Schubert, Franz 279
Schumann, Robert, 295, 296, 302-304
Schwarz, Egon 133, 147
Schubert, Franz 215, 216
Schultze-Naumburg, Paul 34
Schuschnigg, Kurt von 232
Seelich, Nadja 134, 136, 138, 139, 142, 143, 145-147
Shaw, George Bernard 231
Sherwood, Robert E. 226
Sichrovsky, Peter 140
Simmel, Georg 36

Sobol, Joshua 90, 92
Spencer, David 302
Spengler, Oswald 234
Sperber, Manès 135
Spiel, Hilde 63, 133, 142
Sprengnether, Madelon 89
Steele, Valerie 34
Steiner, Carl 22
Steiner, Gertraud 218
Steiner, Rudolf 37
Stekel, Wilhelm 99
Stifter, Adalbert 5
Strater, Edmund 14
Stratz, C. H. 34
Strauss, Johann 216, 247
Stroheim, Erich von 249
Stone, Irving 90, 95
Süskind, Patrick 190
Thalberg, Hans J. 140
Thomas, D. M. 90, 944
Thomas, Dylan 257
Thompson, Bruce 5
Thompson, Dorothy 227
Todrin, Boris 227
Toller, Ernst 313
Tommasini, Anthony 301, 306
Torberg, Friedrich 135, 139, 142
Trenker, Louis 229, 230, 245
Troll-Borostyáni, Irene von 33, 34
Turrini, Peter 147, 155, 237
Twain, Mark 225, 244, 245, 247, 250
Urzidil, Johannes 155
Veblen, Thorsten 32, 34, 37, 38
Veit, Conrad 249
Vetsera, Maria 278
Viertel, Berthold 229
Vinci, Leonardo da 90, 255
Vranitzky, Franz 155
Waggerl, Hans 140
Wagner, Otto 79
Waldheim, Kurt 134, 145, 155, 187, 296, 299
Wandruschka, Adam 227
Wassermann, Jakob 135
Wegener, Paul 313
Weigel, Hans 133, 135, 141, 155
Weininger, Otto 92, 100, 262
Weinzierl, Erika 236
Welles, Orson 217, 219, 254, 292, 304
Werfel, Franz 121, 155
Wesseling, Elizabeth 89
Wharton, Edith 247, 248
White, Hayden 87, 88, 99
Wiesenthal, Simon 134, 135
Winkler, Joseph 155
Winkler, Michael 49
Wolcott, James 294
Wolf, Friedrich 228
Wolfe, Tom 156, 226
Wolfgruber, Gernot 155
Wouk, Herman 138
Yalom, Irvin 90, 92, 93
Zand, Herbert 218
Zenker, Helmut 314
Zeyringer, Klaus 310, 314
Zola, Emile 60
Zweig, Arnold 89
Zweig, Stefan 48-59, 103, 114
Zwillinger, Frank 135

Ariadne Press
Studies

*Major Figures of
Modern Austrian Literature*
Edited by Donald G. Daviau

*Major Figures of Austrian Literature
The Interwar Years 1918-1938*
Edited by Donald G. Daviau

*Major Figures of Turn-of-the-Century
Austrian Literature*
Edited by Donald G. Daviau

*Austrian Writers and the Anschluss
Understanding the Past –
Overcoming the Past*
Edited by Donald G. Daviau

*Austria in the Thirties
Culture and Politics*
Edited by K. Segar and J. Warren

*Austria, 1938 - 1988
Anschluss and Fifty Years*
Edited by William E. Wright

Jura Soyfer and His Time
Edited by Donald G. Daviau

Rilke's Duino Elegies
Edited by R. Paulin & P. Hutchinson

Stefan Zweig
An International Bibliography
By Randolph A. Klawiter

*Franz Karka
A Writer's Life*
By Joachim Unseld

*Kafka and Language: In the
Stream of Thoughts and Life*
By G. von Natzmer Cooper

*Of Reason and Love
The Life and Works of Marie
von Ebner-Eschenbach*
By Carl Steiner

*Marie von Ebner-Eschenbach
The Victory of a Tenacious Will*
By Doris M. Klostermaier

*"What People Call Pessimism"
Freud, Schnitzler and the 19th-Century
Controversy at the University of
Vienna Medical School*
By Mark Luprecht

Arthur Schnitzler and Politics
By Adrian Clive Roberts

*Structures of Disintegration
Narrative Strategies in Elias Canetti's*
Die Blendung
By David Darby

*Blind Reflections
Gender in Canetti's* Die Blendung
By Kristie A. Foell

*Robert Musil and the Tradition
of the German Novelle*
By Kathleen O'Connor

*Implied Dramaturgy. Robert Musil
and the Crisis of Modern Drama*
By Christian Rogowsky

Ariadne Press
New Titles

Pedro II of Brazil
Son of the Habsburg Empress
By Gloria Kaiser
Translated by Lowell A. Bangerter

Brazil
A Land of the Future
By Stefan Zweig
Translated by Lowell A. Bangerter

The Abbey
By Alois Brandstetter
Translated by Evelyn and
Peter Firchow

The Story of Darkness
By Gerhard Roth
Translated by Helga Schreckenberger
and Jacqueline Vansant

Footloose
By Gernot Wolfgruber
Translated by Robert Acker

The Traveling Years
By Elisabeth Freundlich
Translated by Elizabeth Pennebaker

International Zone
By Milo Dor and
Reinhard Federmann
Translated by Jerry Glenn and
Jennifer Kelley-Thierman

Into the Sunset
Anthology of Nineteenth-Century
Austrian Prose
Selected and Translated by
Richard Hacken

The Morning before the Journey
By Julian Schutting
Translated by Barbara Z. Schoenberg

Three Radio Plays
By Ingeborg Bachmann
Translated by Lilian Friedberg

Allemann
By Alfred Kolleritsch
Translated by Paul F. Dvorak

An Anthology of Plays
By Werner Schwab
Translated by Michael Mitchell

Winds of Life
Destinies of a Young Viennese Jew
1938-1958
By Gershon Evan

The Fiction of the I
Austrian Writers and Biography
Edited by Nicholas J. Meyerhofer

Stories from My Life
By Oskar Kokoschka

Barbara Frischmuth
in Contemporary Context
Edited by Renate Posthofen

Ariadne Press
Recent Titles

Flight from Greatness
Six Variations on Perfection
in Imperfection
By Hans Weigel
Translated by Lowell A. Bangerter

Ephemeral Aphorisms
By Phia Rilke
Translated by Wolfgang Mieder
and David Scrase

Stories from My Life
By Oskar Kokoschka
Translated by Michael Mitchell

Telemachos
By Michael Köhlmeier
Translated by Edson M. Chick

Dona Leopoldina
The Austrian Empress of Brazil
By Gloria Kaiser
Translated by Lowell A. Bangerter

The Stone Breakers
and Other Novellas
By Ferdinand von Saar
Translated by Kurt and Alice Bergel

Quotations of a Body
By Evelyn Schlag
Translated by Willy Riemer
Prefatory Note by
Claire Tomalin

Ornament and Crime
Selected Essays
By Adolf Loos
Selected by Adolf Opel
Translated by Michael Mitchell

The Abbey
By Alois Brandstetter
Translated by Peter and
Evelyn Firchow

The Secret of the Empire
By Heimito von Doderer
Translated by John S. Barrett

The Shadow Disappears in the Sun
By Barbara Frischmuth
Translated by Nicholas J. Meyerhofer

The Holy Experiment and Other Plays
By Fritz Hochwälder
Translated by Todd C. Hanlin
and Heidi Hutchinson

The Jib Door
By Marlen Haushofer
Translated by Jerome C. Samuelson

Gran Hotel Cantabria
By Heinrich von Starhemberg
Translated by Harvey I. Dunkle

Thank You, America
By Charlotte Shedd

Ariadne Press
Drama Series

*Professor Bernhardi
and Other Plays*
By Arthur Schnitzler
Translated by G.J. Weinberger

*Paracelsus
and Other One-Act Plays*
By Arthur Schnitzler
Translated by G.J. Weinberger

Three Late Plays
By Arthur Schnitzler
Translated by G.J. Weinberger

The Final Plays
By Arthur Schnitzler
Translated by G.J. Weinberger

*Seven Contemporary
Austrian Plays*
Edited by Richard H. Lawson

*Anthology of Contemporary
Austrian Folk Plays*
Translated by Richard Dixon

*New Anthology of
Austrian Folk Plays*
Edited by Richard H. Lawson

Prince and Plays
By Henry Gregor
[Heinrich von Starhemberg]
Translated by Harvey I. Dunkle

*Shooting Rats,
Other Plays and Poems*
By Peter Turrini
Translated by Richard S. Dixon

*The Slackers
and Other Plays*
By Peter Turrini
Translated by Richard S. Dixon

Dirt
By Robert Schneider
Translated by Paul F. Dvorak

*Siberia
and Other Plays*
By Felix Mitterer

*The Wild Woman
and Other Plays*
By Felix Mitterer
Translated by Todd C. Hanlin
and Heidi Hutchinson

*The Holy Experiment
and Other Plays*
By Fritz Hochwälder
Translated by Todd C. Hanlin
and Heidi Hutchinson

Five Plays
By Gerald Szyszkowitz
Translated by Todd C. Hanlin,
Heidi Hutchinson and Joseph McVeigh